Amy Johnson

Other Books by the Author:

Marie Lloyd, The One and Only

Amy Johnson

MIDGE GILLIES

Weidenfeld & Nicolson
LONDON

First published in Great Britain in 2003
by Weidenfeld & Nicolson

A CIP catalogue record for this book
is available from the British Library.

ISBN 0 297 82982 3

Printed in Great Britain by
Butler & Tanner Ltd, Frome and London

Contents

Acknowledgements

This book could not have been written without the immense help and support of Amy Johnson's nieces, Mrs Susan Crook and Mrs Judy Chilvers. This is in no way an 'authorised' biography but both Susan and Judy have shown me great kindness and hospitality and I am grateful for the chance to get to know them and their family.

Although neither Susan nor Judy knew Amy, the book is nevertheless about their family and I am conscious that inviting a biographer into one's home must be an unnerving experience. I hope that they will feel I have managed to convey the great courage and panache that made Amy such a popular hero and her legacy so enduring. Extracts from the Amy Johnson Estate are quoted with their kind permission.

One of the unexpected pleasures of researching this book has been the weeks I have spent in the Department of Research and Information Services at the Royal Air Force Museum in Hendon. The museum is well worth a visit, not least because it contains an Airspeed Oxford similar to the aircraft that Amy flew on her last trip. Everyone at the museum has shown me the greatest kindness and patience, but I owe a special debt of gratitude to the Museum's Senior Keeper, Peter Elliott.

Peter has catalogued the Amy Johnson archive over several years, and mostly in his lunchbreaks, so that, despite being a large collection, it is a pleasure for a researcher to find their way around. He has answered countless queries and allowed me to draw on his immense knowledge of aviation. He was also kind enough to read a draft of the manuscript; his comments and suggestions were invaluable but any errors that have slipped through the editing net remain my responsibility.

I have also been most fortunate to have the help of several experts in Hull. David Smith, Specialist Librarian, Local Studies at the Central Library, has shared his considerable local knowledge with me and has always been quick to answer any queries about Hull or to send me relevant newspaper cuttings. Without his help my research would have been much harder and much less enjoyable. He also read parts of the manuscript; again, any remaining errors are mine, not his.

Martin Taylor, Hull's City Archivist, Christopher Ketchell, of the

Local History Unit, Hull College and joint founder of the Amy Johnson Appreciation Society, and Dr David Neave of the University of Hull, all added to my knowledge of the city that helped form Amy's character.

I am grateful to all the librarians and archivists whose institutions are mentioned in the 'Sources' section at the back of the book. Ron Davies, Museum Curator at the Smithsonian National Air and Space Museum; Vanna Skelley, Archivist and Information Manager at the Castrol Archive; Dr Helen Mathers, Centenary History Research Fellow, University of Sheffield; Judith Bourne, LL.B, LL.M, barrister, Senior Lecturer at London Metropolitan University; and Max Tyler, Historian of the British Music Hall Society, were particularly helpful.

Other writers have been generous with their support and in sharing their contacts. I would particularly like to thank: Graham Coster; Colin Cruddas, custodian of the Sir Alan Cobham Archive; Eva Fitzpatrick; Michael Holroyd CBE; Ian Mackersey and Roy Nesbit.

Chris Weaver and other members of the Canterbury branch of the British Sub-Aqua Club were kind enough to take me out to the spot where Amy's aeroplane went down, and Tim Burt arranged for me to meet his grandfather, the distinguished aviation expert, Sir Peter Masefield.

Writing this book has allowed me the privilege of speaking to several remarkable pilots: Lettice Curtis, Jennie Broad, Diana Barnato Walker, MBE, Commodore of the Air Transport Auxiliary Association, and Nancy Bird-Walton.

I am grateful, too, for everyone who has written or phoned to share their reminiscences, knowledge or photos of Amy Johnson, especially Peter Berry, Lawrence Hole, David Mooney, and all members of the Amy Johnson Appreciation Society, notably Peter Little. I spent a particularly enjoyable afternoon with Patricia Stewart whose mother, Gwyneth Roulston, was part of the close female group that meant so much to Amy. Meeting her gave me an invaluable insight into Winifred Irving, whom she was fortunate enough to count as a close family friend. Jean Baudouin and his family also showed me great hospitality.

All my friends have been very supportive, but in particular I would like to thank the following: Peter Bently, Dr Kathryn Hughes, Ann-Janine Murtagh, Bridie Pritchard, Jay Sivell and Dr Rosy Thornton. In the early days of this book Jenny Burgoyne and Sarah Mnatzaganian allowed me time to think by entertaining my baby daughter, and by sharing my growing fascination with Amy. As the book and my daughter grew, their practical support and interest in both have been an inspiration. Veronica Forwood doggedly pursued Amy's life in France, allowing me to glimpse another side of Amy's character and to confirm my suspicions of why Veronica is such a good journalist and friend.

The research has involved considerable travel which would not have been possible without the generous support of the K. Blundell Trust. As ever, the Society of Authors remains a vital source of information and support.

Francine Brody, my editor at Weidenfeld & Nicolson, has shown a rare combination of vision and efficiency and my agent, Faith Evans, has driven the project forward with her usual skill and verve. Lucie Sutherland's comments on the text have been extremely helpful.

It is impossible to find words to thank the three people who deserve it most. My parents, Renee and Donald Gillies, lived and fought through the war that killed Amy; for them this book is not history but real life. My husband, Jim Kelly, probably feels as though Amy has shared our lives for the last three years. Despite sending me up in a biplane, he remains one of only two people for whom I would risk a long-distance flight. This book is dedicated to that other person.

List of Illustrations

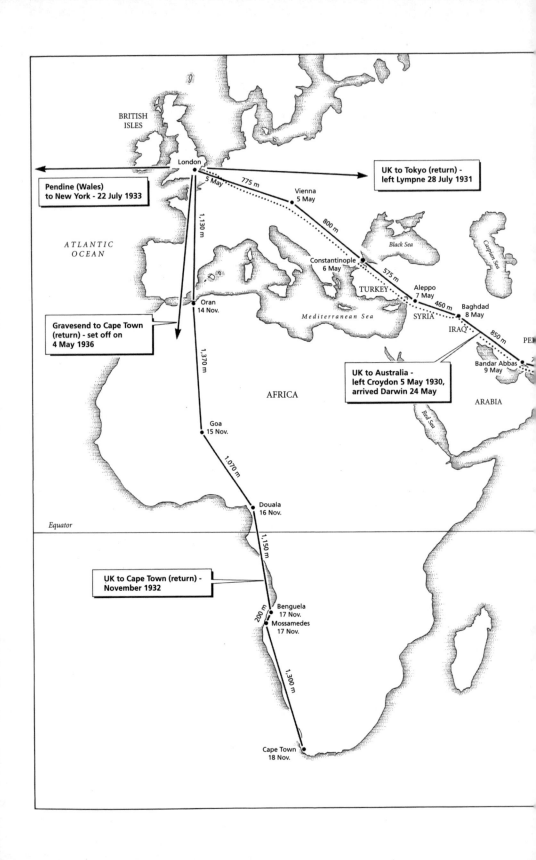

BRITISH
ISLES

London

5 May   775 m   Vienna
5 May

Pendine (Wales)
to New York - 22 July 1933

UK to Tokyo (return) -
left Lympne 28 July 1931

800 m

ATLANTIC
OCEAN

1,130 m

Black Sea

Caspian Sea

Constantinople
6 May

575 m

Aleppo
7 May

460 m

Baghdad
8 May

Oran
14 Nov.

Mediterranean Sea

TURKEY

SYRIA

IRAQ

850 m

PE

Gravesend to Cape Town
(return) - set off on
4 May 1936

1,370 m

AFRICA

UK to Australia -
left Croydon 5 May 1930,
arrived Darwin 24 May

Bandar Abbas
9 May

ARABIA

Goa
15 Nov.

Red Sea

1,070 m

Equator

Douala
16 Nov.

1,150 m

UK to Cape Town (return) -
November 1932

200 m

Benguela
17 Nov.

Mossamedes
17 Nov.

1,300 m

Cape Town
18 Nov.

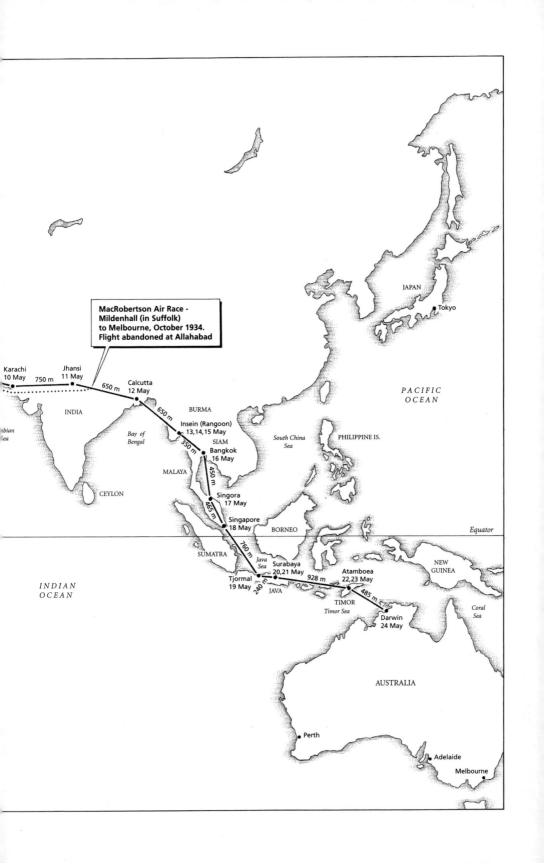

MacRobertson Air Race -
Mildenhall (in Suffolk)
to Melbourne, October 1934.
Flight abandoned at Allahabad

JAPAN

Tokyo

PACIFIC
OCEAN

Karachi
10 May   Jhansi
                11 May
        750 m   Calcutta
                   650 m   12 May
                                650 m   BURMA
INDIA   Insein (Rangoon)
                                         13,14,15 May
               Bay of   SIAM
               Bengal   350 m   Bangkok
                                         16 May
                      MALAYA   450 m

CEYLON   Singora
                              465 m 17 May

                           Singapore
                           18 May

South China
Sea

PHILIPPINE IS.

BORNEO   Equator

                      760 m
        SUMATRA   NEW
                   Java   GUINEA
                   Sea   Surabaya
              Tjormal   20,21 May
INDIAN   19 May 240 m 928 m   Atamboea
OCEAN   JAVA   22,23 May
                                                485 m
                                     TIMOR
                             Timor Sea   Coral
                                         Darwin   Sea
                                         24 May

                                     AUSTRALIA

arabian
Sea

            Perth

                   Adelaide

                   Melbourne

For Rosa Gillies Kelly

Preface

The meaning of the word 'solo' has changed dramatically in the seventy years since Amy Johnson became the first woman to fly alone from England to Australia.

Towards the end of the writing of this biography the word again returned to vogue, although used in a context that the record-breaking pilots of the inter-war years would hardly recognise. The most spectacular example appeared in the case of Ellen MacArthur, who won the gruelling Route du Rhum transatlantic race in a sixty-foot yacht.

On the face of it, the two women, at the peak of their careers, appear to have much in common. Their sex, age (both twenty-six) and size held equal fascination for the press; the French adored both. In their epic journeys they survived on very little sleep, battled through raging storms and used ingenuity and physical strength when things went wrong: MacArthur climbed to the top of a mast to repair damaged rigging; Amy sat on the tail of her plane when a desert storm threatened to blow them both away. But there the similarities end.

Jason, the second-hand biplane that Amy flew to Australia, was half the size of MacArthur's boat, *Kingfisher*, and took her over areas of jungle and desert that had yet to be mapped. Amy carried no radio and was often alone in the air for periods of ten hours at a time over nineteen days; MacArthur's fans followed her thirteen-day voyage via her own website and she received 1300 e-mails in the final two hours of her journey. Amy relied on weather reports that were as accurate as a piece of seaweed pinned to the back door; MacArthur spent a five-figure sum on satellite phone calls to two expert meteorologists.

Ellen MacArthur was 'solo' in the sense that she could not have been plucked to safety if something had gone wrong in the middle of the Atlantic, but the electronic and satellite umbilical cord that provided mental and technical succour during the race was unimaginable to Amy, who had to resort to reciting nursery rhymes to fend off boredom and fear.

Nevertheless, both women share the same heroic 'aloneness'. Gadgets have made most of the world much smaller, but parts of Amy's route to Australia have actually become even more impenetrable since *Jason* droned his way across it. I have visited two of the points on her journey: Croydon and Karachi. Most travel agents would laugh if I suggested visiting Baghdad, Bandar Abbas or Rangoon; if I persisted in going, it would take more than a mobile phone and an e-mail address to rescue me.

Amy Johnson disappeared at the age of thirty-seven, the same age at which I started researching this book. Today she would still rank as an extravagantly well-travelled person; of all my acquaintances I can think of only one – a foreign reporter for a French news agency – who could rival her experience. That this remarkable woman from Hull, who lunched with the President of the United States, had songs written about her and inspired Paris designers, should end her life in the Thames Estuary on a winter's afternoon seems as startling as any of the other headline-making events in her life. That her life should begin and end at two unassuming east-coast estuaries makes the thirty-seven years in between all the more intriguing.

Prologue

Sunday, 5 January 1941, 3.30 p.m.
The Thames Estuary

'Hurry, please, hurry . . .'

The voice was high-pitched and clear and might have belonged to either a boy or a woman, except that the three desperate words were spoken with all the precision of a BBC announcer.

Minutes before, the crew of HMS *Haslemere*, a trawler in wartime Convoy CE21, had watched as a bright yellow plane circled a parachutist fluttering towards the water. The plane was eerily quiet, its engines silent as it glided towards the sea before settling momentarily on the water's surface and then sinking under the waves.

The woman who spoke the words was sexless in the heaving wintry sea, the torso clothed in a heavy uniform, the face partly hidden by a pilot's helmet. She rose up and down on the swell, struggling to keep her head above the giant grey waves that batted her about like a child's ball washed out to sea. Hopelessly she reached out an arm towards the *Haslemere*'s towering side as it lunged towards her through the driving sleet.

The crew scuttled around the deck in a frenzied attempt to position the ship so that they could help the pilot but avoid running aground. They knew the sea well enough to realise they had little time: if the freezing cold did not kill the woman, the waves would, but they dared not take the ship too close in such unstable conditions. For hour-long minutes they played cat and mouse with the current, throwing rope after rope towards the figure, each line teased back towards them by the powerful water. One crew member clambered over the bulwarks to cling from the outermost edges of the ship, his taut body stretched to its limits, fingertips aching to reach the woman. Through the spray he glimpsed a leather pilot's helmet framing neat eyebrows and luminous blue eyes above high cheekbones and a mouth contorted with fear.

'Hurry, please, hurry . . .' The three words rang in the crew's ears as the current pushed the woman dangerously close to the ship. A sudden swell sent the *Haslemere* lurching forward; the crew were unable to pull it back in time and the ship's stern crashed down on the woman who was sucked into the blades of the propeller.

Lieutenant-Commander Fletcher, the *Haslemere*'s thirty-four-year-old captain, broke the morbid silence by scrabbling to tear off his duffel coat and boots. They could see another body in the water, further from the ship but still within reach of the convoy. At least two men on the *Haslemere* were convinced that the helmet and scarf were similar to those worn by a member of the Luftwaffe. Fletcher abandoned his command to dive into the icy sea.

From a distance Fletcher appeared to support himself on the figure for two or three minutes before leaving it to strike out for the *Haslemere*'s lifeboat that was battling the waves to reach him. 'For God's sake, lad, tell them to pull!' he shouted to the oarsman as the waves tossed him in and out of view. A naval motor launch overtook the rowing boat and one of its crew heaved Fletcher aboard with a boat hook. He was limp and silent; a sailor's desperate attempts at artificial resuscitation kept him alive but failed to rouse him from his comatose state. Fletcher never regained consciousness and died five days later from exposure and shock at the Royal Naval Hospital, Gillingham.

A few personal possessions – a logbook, Christmas presents still in their wartime wrapping paper and two bags – were washed up at various points close to the pebbly shore of Herne Bay. Later that day another ship spotted a piece of plywood about ten feet by four feet floating in the Thames Estuary; it was covered with yellow fabric and the figure '5' was clearly visible on it. The personal effects were Amy Johnson's; the wreckage came from the plane she had been flying.

On Tuesday morning the newspapers announced that Amy Johnson had bailed out of her plane over the Thames Estuary and that she was missing. The same evening the Admiralty issued a press release saying that the *Haslemere*'s crew had spotted two people in the water and that one was a woman. The statement turned the tragic loss of a national hero into something more sinister. There were rumours that she was on a secret mission or fleeing the country with a German. The press dubbed the second body 'Mr X'.

The Ministry of Aircraft Production denounced the Admiralty's statement and asserted that Amy Johnson had got lost in bad weather. But it was too late to stop the deluge of rumour and counter-rumour, and the aftermath of her death only added to the suspicion of a cover-up. Inexplicably, both the handbag belonging to one of the world's most famous pilots and the salvaged wing went missing soon after their discovery. No adequate explanation was ever given for their disappearance. Mr X's identity remained a mystery for more than sixty years and Amy Johnson's body was never found.

PART I

Beginnings

Chapter 1

The Land of Green Ginger

Hull is a city out on a limb. It is not the sort of place you stumble upon by chance; nor is it a place to visit without a specific purpose in mind. It sits some thirty miles inland from the North Sea on a great gash of a promontory created by the mighty Humber Estuary. Looking out onto the vast expanse of muddy water feels just like looking out to sea; Hull is exposed and alone. It is a place of comings and goings a place where journeys begin rather than end.

When Amy Johnson was born on 1 July 1903, Hull had been a city for six years. Its full title of Kingston-upon-Hull refers to the less spectacular river that winds its way south to the estuary. Amy was born into a city with a great deal of civic pride. At school she learnt about its most famous sons: anti-slavery campaigner William Wilberforce and poet Andrew Marvell. Hull's remoteness from the national seat of government made it defiant rather than insular. Red telephone boxes, that most English of English landmarks, never made their way to the city; instead public telephone calls are made from off-white cubicles operated by an independent exchange that was set up the year before Amy's birth.

Travel was in her blood. Her paternal grandfather, Anders Jorgensen, was blown into Hull in the mid-nineteenth century from Fyn, one of a clutch of islands entrapped by the Danish mainland of Jutland and the rest of Scandinavia. Jorgensen was the son of a well-digger in the village of Saltofte near Assens, on the west coast of Fyn. Fishing was the only means of escape and the teenage Jorgensen joined one of the boats that stalked the North Sea.

A thriving Scandinavian community already existed in Hull, the port's position on the east coast making it ideally placed to trade with Russia and the north Baltic states. It might well have remained a sleepy medieval port had it not been for the canals that emerged in the late eighteenth century and which filtered exports from Britain's industrial heartland in the Midlands and Sheffield to northern Europe. By 1858 there were regular steamship sailings to Copenhagen and the booming railway industry had increased the demand for timber from Sweden.

Iron, grain and linseed from Scandinavia were already in demand. As
the century progressed Hull became a funnel for immigrants who
either planned to settle in Britain or take the train to Liverpool, where
they sailed for America. Ola Månsson, a Swedish politician accused of
embezzlement and extra-marital affairs, passed through Hull at about
the same time that Jorgensen decided to settle there. In 1859 he arrived
with his mistress and son on their way to a new life in America.
Månsson's grandson, who was born a year before Amy, was Charles
Lindbergh who, in 1927, became the first person to fly solo across the
Atlantic.

Like the business of record-breaking flights, Hull's livelihood – first
whaling, then fishing – depended on weather. All three pursuits were
waiting games. Whaling, for oil and bone, was highly dangerous, and
between 1772 and 1852 4 per cent of Hull's whaling ships never
returned. Gradually fishing started to replace whaling as the main
source of trade, spurred on in 1843 by the discovery of 'Silver Pits', a
spot fifty miles out in the North Sea, close to Dogger Bank, where flat,
mottled sole lay· waiting to be scooped up in previously unimaginable
quantities. The rich hunting-grounds lured fishermen in their smacks,
small fishing-boats with bright red sails, from Brixham in Devon and
Ramsgate on the south coast.

Jorgensen served an apprenticeship with one of the local trawlers in
an environment so cruel that, in 1882, a parliamentary select committee was set up to investigate working conditions. He adopted British
nationality and changed his name to the more manageable Andrew
Johnson. His final act of assimilation was to marry the stepdaughter of
a Brixham skipper, Mary Ann Holmes, or Polly, as she was known.

Polly, like her new husband, was someone trying to overcome a difficult start in life. Her father, Thomas Holmes, had been a stoker on a
merchant ship sailing off the west coast of Canada. His naked body,
partly decapitated, was found in bushes after he went missing during
shore leave.[1] A native American Indian was hanged for the murder,
although he denied it to the last.

Johnson had not left his homeland simply to remain a poor fisherman, and he was determined to escape the poverty he had been born
into. His first goal was to become a skipper, then he set his sights on
buying a boat. While London smacksmen earned a weekly wage, no
matter how much fish they brought back, most Hull fishermen
received a share of their total catch, making it possible for industrious
and thrifty men to save up enough to purchase a boat. Johnson was
hard-working and careful with money, and managed to buy first one

and then two smacks. He was a businessman at heart and astute enough to recognise that sending fishing-boats out into the unpredictable North Sea would never offer a secure living. Instead he decided to spread his risk by providing specialist services to different markets, something which was feasible once ice became widely and cheaply available after the establishment of the Hull Ice Company in 1864.

Together with a Norwegian partner, Johnson set up a business that capitalised on local skills of curing and smoking. The firm, Andrew Johnson Knudtzon, which was known simply as 'AJK', imported fresh herrings and salmon from Scandinavia and exported haddock and salted cod, the latter finding a ready market in Catholic countries, where it was deemed suitable to eat on fast-days and Fridays. After only a few years the business's Norwegian founder died, leaving Johnson and his ten children to build AJK into a tightly-run family concern based at the new St Andrew's Dock which opened in 1883.[2]

By the time John William, the first of Johnson's six sons and Amy's father, was born in 1877, Hull was Britain's third largest port. Will, as he was known, was smaller than the tall, bearded patriarch who had started AJK, but he inherited his father's business acumen and taste for adventure. He started work in the family firm aged fifteen, and by the time he was twenty-one business was so good that he could afford to indulge his thirst for travel. Joining the Klondike gold-rush promised to fulfil his twin aims in life of making money and finding adventure. The expedition turned out to be a particularly harsh introduction to both.

Will was one of a party of four local men who set off for the inhospitable corner of north-west Canada after a celebratory concert at the Liberal Hall in Hull, attended by 500 men who made speeches and sang 'Auld Lang Syne'. They were naive travelling companions who viewed the trip as a bit of caper, entertaining one another with pillow-fights, gymnastic displays and playing the banjo. Will was the most serious of the group and, during the week or more that it took them to cross Canada, his main concern was changing the film in his camera under a blanket or asking one of his friends to use a coat to block the light from the window so that his photos were not over-exposed. He emerges as a young man intoxicated with the thrill of embarking on the first real adventure of his life; but whose natural romance is constantly held in check by a need to impose order. He fingers the dollars and cents in his pocket with awe, a constant reminder of their exotic location, but at the same time keeps a meticulous note of everything the party buys: 'four canvas bags . . . four cowboy hats . . . oats for horse . . . curry powder . . . magnifying glass . . .'

When they finally arrived at Atlin, British Columbia, they found a cluttered city of white tents and log cabins, freezing conditions and hopelessness. The sound of the steamer was the only noise that lifted the gloom, and even then it could bring false hope: one boat carried seven 'stiff uns' who had died from fever. Men dropped dead from exertion and even the group's horse seemed to have run out of patience, kicking a fellow prospector close to the heart. The map reminded them that this was a place where men took second place to nature. Among the unexplored mountains there was a Moose River, Little Sheep Creek and Reindeer Mountain.[3]

Will's journal[4] drifted in and out of shorthand, as if there were some thoughts too dangerous to share – or perhaps he wanted to keep secret details of where they were prospecting. He started to read the Psalms and a chapter of the Bible each day and became obsessed with mosquitoes and the cold. His greatest fear was realised when he fell through a hole in the ice. As he clawed at the river's slippery, frozen ceiling, a man trying to save him fell in before they were both rescued. The ordeal strengthened Will's already deep-rooted faith in God: 'I believe we are in the Lord's hands and you know with His guidance no harm can come to us, in fact I have had proof He is guiding us and keeping us from harm,' he wrote to his brother and sister.[5]

Will's prospecting days failed to dampen his taste for travel, but he never forgot that seeking adventure was a serious, often life-threatening, pursuit. On his return home he was more of a risk-taker than many men from his background, but the ordeal had quashed some of his natural romance. From now on opportunities were assessed with a businessman's rigour, not a dreamer's impulsiveness.

When, in September 1902, Will chose a wife, he picked a woman he loved, but also someone familiar with the mores of a social class slightly higher than his own. In two generations Amy Hodge's family had fallen almost as far as Will's had risen. Her grandfather, William, was born in 1805 on a small farm near Kilnsea on the isolated Spurn Head peninsula to the extreme east of Hull. At twenty William turned his back on farming to take a job in the booming linseed-crushing industry.[6] Mills were scattered along the River Hull to take delivery from boats and barges and process the raw material for the paint and candle industries and for cattle-cake. He worked his way up from foreman to manager before setting up a lucrative business with his brother.

In his fifties, William, now stout and bewhiskered, started a career in local politics. He was elected a town councillor and then alderman. In

1860 he became mayor and it was his casting vote that decided that Hull should have a grand new town hall. During his second term he laid the foundation-stone for the new building and entertained a large party at the Victoria Hotel. Later he bequeathed a statue of King Edward I to sit in the hall.

William needed a home in keeping with his new status in life, and in 1861 he bought Newington Hall, situated on the south side of the Anlaby Road. The house was built in 1842 by the son of a Hull grocer and was known locally as 'Bacon Hall' after the food that funded its construction.[7] It was an unashamedly ostentatious home built in the Greek Revival style. The main entrance was guarded by four Corinthian columns and inside a huge hall rose the full height of the building to a central skylight. A sweeping cast-iron staircase with a mahogany handrail led to the first floor and its seven bedrooms and two dressing rooms. On the ground floor there were drawing, dining and morning rooms. Outside, gravel paths cut through the well-kept lawns to an aviary, stables, kitchen garden, Swiss-style cottage, vines, coach and cow houses.

William's generous acts of philanthropy reinforced the message of Newington Hall – that the Hodges were doing very well for themselves. He funded chapels devoted to Primitive Methodism throughout the east of England, but his cash-flow could not keep up with his ambitions and, towards the end of his life, with his second wife and their five children, he abandoned Newington Hall for a more modest house in Coltman Street, not far from St Andrew's Docks. It was here, in November 1867, that he died following a series of strokes.[8]

His eldest son had none of his father's hard-work ethos or business sense. He made several trips abroad, leaving his wife to look after their eight children, and although he invested some of his money in timber, he was forced to sell off his father's seed mills. Newington Hall looked down on the family as a painful reminder of the status and wealth they had let slip through their fingers, until the house was demolished five years after Amy Johnson was born, leaving her with tales of lost wealth and days when the family dined off a silver table service engraved with their newly acquired crest.

This helter-skelter down the social ranks left Amy Hodge, who was known as 'Ciss', an insecure and twitchy young woman. When, aged twenty-one, she married Will Johnson, she recognised that she was marrying 'beneath' her family, but had the sense to realise that the Johnson name, unlike her own, was on an upward trajectory. Will was someone who would protect her and who had a healthy respect for money. Despite his steadying influence, Ciss never managed to shake off the feeling that something dreadful was just around the corner. She suffered from 'nerves' and was obsessive about the cleanliness of her house. Her one release was playing the piano or practising the organ at their local Methodist chapel.

Will and Ciss's marriage was immediately fruitful and Amy Johnson was born in the summer of 1903 at 154 St George's Road. At Kitty Hawk in North Carolina on 17 December that same year, Orville Wright, lying next to the engine of a spindly biplane, lurched into the air for twelve seconds, while his brother Wilbur looked on. This first ever flight in a heavier-than-air contraption went completely unnoticed by the rest of the world. It was three years later, when the brothers recorded the first passenger flight covering two and a half miles, that news of their achievement began to seep out. Even then it was only France, a country which celebrated the wonder and potential of flying, that was in any way interested. This enthusiasm appeared premature when, on 17 September 1908, the Wright brothers' plane crashed, killing Lieutenant T. E. Selfridge in an accident that become the first fatality in powered aviation.

Irene Johnson was born eighteen months after Amy in the same stolid, terraced Victorian house a few roads west of where Ciss had spent the latter part of her childhood. Amy later remembered her birthplace as 'an ugly suburban street',9 but the road was too close to the docks to fulfil this genteel description. The Johnsons lived in what was known as the Hessle Road area of Hull and, although St George's Road was one of the more affluent streets, the stench of fish still hung in the air and the fishing community's traditions ruled every aspect of life.

Amy grew up in a place dominated by one of the most hazardous industries of its day and where every journey had its own ritual. Superstition forbade fishermen's wives from waving their menfolk off to sea and washing was banned while they were away, lest they 'wash' their breadwinner overboard. It was unlucky for a fisherman to look back after he had left the house and there was a whole catch of words that were deemed inauspicious, including 'pig' (probably because the animal was revered by pagans and seen as unclean by Jews) and 'dog' (possibly because the word is 'God' spelt backwards and because dogs were thought to be able to foresee the approach of death).10 Middle-class families like the Johnsons found a more formal comfort in the many Nonconformist chapels dotted around the area.

Stormy weather was the most obvious enemy, but the North Sea was always capable of producing some unimagined horror. The most shocking incident occurred in the early hours of Saturday, 22 October 1904. A fishing fleet of some forty ships was trawling near the Dogger Bank, two hundred miles from Spurn, when the Russian Baltic fleet appeared out of the darkness and bombarded the Hull vessels for nearly twenty minutes. The Russians had mistaken the ships for the Japanese, with whom they were at war, despite one fisherman holding up a fish in a desperate bid to highlight their occupation. Two men were killed and seven injured in the debacle, which caused outrage in Hull.

When Amy was six the family jumped a few streets east to a road called Boulevard and then, in 1910, putting more distance between them and the docks, to 48 Alliance Avenue. Two years later Molly was born, once more dashing Will's hopes of a male heir for the fishing business. This latest and, so Will and Ciss believed, last effort to produce a son cast Amy in the role of heir apparent.

Outwardly, Will was a sociable man. In 1914 his father retired and Will officially became head of the family business – a role which he had in effect been filling for several years. Hull was quick to make the transition to steam but the heavy capital investment necessary to buy new boats meant there was no room for the smaller entrepreneur; the fishing industry was now concentrated in the hands of a few wealthy individuals. As the business became more and more successful Will embraced the trappings that went with this success: he joined the Rotary Club and became a Freemason; he played golf and attended functions at the Chamber of Commerce. He became a pillar of Hull's business community and enjoyed what money could buy, purchasing a six-horsepower twin Rex 1914 motorbike with sidecar for £50, until the day when he could afford a car, when he bought two – a Standard saloon and a two-seater Morris Oxford.

Will was a stalwart supporter of Hull City Football Club, but he enjoyed the games in a detached and private way; he was not the sort of man to lose control, even on a football terrace. Despite his busy social diary, he was a loner with few close friends. He could only properly relax at home, where he played chess, filled his stamp album and kept a meticulous account of his life that included how much he spent on family presents and a record of his daughters' school marks. Will was not a distant Edwardian father and felt no inhibitions in romping on the floor with his daughters pretending he was a bear, but he was also capable of being a strict patriarch.[11] He enjoyed his all-powerful position as head of a household of three daughters, laying down rules and then allowing them to be broken. His inconsistencies and Ciss's obsession with maintaining standards of decorum led to a volatile, door-slamming atmosphere at home.

Ciss was prone to violent mood swings and Will's vacillation between disciplinarian and doting father left the girls confused about what was expected of them. In many ways they were spoilt: friends envied their fashionable clothes and family outings to the theatre, cinema and occasionally the opera, but Will's generosity was rarely unconditional. Gifts, especially of money, were usually preceded by negotiations and lectures; cash was used to make a point. Will kept his lawn as neat as the neighbours' by paying Amy to get down on her hands and knees to forage for daisies; harvesting a hundred tiny flowers earned her a penny.[12] He also paid her to learn a church hymn off by heart, convinced that the indoctrination was money well spent.

She was a restless tomboy, snatching every opportunity to escape or subvert the hushed decorum of her home and locking herself in the bathroom to avoid talking to visitors. A photo of her as a small girl shows her sitting in a typical Edwardian pose, the elbow of her right arm resting on the open book she is supposed to be reading. The face is that of a little girl, sweetly innocent with long, brown hair trailing down her back in ringlets. But her body language is uneasy: her left arm is draped limply over her lap, her feet are crossed at the ankle and she is slouching as if poised to slip off the chair and run into the garden the minute the photographer has finished. All kinds of physical exertion – the more dangerous the better – mesmerised her to the point of addiction and her boyish obsession with sport provided an unintentional reminder of Will's longing for a son. She later claimed that at the age of twelve she would steal rides on her father's motorbike when he was at work, and when Ciss was out she and Irene turned the most hallowed room in the house, the front parlour, into a race-track, hurling themselves from sofa to table to piano in a game whose only rule was to avoid touching the floor. One contest ended abruptly when they were discovered trying to swing from the gas fitting that hung from the ceiling.

Amy preferred muddy hockey to the more sedate and socially acceptable tennis, and she went to gym classes two or three times a week at the Young People's Institute. Here she chose the most energetic and perilous activities, sailing through the air on the trapeze, leaping over the wooden horse and hurling herself at the springboard. Her headmaster, though, viewed Amy's delight in swimming as unladylike and quashed her attempts to form a girls' club; she responded by persuading Will to hire the local baths so that she could host a gala for female swimmers.

Only boys shared her craving for physical activity and only they were prepared to indulge her need for competition. At school male pupils were strictly separated from females and Amy's sole chance of meeting boys was going to and from school or at the nearby sweetshop. She impressed them by being the one girl capable of bowling overarm at cricket and by her fearlessness in playing 'chicken', a game in which a cyclist careers towards a brick wall before skidding away at the very last moment.

Amy's membership of the boys' gang ended abruptly at the age of fourteen with an accident that blighted the rest of her life. The girl who could bowl like a boy failed to catch the hard leather missile that hit her full in the mouth, leaving her with a broken tooth, a bad lisp and an inferiority complex. Her two front teeth were replaced with badly fitting dentures. So began a life-long obsession with her appearance and with dentists: 'There was no doubt that my looks were seriously impaired from the point of view of my male class-mates and, from being the ringleader, I quickly adopted a most unfortunate inferiority complex which followed me through the rest of my life and probably had a most important bearing on my future actions and character.'[13]

This brutal loss of status, which cruelly coincided with the disorientating arrival of puberty, left Amy feeling resentful and withdrawn. A teenage heaviness crept up on her; she became plump with thick eyebrows and chubby cheeks, looking out of her hockey team photo with a brooding hostility. School had always bored her; up to the age of twelve she went to a series of genteel establishments run by spinsters with little imagination or desire to push bright pupils. Lessons presented no challenge and she came top of the class in most subjects with little effort. Boulevard Secondary, where she was put in a class with children much younger than herself, was even more stultifying and she spent her time devising acts of rebellion. It was no coincidence that when, in 1920, Irene was moved from Boulevard to the more refined Hull High School,[14] Amy launched a campaign against the compulsory wearing of straw hats, known as 'bangers'. Significantly, girls at Irene's school wore the more sophisticated soft panamas. Confident that her fellow students would follow her lead, Amy turned up at school wearing a panama fitted with her school's badge and ribbon. But she was a lone rebel made to sit by herself outside the headteacher's room for several hours. After this humiliation she started to skive off school for long, lonely cycle rides in the countryside or to immerse herself in the girls' adventure books of Angela Brazil or the darkened escapism of the cinema.

Her status at home was also changing as her parents became preoccupied with their second daughter, Irene, who was emerging as a flighty, irascible girl. Irene was pretty and vivacious and enjoyed dressing up and amateur dramatics. During Christmas charades she was the whimsical fairy who represented the fresh new year while Amy played the dour old man of the retreating months. But Irene was also moody and often sank into dark depressions that cast a pall over the entire house. As the eldest child Amy felt a strong responsibility towards her younger sisters but she also resented the attention lavished on Irene.

His two daughters' violent mood swings were among the many worries that gnawed away at Will Johnson during the second decade of the new century. He was thirty-nine when war broke out and he recorded its progress with grim detail in his diary, intertwining national with personal events. At 3.45 p.m. on Thursday, 11 January 1917 his brother Bert was killed in France. In April potatoes were 'almost unobtainable' and in June fifteen aeroplanes attacked East London in broad daylight, leaving a hundred people dead and four hundred injured.

The First World War signalled excitement and change for Amy; even everyday objects appeared in a new light. The upper windows of trams were painted sepia, the lower decks were fitted with curtains, and streetlamps were disguised in two tones of blue. There were no official air-raid shelters and people were advised to hide under the stairs. Some ignored the warning and gathered in one of Hull's parks, taking pets and joints of ham with them; others simply lay down in ditches.

Amy enjoyed the excitement of air raids – the excuse to stay up late, playing games and drinking hot chocolate while the family took shelter in the cellar. The raids failed to inspire in her any thoughts of flying, as she later pointed out: 'The popular Press adopted the line that it was this early acquaintance with Zeppelins which first put the thought of flying into my head. I do not for one moment believe that to be true. I was far more likely to have felt an intense hatred of them and their awful power.'[15]

Children were warned to talk in whispers to stop the Zeppelin crews, floating high above the clouds, eavesdropping on their conversations, and it was seriously suggested that clocks should be stopped in case their ticking guided the airships to their target. On the night of 6 June 1915 at 10 p.m. such paranoia proved to be justified. There were two 'official' forms of air-raid warning: an urgent buzzing sounded and electric lights were dipped. The streets became eerily deserted. By midnight the citizens of Hull could hear the low purring noise of an approaching Zeppelin, followed by the ghostly clanging of its signalling bells. Two bombs dropped harmlessly in the dock area to the east of the Johnson house, but the Old Town, with its tiny alleyways such as the Land of Green Ginger and its mainly working-class houses, was less fortunate. Forty people were injured and twenty-five killed.

The bombing led to accusations that London had not bothered to give Hull proper defences against German attacks. Suspicion became a way of life. A stranger, especially if he had a beard, was assumed to be a spy and anyone unfortunate enough to bear a German-sounding name became an outcast. Later in June 1915 there were ugly attacks on shops in the Hessle Road area of Hull; most were pork butchers and all were owned by families with Teutonic names such as 'Schumm', 'Steeg' and 'Hohenrein'.

As the war continued most fish and chip shops in Hull shut. The Government requisitioned many ships and catches arrived in vessels sailing under the flags of neutral countries. AJK's herring trade with Norway kept the business going and Will's work in the food industry meant he avoided being called up, but the strain of running a family business in such difficult times was almost too great and he became ill with a skin disease called erysipelas. The Johnsons' home became one of lowered voices and a nurse moved in to care for Will. The three girls watched in horror as the illness stoked up their father's pallid face into a scarlet crustiness that eventually gave way to painfully peeling skin. While the disease took its course Will was transformed from a bustling little businessman into a reclusive invalid who hid away from the outside world.

The end of the war hastened Will's return to good health. He fitted in more comfortably in post-war Britain than the men returning from the trenches: his mind was not clouded with images of mud and mutilated bodies. Peace meant a resumption of full trade and enabled the Johnsons to make their final, and most ambitious, move in Hull, to 85 Park Avenue. The change of address took them still further away from the docks and their mercantile roots to one of the most select areas of Hull, still known today as The Avenues.

The area, in the north-west of the city, is made up of four wide, tree-lined boulevards that run parallel to one another. The houses are individual, even quirky, Victorian red-brick flights of fancy, many of them turreted. When Amy lived there the road intersections were adorned with six fabulous cast-iron fountains depicting mermaids and herons. Nearby Pearson Park, known as the People's Park, offered a tranquil escape to the east. This was a distinctly well-to-do area where emotions were kept constantly in check. Middle-class families formed a cordon sanitaire around them: the Johnsons had solicitors and businessmen, even an American ambassador, as neighbours. During the war Dorothy L. Sayers, then a French teacher at the school Irene was to attend, lodged at 80 Westbourne Avenue, the next road running south from Park Avenue. Sayers, who had moved to Hull to take up her first job after graduating from Oxford, was surprised by the quality of the shops and the fact that the city had at least one decent café.[16] 'I don't think Hull is a bad city, though ugly and dreadfully dirty – I mean in the way of smuts and things,' she wrote in a letter to a friend.[17]

Will and Ciss's fourth child, Betty, was born in May 1919. It seems unlikely that the birth was planned.[18] Like most sixteen-year-olds, Amy probably felt a mixture of jealousy at the new arrival and embarrassment that her parents were still reproducing. She became more and more reclusive, lost in daydreams of travelling round the world. Once when she went to the cinema an aeroplane featured in a newsreel item and she was so captivated by it that she sat through the whole programme twice to see the aircraft again. 'For some strange reason that aeroplane appealed to me enormously. It seemed to offer the chance of escape for which I was always looking.'[19]

She discovered the Blackburn Aircraft Factory at nearby Brough and began to cycle out by herself to watch, from a distance, the planes being assembled. Amy was too shy to walk through the factory gates and the planes remained tantalisingly out of reach. Until one summer after the end of the war.

Chapter 2

Joy-riding

(1919–25)

The battered Avro 504 biplane that tottered through the summer sky was the first plane its passengers, waiting on the grass below for their 'five-bob flip', had ever seen. The makeshift airfield, a meadow hired for the day from a local farmer, had a tent in one corner where the pilot's wife sold tickets; red cans of Shell petrol were strewn on the ground. The heady perfume of crushed grass and spent engine oil hung in the air. To the former RAF pilots who flew the Avros this was the scent of post-war England. The airmen were only eking out a living, but at least they had an occupation. To the customers who clambered up the shaky wooden step-ladder into the cockpit, the women clutching their cloche hats and billowing dresses, the fifteen-minute spin represented the spirit of what became known as the 'carefree twenties'.

Writing in 1938, Amy remembers one 'never-to-be-forgotten weekend, when the war was over' in that 'queer era of joy-riding' when an old, wartime plane came to a field near Hull and offered flights for five shillings a time. She pooled her birthday money with Irene's spare cash and they climbed together into the ageing plane.[1]

'Oh, the disappointment!' she wrote later. 'I don't know for what I had hoped. Maybe I thought it would be ten times as exciting as a swing-boat at the fair, but it was not. There was no sensation. Just a lot of noise and wind, smell of burnt oil and escaping petrol. My hair was blown into a tangled mass which could not be combed out for days and I was almost – not quite – cured of flying for ever.'

The joy-riding pilots, who had left what, on 1 April 1918, became the Royal Air Force when the Royal Flying Corps merged with the Royal Naval Air Service, were among the lucky ones able to earn some sort of living from the skills that had kept them in the skies during the primitive, early days of aerial warfare. The end of hostilities produced a group of dispossessed men who returned home to a foreign country. In many cases their jobs had disappeared and they were incapable of sharing with their friends and family the horrors they had seen: the hideousness was too great to voice and the rest of the country wanted to put the Great War out of their minds.

Years in uniform meant they literally spoke another language, the language of army slang and trench banter. The awful, unspoken truth of the war's futility and savagery began to emerge over a decade later in books such as *Testament of Youth*, *All Quiet on the Western Front* and *Journey's End*.

Many out-of-work pilots bought up ex-wartime planes: the Avro in Britain and the Curtiss Jenny in the USA. Joy-riding – or barn-storming, as it was called in America after the itinerant actors who travelled the country, often performing in barns – gave pilots the chance to fly regularly and so retain their licences. It offered a wandering, undisciplined lifestyle that suited demobbed pilots better than clocking on or living on the newly termed 'dole'. The public was fascinated by the rickety planes that swooped down on them and offered them thrills and spills while the weather lasted and then, just as quickly, disappeared.

Many people believed a trip in a plane could ease ear problems – and often the change in pressure did provide relief. Others were simply curious to see what their home looked like from the air. One male passenger, whom Charles Lindbergh took up during his early flying career, expressed a desire to urinate over his town and the people in it.[2]

As flying circuses became increasingly common, crowds demanded ever greater feats of daring; wing-walking was superseded by stuntmen and women dancing the Charleston in mid air. Planes strafed spectators with flour bombs and, in Atlantic City, ten thousand people watched a man leap from one aircraft to another. Under the skilled guidance of the devoted pilots planes became performing pets. They were coaxed into holding conversations while they waited on the ground, dipping their noses in agreement or twitching their wings in a quizzical fashion in reply to questions rattled out from a tinny loudspeaker. The machines played the straight man in a crazy world of Keystone Kop characters. Crowds watched while an apparently genuine policeman chased a burglar towards the plane. The villain leapt into the Avro and took it high above the field, the policeman dangling from a strut for just as long it was safe. If the flying circus was big enough the criminal might even parachute from what appeared to be an empty plane, leaving a concealed pilot to take the controls.

Planes were exotic and playful and fitted into the post-war mood: after four years of deprivation and worry, people wanted to enjoy themselves. During the summer of 1919 thousands flocked to the seaside in a 'holiday scramble' and tales of derring-do, of people risking their lives to make the world smaller, generated huge interest. In a year in which three separate attempts were made to cross the Atlantic, Captain John Alcock and Lieutenant Arthur Whitten Brown became the first to fly the ocean non-stop. Their already heroic journey assumed superhuman proportions when Brown pulled himself up in his seat to kneel on the edge of the fuselage so that he could reach out into the bitterly cold air to wipe snow off the glass face of the petrol-flow gauge that was mounted on a strut just out of reach of the pilot. He repeated the hazardous balancing act some six times.[3]

Despite the end of hostilities, 1919 was not a carefree year. In the summer a virulent form of influenza broke out that turned into a pandemic that would claim more lives than the First World War. Hull trawler engineers went on strike and Will Johnson was left worrying about the lack of fish arriving in the port. Wartime shortages meant Amy and her sisters experienced a Christmas with very few sweets or toys.

As Amy neared the end of her final year at school, her parents could not make up their minds what to do with their intelligent, restless elder daughter. For Ciss there was but one course of action: Amy should do as her mother had done and learn how to run a home. But Amy, with her celluloid-fuelled dreams of travel and adventure, nurtured ambitions beyond housekeeping. Apart from sulking, there were few ways in which she could make her displeasure known. When she did respond she chose a shocking and long-lasting act of defiance.

In the twenties short hair equalled independence, and when Amy hacked off the two plaits, each ending in her school's maroon bows (a colour she loathed), she was making a very public statement. Will punished her for the assault on the long, tumbling ringlets that Ciss had spent years brushing and curling by forcing her to stay on at school for an extra year until her hair had grown to a less defiant length. His decision sharpened Amy's resentfulness by thrusting her into the anomalous position of a nineteen-year-old who was still at school, too old to mix easily with fellow students and bored by the classes that she had found tedious the first time round.

She was on the look-out for anything to relieve the tedium of her enforced return to the classroom; Hans Arregger did much more than that. They first met at a party given by her aunt Evelyn who had been widowed during the war and who lived twenty miles north of Hull at Bridlington, a town in which seasonal kiss-me-quick exuberance jostled with middle-class decorum. After the First World War 'Brid' ranked as one of the top ten most popular seaside resorts in England and Wales; at the height of the summer thousands of holidaymakers flocked to its exposed North Sea beaches. Though certainly no Blackpool or Margate, it was more popular than Torquay and Skegness and had a core of permanent residents who worked in Hull and liked to think of themselves as professionals. Hans, who rented accommodation in Brid, commuted daily to the city. A Swiss by birth, he spoke French, German and Italian fluently in a loud, strong voice; his English was passable and he was able to read, but not converse in, Spanish. His ease with languages won him a job at Hull's Swiss consulate where he helped tend his country's trading links with northern Europe.

Hans was the eldest of two sons in a family of six children. Their father had run a small business until his death in 1915 and his widow lived with her four daughters in a large flat in Lucerne. Hans, who was born in 1895, had attended the officers' training school in Basle and patrolled the country's borders when the First World War was raging around neutral Switzerland. These war years were the most carefree of his life: he rode horses, skated, drove his motorbike and played the piccolo. Hans did not like being pinned down and the thought of assuming the role of head of the household following his father's death appalled him. He neatly side-stepped the issue by leaving the country to work at the Swiss consulate in Amsterdam before moving to Hull in 1921.

During his first summer in England Hans met Amy's aunt and her son John at a tennis club in Bridlington. The experienced man of the world and ex-army officer barely noticed Evelyn's gauche young niece; he later remembered her as having eyes that 'popped out' and that her sister Irene was much prettier. Amy had yet to succumb to anything other than a schoolgirl crush but Hans's short, stocky physique instantly attracted her.

His maturity and otherness appealed at a time when she was being forced to return to the childish sameness of her schooldays. She liked the fact that he was eight years older than her, but his exoticism, marked by a curious Swiss/French accent and sullenness, appealed most.

Everything about him was different and unconventional. His manners were precise and continental; he held himself erect and bowed slightly when introduced to people and was full of little gallantries, greeting women with a kiss on the hand. Such theatrical gestures aroused Amy's romantic nature but instantly alienated her down-to-earth father. Hans dressed with a neat, almost spiv-like precision; when he smoked he clenched a cigarette-holder between his teeth so that it stood to attention in the corner of his mouth. In Hull he was well known for his hats: in winter he wore high Italian Homburgs made from beige or creamy velours; in summer he switched to straw boaters. His appearance was seen as deeply eccentric and passers-by openly stared at him in the street. Hans was older than Amy, foreign, Roman Catholic, given to intellectual musings and in trade. Short of being German – which he might as well have been, given his name – he could hardly have been further from the suitor Amy's parents had in mind – which, of course, made him all the more attractive. For years she had been searching for a challenge and capturing Hans gave her a purpose in life.

There was a gap after their initial meeting but Amy made sure they 'bumped into' each other by joining a group that met in Hull to practise their French. Hans spotted the advantage of having someone at hand who could help improve his English and he enjoyed the company of women, but it was Amy who did all the running. Letters from Amy to Hans show that they had started a relationship by March 1922.

Amy's future was decided that summer. Encouraged by the Boulevard's Principal, her parents agreed that she should go to Sheffield University as the first step towards what was at that time the most common career for female graduates – a job in teaching. In 1910 the Board of Education offered grants covering all fees and financial help towards living expenses to students who agreed to become teachers after graduation. Amy was no longer marking time: she would soon be leaving home, and while she was still in Hull she had a daring relationship to explore. The knowledge of these two escape routes imbued her life at home with a rare calmness.

In June she wrote to her father, who was away on one of his frequent business trips, telling him how she liked to sit on the stairs and sing to their dog, Patch. She told him about a newspaper advertisement that Irene had spotted and which the two sisters found hysterically funny. The advert was trying to sell a type of baby's bottle: 'When a baby has done drinking, unscrew it and put it in a cool place under the tap. If the baby does not thrive on fresh milk, it must be boiled.' The two sisters concocted their own advert: 'For sale. A splendid pram suitable for stout babies. If the baby is too small to fit the body stuff it with cushions.'[4]

Once she had left home Amy's letters to Hans grew in length and frequency as the intensity of their relationship deepened; sometimes she wrote more than once a day. Most of the several hundred letters she sent have survived and are held in Hull's Central Library; a legend persists that the missing letters mysteriously disappeared because of their content.

Hans's replies, too, have vanished, so that the account of their relationship is inevitably one-sided. Amy's outpourings to Hans reflect her deep insecurity in a relationship that never settles into mutual trust and in which she is aware that she is making all the running. Hans was so far removed from her limited experience of men that it was as if Rudolph Valentino had stepped down from the silent screen. She knew that to him she was no more than a dizzy schoolgirl, but her attempts to provoke jealousy in him always ended in petulant outbursts that merely confirmed her immaturity. While Hans dominated her thoughts, he found it easy to pick up and drop the relationship at will; at best it was an amusing distraction, but when Amy was at her most insecure it became an irritation.

Hans found many uses for Amy; their early love letters were at times little more than a correspondence course in the English language in which Amy rejoiced in her superior knowledge and corrected his grammar with meticulous care. They both enjoyed the theatre, dancing and literature and discussed them at length, although for Hans such conversations were first and foremost a way of improving his English. He viewed her as a well-connected scion of an important business empire and a useful escort for an outsider trying to infiltrate a social elite. Beyond these motives, her attentions flattered him and he found her innocence intriguing. Her refusal to sleep with him added a frisson to the situation.

He was fully aware that he had the upper hand in the relationship and took a cruel delight in teasing her about the other women in his life; Amy's insecurity was so raw that even the mention of his landlady inflamed her jealousy. When he told her he planned to teach French in his spare time she immediately asked whether his students would include 'some charming lady pupils'.[5]

Her only hold over him was their agreement that she would correct his English, while he would improve her French. Hans persisted in writing solely in English, despite Amy's usually sarcastic comments about his style. She could not resist drawing attention to this one area where she was more confident than him: 'I have decided irrevocably, – (will you have to look this word up?) – to take French, English, Latin and modern history [at Sheffield University].'[6]

Amy soon grew tired of the effort of writing in his language and slipped into a sort of Franglais – 'Votre letter est "hopeless" à corriger'[7] – and, after a fortnight, she gave up altogether, saying it was 'really too much bother' to write in French when she had to listen to lectures in the language all day.[8] She always found the energy, though, to correct Hans's English and to underline his mistakes:

> 'As to <u>disgusting my face</u> by wearing glasses', 'As to make my face more disgusting by . . .'
> Successful has only one 'l' – as all compound words.
> 'Scenery' has no plural and 'co-spectators' should be 'the rest of the audience . . .'

she tells him as she runs through his errors, point by point.[9] But Hans is a natural linguist and it soon becomes harder to find fault; Amy has to resort to pointing out nuances. 'Banal talk', she says, is 'a purely dictionary word and very rarely used . . .'[10] 'It is preferable to use "excellent" before a noun, rather than "very good".' 'If you ask me to be "good enough" to do something any more I'll give you up as hopeless. It's too pedantic for words! And it's a very patronising expression, too, if you know what that means. I don't care to be patronised by anybody, and least of all by you. Say "Would you mind" or simply "please".'[11]

Sheffield was barely seventy miles from Hull but it might as well have been a different country. Instead of the wide open estuary and a community ruled by the sea, Amy was surrounded by stark hills. The steel industry dominated Sheffield and its workshops and factories belched out a pall of smoke that hung over most of the city. The university had a frantic, excitable atmosphere in the early 1920s. Many of its students were ex-servicemen making up for lost time and their exuberance worried the authorities to such an extent that midday dances were banned because of concern about their effect on academic work.

Amy was one of nearly 200 female students studying side-by-side with almost 600 men. She was in demand, and this demand was most obvious on the dance-floor where she learnt to foxtrot and waltz. Most dances were held at Firth Hall, a tall, daunting, red-brick building that sat at the top of a hill looking down on the city with gothic foreboding and where a tutor checked that women students were suitably attired. As there was not enough accommodation for the women, they were forced to lodge with various approved landladies who acted *in loco parentis*, providing meals and watching the behaviour of the young students.

Amy moved more often than most of her contemporaries, always searching for somewhere to live that was cheaper or more convenient. Grange Crescent Road was close to the cemetery, Thompson Road bordered the peaceful Botanical Gardens, Moncrieffe Road took her furthest from the university and her final city address in Glossop Road was a short walk from Firth Hall.

The comforting knowledge that she had a lover, and everyone knew it, allowed her to appear more sophisticated than she was, while Hans's absence left her free to indulge in student pleasures as if she were single. She existed in two distinct orbits: the heady student world of new experiences – amateur dramatics, dances, debates, hockey and intense friendships – and the pull of her Hull life – Hans, her parents and her wilful younger sister. Amy suffered bouts of homesickness in her first weeks away from home and her gloomy state of mind deepened when a nineteen-year-old medical student fell to her death from the top of a staircase, probably in one of the towers that Amy passed daily. The girl was alone at the time and it was never clear whether the death was suicide or a terrible accident. Amy felt horror and fascination in equal measure: 'I simply daren't go near the banisters though when I am at the top I always feel compelled to look over and see how far down it is. It seems to draw you somehow and it's getting on my nerves.'

Amy was not a natural scholar, but she was intoxicated by the atmosphere of academia and startled the professor of economics, Douglas Knoop, by taking a photograph of him in his cap and gown. She could only concentrate on a subject in short, intense bursts and her attention span lasted weeks rather than months or years. 'I'm nearly grey with worry and thin as a matchstick with work,' Amy wrote a few weeks after arriving at Sheffield.[12] She was shocked to discover that she faced an exam at the end of her first term and that failure would make her ineligible for an honours degree. The results arrived just after the Christmas holidays. 'I've never failed before and it's a horrid feeling,' she told Hans.[13] Her main concern was disappointing her father; she tried to persuade the university authorities to allow her to switch to English so that she could say she had simply transferred subjects, but they were not prepared to bend the rules and she settled for an ordinary degree in French, Latin and Economics.

When, at the start of her second year, Winifred Irving bounced into Amy's life, she experienced for the first time the joy of a close friendship with a woman who was her intellectual equal and as physically adventurous as she was. At twenty-one years of age Amy had found a soulmate outside the clutches of the Johnson family. The most significant friendship of Amy's life began by chance when the two women walked home after lectures through the hilly backstreets of Sheffield. They instantly fell into an easy conversation during which they discovered a mutual love of books, dancing, clothes and hockey.

Winifred was tall with bobbed hair and a long face. Her attractiveness stemmed from her energy; she was lively, outspoken and down to earth. She made friends easily and sustained friendships over several years with casual acquaintances made when she was out walking. Elegance evaded her and she sometimes accidentally revealed an excess of leg in a period when hems were still well below the knee. When she entered a room she 'planted' her feet deliberately on the floor, as if to confirm the impression that she was steadfast and reliable. She was a good listener but her advice was always practical; she had no time for 'moping around'. She spoke in a rich mixture of Yorkshire with a trace of Scottish picked up from her engineer father and had a quaint way of ordering her words. The family were Plymouth Brethren and their home in a respectable suburb of Sheffield was a strict, silent place where entertainment of any sort was forbidden. The discipline she had learnt at home allowed her to focus on her studies while still leaving room to enjoy herself. She began by studying French, modern history and geography and easily passed the exam allowing her to sit for an honours degree in economics.

She quickly became the leader of a close-knit group of female friends made up of Amy, Gwyneth Roulston and Constance Tupholme. Constance, or 'Tuppy' as she was known, had gone to school with Winifred and was studying classics. Her father managed a furniture business and she considered herself of a slightly better class than the other three, which probably explained her tendency to bossiness. Gwyneth went to Boulevard with Amy and was a year younger. Her mother had died when she was small and an elder sister had raised her. Gwyneth was not sporty and was quieter than Winifred but her intellectual equal. Amy was the group's loner. The ever-present spectre of Hans, who visited Sheffield once but whose letters chased Amy round the thirty or so lodgings she stayed in as an undergraduate, set her slightly apart from the other girls. She was always holding something back; only Winifred could penetrate her protective shell.

A passion for clothes united the four girls. Amy, Winifred and

Gwyneth were a similar size and augmented their wardrobes by swapping clothes. Winifred and Tuppy had a horror of navy blue because it was the colour of their school uniform, preferring brown, whereas blue was Amy's favourite colour. 'A.J.' or 'Amy J.', as she was called, was well known as a stylish dresser and her navy gabardine dress with 'swing strips' in its skirt was much talked about. She wore it with flesh-coloured artificial silk stockings and bar shoes decorated with bows attached by safety pins. During Rag Week Amy chose an animal suit that was so tight that she dared not sit down in it.

Amy poured out the minutiae of student life in a torrent of excitement to Hans, who must have found it rather childish and far removed from the real world of commerce that he viewed every day from his dockside office in Hull. While Amy bounded down the stairs of her lodgings hoping to find a letter waiting on the hall table, Hans was more circumspect about their correspondence. He waited until after lunch to read her letters in the office as part of a typically exotic ritual of coffee and Turkish cigarettes.

Their correspondence covered favourite authors, such as Arnold Bennett and George Bernard Shaw, and Hans introduced her to Players cigarettes, but they proved too expensive and Amy was soon 'reduced to Woodbines' until her allowance arrived. The most pressing subject on the agenda for Amy was marriage. University was only ever a stopgap. Barely nine months after they had started going out Amy made the first of what she believed was an oblique reference to marriage by telling Hans about the Hallowe'en superstition that anyone who looked in a mirror would see their future husband. His response was to mention his new landlady, Mrs Baker. Instead of dreaming of her future husband, she was haunted by the spectre of Mrs Baker. Even when Hans reassured her about his landlady, Amy demanded to know whether she had any grown-up daughters.

Hans's priority was to move the relationship onto a more physical level. It was a subject where she felt completely out of her depth, but one which she was keen to learn more about. She told him she had been talking to a university friend about a visit to Paris. 'I've a hazy notion now what you were driving at the night before I came away. Remember? But I've come to the conclusion that the only thing for me to do is to float over to the continent to acquire my knowledge in French as the English language does not afford facilities for such conversations etc.'

From later letters it is clear that Hans persuaded Amy to have sex with him in 1924, two years after they had first started going out together. She did not doubt that the act was a precursor to marriage and it remained a vivid event in her mind for years to come. 'Up to the time of that drive to Brid. on Easter Sunday two years ago you only felt a very slight interest in me, although I suppose you knew it was arranged that we should get married some time,' she wrote later.[14] Either Hans misled her about his intentions, or she allowed herself to assume too much – probably a bit of both. Hans was sexually experienced, but for Amy sleeping with him was a huge step and one which she assumed would bring the reward of marriage.

Although at the beginning Amy did not mention the fear of pregnancy, sex, even with contraception, was a highly hazardous pastime in the 1920s. Marie Stopes' controversial book on birth control was published with the coy title of Married Love in 1918 and in 1921 Stopes opened her first birth control clinic in London. Her book sold over a million copies, many to couples whose key interest was patently unmarried love. A very public libel trial in 1923 provided further publicity for Stopes' ideas and despite her strict family background Amy almost certainly saw a copy of Married Love.

It was exactly the sort of book that a young, independently minded woman like Amy would have been fascinated by. Stopes disapproved of married couples sharing a room: she felt it was impossible for a wife to maintain her aura of mystery if her husband saw her 'screw up her hair into a tight and unbecoming knot and soap her ears'.[15] The question of whether or not to co-habit in the marital bedroom was one which intrigued Amy and which she discussed with Hans. Like most women of her day, Amy left contraception up to her lover. Their sexual encounters had to be planned carefully and usually involved a great deal of subterfuge in which Hans's motorbike played a key part, Amy clinging to him as they roared away from Hull.

During the summer of 1923 Amy and Irene went away together for a short holiday on the Isle of Man. It became a lonely and depressing break for Amy when Irene abandoned her to go off on a day-trip to Dublin with a man she had met. Amy had no scruples in relaying Irene's Irish excursion to their mother, adding: 'Irene's by far the favourite here. She's awfully popular. I felt somewhat left out of it. But never mind, she's nearly two years younger than I am.'[16]

Irene's violent mood swings led to a tense atmosphere at home. She had ambitions to be an actress and melodrama was part of her personality. Once she returned at midnight and announced that she had tried to drown herself by the rather half-hearted technique of lying in a ditch. There was insufficient water but Will and Ciss could not afford to ignore the gesture. They were concerned enough to call in a doctor who suggested that Irene be sent to recuperate in Harrogate for three or four months.

Amy felt a mixture of anxiety for her sister tinged with jealousy at the attention she was attracting. Winifred, who got to know Irene when she visited Amy, described her as 'sly' and 'superior'.[17] Irene enjoyed intrigue and boasted to Amy of a secret visit to a London dance; Amy wrote with admiration that Irene, who had just had her hair shingled in the latest style, looked 'awfully sweet'.[18]

Ciss did not like it when her daughters slipped through her fingers. She expected Amy to write to her three times a week and, when she failed to do so, called her 'everything imaginable'.[19] 'Mother doesn't write very cheerful letters,' Amy told Hans.[20] Ciss was particularly anxious about religion and worried that Amy might find the novelty of Hans's Catholicism too tempting. She asked an aunt to bring up the subject of religion with Amy, but Amy wrote furiously to tell her mother that she did not belong to any denomination.

Amy's desire to be independent did not prevent her, on other occasions, from confiding in her mother about her money worries. Independence, too, had its limit and she often asked her mother to send her clean underwear and other items from home. Will, by comparison, treated Amy more like an adult and surprised her by writing a long letter in which he described his feelings of solitude. She wrote to Hans, 'I understood him more when I read that sentence than I've ever done before, because it's just how I feel here. Of course it isn't lonely in that sense, but it is the feeling of being alone in a crowd.'[21]

By the summer of 1924 Amy and her friends had grown tired of Sheffield and what now seemed like juvenile student pastimes. Once they put their heads above the parapets of student life they were dazed to find they were living on the edge of the stunning Derbyshire hills. They began cycling across the Peaks, gradually venturing further afield and going camping. The first time Amy stayed overnight in a tent she took her nightdress case with her, but she soon started to enjoy 'roughing it'. The girls discussed Freud, Marx and the English philosopher Alfred Whitehead in between earnest drags on their cigarettes, which they held in the corner of their mouths as they lit campfires and erected their tent.

They set up camp at a spot near Baslow on the edge of the Chatsworth estate which Winifred had found on a solitary bike ride and named Fir-Tree Island, Fairy Glen. It was a damp, over-grown, insect-infested area and Amy had never been happier. The setting combined her two childhood fantasies: a woodland, fairy-tale setting and the adventure of an Angela Brazil book. She wallowed in the waterfalls and wild flowers; being wet and unkempt added to her pleasure. She sat smoking Player cigarettes to ward off the midges, wearing a gym tunic, tortoiseshell-print shoes and drenched stockings. Knowing that her mother would 'have a fit' if she could see her unpowdered nose heightened her enjoyment. She wrote jubilantly to Hans: 'If you've any soul left at all, you couldn't help but like it,' adding, 'I never have been able to find out what sort of a soul you have got – if any.'[22]

Hans, who had left the Swiss consulate and was working for a business that traded in fruit, sent her pears, peaches, primroses and Toblerone. She ate so much of the Swiss chocolate, with its distinctive, triangular, twenties design, that she started saving tokens to join the manufacturers' profit-sharing scheme. The peaches, too, featured in several letters; Amy found a deep significance in their bruises and perhaps to her they represented a loss of innocence. By March 1925 Amy told Hans: 'I shall never be really happy 'til I have a home of my own . . . oh, you're the nicest, dearest person I've ever met, or ever could meet.'[23]

Less than a week later Hans and Irene exchanged letters in which they arranged to meet. It seems unlikely that Amy knew of this meeting. Irene's predatory nature and love of intrigue suggests that she was, at the very least, flirting with Hans. He later confirmed that Irene had shown an interest in him and that Amy had tried to prevent them becoming close friends. Hans felt cornered by Amy's intense feelings and he could well have welcomed a less demanding relationship. In April 1925 she wrote, 'I've only just realised how many of my thoughts and plans I've unconsciously built round you,'[24] and, a few weeks later, 'I woke up this morning with the strangest feeling that you were kissing each of my eyelids in turn, as you often do . . .'[25]

In May 1925 Irene wrote to tell Amy that a Frenchman had fallen in love with her and they were about to fly to Paris to live a 'wild Bohemian life'. Amy commented to Hans, with no sense of self-awareness, 'She'll wake up soon.'[26] The two sisters were again competing; both had foreign boyfriends, but Irene's was a much more sophisticated Frenchman.

Relationships between Irene and her parents had deteriorated to such an extent that Irene had moved out of their home and taken lodgings in Anlaby Road, Hull. 'Mother's ever such a dear – I don't know how Irene can hate her so much,' Amy wrote to Hans.[27]

As her final exams approached Amy escaped to the rural quiet of

Hathersage, a small Derbyshire village of higgledy-piggledy stone houses about ten miles from Sheffield. Dampness seeps through Hathersage, with its constant soundtrack of hurrying water; the air, especially compared to the polluted atmosphere of 1920s Sheffield, was clear, almost astringent. Amy rented two rooms in Crossland Road, close to the churchyard where Robin Hood's right-hand man, Little John, is buried. Hans sent her forget-me-nots from Switzerland and Ciss posted her chocolates while her sister Molly wrote her silly, girlish letters that made her laugh.

The cottage's one drawback was its insects, which Amy detailed to Hans in a 'list of slain on first campaign': one Johnny long legs, one moth, one fly with 'elongated legs' and two 'big brown horrible cockroaches'.[28]

Although she was fond of mice, insects, especially beetles, horrified her and she taped up all the cracks in the walls and ceilings to keep them at bay. As she was writing to Hans one day she spotted a cockroach trundling over the Toblerone she kept high on a top shelf.

In Amy's opinion she passed her exams by the 'barest margin' and only through intense 'cramming' the week before. Afterwards she pawned her books and went 'dance mad' before joining her family at Bridlington, playing on the sand with Molly and eating Toblerone. As well as chocolate, Hans sent her copies of *Punch*. She was desperate for him to realise that she grasped the magazine's jokes: 'I'm awfully keen on *Punch*, it's really humorous and not silly.'[29] Even her sense of humour was no longer her own.

Hans's business took him to the North-west and they managed to fit in a furtive meeting at the sumptuous Adelphi Hotel in Liverpool. The six-storey Neo-Grecian building reeked of glamour and expectancy, a haven for music-hall stars, actors and wealthy businessmen before they boarded a liner for America. The visit gave Amy a brief taste of a more exciting life but she was at a loss as to how to move their relationship away from this series of clandestine meetings and onto a more stable basis.

Chapter 3

Sibling Rivalry
(1925–6)

When Amy left Sheffield University in the summer of 1925 she and Hans had been seeing one another for nearly four years. By the standards of the time she appeared to be in an enviable position. The war had killed off one in seven eligible men and maimed or seriously injured thousands more. There were simply not enough males to go round and the imbalance led to what became known as the phenomenon of the 'surplus woman'.[1] Given that she was lucky enough to have found a single, healthy man, marriage seemed to everyone, including Amy, the obvious next step. Everyone, that was, except Hans.

While Amy marked time, Irene's life sped on. She was now seeing Edward Pocock, a family friend since childhood. They appeared to be in a 'steady relationship' and Hans enraged Amy by referring to him as 'prospective family'. She responded: 'If you still envy Teddy and prefer to worship Irene's gay spirit, you can do. I'll repeat mother's motto, "Live and learn". Irene's charming and adorable and I suppose I'm hatefully jealous of her – she always outshines me.'[2]

Ciss and Will were relieved that Irene had found someone as cheerful and easy-going as Teddy, a young man who enjoyed playing the piano and singing, and who seemed prepared to put up with Irene's mood swings. In short, he was the exact opposite of Amy's brooding boyfriend. Socially Teddy was not the perfect match for a member of the Johnson family but he seemed well balanced and he was local to Hull. He worked as a clerk for Shell-Mex in a job that offered a steady, if unspectacular, income. Teddy's parents were on the stage and in their spare time he and Irene played at being 'performers'. At parties Irene sang while Teddy accompanied her on the piano. They dreamt of turning professional but Will and Ciss assured themselves that these theatrical ambitions would fade once they settled down together. Amy was less gracious, suggesting to Hans that Teddy was merely a cover for the other, clandestine, relationships that Irene carried on in London.

Both Irene and Amy had decided to give up the idea of teaching.[3] In Amy's case she persuaded her father to repay the Board of Education's grant of £100. The head of Irene's training college wrote to Will Johnson in May 1924 saying that if Irene returned there was 'every possibility of another nerve storm and breakdown'.[4] Irene followed the inevitable path of taking a secretarial course but toyed with the idea of acting. Amy, too, spent much of the summer at a secretarial college brushing up the skills she had learnt during university vacations. Coincidentally, one of the pieces she took down as shorthand practice was a description of Alcock and Brown's flight across the Atlantic. By early August she had found a job as a shorthand typist with the accountancy firm of Frank Hall. The offices sat snugly in Bowlalley Lane, close to the Land of Green Ginger, tucked away between the city centre and the old dock area in a warren of Dickensian streets littered with the debris of the wholesale food trade. For Amy the new job's main advantage was that it was a ten-minute walk from Hans's office in Humber Place and his flat in Wellington Chambers.

The stuffy rigidity of office hours, clock-watching and hierarchy was a shock after the freedom of three years at university. As she had been in her final school years, Amy was again a misfit: both her age and her degree set her apart. She had too much education and not enough training. Her office skills were inadequate and she constantly faced the humiliation of having to ask her boss to supply the missing words when she could not read back her shorthand. Financial statements had to be typed without mistakes or corrections; she rarely managed either. At the end of September she fainted in the office and was sent home. In later years she described her collapse as a nervous breakdown, but Ciss was convinced that she had been starving herself to retain a fashionably thin, flapper silhouette and that rest and good food were the answer. Amy's parents' response was to send her away to recuperate. And, as they had done with Irene, they chose a genteel resort known for its restorative qualities.

Bournemouth out of season was a depressing place for a young woman with too much on her mind. It was an obsessively neat town with wide streets and few distractions apart from the pine trees that its residents were so proud of. The cosy domesticity of the Eddison family at Kingsmead, East Avenue, was exactly what Amy was trying to avoid. She was brought breakfast in bed every morning and at first her escape from the drudgery of office work came as a huge relief, but spending hours gazing out of her bedroom window at the pine trees only gave her time to dwell on her problems. The Eddisons, who had five children and were house-hunting, reminded her of what she desperately wanted. She complained to her mother that although their five-year-old daughter Bunty was 'awfully sweet', she was not in the mood for 'energetic, chattering children'.[5]

During her time as a typist she had seen Hans regularly and there was no need for letter writing. But now that they were once more apart she resumed her old habits, peppering her letters with hints. She talked of the tradition of sleeping with a piece of wedding cake under the pillow so that she would dream of her future husband and imagined furnishing her own home, commenting on the Eddisons' sleeping arrangements – in separate rooms – a practice she now disagreed with. 'Your idea is nicest – two beds in one room,' she told Hans.[6] She visited the Ideal Home Exhibition, which had become a regular event in London since 1908, and started to collect little household items such as tea towels for when she had her own home. Her romantic imagination ran riot and she dreamt of living in medieval times: 'You'd be my knight, of course, and kill nasty dragons (dentists, etc.) and then we'd be married and live happily ever after.'[7]

By the end of October Amy was deeply depressed and suffering violent mood swings which were partly due to what she described to her mother as her 'bad week', referring to her periods. She felt discontented with everything; she was even inexplicably convinced that her own first name somehow branded her as being 'too hasty'. Being nothing if not a seasonal lover, Hans sent her figs. Amy's frame of mind was made worse by the fact that all news from home was dominated by plans for Irene's twenty-first birthday party. Whereas Amy had been content to allow her coming of age the year before to slip by largely unnoticed, Irene wanted a typically theatrical event: a party of forty friends to toast her health in champagne. Talk of the event was endless. Will was only prepared to contribute £5 towards the party – the exact amount he had spent on Amy's birthday – but then relented and bought Ciss and his four daughters new dresses. Amy tried to dismiss the party as an 'awfully silly "do"' and insisted that she was glad she had not had one herself, but added that she would not have been allowed such a celebration.[8] Although she did not admit it, she would have found it difficult to muster enough friends of her own for such a grand affair.

'I know everyone, including you, stands enslaved and enraptured by her vivacity and charm,' Amy wrote to Hans, 'and I'm in dire disgrace all round because I dared to express my feelings about Irene's dance.'[9]

Amy, who was already unable to sleep because of her debts, was worried about the expense of buying Irene a birthday present. She owed Hans £12 and had spent a further £33 on clothes. She felt in direct competition with Irene on every level; even her sister's ability to tango rankled. Irene fuelled Amy's resentment by admitting that she had seen Hans to talk over Amy's ill health. 'And how dare you discuss me with Irene,' Amy fumed at him. 'I'm furious about that – can quite imagine the rotten things that would be said.'[10]

In a pitiful attempt to increase Hans's standing with her parents, Amy wrote to her mother telling her that the Eddisons had taken a 'great fancy' to him and that he was a 'great hit' with the children. 'They say he's a very sensible man, with practical views and plenty of common sense. Mrs Eddison advises me to take him whilst I've got the chance and not go to America, but I don't at all agree.'[11] Ciss's response was to write back with news of the flood of presents Irene was receiving for her birthday. Her mother's lack of emotion and subservience to her husband annoyed Amy intensely. She felt deeply hurt by her mother's 'nasty' letters in which she borrowed business terms from Will in a way that made her words seem heartless and cold: 'Your letter has safely come to hand . . . I note your remarks re dance.'[12] Ciss had also given Amy the impression that she must find a new job soon as she would only be in the way at home.

Hans encouraged Amy to consider working in America as a way of providing a 'cooling off period' in a relationship which, on Amy's side, was bubbling out of control. Its physical aspect continued via more clandestine meetings: in London and, on her return to Hull, even as far away as Loch Lomond in Scotland. For Amy each encounter took her closer to marriage: 'The part [of the weekend] I enjoyed most was when you were so pleased I came to you at 3 a.m. one morning. It was delicious to feel I could make you as happy as you seemed to be then. I'd come miles to make you feel like that again.'[13] She described their trip to Scotland as 'their honeymoon' and delighted in any reference to Hans's home country of Switzerland.[14]

While she rested in bed she caught up with the books she had been too tired to read when she was working in the office. She described to Hans the 'most glorious feeling of possession' when she bought a new book and recommended he tried her favourites such as Rose Macaulay's *Told by an Idiot*.[15] She teased him for claiming he had understood a recent production of George Bernard Shaw's *Saint Joan* better than any other member of the audience and told him about a lecture on Ibsen she had attended in Bournemouth.

Her fascination with words drew her to advertising and she regularly flicked through magazines to see how she could improve the adverts. When she returned to Hull in November she wrote to all the main advertising agencies in the city asking for the chance to study copy writing in return for a nominal salary. A new agency called Morison's in Albion Street offered her the position of secretary for thirty shillings a week. She snapped up the chance to escape from a home where she was still taking second place to Irene's achievements. Irene had been given the job of manageress of a new direct-mail advertising department at Bold & Lowthorp's. Amy had seriously considered direct mail and now regretted not following up her idea.

At Morison's she was once more an outcast: the other typists resented her apparent privileges and gave her the most temperamental typewriter and the least comfortable desk and chair. But her 'privileges' consisted of staying late, sometimes until 10 p.m., to stuff envelopes. After she had addressed a thousand envelopes and a hundred postcards in two days she wrote to Hans, who was away on business in Hamburg, saying: 'I've become an addressing machine.'[16] The one perk of her job at Morison's was that she was responsible for the foreign magazines that arrived at the ad agency and offered glimpses of a life outside England: pictures of people 'as per nature', adverts offering cures for diseases and 'all sorts of things [presumably condoms] like those you bought somewhere', she confided to Hans.

By early 1926 Amy was frustrated both in her work and her relationship with Hans. 'You would accept me gladly as a mistress, but not as a wife,' she wrote to him one Sunday night. 'After that drive [to Bridlington], when you presumed somewhat on my ignorance, your interest gradually increased. You found yourself attracted towards me physically, and enjoyed teaching me things I ought to have known.'

Hans managed to placate her by finally agreeing to take her to meet his family in Lucerne and by promising to discuss their future on her next birthday. He drifted through the two-week holiday in June 1926, seemingly oblivious to the importance that the women in his life attached to the visit.

The Arreggers lived in a fairy-tale Swiss home with geranium-filled window-boxes and a view of the mountains. Amy's prospective mother-in-law even turned out to be a white-haired old lady who enjoyed working at her spinning-wheel. Frau Arregger was stoical and dignified and Amy was struck by the contrast with her own mother, who would have collapsed under the strain of holding together such a large family by herself.

Throughout the visit Amy tried too hard. She insisted on climbing the giant mountain that dominates Lucerne in a seven-hour hike that meant leaving the house at four in the morning. Nearly 7500 feet high, Mount Pilatus towers over the area, a harsh jumble of sharply defined ridges. Its name is said to come from a myth that Pontius Pilate was flung into a small lake near its peak and that his spirit still haunts the summit, ready to bring damnation on the area if disturbed. Pilatus is still a popular tourist attraction because of its spectacular Alpine views, but few people attempt to reach the top by foot. When Queen Victoria visited in 1868, a mule did the hard work. As Amy struggled to keep up with Hans and a friend who accompanied them, she suddenly became paralysed with fear until Hans managed to wrench her out of her terror by shouting at her several times.

Amy's birthday was the ideal day for a marriage proposal. Hans took her and a few of his closest friends and their wives to a small restaurant to celebrate. The meal was an awkward occasion in which everyone except Hans was confused by Amy's status. His friends gave her a blue vase and two pictures of Lucerne, presents obviously intended for their marital home.

Hans had already confided to his best friend that he had no intention of marrying her but that she was refusing to face up to reality. He even contrived to sit next to his friend's wife at lunch, rather than Amy, and scurried off as soon as the meal was over, leaving Amy to wander into the family church where she prayed in desperation that Hans would remember his promise about discussing their future. That evening she lingered on the stairs hoping that he might sense that she was waiting for him to say something. But Hans always found such subtleties easy to ignore.

Returning to Hull felt anticlimactic. Her parents had opposed her visit to Switzerland and Will had refused to pay for the trip, but they, like everyone who knew Amy, must have assumed that the visit was the precursor to some sort of announcement. Instead Amy returned to a tedious job and a life where she had little status. In Switzerland she had been treated by Hans's friends and family as his fiancée; in Hull she had no special standing among the few friends he allowed her to meet. She began to detest the cheap brass 'wedding' ring she was forced to wear during their clandestine weekends.

During the autumn of 1926 Hans spent several months on business in Hamburg, Prague and Italy. Although Amy made no comment to him about the General Strike of May 1926 and the tramworkers' protest in Hull, it was a time of uncertainty. Hans was particularly anxious about money – not least because he was desperate to trade in his motorbike for a car. While he was away trying to drum up more business abroad, Amy exchanged letters with his mother and sisters. In response to a direct question from his mother, Amy assured her that if she married Hans she would convert to Catholicism. She started to spend more time with Molly since Irene was now preoccupied with her forthcoming marriage to Teddy. Will had lent them £200 so that they could buy a home, and they chose a brand-new house in Lake Drive to the far east of Hull. The transaction left Irene and Teddy heavily in Will's debt, and Irene wrote to him: 'I am very anxious that you should realise that I really understand the value of money. Teddy and I are both very very grateful . . .' She assured him that they were not squandering the cash on 'pretty furniture'.[17] Amy's only comment on the house was that she would have preferred a flat.[18]

While Hans was away she went often to the theatre and cinema. On bleaker days she compounded her gloom by turning to the plays of Strindberg or went for solitary bike rides in which she pretended Hans was there and that they talked without quarrelling. By the end of November 1926 she had decided she wanted to leave home and contacted several advertising agencies in London, looking for a job. On Christmas Eve she wrote to Hans, who was with his family in Switzerland, telling him that she was concerned at his plans to travel through an Italy whipped into a frenzy by the posturing of Benito Mussolini. Nearly two years after leaving Sheffield there was still no sign of Amy getting married. If her life was going to change she would have to do something about it herself.

Chapter 4

London

(1927)

By the spring of 1927 Amy's life in Hull had become intolerable. Ciss was convinced that something awful was about to happen – at the very least her daughter was poised to convert to Catholicism, if not to announce something even more shaming – and Will could not overcome his profound disappointment at Amy's infatuation with a foreigner. In March he offered her £50 and a ticket to visit his brother Tom in Canada, in the hope that the journey would provide sufficient distance to allow the affair to fade away; cleverly, he also reckoned that the voyage might appeal to her sense of adventure.[1] If, however, she turned down his proposal she must leave the house immediately and with no money. He gave her two days to make up her mind.

The ultimatum represented exile but it came when Amy was ready for a clean break. In Hull she would always be the eldest daughter of a respected fish merchant; she needed a new setting to formulate a separate identity and one which she hoped would provide Hans with the impetus to seal their relationship. When her father called her into his study to ask her what her decision was, she knew that in rejecting a ticket to Canada she was rejecting parental control. Will was devastated by her choice, which in one blow knocked him off his pedestal as all-powerful head of the Johnson family and deprived him of the daughter he loved. Although he had threatened to cut off all financial help if she turned down his offer, he immediately unlocked his desk and took out £10 to help her through her first days in the world outside Park Avenue.

London in the 1920s was a behemoth far larger than any other European city; an urban sprawl greater even than New York. It was a place that most people could not afford to visit, and Amy's trips to the Ideal Home Exhibition and her clandestine stays with Hans in London hotels gave her an unusual insight, but it was still alien territory where she had no friends and where her family name meant nothing. It was apart from the rest of the country and especially from the North, a city that had little experience of the Depression that was tearing apart communities in industrial Britain. Only 1 per cent of London's blue-collar workers earned a living from the 6 most endangered industries – shipbuilding, coal, cotton, wool, iron and steel.[2] The capital was in the happy position of relying on service and consumer industries that thrived amid falling prices and rising wages. It was bustling and confident, spreading its tentacles north-west into Metroland through extensions to the underground and better road and rail links.

Amy trudged the mile or so from Kings Cross railway station to Bloomsbury, carrying a suitcase that contained everything she thought she needed to start a new life. Her home was a gloomy hostel where the lights were turned out at 10.30 p.m. A photo of Hans and his gifts of a manicure set, perfume and a lucky black cat helped to make the room slightly less impersonal. Escaping from the hostel became a priority. She approached several advertising firms and put her name down for a Swiss recruitment agency. Finally, John Lewis offered her a place on its 'Learnership at Peter Jones' scheme at its upmarket Chelsea store.

Peter Jones in 1927 was a fussy Victorian building with cluttered shop windows protected by a long awning that swept round from Sloane Square to the King's Road. It was not until 1934 that today's majestic curtain wall of glass and metal replaced the old department store. When Amy joined Peter Jones the shop was still fighting to turn the tide after years of static or falling profits. John Lewis bought the shop in 1906, walking from his Oxford Street shop with £21,000 in notes in his pocket to pay for the deal. But Lewis despaired of what he called 'that bucket of a shop' and handed it over to his son, who redecorated it and introduced radical new working arrangements.[3] He cut hours, introduced profit sharing and gave staff a third week's holiday. The Learnership scheme was his idea and was aimed at attracting senior civil servants, university graduates like Amy and debutantes.

Standing outside on the pavement of Sloane Square, Amy caught glimpses of the shop's exotic interior, its 'beautifully arranged rooms with gorgeous carpets' and its walnut staircase.[4] The shop girls looked smart in their dark fawn dresses with contrasting light fawn silk collars. Amy's only qualm was that black would have suited her better. Peter Jones was 'one of the most exclusive shops in London', she told Hans, and at first she was seduced by the texture and colours of the silks that surrounded her.[5] She loved the feel of the crêpe de Chine, the georgette and chiffons, and the exotic-sounding names of new fabrics such as Kasha (a mixture of flannel, goat-hair and wool), 'art silk' (rayon) and 'flamingo' (a silk-and-wool mix that looked liked crêpe). Measuring out the great rolls of fabric felt like playing shop with her sisters. The customers who swept into the department store were glamorous creatures unlike anyone she had ever seen in Hull: confident 'modern' types with flat chests and daringly short dresses. Amy was made stock-keeper and completed her first sales of Japanese silks after two weeks, which, she boasted to Hans, was very unusual. 'Everyone's extraordinarily nice,' she told him. 'I think shopgirls in a good class shop are amongst the nicest girls there are. All I know at Peter Jones are nice – tho', of course, not the kind one makes intimate friends of.'[6]

Amy started work at 9 a.m., had lunch at 2 p.m. and finished at 6.15 p.m. Apart from a twenty-minute break, she was on her feet all day and spent the evenings trudging round London looking for accommodation. She was desperately short of money – but so was Hans – and she sent him £5 of the £17 she owed him. Despite her lack of funds, she could not resist buying a tea towel and was distraught when she left it on the tube. Hans was a lifeline while she was awash in this new, foreign city. She frequently wrote him sixteen-page letters and started buying writing paper by the pound.

Slowly Amy realised that the Learnership scheme was a way of persuading naive sales girls to pay for their training, rather than the fast-track route to a managerial position that she had hoped for. Each week the value of the trainee's services was assessed and charged against a remuneration account of £3. Inevitably, the trainee's contribution was small during her first weeks and she built up a debt which, in theory, would be paid off as her expertise increased. Amy had four weeks to decide whether to continue at the store or leave. If she stayed beyond the month, she was expected to pay back the money she 'owed'. She wrote to Hans and her father for advice; both urged her to leave before the month was up.

Amy also turned to her step-cousin, Olive Birkbeck, for advice. Olive was originally from Leeds but had got a job as an assistant in the stationery department of the *Times* Book Club in Wigmore Street. The two women bartered confidences at one of Lyons' Corner Houses in the West End of London. The restaurants, which could seat 3000 customers, offered ordinary people – mainly shop girls and typists – a bite of luxury and a chance to daydream over prolonged cups of tea. Waitresses, or 'nippies', darted round in their black-and-white uniforms serving inexpensive food against a backdrop of music and the babble of the diners. Olive, who was engaged to be married, was happy to provide both career and relationship advice. Amy wrote to Hans about

Olive's fiancé: 'She's not madly in love with him, but like me – and all other normal girls I suppose – she's a horror of being left an old maid.'[7]

Olive provided a bridge between the new 'London' Amy and her family in Hull and paved the way for a reconciliation. Ciss took them both to Gatti's restaurant and Amy enjoyed the responsibility of choosing the wine. The main preoccupation at home was Irene and Teddy's wedding day, which had been set for 28 May 1927. Amy could not resist telling Hans what Olive and many others felt about him: 'They all say the same thing – "A charming boy, but not a marrying man." I'm fed up with such talk and I wish the institution of marriage was at the bottom of the sea. And if Olive tells me many more things about you – "all for my sake" – I think I shall lose my temper.'[8] Amy was particularly sensitive about their relationship because she had allowed her jealousy over Hans's landlady to escalate and Mrs Leach made regular appearances in her nightmares.

Olive was determined to find Amy a better job. When an interview at the *Times* Book Club library came to nothing and Harrods said it had no vacancies in its advertising department, Olive arranged for Amy to meet Vernon Wood. Wood was a distinguished partner in a City law firm and as a leading businessman in the North of England he had known the Johnson family since Amy was a child. Will respected and admired him as a man who had found commercial success while retaining his thick Lancashire accent. Amy showed Wood the John Lewis Learnership contract over dinner with Olive at the Holborn restaurant. The strange mixture of intelligence, wilfulness and naivety that he saw in Amy intrigued Wood, and the next day he wrote to her outlining his worries about the Learnership scheme and offering her a position as a typist at his firm of Messrs William Charles Crocker. The pay was £3 a week and there was the chance of more interesting work as she gained legal experience. She started work at Crockers on 11 April 1927. At about the same time Irene was admitted to a sanatorium with scarlet fever.

Crockers sat proudly in slick, modern offices at 21 Bucklersbury. Its five-storeyed building was close to Mansion House, in the very heart of the City of London. Amy described the offices, with their Dictaphones and 'intercom' system, as 'topping'. The typists who worked there were part of a growing band of women who were making the important, if unsung, role of the clerical assistant their own. In 1911 only a fifth of clerical workers were women; by 1931 they accounted for over half – although their pay lagged behind that of their male counterparts.[9] During the Great War they had stepped in to fill the vacancies

left by men at the front. The contrast with the long hours and drudgery of domestic service made life in an office much more attractive. By
the time Amy joined Crockers, typing was seen as women's work.
Unlike the secretaries at Morison's, the women at Crockers were
upbeat and confident. The firm was thriving and law, like most professional services, was spared the worst of the economic downturn that
was hitting heavy industry. Crockers specialised in corporate work and
later won a name for itself by uncovering insurance frauds such as the
case of the 'Margate Murderer' who in 1929 claimed a large sum of life
insurance from Cornhill, one of Crockers' clients. He was later
hanged.

Amy's relationship with Wood gave her the sense of stability and
confidence that had been lacking in her two previous office jobs.
Unusually for the time, Wood was eager to nurture talents that
belonged to a woman. The fact that Amy had been hand-picked by
Wood to work at Crockers might have made her susceptible to the jealousies that she had suffered at Morison's and Frank Hall's offices,
except that Wood pushed her harder than other secretaries. Amy complained to Hans that Wood was a 'slavedriver' who kept her in the
office from 7.15 a.m. to 7 p.m. But she admired his intellect and power.
She told Hans that she could understand someone being in love with
him. Amy enjoyed the arcane world of law; she liked the fact that
everything had an answer and she relished the profession's neat for-
malities. 'I made a beautiful schedule and it looked most professional,'
she told Hans.[10] She began to study company law so that she could help
when the firm next prepared a client to join the stock market.

As her expertise increased, Wood's interest turned into an informal
apprenticeship. He made her complete a précis of the complex articles
of association for two companies and compared her version with his,
taking time to explain where and why they differed. He sent her home
at weekends with legal conundrums: a company was keen to buy a
rival but one investor in the take-over target refused to sell his £1000
worth of preference shares – could anything be done to break the dead-
lock? She was clearly more than a secretary and had started to draft
complicated legal documents. When Crockers tried to trace hidden
bonds in a criminal case, she joined the chase.

Wood's interest in her legal schooling allowed her to escape the
office, which she found so claustrophobic that it gave her a headache.
He encouraged her to visit the courts so that she could follow a case
they were working on. Her reputation as a bright and willing typist
grew within the office and she was in demand among senior members

of the firm. There was only a slim chance of her ever qualifying as a solicitor (in 1921 there were just seventeen female solicitors in England), but as her knowledge increased, so did her status and pay. Barely six months after joining she was given a ten-shilling rise.

As well as securing her a good job, Olive helped Amy to escape from her Bloomsbury hostel after three weeks by introducing her to a middle-aged couple from Yorkshire who were looking for a lodger. They lived in West End Mansions, a tall red-brick building in the village-like setting of West Hampstead that crouched at the bottom of a hill and looked out onto a small green close to a bus terminus.[11] It was conveniently placed for Amy to get to Crockers, and a forty-minute walk took her to Hampstead and the Heath's wide, open space that she craved. Living with the couple, who were devoted to each other, again gave her the chance to observe marriage at close quarters.

Amy and Hans met every fortnight when he came to London on business; he had lost a lot of money speculating on potatoes and was constantly looking for new ways of increasing his income. For once, insecurity dogged Hans – though of a financial, not an emotional, kind – and Amy provided a release from these troubles. Her move to London gave the relationship a new impetus and some of the sophistication of her cosmopolitan setting rubbed off on her; she was aware of and influenced by the way fashionable people dressed and talked and the sort of music they danced to. Her meetings with Hans had changed; landladies kept a watchful eye over them but they were untroubled by the fear of bumping into someone they knew who would report back to Amy's family. Deception was much easier. They spent their Easter 'honeymoon' in Dolgellau, Wales, and Amy told her parents that she would be visiting Southend to stay with the family of a girl she had met at Peter Jones.

Hans and Amy appear to have switched to a different form of contraception around this time and Amy was tormented by a fear of falling pregnant. She had no qualms about sharing her worries with Hans in an intimate description that most women of her time would have found difficult to mention even to their doctors. Fears about her health turned into hypochondria. She was convinced she had pneumonia; she longed to see Sybil Thorndike at the Golders Green Hippodrome but was too anxious about the four cases of smallpox that had been reported to risk sitting side-by-side with potentially infectious strangers in the theatre or on the underground. The city's darker side was closing in on her. On her way to work one morning she glimpsed a newspaper vendor's stand near Moorgate that screamed out details of the 'Trunk

Murder' at Charing Cross. Over the next few weeks Londoners were mesmerised by the mystery of the woman's body found in a trunk at the railway station's cloakroom. The corpse had been hacked into five parts and neatly packed under brown paper along with various pieces of clothing, a duster and a handbag. Despite the body's butchered state, the police constable called to investigate the smell emanating from the trunk only allowed the body parts to be moved to the mortuary after a surgeon had pronounced the victim dead. Thoughts of 'the beastly trunk' kept Amy awake as she lay listening to the strange night noises in her lodgings: the creaking cistern and the nocturnal prowlings of a cat. Her feelings towards her room were not helped by the fact that her landlady insisted on dishing up rhubarb pudding every night.

Hans sent her frank bulletins about his business and Amy took this desire to share his concerns as proof that they were partners. She replied with sympathetic diatribes against the potatoes that were causing his worries and a description of her own day-to-day life. At Crockers she was climbing up the secretarial hierarchy and confident enough in her status to start complaining about the men she worked for. One partner she was asked to help was 'not nice to look at and is rumoured to be an absolute slave driver and awfully inconsiderate'.[12] The financial district, especially on a Saturday, intrigued her – a curious, barren place populated by lone policemen who tramped through the sleet and wind. Law stimulated her mind in a way she had not experienced before but she found the physical restraints of office life at times unbearable. The room she worked in was 'beastly' with no ventilation or windows. 'It is the heat and sunshine I so love and feel I need,' she told Hans.[13] 'I just hate streets and houses and tubes and buses and people and stuffy rooms and typewriters – I wish I could climb up a mountain and be high above all these things and where there's light and air and sunshine.'[14]

She was also struggling to come to terms with what she wanted from Hans. Intellectually, she could justify an 'open' relationship based on independence for both sexes, but emotionally she craved a conventional marriage. Her loyalty to Hans had driven her from the family home, but her desire to leave Hull was partly fuelled by a need to strike out on her own. Most women of Amy's time saw marriage as their goal, if not duty, in life. It was natural for Amy, given the length of their courtship, to assume Hans intended to marry her. She clung to this hope – despite what may appear, to modern sensibilities, to be obvious clues – and used Hans's business worries to justify their separation and her evenings sitting in her pyjamas in her room in West Hampstead.

Hans's jealousy of her close working relationship with Wood – a highly successful businessman compared to Hans, who was struggling to avoid bankruptcy – convinced her that Hans was simply trying to knock himself into sound financial shape so that he could propose to her.

Hans's money problems made Amy more sympathetic about Irene and Teddy's wedding predicament. Irene was still recovering from scarlet fever and her weight had dropped to seven stone, but Will refused to foot the bill for the extravaganza that Irene wanted, casting a shadow over the event. Amy wrote to Hans:

> It was unfortunate there was all that trouble about Irene's wedding, because it has placed poor Father in rather a false light as regards his generosity. He really is generous in his own way, and if Irene had only got married according to his ideas, he would have acted differently about the money question. But, of course, he doesn't regard it as his duty to set Irene and Teddy up in their house – he thinks it disgraceful that he, and not Teddy, should be providing the money. I used to see things like Father does but now I see them differently. I can see that it's his duty to start them off . . . and that it is not disgraceful of Teddy to let him.[15]

The wedding was a quiet ceremony to which only close family members were invited. At a time when weddings were low-key events, Amy's decision not to go was reasonable: she could not afford the train journey to Hull and did not feel able to ask for time off from a job that she had started so recently. Instead she sent the couple an assortment of 'useful things' including a pair of pure linen hand-stitched single sheets.[16]

But Amy's patience cracked under the strain of watching her sister garner everything she had waited so long for. Irene had a full hand: husband, house, new clothes, an easy job, car, even regular games of tennis. Two days after Irene's wedding Amy's anger and frustration with Hans exploded:

> Do you realise, darling, that for a long time now you have been repulsing me? I don't know whether it's because you have ceased to be in sympathy with me, which of course means that you no longer love me in the real meaning of the word (I know you do physically – there has never arisen any occasion when I've doubted that – but physical love alone is so unsatisfying), or whether its simply that your mind is so absorbed in business you can't see on – beyond it. When you come here and we have finished eating and drink-

ing and satisfying our physical love and somehow there is always something more I long for . . . I believe that I have been making you my religion. I have been worshipping you, giving you the whole of my thoughts, acting on your code of right and wrong, confessing to you my sins.[17]

But Amy could not quite bring herself to throw away all those years of waiting, and since Hans refused to be drawn into an emotional discussion of marriage, Amy approached it from an academic stance. She read Shaw's *Getting Married* and *Mrs Warren's Profession* – confessing herself baffled by the nature of Mrs Warren's work. *Getting Married* set her thinking about the ceremony itself. The play takes place on the wedding day of a bishop's daughter. As the guests arrive the bride and bridegroom are nowhere to be found. Eventually it emerges that both have been sent an anonymous pamphlet entitled, 'Do you know what you are going to do? By one who has done it'. The couple refuse to get out of bed until they have read the article, which sets forth the dangers and anomalies of marriage. While they wait the guests discuss marriage. On 8 May, 1927 Amy wrote to Hans:

It is unnatural to imagine that a marriage service is like a magic spell enabling two people to live peacefully together for the rest of their lives in complete love and accord . . . So long as the marriage vows are so stupid as they are at present I think the only way to help these natural <u>difficulties</u> and enable two people to retain their interest, and love for one another is for a greater measure of freedom to be agreed on between the two than the words of the marriage service (hopelessly outdated) confer.

As summer approached Amy found London stifling. She retreated to any patch of greenery she could find: writing to Hans as she sat on Hampstead Heath or from St James's Park, Hyde Park's Rotten Row or Kew Gardens. She longed to go for a bike ride to escape the city's oppressive heat and would have liked to have joined a tennis club, but the fees were too high. Her landlady had asked Amy to pay an extra thirty shillings for evening meals and she took packed lunches to the office to economise. She went swimming regularly. 'I'd give anything to have some good strenuous games,' she told Hans.[18]

Just as Amy was complaining to Hans that she was in desperate need of 'satisfying company' she received a postcard from a university friend who was teaching in Leighton Buzzard, a small town about thirty miles north-west of London. Amy was shocked to discover that her friend was having an affair with her boss, whom Amy summed up as: forty,

'ugly, awkward, narrow but genial and kindhearted'.[19] She was desperate for him to leave his wife, but the resultant scandal would end his
teaching career. Amy suggested they ran away to the United States or
Australia but was blind to the parallels between her friend's situation
and her own, and wrote to Hans:

> If poor [friend's name] weren't so deadly serious about it I'd be awfully
> amused at the whole thing because it's easy enough to see what has hap-
> pened . . . I'm afraid I haven't any sympathy for [ ], except that I know she
> can't help herself – but she doesn't make any effort to do anything or make
> any decision. She can't get beyond the idea that she wants to marry him and
> can't – I feel a wee bit disgusted (which is priggish of me) and a bit impatient
> with her . . .[20]

The next time Hans was in London, on his way to Lisbon, they booked
into an hotel using his business partner's name, Raymond; Amy told
her landlady that she was going to visit a friend. Afterwards Hans sent
her pressed flowers and peaches and she consoled herself by looking
forward to two major events: a flying exhibition at Hendon in North
London and Winifred's arrival to share a flat with her until Hans moved
to London.

Chapter 5

A Room of One's Own
(1927–8)

The jerky, stylised, frantic Charleston arrived in England in 1925, adding to the repertoire of energetic dances available on both sides of the Atlantic. Dancers rushed to halls after work to indulge in the latest craze, from the Bunny Hug and the Black Bottom to the Wob-a-ly Walk and the Kickaboo. Enjoyment had an urgency to it, as if people were making up for the austerity of the war years. Amy, who had loved dancing at Sheffield, could barely manage a shuffle, unable to shake off the weight of her infatuation with Hans. The arrival of Winifred began her rehabilitation. It was difficult to be introspective with Winifred around. Her engagement had been called off, but rather than sinking into despair, she was determined to squeeze every drop of pleasure out of London that she and Amy could afford. Their small flat in Oxford and Cambridge Mansions, Marylebone High Street, was an easy bus ride to the West End of London and they went frequently to the cinema and, usually when someone else was paying, to the theatre. They saw a stage production of *Mrs Warren's Profession* and Ciss took them to *The Boyfriend*, Sandy Wilson's carefree flapper musical.

Winifred complemented Amy's character perfectly; she even disliked milk chocolates, leaving Amy with a free conscience to devour single-handedly the boxes of confectionery that Ciss bought them. Aunt Evelyn and Amy went to *The Yellow Mask*, a fashionable Edgar Wallace thriller set to music, and like the million other people who flocked to see *Ben Hur*, Amy was mesmerised by the new silent film with its occasional bursts of colour and was so enraptured that she saw it twice.

Winifred started to play hockey again, reminding Amy that sport had always helped purge her demons. Amy swam at the club opposite their flat every Monday and took up tennis again, borrowing a racquet from Wood to play at the McVitie's factory, where Winifred worked in the welfare department at the huge Park Royal industrial estate in Willesden, north-west London. Winifred's gregariousness meant that she often had a girlfriend to stay the night and their already cramped

flat grew smaller with the appearance of a camp bed. When they were
short of money they sat at home in front of the gas fire; Amy smoked
while Winifred read poetry to her. Being seen with a cigarette was now
an essential fashion statement, its popularity boosted by advertisers'
promises that smoking curbed the appetite and eased sore throats.

While they waited for potential husbands to declare their hand, they
played at home-making within the bare, distempered walls of their flat
and, like thousands of housewives around Britain, delighted in their
new, labour-saving electric iron. They lived in a bustling part of
London, north of Oxford Street but far enough from the centre to have
retained its patches of greenery, trees and old churches. Amy frequently came home to Winifred's one pair of pyjamas drying in front
of the fire. When Winifred was not there Amy busied herself by
dusting, cleaning the silver or baking cakes. She read *The Cathedral* by
Hugh Walpole and Shaw's *Pygmalion*. Her parents put pressure on her
to return to Hull for their silver wedding celebrations but relations –
particularly with her mother – were still fragile. Any mention of Hans
would wreck the celebrations and she urged him to stay away: 'I know
so perfectly well that I shall come and see you often and that mother
will be mad. I've realised lately it was mother who caused all the
trouble and I don't think father would ever have acted as he did if it
hadn't been for mother . . . I really, honestly believe that given the
opportunity and an excuse mother would kill you.'[1]

Will tried to compensate for Amy's banishment by spoiling her on
his trips to London. He took her shopping at Swan & Edgar's department store on Piccadilly Circus where he bought her a jumper, a suit
and gloves which, he recorded in his diary, cost £3.5.0. They went to see
a comedy called *Yellow Sands* at the Haymarket and he treated her to
chocolates and lilies. Freed from the constraints of his respectable,
middle-class image in Hull, Will was less strict and judgemental. He
asked her whether she smoked and when she said she had almost given
it up he seemed relieved, although Amy felt he would probably have
given her a cigarette if she had asked. She was sure that he had guessed
that she and Hans were sleeping together. Back in Hull Will was less
relaxed. He lectured Amy on punctuality and told her he had written
on her behalf to apologise to someone she had offended. 'They are still
trying to direct my life even now I've left home,' Amy complained to
Hans.[2]

Hans was only interested in her new home with Winifred as a possible business address for his firm in London. For her birthday he sent
Amy a pound, like a dutiful uncle who was out of touch with his

niece's likes and dislikes. She used the money to buy a small, dark brown crocodile leather case lined with pale grey material and decorated with tiny red rose-buds. She had it initialled with the single letter 'A', saying she hoped one day she could add the rest of Hans's surname. He made no attempt to hide the way their lives were diverging and decided to spend his one holiday that year on a trip to Scotland with some friends.

His decision initially plunged Amy into a black mood but she soon surfaced when Winifred invited two 'charming boys', one of whom worked at McVitie's, to their flat. Her jealousy was directed at Hans's social life rather than the women in it; she envied him his smart clothes and the dances and parties he attended while she had yet to wear her evening cloak in London and had only worn her smart grey dress once. The city no longer frightened her; she felt proud and excited to be living in the capital and she enjoyed window shopping in Piccadilly and Regent's Street. She had a passion for knick-knacks and, peering through the window of a brasswear shop, longed to buy candlesticks, ash-trays and a cigar-box. Instead she settled for a toasting-fork decorated with a cross-legged devil. One night in early December after posting a letter to Hans she wandered round London till midnight, gazing at the Christmas lights.

Her responsibilities at work were increasing. Amy had been asked to train a new girl and regularly sat in on client meetings and conferences; she went to Somerset House to carry out important searches and Wood put her in charge of all the annual returns of his private company clients. She attended evening classes in advanced book-keeping, income tax and banking. The effort was paying off: 'I feel I've got more status now at the office and am glad of it because I don't like to be just one of the crowd.'[3] But, she told Hans, 'in spite of being a "business woman" and getting old I do badly want spoiling and making a fuss of and I never get it.'[4]

New Year's Eve 1927 gave her a taste of what it felt like to be spoilt and proved a turning point that set the tone for 1928. Hans had been invited to see the year in with friends near Hull and Amy went to the theatre with a group of eight friends. They sat in the royal box and the other theatre-goers could not resist stealing glances at them. Amy worked out that she was sitting in the very same seat that Princess Victoria had occupied only a few hours earlier. Afterwards Amy and her friends stayed up until 3 a.m. playing games. It was the first time since university that she had enjoyed herself in a group of people; it left her in a 'queer' mood and convinced her that something was going to happen.[5]

Feeling wanted allowed her to treat her 'open' relationship with Hans more calmly. She bragged to him of 'Our Little Boyfriend', a young man whom Amy and Winifred had 'adopted'.[6] Amy spoke patronisingly of him as 'A most delightful child in some ways whereas in others he's older even than I am. He thinks I'm all the nice things you could never see in me, but he really is most interesting and I thoroughly like him.' 'Her little friend' drove her to Oxford and took her to a Greek restaurant in Tottenham Court Road.

Amy was in such a buoyant mood that when Winifred ran out of money and they were forced to quit their flat at two weeks' notice she took the sudden departure in her stride. 'Goodbye to our little home,' she wrote cheerfully to Hans, adding, 'The less I say about our new domicile the better.'[7] They moved in the pouring rain to a YWCA hostel near Oxford Circus. Ames House at 44 Mortimer Street was run like a strict girls' boarding-school; it was a tall red-brick building with narrow windows. Curtains divided the rooms into cubicles that did little to smother the nocturnal sounds of rows of strangers. Residents had to be in by 10.30 p.m. and lights-out was 10.45 p.m. There was one communal drawing-room whose walls were covered with religious tracts. Hymns were played almost continuously. Moving to the hostel turned out to be a false economy as Winifred and Amy loathed it so much that they spent much of their time trying to avoid going home. Winifred sat smoking in the drawing-room but Amy was driven mad by the hymns, especially when some of the women started to hum along to them. She preferred to go for long walks.

Amy's fear of heights made the nearby building work much more threatening than the hostel itself.[8] Her cubicle had a window that looked down onto the gaping hole where the construction work was going on. She was terrified one night when there was a terrible banging from the building site that sent a mirror crashing to the floor. Shortly after this experience their patience snapped and, despite the obvious expense, Winifred and Amy took off to Paris for a break. On their return they rented a single room at 24 Castellain Road, in Maida Vale, north-west London. Their new home was a well-furnished flat in a tall house with big windows that overlooked gardens and a tennis court. Maida Vale had a hushed residential feel to it; the roads were wide by London standards and studded with large, white, wedding-cake-like houses. The canal made it feel continental and it was close enough to Stag Lane airfield, near Hendon, for Moths to be heard droning overhead, a noise that most of the neighbours loathed but which Amy found exhilarating. 'I envied these pilots,' she wrote later.

'I longed for the freedom and detachment it seemed they must enjoy.'[9]

When Irene sent Amy a 'very cheerful' letter[10] in which she said she was enjoying her new job at the *Hull Evening News*, Amy was contented enough to praise as 'really very good and original' an article Irene had written for the children's page.[11] Teddy and Irene had developed a thought-reading act and were hopeful that they could secure a booking at the Bridlington Spa for £10 each. This represented a huge amount of money, but Amy, who had just been given a rise that took her pay to £5 a week, seemed genuinely pleased for her sister. She found it harder, though, to hide her jealousy of Irene's social life of at least two parties every night. Amy was doing well at Crockers, but sometimes worked until 9 p.m. Mr Wood was a 'great sport' and teased her, saying, 'I can see what will happen in a few years when I'm an old man – you'll bring me everything and all I'll do is sign.'[12]

Now that she was surrounded by people she liked, at home and at work, Amy enjoyed being by herself. She took a holiday in Newquay, a resort on the north-west coast of Cornwall that the Prince of Wales had made fashionable by his visits. Each day she walked between ten and fifteen miles, gathering shells for her sister Betty along the way. At the hotel she gained a reputation for her unfailing sense of direction after negotiating her way along roads that bore no signposts to the 'lost' church of St Piran's at Perranporth, a desolate, windswept spot by the sea six miles south-west of Newquay. The sixth-century chapel, which is supposed to mark the burial site of a saint who is said to have crossed from Ireland to Cornwall on a millstone, is barely thirty feet by seventeen and is hidden in a mass of sand-dunes and rabbit-warrens. The remains were rediscovered in 1835 but buried again by the vigorous sand some fifty years after Amy's visit. Today the site is marked by a cross on top of a mound which, despite the help of tourist signs, is still difficult to find.

Days spent alone with the circling seagulls gave her time to look dis-passionately at her relationship with Hans. After an initial twinge of homesickness when she missed Winifred, she began to enjoy her own company; the realisation that she could be happy without help from other people came as a shock. The fresh air and solitude pumped up self-esteem that a hopeless love affair and the London fog had almost extinguished. By the time she returned to London she had mustered the resolve to attack a relationship that had blighted her adult life. Her determination was strengthened by Winifred's news that her former fiancé had married someone else. When Amy bumped into the couple in a Greek restaurant she came face to face with the fickleness of men.

The chance encounter prompted her to fire off a seventeen-side dia-
tribe to Hans:

> [Sex is] all men want with girls, you can see it all around you in the painted
> faces of nearly all the girls you meet and in the staring desiring eyes of the
> men who pass you in the street. How I loathe them all and how I despise
> myself for being just the same as they. But please don't mistake [me] – I owe
> all my knowledge to you and I am grateful to you for your training and for
> the worldly knowledge you have given me. If I <u>could</u> I wouldn't wish again
> to be the stupid little innocent I was when you first knew me. I used to think
> it was <u>hurting</u> you and I was so sorry for you and felt so tender towards you
> because I thought you were hurting yourself for the sake of giving me enjoy-
> ment – oh, isn't it too funny.
>
> The only thing which has kept us together for so long has been your
> intense desire, and my reciprocatory desire, for sexual intimacy (loathsome
> words) . . .[13]

From then on Amy's letters to Hans were matter of fact, even about
each other's romances. Amy teased him about his 'broadcasting friend',
saying that Liverpool University, where the girl had studied, was infe-
rior to Sheffield. She played woman of the world, asking his advice
about a female friend who was twenty-two, pretty and aware of the
facts of life but unsure about whether to go out with an innocent
eighteen-year-old boy and 'initiate him'.

Such predicaments were part of the lifestyle that Amy and Winifred
threw themselves into; their weekends and evenings were booked up
long in advance with dances, tennis matches and visits to the cinema,
where they saw Charlie Chaplin in *The Circus* and Harold Lloyd in
Speedy. She was making up for lost time, cramming all the sensual
pleasures that London could offer into as short a time as possible. She
could now not imagine being happy anywhere else than the capital. On
a typical Saturday evening she dined at the Trocadero near Piccadilly
and then went to the Prince of Wales theatre to see the play of Anita
Loos' hugely popular book, *Gentlemen Prefer Blondes*, before returning
to the Trocadero for a late-night cabaret. The play suited her mood perfectly: 'Awfully funny and very entertaining, no plot, no hero or
heroine – but just good.'[14] Although she had very little sleep, she did
not seem to need it. She went to Soho in search of clothes and bought
a pale-green, high-waisted evening dress with a full skirt and tight
bodice.

The men Amy met were always 'boys'; she enjoyed, at twenty-five, being the older, experienced woman. She liked the fact that she had a 'past' and, after seven years of playing the innocent to Hans's man of the world, she was now the one with the experience up her sleeve. One boyfriend worked at the Board of Trade and had a car like her father's, which he allowed her to drive. A German 'boy' took her to the cinema. At a cricket match arranged by Winifred's hockey club Amy was introduced to a tall, good-looking young Scot in cricket flannels and green blazer. He was an articled surveyor who often visited Crockers on business. Amy was blasé about the relationship, writing to Hans: 'I'll give him carte blanche and have firmly decided I won't be the one to initiate him into the ways of the world. I prefer to pit my experience against the experience of others than to teach the young and innocent. I'll tell you how the affair progresses.'[15]

But one athletic young man was not enough; Amy was also sipping cocktails at the Criterion with a man whom she described to Hans as someone 'just back from Africa'.[16] They went on to Café Marguerite for dinner and a cabaret at Romano's, a bohemian, late-night restaurant in the Strand frequented by music-hall stars and jockeys, where they finished at two in the morning with whisky and soda and pâté de foie gras. Even Winifred was shocked by Amy's excesses and said it was 'enough to make her ill'. 'My [boy]friend admires me because he thinks I'm a "good girl" and seems greatly intrigued thereby – I think I've managed to keep up the impression,' Amy wrote.

Even summer in the city, which normally made Amy long for the countryside, raised her spirits. 'You would hardly know me now,' she wrote to Hans. 'I have changed such a lot – I am enjoying life very well and on the whole getting a lot out of it – it is glorious to be alive when the sun is shining, but even when it's not I am still happy – in spite of very hard work and late hours recently at the office.'[17]

But her hectic social life left her short of money. She broke a tooth and struggled to find £6.6.0. to pay the dentist. She could not afford to join a eurhythmics class but bought a gramophone player using hire-purchase so that she could roll back the carpet and practise dancing. Despite lack of funds, she planned a walking holiday in August with Winifred and Gwyneth in a grand tour of Grenoble, Turin, Milan and Lucerne. Winifred owed her money, and although she eventually paid her back, it was always a long wait. 'If I weren't so fond of her I'd get awfully fed up over this money business,' Amy wrote to her mother.[18] Amy still owed Hans £3.

She craved excitement and new experiences. For months she longed to see *Wings*, a new, swashbuckling Hollywood movie about the pilots of the First World War. Clara Bow, the Hollywood star with the heart-shaped face and vulnerable, startled expression, worked as a volunteer ambulance driver while her boy-next-door lover performed daring aerial dogfights. It was the first time that a film had effectively moved the action from the ground to the air in scenes that were so convincing that, at its London première in April 1928, several ex-First World War pilots admitted kicking the seat in front of them as they instinctively groped for the plane's controls. While she waited for the film Amy visited the Hendon Air Display and wallowed in the romance of T. E. Lawrence's desert adventures in a book that Wood lent her.

'Winifred and I have decided that utter boredom is responsible for more crimes than wickedness,' she wrote to Hans.[19] It was during one such weekend moment of boredom, in late April 1928, that Amy found herself on the top deck of a bus rattling its way north to Hendon, where she thought she might watch some planes at the aerodrome there. The bus wound its way through Golders Green to Stag Lane, home of the London Aeroplane Club. The aerodrome was little more than a clutch of hangars and a small clubhouse bordered by suburban houses. Amy got off the bus, walked through the gates, past the primitive sheds where the De Havilland planes were built, to a pavilion with deckchairs outside. The muddy field was full of people contentedly watching yellow planes land and take off, or sauntering from the hangars to the pavilion in search of a pink gin.[20] Amy walked over to one of the deckchairs and sank into it. She had finally arrived.

Chapter 6

The Lipstick is Mightier than the Joystick
(1928–9)

On 18 June 1928 Amelia Earhart became the first woman to cross the Atlantic in a plane. At thirty, she was an experienced pilot and one-time holder of the world altitude record, but when she landed on British soil she did so as a token woman. She had spent the twenty-four-hour and forty-nine-minute crossing crouched between fuel tanks at the back of the Fokker plane while Wilmer Stultz and 'Slim' (Louis) Gordon guided the aircraft across the Atlantic. When the plane landed – not in Ireland, as they had expected, but at Burry Port, Wales – 2000 people turned up to welcome the Americans. Many reached out to try to touch Amelia's clothing as if it had mystical properties.

Amelia herself thought she had been as useful as a 'sack of potatoes'.[1] The *Church Times* believed her presence 'added no more to the achievement than if the passenger had been a sheep'.[2] Even so, there was immense interest in her. She met George Bernard Shaw and danced with the Prince of Wales, who had recently acquired a pilot to ferry him about the country – much to the consternation of the press, who thought this too risky a means of travel for the heir to the throne. Nancy Astor, an American by birth and Britain's first practising female Member of Parliament, befriended Amelia and took her to lunch at the Women's Committee of the Air League of the British Empire. Although she disapproved of Amelia's boyishly short curls, she was interested in her previous career as a social worker in Boston.

Journalists found it difficult to pigeon-hole the serious-minded pilot with the freckles who was happy to be photographed wearing a bulky flying suit and a helmet as unflattering as the ugliest of swimming hats. British female pilots were easier to categorise. They were either 'flying flappers', typically actresses, who took to the air for publicity; or members of the aristocracy – rich, eccentric women who saw flying as an extension of the hunt or the tennis court. Stag Lane had both types but Amy was aware of neither on her first visit to the airfield. Her overriding impression was a sense of belonging. She was surprised at the friendliness of the pilot she started talking to and how easy, and inexpensive, he made learning to fly sound. Joining the London Aeroplane Club involved a flat fee of £3.3.0., there was a further subscription of £3.3.0 and an hour's lesson cost 30 shillings. Most people applied for their pilot's licence after about eight hours' tuition and, once they had qualified, they could hire planes for a pound an hour.

Amy had been looking for something to join for months; a tennis club or eurhythmics class were the most obvious choices. But flying would set her apart: it was something a girl from Hull simply did not do. She wrote ecstatically to Hans, 'I'm going to learn to fly!' and confidently expected to take her first lesson the following weekend.³ Hans disappointed her by exhibiting no opposition to her plans and she was further dismayed to hear that the club had a long waiting list. While she waited to start her tuition she joined as an associate member and went regularly to Stag Lane to wallow in the atmosphere. When her father visited her she discreetly introduced the idea that she might quite like to learn to fly. Will, who had already flown abroad on business trips, was fascinated by the new means of travel and did not put her off the idea.

As well as the London Aeroplane Club, Stag Lane was home to the De Havilland School of Flying, whose main clients were RAF Reservists. In fine weather planes from the club managed a thousand landings a day.⁴ Amy had originally written to the School asking for details of flying lessons but had abandoned the idea when she discovered that they cost £5 an hour – the same amount as her weekly pay. The London Aeroplane Club was able to offer much cheaper lessons because it was subsidised by a Government keen to increase the number of qualified pilots and the general awareness of the importance of flying, or 'air-mindedness'. Air Vice-Marshal Sir Sefton Branker, Director of Civil Aviation at the Air Ministry, had three years earlier introduced grants to light-aircraft clubs to help them buy planes and train pilots. 'Branks', as he was known by his friends, had served in the army in India and claimed to have been the first person to use aerial reconnaissance when he took a plane up in 1910. He was a passionate advocate of aircraft at a time when many people saw flying as a passing fad. When the *Daily Mirror* criticised the Prince of Wales for going up in a plane Branks wrote to the editor pointing out that *The Times* had been similarly horrified when Queen Victoria took a train to Slough in 1842. He believed that while the British Empire had been founded on the strength of its navy, its future depended on its power in the skies. Branks made several well-publicised visits to Stag Lane and to other flying clubs around the country. But air-mindedness would quickly evaporate unless the keen amateur had a plane that was easy to fly and inexpensive to run. That plane arrived on 22 February 1925 when the first De Havilland Moth appeared over Stag Lane.

De Havilland, the son of a vicar from Hampshire, trained as an engineer before joining the blossoming motor industry. He was an inveterate tinkerer and soon after his marriage built a plane using piano wire and bicycle parts. His wife sewed the fabric together in a Kensington flat using a hand-turned Singer sewing machine. In 1910 she became one of the first ever air passengers when she sat in the second plane her husband had ever made with her eight-week-old baby on her lap. The War Office bought De Havilland's plane and employed him as a test pilot at Farnborough. During these early years of flying accidents were always treated with matter-of-factness and the teeth De Havilland lost after one crash were returned to him in an envelope. He eventually set up his own company in 1920 at Stag Lane. When the Reserve School opened three years later the De Havilland company was able to build up a reputation for servicing planes that eventually enabled it to move into manufacturing.

The early Moths were designed as a type of aerial sports car. There was just enough fuel capacity and luggage space for the owner and his fiancée (pilots were mostly men) to fly to Paris for the weekend at a cruising speed of seventy miles per hour, sitting one behind the other in two open cockpits. The plane could be towed behind the family car and its wings folded back for storage in the garage. By 1930 women's magazines were running articles such as 'Keeping an airplane of one's own'[5] in which Sicele O'Brien, an aristocratic pilot who continued to fly even after losing a leg in a crash, confidently told readers that a 'girl' could fold open a plane single-handedly in less than two minutes.

Taking a Moth for jaunts around the world became the equivalent of the Grand Tour for the wealthy, who either learnt to fly themselves or hired a pilot. Mostly they avoided crossing large stretches of water but simply crated up the plane and took a ship. According to *The Tatler*,[6] the Gipsy Moth made Baghdad seem as close as Balham and Tunis as near as Tooting, and much less tiring to reach than travelling by tube. Aristocrats flew between their stately homes. The Duchess of Bedford, who suffered from ringing in the ears that could only be relieved by a noisy open cockpit, hired a pilot to shuttle her in a Moth between Woburn Abbey and her mansions in Scotland and Cornwall while she sat knitting behind him. Later, when she learnt to fly herself, her instructor was only ever allowed to address her as 'Your Grace', even if the plane was about to enter a spin.

De Havilland's design dominated flying competitions such as the King's Cup to the extent that they were described as 'Moth-eaten'. The London Aeroplane Club was one of twelve flying clubs that received Government subsidies to help them buy DH Moths at £650 each. The clubs could claim £2000 from the Government if they could match the figure through membership fees or other fund-raising. Every time a member 'took their ticket', or gained the basic 'A' flying licence, the club received a further £50 subsidy. The incentives proved so effective that most flying clubs could not keep up with demand. The London Aeroplane Club had only two instructors and Amy had to wait until mid September for her first flying lesson. She wrote several times to the club's secretary, Lieutenant Commander Harold Perrin, pleading to be allowed to start sooner. But Perrin, a punctilious and powerful man with short-cropped curly hair who was also Secretary of the Royal Aero Club, ignored her requests. He was not keen on women pilots and did not like anyone who tried to buck the established order.

The summer of 1928 was a long, hot one in which sun-bathing became popular for the first time. Amy had not seen Hans for several months but, out of the blue, he suggested they meet. The end of their relationship was not distant enough to remove all traces of bitterness, but they had slid into a semi-flirtatious bantering that replaced the previous bickering. They had reached that half-way house when their shared history meant they were still the closest of friends, but a residual physical attraction made a straightforward friendship problematic. The balance of power had tipped in her favour: London was her home, not his, and she had a string of romantic encounters to boast about. She was curious about Hans's latest conquest and prepared to feel a twinge of jealousy. Her new-found confidence and her anticipation of a relaxing evening made Hans's news all the more devastating. Amy expected their dinner-date to confirm her view of herself as someone who had thrown off the painful memories of the past; instead it ripped open a wound that had only just begun to heal.

Winifred was surprised when she heard her return from her meeting with Hans much sooner than she had expected. Amy threw herself on her bed and, between Amy's wrenching sobs, Winifred extracted the reason why Hans had been so anxious to see her. Hans had married on 14 July 1928 at St Patrick's Roman Catholic Church in Hull. His bride was a twenty-five-year-old from Mossley in Manchester who worked for the BBC. This was the 'broadcasting friend' and graduate of

Liverpool University whom Hans had introduced into his letters to Amy a few months before.

Amy had only recently come to terms with the idea that Hans was seeing other women. She was totally unprepared for and unable to cope with the news that the man who for years had been at the centre of her fantasies of marriage was now married to someone else. She had reconciled herself to their separation with the argument that others had put forward for years: that Hans was simply not the marrying type and that if he would not marry her he would marry no one. The confirmed bachelor had just walked down the aisle.

It is impossible to know how much Hans told her about his new wife, whether Amy demanded to know and, if she did, whether she was too shocked to take in any of the details. It was not the last time she and Hans met but he abandoned her that summer's evening with a Pandora's box full of unanswered and unanswerable questions. Every scrap of information that she had gleaned about the new Mrs Arregger gnawed away at her. She was exactly the same age as her and, like her, had gone to university. Amy had asked Hans for a photo of his new girlfriend; if he sent it she never acknowledged it in her letters. She must have wondered when exactly the affair had started, probably on one of Hans's business trips to Manchester or Liverpool, and most likely when he was still sleeping with Amy.

Hans may or may not have chosen to tell Amy about the most devastating aspect of his marriage: that his new wife was pregnant. Their son was born on 18 January 1929 at Westcliff-on-Sea when the couple had moved to Thorpe Bay. It took ten years for Amy to write down her thoughts on Hans's marriage, and even after a decade the bitterness remains fresh: 'The young man finally married someone else and settled down into a rut which would sooner or later have driven me crazy.'[7]

Amy stumbled through the rest of the summer. Flying represented the only release from a dead weight of disappointment and hurt. The planes that danced across the skies above Maida Vale gave her need to escape a greater urgency. Two days before her first lesson on 15 September she wrote to her father, who had just returned from a business trip that included Lowestoft in Suffolk, where he had opened an office, and Norway. She complained that she and Winifred had both been suffering from colds and that Winifred, who was working too hard, had developed pneumonia. Amy had become so alarmed that she had called an ambulance. She told her father that, apart from the one hour she spent each week at Stag Lane, her life was devoted to the office and that she came home only to eat and sleep:

It makes me happy to be taking these lessons and gives me an interest in an otherwise very monotonous life and gives me a chance to meet people . . . I think you will agree that I shall be happiest living my life in my own way and learning through my own experiences and so long as this doesn't entail my having to fall back on you financially, I shouldn't think you will object. You see, I have an immense belief in the future of flying.[8]

Stag Lane was the ideal place for anyone searching for an antidote to monotony: its strange mixture of social classes and personalities gave it a unique atmosphere. As in the RAF and the public schools, which produced many of its members, nicknames were commonplace, if not compulsory. When Amy dyed her hair she was called the 'Platinum Blonde'; later she became 'Johnnie' or 'John'. Both were preferable to 'Bottle Johnson' – the title given to a female pilot who suffered from thick calves. There were two 'Nathans': 'Nasty Nathan', who was Italian, and 'Nice Nathan', who was British. The giggling young debutantes who flocked to Stag Lane were known as the 'Beauty Chorus' and the group of music-hall stars who joined the club were 'The Variety Act'. The airfield itself was known as 'Stuck Lane' because of the mud that dogged flyers through the wet months. Flying had its own language that added to the sense of a closed clique. A 'daisy bender' was a good landing, a 'shepherd's crook' a particularly tricky aerial manoeuvre.

There was always someone or something to see at Stag Lane and, for Amy, the attraction of this exotic new world was that it was set in the open air. De Havilland strode around the aerodrome in his crumpled hat and full-length leather coat and Lady Heath used the aerodrome's wide, open space to practise her javelin throwing. Nearly every day a gleaming Bentley or Buick delivered its glamorous occupants to this least glamorous of venues. Miss Gillie Flower and Miss Edna May, two giggling actresses appearing in the comedy So This is Love at the Winter Garden, played aerial golf from De Havilland Moths high over Stag Lane. Bags of flour acted as balls that they dropped from their planes, hoping to hit a white circle marked on the ground. The purpose of the exercise, of course, was publicity.

Flying in the late 1920s was a 'hot' topic that newspapers and magazines could not afford to ignore. When Lindbergh crossed the Atlantic in 1927, 'Aviator hats' became popular, and fashionable London stores like Selfridges, Burberrys and Dunhills designed flying clothes for women in much the same way that they had suggested outfits for the new lady motorist. Since sitting in an open cockpit was a chilly pursuit, the new outfits had to be constructed from unbending leather and looked about as attractive as boiler cladding.

Aeroplane manufacturers were good publicists and journalists were willing victims of their publicity stunts. In June 1927 a plane setting off from the newly opened Croydon Airport raced the *Flying Scotsman* which started from King's Cross railway station. The plane won, despite at one point following the wrong engine, and probably helped by the fact that the train-driver was seventy-nine. In March 1928 *The Tatler* began a regular page covering aviation news called 'Air Eddies'. It was a mixture of serious comment on the development of the new form of transport and gossip about the aristocrats and celebrities who indulged in it. It featured pictures of the two flying golfers and one of Will Hay, the music-hall star, who flew his Gipsy Moth from Stag Lane. Major Oliver Stewart, an ex-RAF pilot who wrote 'Air Eddies', gave particular prominence to women pilots, who were hardly out of the news in 1928. In a year that saw the banning of *Lady Chatterley's Lover* and *The Well of Loneliness* (the latter depicted lesbian love, albeit obliquely), there was considerable debate about the 'modern woman'. The aviatrix was part of that debate and although he could not resist taking a pot-shot at the woman pilot, Stewart did so with affection:

> Unfortunately instead of concentrating their energies upon the ethereal problems of dress, women tend increasingly to turn their attention to trivial and flippant pursuits like running insurance companies, politics, the law, aviation, medicine and so on . . . Consequently there are too many women who wear their hats at stalling angle, and whose garments bristle with exposed kingposts, struts and bracing wires. Their interests and energies are being wasted on some such activity as aviation, and they will be persuaded to mend their ways only when they have learned the truth that the lip-stick is mightier than the joy-stick.[9]

Luckily for Stewart, the women pilots who dominated the headlines were (with the exception of Amelia Earhart, who did not count because she was foreign) overwhelmingly from the same class as most of his readers. One of the most famous was Lady Heath, a formidable pilot who earned the nickname 'Lady Hell of a Din' because of her perceived talent for self-publicity. Her exploits produced copious column inches but she was also responsible for fighting many important battles for women pilots and the din that she made was usually designed to remove obstacles put in their way.

Lady Heath was born in Ireland[10] and studied science at Dublin University. She started flying when she was twenty-two and gained a commercial pilot's licence. When, in 1924, the International Commission for Air Navigation banned women as commercial pilots, Lady Heath succeeded in having the ban lifted by demonstrating that she was capable of flying at all times of the month. She breezily announced that flying was as easy as Charlestoning and dressed for the cockpit as she would for the dance floor.

When she became the first woman to fly solo from South Africa to London in the spring of 1928, her luggage included a tennis racquet and evening dress. She wore a fur coat to protect her neck from the sun and struggled into two inflated motorbike tyres when flying over water, believing that the tyres would support her if she crashed into the sea. Instead, they burst as her plane gained height, leaving her with shreds of rubber around her neck. Arriving at Croydon Airport, Heath told waiting reporters that she had managed to repair her appearance by powdering her nose and donning silk stockings in mid air. It was only after a bullet hole was discovered in one of her wings that she realised she had been shot at – probably over the North African coast.

While Lady Heath was flying back from Cape Town, Lady Bailey was on her way from Croydon in the opposite direction.[11] Bailey was also Irish and, like Heath, had the advantage of a rich husband so that when her plane was written off in Tanganyika she could send for a replacement, knowing that her husband, the South African industrialist Sir Abe Bailey, would pay for it. When she eventually arrived in Britain in January 1929 she became the first woman to make the return journey and did so across the untried routes of central Africa and the Sahara. Bailey obtained her pilot's licence at Stag Lane in 1926. She was an unflappable woman who preferred a tweed suit to an evening gown. Geoffrey De Havilland was with her at Stag Lane when she slipped on wet grass and fell forward into a spinning propeller. Such an accident would normally be fatal but Bailey was merely scalped. Ever the gentleman, De Havilland retrieved the missing patch of skin and hair and made sure that Bailey's head was cleaned and bandaged.

Amy had her first flying lesson at Stag Lane on 15 September 1928. It was not a sensible time of year to start tuition as the onset of winter inevitably limited the number of days when the weather was fine enough to go out. Stag Lane's position in a low-lying hollow meant that a thick mist frequently descended on the airfield, grounding the planes and sending disgruntled members to the club-house. But Amy was too impatient to wait for the spring; she wanted to be in the air.

Her first instructor was Captain Matthews. When she climbed onto the wooden wing of his training Moth, stepping over the bolts that held the wings in place until they were ready to be folded away, she did so with grim determination. She was not a flying flapper out on a weekend jaunt – the lesson was expensive and she wanted to make the most of it. Matthews barked instructions at her down a Gosport speaking tube as he sat in the front cockpit of the Cirrus II Moth. To Amy, sitting taut in the cockpit behind Matthews, the commands were incomprehensible squawks of anger until she realised that her flying helmet was too big and that the reason she could not make out his commands was that the tube connecting her to her instructor did not fit snugly over her ear. The distant, distorted voice buzzing around her neck added to her feelings of disorientation.

Flying in a Moth for the first time produces a sensation of claustrophobic exposure. The claustrophobia comes from the design of the cockpit, a high-sided capsule that encloses the pilot's whole body in a space not much bigger than the driver's seat of a Mini car. Amy, who was only five feet four inches tall, could barely peep over the side. She kept her goggled eyes fixed on the helmeted head of Matthews that she could see through the windscreen in front of her, trying to match his body movements with the disembodied voice that had found its way into her cockpit. The wire bracing between the two sets of wings sang in the wind above the rumble of the engine. If she raised her hand for a moment above the side of the cockpit, it was battered by the force of the air outside the plane. The same cockpit that can make the learner feel so enclosed can also produce a feeling of exposure. The dual-control joystick and rudder pedals on their long metal struts dart around in sudden, mysterious movements orchestrated by the instructor. Light seeps through the fabric floor. The thin dashboard is the only immovable object to cling onto.

Matthews did not believe in encouraging his pupils and there were times when Amy felt that she was making no progress at all. Like most novice flyers, she was too heavy-handed; it took time for her to realise that the Moth responded to what felt like a barely perceptible touch of the joystick. As a guideline she was taught always to try to keep the plane's nose on a level with the horizon. Her lessons were less of an ordeal when she was taken up by Captain James Valentine Baker, the club's chief flying instructor. He was only eleven years younger than Amy's father and spoke with a soft, Welsh accent. Baker had fought at Gallipoli and still suffered from a bullet that was lodged too near to his spine to be safely removed. The wound did not prevent him from learning to fly and he went on to win the Military Cross after reputedly shooting down fifteen German planes. When the war ended he worked in the Dutch East Indies and Chile before returning to Britain to teach flying. The extraordinary events Baker had lived through had left him with a matter-of-factness when it came to everyday flying. He had nothing to prove and it took a lot to ruffle him; he enjoyed frightening less experienced pilots by flying low over cabbage fields.

Baker communicated with his pupils through a set of neat little hand signals that made him look like an in-flight book-maker. When a pupil performed well he clapped his hands in the air to praise them. The only time he spoke was to let the pupil know he had handed over control of the plane, saying, 'You've got her.' He felt no need to prolong his position as instructor and encouraged his pupils to try out their skills as soon as possible. His confidence was catching and his students learnt quickly.

Baker suggested that Amy should try 'turns' in the first weekend of November after three and a half hours of tuition. A 'turn' is a delicate operation in which the pilot applies pressure to the rudder with one foot while moving the joystick with their hand; if they are too heavy-handed the plane careers out of control. A steep turn feels as though you are about to tumble out of the plane, and most people instinctively contort their body so that it remains parallel with the ground, rather than relaxing into the plane's movement.

Bad weather and the expense of Christmas forced Amy to take a two-month break from her flying lessons, although she continued to trek through the dreary suburban hinterland to reach Stag Lane at least once every weekend. She liked the atmosphere of what was now a thriving social club with a bar that had become slightly plusher and with a proper restaurant. The pavilion had a roaring fire and served tea and ham sandwiches. When the weather was very bad skating was popular at nearby Elstree Reservoir and Amy enjoyed snowball fights among the sheds. Watching planes was the next best thing to flying in one and Amy was beginning to wonder what made them work. Women were strictly banned from the sheds where the planes were serviced, but this prohibition made the world on the other side of the door more inviting. 'Hangar talk', with its reference to arcane terms such as 'gudgeon pins', 'D.I.' (Daily Inspection Certificates) and 'distributor points', fascinated her, and she was intrigued by the processes that transformed the neat ground engineers into dishevelled, oil-splattered individuals.

Magazines that Christmas welcomed the festive season with illustrations of a biplane soaring above a bemused Santa Claus struggling to keep up with the new competitor in the sky. Amy went home to Hull by train. The festivities started off dramatically when the maid found the dining-room on fire the day before Christmas Eve. Will gave Amy and Irene leather coats that cost £5.5.0. each; Molly was given a bag costing £2.10.0. and Betty received a dog. Ciss's present was an expensive gramophone. Amy was more than usually content on her visit home; Winifred visited on Boxing Day and stayed the night while Gwyneth came to tea. She knew that her leather coat would be much admired at Stag Lane. Will reported in his diary, 'a very happy time'.[12]

Flying lessons started again in the second week of January, this time exclusively with Baker. On 10 February he began to teach Amy about landings, forcing her not to look out of the plane at the fast-approaching ground. But heavy frost and snow meant she was unable to consolidate what she had learnt and she went up only five times during the next two months. In March she wrote to her mother, 'I've almost forgotten what it feels like to be full of beans and life and vitality' and told her she was taking 'hypophosphates' to boost her energy levels.[13]

By April Baker was prepared to let Amy go solo but this time fog thwarted her. Just as the weather cleared Baker left for a new job at Heston Aerodrome and Amy was back with Matthews, who insisted on putting her through her paces himself before letting her go solo. They went over and over the techniques of recovering from spins and stalls. Although both can be exhilarating, they are a long way from 'proper' flying, and spins, in particular, can make a new pilot feel dizzy and nauseous. Just as she seemed about to be put out of her misery, Matthews was taken ill and Amy's debut was delayed again. In the meantime Major Herbert Gardner Travers took over as chief flying instructor.

By this time Amy's patience had been stretched to breaking point and she was not prepared to start the whole process of proving herself to a third instructor. Unfortunately for Amy, patience was Travers' strong point. He was a cautious person with a keen sense of responsibility that had been heightened by his experiences in the trenches of the First World War and by a tragedy that he had witnessed just a few months before joining Stag Lane. Travers' daughter, Eva, remembers Amy as a young woman who was 'furious with life'. That fury quickly became focused on the man who was standing in the way of her desire to be left alone in the skies.

Travers was thirty-eight, but seemed much older. He was a typical son of the Empire whose mother had been born in a ditch during the Indian Mutiny while a mutineer snatched the rings from his grandmother's fingers. During the First World War he was stranded on the front line one freezing December day when his machine-gun jammed and exploded, sending shards of metal ripping into his right hand, wrist and arm. He lay with blood seeping out of him until a Quaker stretcher-party risked enemy fire to wade through the mud to drag him to safety. He narrowly escaped having his arm amputated, although it never recovered and withered into a wasted stick. A year later he was back in France as a pilot where he earned the Distinguished Service Cross, becoming a major when the RAF was formed.

Before joining Stag Lane Travers had worked as a temporary instructor at the Cinque Ports Flying Club at Lympne on the south coast. On his very first day's flying in October 1928, in a brand new Moth, a pupil went up alone immediately after a lesson with Travers. The man's seat-belt snapped and he plunged to his death. In March 1929 Travers was giving his wife a flying lesson at Lympne when, at 150 feet, the Moth's engine failed and they were forced to land in a field. The plane flipped over and Travers was pinned under the wreckage, hoping the aircraft would not burst into flames. The official accident report suggested that the plane had run out of petrol. It was the ground engineer's job to make sure that there was enough petrol, but it was the pilot's responsibility to check the supply before take-off. Travers resigned shortly after the incident. At Stag Lane he earned a reputation as a worrier; it is easy to see why.

Travers was a physically intimidating man. He was a foot taller than Amy with startling blue eyes, blond hair and a long nose that gave him a distinguished air. During cold weather he wore a duffel coat with the hood thrown back to reveal his 'lucky' leather flying helmet that he had had since the war; he smoked a pipe using his 'good' left hand. Pupils sat waiting for him on a wooden bench outside his tiny office, straining to see the church spire at Harrow which Travers used as a guide to determine whether the skies were clear enough for flying. 'Today no see – no fly,' he told disappointed pupils in the clipped, pidgin English of the RAF.

He had a methodical approach to teaching. Since so many pupils became confused about how to use their feet to work the rudder, he made them practise on the ground. Travers used hand signals, or 'voice savers', as he called them: two hands held up with open palms meant the pupil had entire control, one hand held on edge meant straight ahead.

He believed that the flying instructor must be 'a very quick judge of the probable home life and habits of new pupils'.[14] His assessment of

Amy was that she was in too much of a hurry. His daughter Eva believes he thought Amy 'grim and unattractive . . . with a chip on her shoulder as thick as three cubic feet of best B.C. lumber'.[15] Amy had never experienced such close contact with anyone from Travers' class before and he unwittingly made her feel self-conscious about her background and her accent. She took his clipped, upper-class way of speaking as a sign of an easy life. But Travers was neither a snob nor a chauvinist, he was just cautious. He had several female pupils such as the New Zealander, Jean Batten, who, like another of Travers' students, the future Sir Francis Chichester, was to fly solo from England to Australia. Other learners, with less to prove than Amy, got on well with Travers. When the publisher Hamish Hamilton qualified to fly, he sent Travers several new books as a thank-you. Jobling Purser, maker of Pyrex oven-to-tableware, inundated the Travers family with his product when he received his 'A' licence.

A few instructors reckoned it was possible to go solo after twelve hours of dual control; but several novices who went on to be distinguished pilots were much slower, and Francis Chichester took twice as long. Amy finally went solo on 9 June 1929 when Matthews was back as her tutor. It was two months after Baker had first said she was ready, and following fifteen hours and forty-five minutes of tuition. After such a protracted wait it seemed incredible that she was to be left alone with the plane. She checked each of her instruments in turn and tugged at her safety harness to make sure it was properly secured. A mechanic removed the chocks that held the plane in place and gave the propeller a hefty swing that brought the engine to life. Amy strained over the side of the plane to make sure her path was clear, and the Cirrus Moth ambled over the grass ready for take-off. She went over the drill she had been taught so many times and, with nothing left to check, opened up the throttle. Unleashed, the plane hurtled past spectators watching the novice's attempt and eager for a chance to criticise a woman flyer. Amy was probably too busy going through a mental checklist of what to do to enjoy her first take-off; like most learners, she may have been amazed that the plane had not sensed a raw pilot at its controls. For five minutes she soared over North London, no leather-clad figure in front of her, no dual control between her and the plane's engine.

Going solo took her over the first hurdle towards a career in aviation, and she dared to voice her ambitions. That night, when she wrote to tell her mother she had flown the Cirrus Moth by herself, she talked of sitting for the Private Pilot's 'A' licence that would allow her to take her parents up. The main qualification was having done three hours of solo flying in the last twelve months. In Amy's case being able to clock up the remaining two hours and fifty-five minutes depended on the availability of planes and the money to pay for taking them up. Flying had become a drug and Amy was impatient for her next 'fix'. Sitting in the clubhouse exchanging gossip with other club members while the fortunate few droned overheard in their yellow Moths was no longer enough; she wanted to know what went on on the other side of the hangar doors.

Chapter 7

Behind the Hangar Door
(1929)

The sheds where the planes were repaired and cosseted represented the 'downstairs' of a social structure as complicated as the multi-layered hierarchy of an Edwardian stately home. It was an all-male preserve visited fleetingly by pilots when they wanted to discuss a problem they were experiencing with their 'machine', in much the same way that a lord might drop by at his stables to chat about the health of his favourite horse.

Only pilots who were truly obsessed with flying lingered longer than necessary in the hangars; most preferred to treat the engineers as boiler-suited servants. The hangars were grubby places run by men outside Amy's middle-class background – and as such could hardly have been more attractive to her.

Improving her flying skills would only take Amy so far: more solo trips and, if she obtained her 'A' licence, the possibility of taking passengers up with her. If she ever hoped to earn a living from flying, she needed to understand how a plane worked and what to do if it did not. Engineering know-how was essential for longer solo trips and if she wanted to act as a De Havilland agent; it was a skill as practical and portable as typing and one that could take her round the world. The only problem was that the Air Ministry had yet to issue a Ground Engineer's licence to a woman. Lady Heath had trained as an 'air mechanic' in America and was authorised by the US Department of Commerce to carry out work on planes, but even she had allowed her 'ticket' to lapse. If Amy qualified as an engineer she would be the only woman in the world to hold the title; most pilots thought her chances of achieving this remote and fanciful.

Jack Humphreys, who had been chief engineer at Stag Lane for two years when Amy first went solo, offered a way into the hangars. In terms of Stag Lane's hierarchy, he was a quasi-butler, someone whom the owner-pilots respected for his engineering skills and ability to keep the busy airfield running smoothly. He mixed freely with them without ever becoming one of them.

From behind the hangar door Jack ran a tight ship. His job was a matter of life and death: if his team of engineers did not look after the planes properly they would fall out of the skies. Jack was responsible for maintaining standards and discipline among his men while ensuring a happy and productive atmosphere. It helped that he had spent all his working life in exclusively male worlds. At sixteen he joined the Royal Flying Corps as a fitter-mechanic and served on the Russian front. After the war he worked for Shorts aircraft company before joining De Havilland. At Stag Lane he stood out from the well-dressed club members who quizzed him about the state of their machines. They respected him despite the fact that he looked a bit like Charlie Chaplin with his twitching moustache, thick hair and oily overalls that were several inches too short in the leg. He lived by an unbending black-and-white moral code and once someone or something earned his loyalty, his devotion was unswerving, a trait that left him vulnerable to abuse.

The engineers were suspicious of anyone who trespassed on their territory. They whistled, sang and traded mild abuse in their stark, echoey workplace, falling silent when anyone from outside their ranks entered. Their silence, ostensibly from respect, always gave the newcomer the uneasy feeling that they would be talked and laughed about as soon as they had left. When Amy first peered into their gloomy workplace, the ground engineers had no idea how to treat her; they felt uncomfortable about swearing or continuing with their usual bluish banter. They could not believe that she was interested in mechanics and were baffled by her persistence in turning up despite their frosty reception. Usually they enlisted the help of a male pilot to guide her back to the clubhouse where she belonged.

Only Jack was intrigued. He later admitted that he abhorred the idea of teaching a woman engineering and that he was at first unsure how to talk to Amy.[1] He could tell that she was genuinely interested in learning more about how a plane worked and his love of mechanics meant he could not resist responding to her questions. Jack had a close working relationship with Baker, who told him all about Amy's progress in the air. Once she got to know Jack, Amy felt completely safe with him. He was two years older than her and married with a young son. He was a Freemason like her father and quickly became a mentor in the way that Vernon Wood was, teaching her about engines and setting her tasks. It was not long before she had told Jack about Hans and, as they began to spend more time together, Jack got used to the black moods she sometimes sank into, when he complained that he could do nothing with her. Although he never appeared anything other than the cajoling chief engineer who treated Amy like a tomboyish, younger sister, Jack's feelings towards her gradually deepened into affection.

Jack's patronage of her gave Amy a degree of acceptance in the 'sheds'. She started to enjoy being part of their rough and tumble and to take her turn with the boxing gloves when there was time for a sparring match; the languid life of the clubhouse seemed tame by comparison. In the hangars she was known as 'Johnnie', a sexless nickname that pigeon-holed her as 'one of the lads', whereas among the pilots she was always the typist who had to scrape and save for her lessons. Her passion for flying gave her a link with the other club members but that was as far as it went; they were not about to ask her back to their country seats or their Mayfair flats. The only pilots with whom she felt at ease were the 'Variety Act' – the music-hall stars who were drawn to Stag Lane rather than the socially exclusive clubs of Heston and Brooklands. Performers like the comedian Will Hay and the juggler Tom Elder-Hearne had an ambiguity about their roots that Amy shared. And they knew how to party.

Will Hay is remembered today for the laughable buffoons he created for the variety stage and later the cinema: the inept schoolmaster with the glasses balanced at the end of his nose, and the blustering station-master from *Oh! Mr Porter*. But when he was not in costume or contorting his face into a grimace, he was good-looking in a severe, unsmiling sort of way. His face was heavily lined and he had a taut, athletic body. He carried ropes in his props basket so that he could rig up an impromptu boxing ring to spar in when he arrived for a show; he liked swimming and diving and was competitive at everything he tried: he would only undertake something if he knew he could be the best at it.

At forty-one Will was fifteen years older than Amy and had been married for twenty-two years. His mother was a fish-merchant's daughter and he was born into a strict religious family from the North. His variety act had taken him to Australia, America and South Africa. He learnt French, German and Italian and traded Cantonese lessons from a laundryman in return for his book-keeping services. By the time he met Amy he had become obsessed with flying and kept a Moth at Stag Lane.[2] On stage he used the audience's laughter as a chance to tell his co-stars in hurried asides about his latest flight.

Will combined Amy's two loves: the escapism of the theatre and flying. He was the first famous person she had met and his married status made their friendship dangerous and exciting. She visited Will backstage when he was performing at London's Victoria Palace, and inevitably gossip about them grew both in music-hall circles and at Stag Lane.[3] At first Jack saw the endless round of parties as a useful safety valve to release some of the bitterness Amy felt about Hans. But the topsy-turvy world of variety stars, whose working day started in the middle of the evening, meant Amy began to turn up for her sessions with Jack tired and unable to concentrate. Jack's ramrod-straight moral code was offended by the thought of a single woman gallivanting with an older, married man; he may have been jealous, too, that his position was being usurped. When Amy seemed in danger of crashing head-long into an affair, Jack told her bluntly either to end the relationship or get out of his hangar.

Whether or not the friendship had developed beyond the platonic stage can only be guessed at. Amy did not feel ashamed of her friend-ship and introduced Will to her father when he visited Stag Lane. The comedian found her father 'bossy and stern',[4] but it is hardly surprising that Will Johnson felt he had to assert his authority in front of his daughter's older, married friend. Amy told Winifred that Jack had been concerned that she would 'get into trouble' and offered to obtain 'abortion powders' for her.[5] In the end the infatuation faded of its own accord. Amy was now much more absorbed in her role as 'greaseboy'.

At the end of March she decided to move nearer Stag Lane and took lodgings at 2 Brentmead Place, at the northernmost end of the Golders Green Road, hugging what is now the North Circular Road and close to Brent Cross. Part of the logic behind the move was to save money. Her landlords were the Percivals, a couple in their mid twenties who offered free board and lodging to a young female who would look after their two small children for two evenings a week and one Sunday a month, but they were not a trusting couple and always locked the larder and hid the wireless when they went out. The decision to move was a momentous one as it meant Amy would no longer have Winifred to come home to. She planned to leave McVitie's in the autumn and had won a scholarship to study social science at the London School of Economics. Amy was still interested in her work at Crockers but it no longer dominated her letters home. In April the firm helped a group of investors to set up a new company to make 'talkies' and Wood praised one of her reports as 'excellent'. But it now took something as novel and glamorous as movie-making to arouse Amy's interest.

While Amy waited to 'take her ticket' she looked around for the next best thing to a plane, something that offered speed and independence. She found it in the motor car. When Amy first went to university there were just 314,000 cars in Britain; by the end of 1929 that figure had leapt to over a million and in 1925 there were for the first time more cars on the roads than motorbikes. The car was still a cold, draughty means of transport, a seasonal hobby that was abandoned during the cooler months, and at the start of the decade cars were so unreliable that a successful chauffeur was also a mechanic; but they were slowly becoming more sophisticated. The Model A Ford had windscreen wipers and could be ordered in more than one colour, and the introduction of the electric self-starter, which replaced the crank-handle, put cars within the physical capabilities of women for the first time. A national speed limit of twenty miles per hour was largely ignored, as was the suggestion that mirrors might make driving safer. The term 'road hog' became a common expression of abuse and during a debate in the House of Lords one peer declared that reckless driving had made taking a walk in London as dangerous a pursuit as coal-mining.

Despite mounting debts, Amy was determined to buy a car. The Percivals sold her their dark-maroon, two-seater Morris Cowley for £65 and her father agreed to lend her £70 to cover the purchase and the money she owed; she was to repay him in weekly instalments. The car was three years old with 'balloon' tyres and a 'dicky seat' that folded down from the tiny boot. It gave her a sense of independence and a way of practising her new-found mechanical knowledge. She now wrote to her father about her growing familiarity with her car's engine – her ability to tune up the magneto and carburettor and to clean the jets and plugs.

Amy went home to Hull for Easter and the whole family travelled to Bridlington to visit Will's parents. On Easter Monday Will watched Hull City draw 1–1 with Middlesbrough and later went to the cinema with Ciss, Amy, Irene and Teddy. The newly-weds were now settled in the home that Will had bought them. Lake Drive is just off the Holderness Road in the east of Hull.[6] The houses were brand new when Irene and Teddy moved in and their neighbours were people clawing at the fringes of respectability: clerks, foremen, master mariners and other tradesmen. Each house had a kitchen and sitting-room downstairs, a pantry, coalhouse and toilet at the back. There were three bedrooms upstairs and, unusually for houses in Hull at this time, an upstairs bathroom. Teddy and Irene's home backed onto East Park which had a boating lake that wove its way through the park. Their Morris car was kept in its own garage.

During the Easter holidays everyone was prepared to play happy families but a few weeks later the old problems bubbled to the surface again. As was so often the case with the Johnson girls, the root of the anxiety was money. Amy seems at this time to have been afraid of her sister and wrote in private to her mother telling her that she had lost Irene's camera and was worried about how to replace it. Irene had become obsessively anxious about money and for two Sundays running in April had flown into a rage during the traditional weekend visits to her parents. She confided in Ciss about her worries and then lost her temper when her mother discussed the matter with Will, who was baffled by the outbursts. He wrote to Irene in May 1929:

> Things have been so happy it seems utterly ridiculous that such unpleasant-ness should be occasioned owing to some misunderstanding over a few shillings. You told Mother you were hard up. Of course we don't know any details but if you have any trouble why don't you out [sic] with it, as you know both Mother and myself are always ready to help our girls in their dif-ficulties or troubles, but there is always a right and wrong way to approach things and I'm afraid you've handled the matter in the wrong way this time. If you have any difficulties do come to dinner on Tuesday and let us discuss it and see what we can do. Best love, Father.[7]

Irene wrote back the next day to say that her mother had got the wrong impression and that she was only worried about 'things which are nec-essary and yet which I feel I cannot afford'.[8] She mentioned expenses with the house and giving the Morris 'a rest'. On 19 June Irene wrote to her father asking his advice about the rates in a letter that betrays a growing paranoia.[9] The council had added £1.10.0. to Irene and Teddy's rates because of their garage but Irene felt this was unfair. Her griev-ance was based on one of her neighbours who did not have a garage and instead dumped wood near theirs. The wood attracted rats, forcing the council to send out men with dogs to kill them. Irene argued that because they had a proper garage they were actually saving the council money because they did not attract vermin. She became obsessed with the rats nesting behind the garage at her and Teddy's expense: thirty-seven were killed by the council men on their first visit; seventeen died in the second extermination. Her father told her that there was nothing that could be done about the council's decision.

Will Johnson at this time was leading a double life. In his red leather diary[10] he jotted down in his neat handwriting a short entry for most days and always included details of the weather. It told the story of a quiet domestic existence: his Rotary meetings, Ciss's organ and choir practice and what everyone bought each other for family birthdays and how much his presents cost. But Will had several escape routes from this mundanity. He went often to the cinema and at the end of March he saw *Wings*. Will now knew how thrilling flying could be. In April 1929 he and Ciss took a plane from the newly opened Croydon Airport to Paris and then continued by train. They were given a guided tour round Rome by car, visited Florence and went for a gondola ride in Venice – despite his qualms about the cost. They bought a bedspread for 1500 lire, a price which Will dutifully recorded in his diary, and on their way home to Hull went up the Eiffel Tower.

The Johnsons were part of a slow trickle of tourists who were starting to use aeroplanes. The first air passenger crossed the Channel in 1919 and by the end of the 1920s there were regular flights between London and Paris. Travelling by air was an unhurried business and more like sitting in the Pullman carriage of a train. Although planes were noisy and airsickness was more common than it is today, comfort rather than economy was the airlines' keyword. The first passengers sat in Lloyd Loom chairs bolted to the floor but these were gradually replaced by upholstered seats. First-class customers chatted at tables covered with linen tablecloths and decorated with fresh flowers as if they were in a nightclub waiting for the cabaret to begin. Waiters dressed in white starched uniforms served meals using silver cutlery and china crockery. Air travel was slowly becoming more popular in the United States too, where the prospect of covering the country's vast distances faster than the train was a huge incentive. Windows were sometimes left ajar in case the cabin became stuffy, although one American airline was forced to bolt them shut because empty drinks bottles thrown out by passengers damaged the fuselage.

Will was too much of a businessman not to realise the potential of commercial flight. As a means of transport it also appealed to his suppressed sense of adventure. He was excited by and proud of his European trip and invited forty-five friends to see the cine film of it. Since so few of his guests had ever travelled abroad, it was an invitation that held none of the dread that it would today.

At the beginning of June Amy let slip in a letter to her parents that it was 'just possible I shall leave Crockers in the autumn'.[11] She often used this tactic with her parents – dropping what was a well-advanced plan into the conversation as if it had just occurred to her; it gave them time to assimilate an idea calmly without feeling that it was a *fait accompli*. She added a handwritten postscript in the corner of the letter, written on 7 June: 'Sorry to hear about Irene. I'm sure there must be some misunderstanding somewhere. Hope it will soon be cleared up.'[12]

Amy spent every spare moment in the sheds that were heavy with the smell of 'dope' and oil and where the highly flammable chemicals made fire a constant risk. At first she was given mundane tasks like sweeping the floor or washing the planes of the forty private owners who kept their machines in lock-up garages at the club. When she showed no signs of giving up, Jack agreed to give her free engineering lessons. She was at Stag Lane by 7.15 a.m. and stayed until 9 a.m.; when her office job was over she hurried straight back, often not leaving until 10 p.m. At Crockers she became a clock-watcher. It was obvious that her mind was elsewhere; her carefully tended nails had become torn and neglected and she sneaked aviation books into the office to read in secret. In one letter to her parents she devoted four pages to a discussion of the state of aviation and air-mindedness in what must have been, even to the most devoted of parents, a tedious lecture, and she gave Betty a model aeroplane for her birthday.

Amy was working hard at converting her parents to the idea of their daughter abandoning a safe job at Crockers for what was, to them, the completely alien world of aviation. On 6 July 1929 she passed a series of practical and oral tests to obtain her Private Pilot's 'A' Licence and a week later she made her first cross-country flight alone. Travers drummed into his pilots the four 'C's that he believed to be vital for this type of flying: compass, clock, chart and common sense. The compass allowed the pilot to check direction; he or she could compare land-marks with the chart and making a note of the time at which they had left would tell them how far they could expect to have travelled in the time. Navigation was not as straightforward as Amy had thought and she became lost, making a forced landing at Stony Stratford.

She had been mulling over ways in which to earn a living from flying for some time. Uppermost in her mind was a scheme to start an agency in Hull to sell and repair Moths. The De Havilland plane had a loyal fol-lowing of owners scattered throughout the country and, increasingly, the world. Geoffrey De Havilland chose the name 'Moth' because he had collected moths and butterflies since he was a schoolboy. As the business grew he drew on his childhood hobby as an inspiration for what became a whole series of planes that included the Tiger Moth, Puss Moth and Queen Bee. As a brand name, though, the word 'Moth' was an unfortunate choice as it is an excruciatingly difficult word for anyone whose first language is not English to pronounce. Despite De Havilland's marketing *faux pas* the plane performed well in a range of different climates and terrains and was viewed with affection by anyone who flew it. Roald Dahl learnt to fly during the Second World War in a Tiger Moth and remembered it as 'a thing of great beauty', an aeroplane with 'no vices' that it is impossible not to fall in love with.[13] During 1929 sales of the Moth leapt by 300 per cent in Europe.[14]

As part of a plan to secure her father's backing for the scheme, Amy arranged for Will to visit Stag Lane at the end of June. He discussed Amy's ideas with Travers and went up with her before making an appointment to meet De Havilland. Will was broadly supportive of Amy's desire to work in aviation but his was the voice of reason constantly probing for the detail behind her dreams. He was quick to find practical drawbacks to her idea of setting up a De Havilland agency in Hull. In between tending his stamp album he wrote to her on 1 July 1929:

> While I understand your enthusiasm yet when it comes to speculation and an investment it does sound another matter. It seems to me PIONEER WORK [sic] and as a general rule Pioneer Work does not pay but sometimes becomes a very costly matter.[15]

He outlined the reasons why he thought the agency would be an expensive venture. The capital expenditure would come to around £2000 and there would be weekly bills of some £30. The only income would be commission from sales and Amy would be competing with the National Flying Services and the local flying club. 'Now Amy, I haven't stated all this to dampen you but merely to give you the business side of the matter.' He told her to put her plan on paper and sent her £5 to soften the blow. Ten days later Will wrote again, urging her to change jobs if that was what she really wanted; procrastination meant she was wasting time and was not fair to Wood. He suggested she become the secretary to the principal of a flying club who might allow her to fly his plane. But Will was adamant he would not lend her any more money:

> If we have ambitions we must make sacrifices to secure them, it might mean living cheaply and doing many things on the cheap until the right moment comes. Many an artist lives in an attic all their lives as a sacrifice to their ambition, always hoping for the right moment of success, which comes to some while others are doing the same thing all their lives without getting the desired success.[16]

Amy replied that typing would never get her into the air. She told him that she was unlikely to marry and reminded him pointedly that he had given Irene money to help her set up home. Amy's latest plan was to launch a De Havilland agency in New Zealand. To do this she needed her 'B' licence, which would allow her to operate as a pilot for money, rather than pleasure, and she spent the summer working towards the hundred hours' flying that was a key part of the qualification. Only a handful of British women, including Lady Heath, held this licence, and they were forced to undergo more frequent medical examinations than men. In July Amy visited the Aero Show at London's Olympia; Jack was at her side explaining technical details and pointing out interesting features. Amy was so absorbed by the exhibition that she went twice.

At the end of June ten-year-old Betty contracted scarlet fever. The sweltering heat made her illness even more painful to watch. Will recorded its steady progress in his diary: '30 June . . . Betty not quite so well . . . 1 July . . . Betty improving . . . 7 July . . . Betty progressing nicely . . . 16 July . . . Betty got up and dressed.' Irene and Teddy occasionally looked after her if Will and Ciss had to go to Bridlington to see Will's parents and on Sunday, 21 July Betty was well enough to accompany them. Irene took advantage of the hot weather to swim in the sea.

On Wednesday, 24 July Irene called on her parents and Will reported her 'very happy'. The next day he set off on a long business trek to Lerwick on the distant Shetland Islands in Scotland, content in the knowledge that his youngest daughter was out of danger and her troubled elder sister was on an even keel. Molly returned home from boarding-school on the Friday and, since Betty had been given the all-clear, the house was fumigated.

Saturday, 27 July 1929 was the day of Shell-Mex's annual outing. Teddy kissed Irene as she lay in bed and then crept downstairs to eat his breakfast alone. As he left the house at twenty minutes to nine he called up the stairs, 'Goodbye, love.' She answered him happily from her bed. Molly, who had not seen her sister for several weeks, visited and stayed until after lunch. As so often happens when tragedy strikes, it was the sort of day that was remarkable for being so ordinary.

Teddy and Irene's housemaid, Florence Carr, let herself into the house that night. It was unusually still in the quiet suburban home, but then Teddy had not yet returned from his works outing. Standing in the dining-room, Florence sensed that something was out of place in the well-ordered house but could not tell what it was. Scanning the room, she noticed the two slight, but telling, details that alarmed her. A note had been left on the table and a cushion was missing from the

Chesterfield. There was a strong smell coming from the kitchen. When Florence recognised it as gas she dashed to the nearest house, and it was this startled neighbour who fought through the mounting fumes to the scullery, where he found Irene unconscious, her head slightly to one side facing the oven. She was declared dead at Hull Royal Infirmary just before midnight. Teddy was told the news when he arrived back at Paragon Railway Station.

Will's diary entry for Saturday reads: 'Fine day. With Len White all day. Left at 5 p.m. for Aberdeen. Moll saw Irene at 1.40 p.m. Irene died between 1.40 p.m. & 10.30 p.m.' During the days that followed Will recorded the practicalities of his life: how he waited fifteen minutes for a train on his way back to Hull from Edinburgh, Amy's arrival on the Sunday, going to fetch Betty and Molly from Bridlington and how Teddy and a friend came to stay with them at Park Avenue. A day rarely passed when he did not mention the weather. There was no outpouring of grief or hint at what he might have been feeling. The only clue that this was an extraordinarily painful time appears in the sprig of stiff white heather wrapped in tissue paper that he placed between the pages of his diary a week after Irene's death.

'I give you the letter back, and no one shall know what was in it except you and me,' Coroner J. Divine told Teddy at the inquest into Irene's death.[17] He was as good as his word and no record survives of the note's contents. The official entry of the inquest simply states the basics of Irene's life and death: her age, address, that she was married and that she died of coal gas poisoning. The verdict was suicide whilst of unsound mind.

The coroner had known Teddy since he was a baby and when he called him as a witness he treated him with the gentleness of an old family friend. 'Now, Edward, I am not going to read this letter, (Witness: Thank you) but I am bound to say for your sake that it gives the happiest conception of the relationship between you and her. The terms in which it speaks of you are terms of which you might well be proud . . .'

Witnesses portrayed Irene as a gifted young woman. Mark Goulden, the editor of the *Hull Evening News* whom she worked for as a secretary, said she had ambitions to be a journalist and he was sure she had a 'brilliant' career in front of her. As is often the case with people who take their own life, Irene appeared cheerful in the days and hours just before her death.

Will mentioned Irene's earlier suicide attempt but added: 'It [her death] has come as a thunderbolt. We felt that she was happy in every way. I saw her the previous Sunday when we were motoring together and she seemed quite happy.'

The Johnsons were a well-known Hull family and the inquest attracted much attention. They were left with the knowledge that their neighbours, business associates, friends and family all knew the details of Irene's death and yet the taboo of suicide meant the tragedy must not be mentioned, or only elliptically. So many people had lost sons, husbands and brothers in the war that suicide seemed a gratuitous act. It was even more wanton because the Johnsons were a lucky family: Will's profession had allowed him to escape the trenches and he had been spared the anguish of waving any sons off to war. Suicide was technically against the law and, more unforgivably, contravened the natural order. No words of comfort were available: Irene had not been in physical pain, she was still young and, worse for the devout Ciss, there was no sense that her death was 'God's will'. The teachings of Freud were seen by 'normal' people as no more than the eccentric out-pourings of a bearded Austrian and there was little awareness of mental health problems. Neighbours whispered that Irene had a lover in London, mounting money problems or some unspeakable disease.

More convincingly, some family members said Irene felt trapped in a marriage that, while not unhappy, offered none of the raw emotion that she craved. Teddy would never be more than a lowly pen-pusher in a dull office job. Inevitably some of these poisonous theories trick-led back to the Johnsons at a time when they were already tussling with feelings of guilt, anger and failure. Their strict adherence to Method-ism made the death even harder to bear: not only had they failed as parents but their faith had failed them. There was the nagging feeling that they were being punished for something; there were so many questions but no answers. Will and Ciss were not emotional people and they had no mechanisms to help them deal with the tragedy. Betty and Molly were still young girls whom they wanted to shield from the depths of their grief. Will immersed himself in the details of the cre-mation and sorting out Irene's affairs. Amy, who stayed with her family until after the service on the following Wednesday, was unflinchingly supportive but she too was unable to confront her complicated feel-ings. She assumed the role of head of the household, trying to cheer everyone along with a breeziness that betrayed the fact that she had yet to take in her sister's death.

Amy's work kept her in London while Will retreated with the rest of the family, including Teddy, to Ilfracombe on the north Devon coast. The short holiday was designed to take them far away from the prying eyes of their Hull neighbours. Amy urged them to be as 'cheerful as possible'. 'If Moll and Bee get fed up,' she wrote to her father, 'please tell them from me that at any rate they've got a roof and a bed and meals prepared for them whilst I am turned out of my digs and have to tramp London to look for a roof to cover me – you know, make the picture real black!!! (I'm alright [sic] really because I'm never stumped!)'[18] She urged 'Muth' to rest and to buy bread rather than baking it herself. At times her words were so excessively cheerful that they appeared one step behind hysteria: 'I wouldn't like any telegrams saying anyone has collapsed!!! So please all go steady and rest and be cheerful, won't you?'

PART 2

Australia

Chapter 8

Where To?

(1929–30)

At the end of August 1929 Amy went with Winifred to the cliff-top resort of Ventnor on the Isle of Wight. She told her father that her 'nerves' were bad and she could not allow them to deteriorate further. For a week she had not felt like flying, but her interest was stirred by the Schneider Trophy, which had been sponsored since 1912 by Jacques Schneider, the son of a wealthy French arms manufacturer, who hoped to encourage the use of planes that were capable of landing on water.

Irene's death gave Amy a sense of urgency and a determination to move on – even if she was unsure quite where to. She had decided to leave Crockers and worked out her notice in an uneasy atmosphere. Wood chastised her for being late, saying that it was her duty to set an example to the younger secretaries. He was disappointed to see his pro-tégée leave and Amy detected a coldness in his manner towards her. On her last day at Crockers she told her father she hated the 'dark stuffy room and the eternal typing, the swindling and unfairness of law'.[1] He replied: 'Business life is hard and cold, so you must not expect anything else.'[2] He impressed on her that leaving Crockers was a big step. 'One can't keep on changing their course . . . I know you are really keen and I know you are clever, therefore make up your mind to make this a success.'

The very day after Amy left Crockers she was sitting in a speed-boat being rocked by the swell from a dashing red seaplane as it skidded onto the water of Southampton's Solent. Amy, her hair dyed a startling blonde, watched from a boat owned by a flying friend, occasionally dipping into the hampers of food supplied by a local hotel. She was one of two women in a party of eight who squinted through the rainbows formed as the sunshine merged with the seaspray. The single-winged seaplane sped round the circuit of the Schneider contest at over 330 miles per hour.[3]

Having finally cast off from Crockers, Amy spent most of her time at Stag Lane. She returned from the Schneider Trophy contest to new lodgings in a pastoral setting that put her within a twenty-minute walk of the airfield and allowed her to sell her car for £40. Oldways, Elmwood Crescent, was one of two thatched timbered cottages perched by a small green. Amy's room had a coal fire and looked out onto an old-fashioned garden and the fields beyond. Her landlords were a couple with two children; the husband sorted mail at the post office and often worked night shifts.

In Hull Will and Ciss were struggling to present a front of normality after Irene's death. Ciss spent whole days practising the organ or went with Teddy to Lake Drive, where they sorted through the detritus of Irene's life. Will complained of aches and pains, and worried about Betty's operation to remove her adenoids and tonsils, and Molly's inability to find a job. Teddy, who had moved into Park Avenue after the tragedy, was eventually unable to stand the claustrophobic atmosphere and left without warning. He later telephoned to say that he was living with his father. The Johnsons took his abrupt departure as a personal slight: 'Can you understand such a man?' Will wrote to Amy. 'We now see what poor Irene had to put up with. I intend to cut him if I see him in the street and if he comes again to 85 I shall tell him many home truths which will make him feel somewhat uncomfortable.'4

Teddy's behaviour shook their fragile attempts at rebuilding a sense of themselves as a family. Amy went on the defensive in a letter to her mother that placed all the blame on Irene's husband and put money at the root of the insult: 'Ted's conduct leaves me utterly disgusted. I told him off in my last letter to him about sponging on other people so he can't plead ignorance.'5

Amy's changing life in London dominated her parents' world in Hull and they were determined to allow her to fulfil her potential as a pilot. A fortnight before Irene's death Will had been adamant that he would not lend Amy money to support her ambitious plans; six weeks later he sent her £50 of what would become a regular allowance. He told her to use it to pay her subscription fees at Stag Lane and the Royal Aeronautical Society (where, thanks to Jack's influence, she had recently become a companion), and her income tax. He wanted her to have a 'clear start' and giving her money helped him to draw a line under the past. 'I am trying to give you your chance,' he wrote, 'and want to do my part, but it is also up to you to do your part and at a certain point (which I hope won't be reached) I shall have to say stop, so take things very steadily, seriously and economically.'6

Her father had, for the moment, eased the financial pressure on

Amy, but she still faced opposition from two influential members of the London Aeroplane Club. Travers and the club secretary, Perrin, were both determined to put Amy in her place. Perrin felt women should not be allowed in the hangars and was annoyed at the interest being taken in Amy. Her obsession with engines was novel enough but her heavy-handed use of hair dye, which earned her the additional nickname of the 'Platinum Blonde', increased the attention paid to her. Travers, too, was determined to curb her ambitions. 'I detest the man, he's a rotten instructor,'[7] she told her father, adding, when Travers took her and Will up for a spin, 'I never have liked him much and now I loathe him. He's doing his best to make things very difficult for me and unfortunately is succeeding.'[8]

But she had a few key allies. Jack refused to bow to pressure to keep Amy out of the sheds and threatened to leave if his hand was forced. He pointed out to Perrin that she was an unpaid and hard-working member of the ground staff. Amy had another ally in Jimmy Martin. He was not one of the traditional flying crowd, but a farmer's son from County Down who had been brought up by his aunt and sister. When his sister moved to England Jimmy followed and lodged with her and her husband in Acton, West London. For the next twenty years he used their kitchen to dismantle his motorbike or work on an invention with the planks of wood he brought home on the bus.[9]

Jimmy was thirty-six when he met Amy. On the surface he was a jolly, teasing man with a big, red face and workman's hands. But his joshing façade masked a certain ruthlessness. He always had a scheme on the go and was convinced that one day one of these schemes would make him a lot of money. Amy was instantly intrigued by the fast-talking Irishman whose optimism provided an antidote to Travers. When Jimmy told her he was building a new type of plane that would be ready by Christmas and which she could fly to Australia, she found it easy to ignore the countless pitfalls attached to such an ambitious plan.

The new plane was to be the first project for Martin's Aircraft Works which Jimmy launched at a disused lino factory at the end of a long, rough lane in Denham, near Gerrards Cross in Buckinghamshire, that he persuaded his brother-in-law to buy. Baker, now working at the flying school at Heston, met Jimmy regularly to discuss the prototype over dinner. Amy, who was to be the plane's test pilot, regularly borrowed Jack's Austin Seven to make the twenty-minute drive to Denham to see how the plane was progressing. Jimmy planned a low-wing design that was easy to fly and look after and which had a low stalling speed. By the standards of its time it was revolutionary: a monoplane made from steel tubing rather than wood, with side-by-side seating and an engine behind the cockpit.

As her plane materialised Amy needed to stoke up interest in her as a potential long-distance pilot so that she could raise money. Publicity was something she enjoyed because it vindicated her choice of careers. One of the reasons for choosing her as a test pilot was that the novelty of a woman flyer would mean the plane attracted more attention. In October 1929 she wrote a piece for the *Sketch* and when the *Daily Express* decided to do a photo spread about women pilots she was determined to appear in it. Her picture was in the *Sunday Graphic* and the *Daily Mail* at the beginning of November.

Amy had still not broached the subject of a long-distance flight with her parents. She flew up to Hull to visit them at the beginning of October and at the end of the month wrote to tell them that she had been offered the chance to study on a private navigation course. The other women taking part were Lady Bailey and Miss Ward, a maths lecturer at London University. Amy pointed out that Bert Hinkler, who held the solo record from England to Australia, had taken an American correspondence course in navigation before embarking on his epic journey. Then she added in one of her throw-away lines that so often revealed her true intentions: 'It may some day make all the difference to my getting as far as India or Australia instead of only Paris!! One never knows . . .'[10]

Having given her parents a fortnight to assimilate the idea, she wrote on 13 November to tell them excitedly that she hoped in the spring to be 'pushing off on a stunt trip to Australia or something of that sort'. She planned to fly in a new plane that was in the early stages of development and which should be ready by Christmas. It was all very secret, she told her parents. To date she had managed forty-two hours solo.

Amy had so far kept her sister's suicide at arm's length. She behaved as though Irene had emigrated to some distant country and the only thing for the rest of the family to do was to deal with the practicalities caused by her absence. She suggested a use for Irene's pink frock and arranged for a tiny gilt frame to be made for Irene's picture. But Irene's birthday in November forced Amy to confront her feelings. She was acutely aware how difficult the anniversary was for Ciss, especially since Will was in America on business:

I try to think of Irene as simply living in some place rather a long way off but where she is happier than she ever was before. It is the folk left behind who have the hard part to bear and you, of course, are bound to suffer more than any of us . . .[11]

The more one thinks about life and death, the more incomprehensible they seem. I don't often think about them as I am not given to deep thinking and philosophy. I believe in taking things as they come and making the most of life whilst one has youth, health and strength.[12]

The suicide of a brother or sister can alter the survivor's attitude to death; suddenly it is no longer a remote, alien concept. Those left behind often behave in what seems a destructive way. They appear to have a special drive and strength; it is not so much that they feel nothing so terrible could ever happen again, but that because the suicide took them to the limits of despair, they have been immunised against a repeat of such profound grief. Siblings, in particular, can suffer from survivor guilt in much the same way that the men who returned from the trenches felt uneasy at their good fortune in staying alive against all the odds. Amy was already intoxicated with flying when Irene died, but after her suicide flying and life at Stag Lane became a physical outlet for the emotions left by her sister's death.

Jimmy Martin said later that Amy had told him she planned to use flying as a way of killing herself after what she saw as her betrayal by Hans. A fatal crash would allow her parents to believe her death had been an accident; Jimmy claimed Amy abandoned the idea because her love of flying gave her a reason to live. The loophole in this theory is that Amy had already decided to learn to fly before Hans married, but Will, Ciss and Jack each had a nagging worry that Amy's bid to fly to Australia might be a suicide attempt. Will ended a letter to Amy in January 1930: 'don't forget the promised motto "BE CAREFUL".' They were torn between their anxiety for her safety and a desire to see her fulfilled; her struggles provided them with a vicarious sense of release.

After Irene's death flying took on a new impetus for Amy; it became a career rather than a hobby, and it was only following her sister's suicide that she took the momentous step of leaving Crockers. She felt she had something to prove and she was searching for a vehicle for her anger and frustration. Put harshly, Amy's life so far had been a failure. She had failed to obtain an honours degree, failed to become a teacher, let an eligible man slip through her fingers and failed as a sister. She needed to do something that would re-establish her self-worth and her family's good name.

Jack helped give a structure to Amy's rather vague ambitions. Under his tutelage she began to study for her 'C' Ground Engineer's Licence – a qualification that would allow her to inspect certain types of aero-engines, including the Cirrus Marks II and III, the Hermes and the De Havilland Gipsy. She worked in the sheds from eight in the morning until dusk every day except Mondays and including weekends. She was allocated her own engine which was her sole responsibility and which she nurtured like a prize plant. Each morning she put on her baggy overalls or a zip-up jacket and as the day progressed her face picked up the grime and grease of the sheds; her hands became stained with the petrol and paraffin that she used to wash down the engine. She learnt to love the mysterious world of the ground engineer in much the same way that she had enjoyed her initiation into the legal profession. 'Tappets' had to be checked for 'clearance', 'rocker fulcrum pins' needed to be 'charged' with grease and 'contact breaker gaps' would only be effective if they were the exact size. All the time Jack was in the background, often wielding a slide-rule, watching her dismantle and rebuild the engine until the process became as automatic as packing and unpacking a suitcase. In the evenings she pored over textbooks. Her main incentive was the promised position of test pilot for Jimmy's new plane that she still believed would be ready before Christmas, but once she heard that Lady Heath[13] had allowed her 'ticket' to lapse, Amy was driven by a new dream.

She was given a few days' notice that her exam would be held in November at Stag Lane. It was an oral test in which a board of five men fired questions at her. She found the experience so worryingly simple that she was afraid she might have failed. But there was no catch and she received her ground engineer's licence on 10 December 1929. Her next goal was to secure a Ground Engineer's 'A' Licence. This would allow her to inspect aeroplanes and would fit nicely with her 'C' licence which dealt solely with the plane's engine. The 'A' licence was just as technical and covered areas such as the correct tension of the bracing wires, the extra weight that a coating of 'dope' (applied to strengthen the canvas covering) adds to a plane, the workings of the ailerons (the movable surface on the rear of each wing that controls the rolling motion) and how to install an air-speed indicator. Amy obtained her 'A' licence on 10 March 1930 and the two engineering qualifications allowed her to upgrade her membership of the Royal Aeronautical Society from companion to associate member.

Her other ambition was to qualify to take passengers up by gaining a 'B' licence. When she took her first flying lesson in 1928 a pilot only needed thirty-five hours of solo to qualify for a 'B' licence, including one cross-country trip of 200 miles and one night flight. The new rules specified 100 hours' solo. Amy took advantage of an interim ruling that allowed pilots to take passengers up after 50 hours' solo and once their application had been approved by the Royal Aero Club. Jack was her first passenger on 13 December 1929; Ciss and Winifred followed in the spring of 1930.

Her mother's decision to become the first member of the Johnson family to fly with Amy was a brave one. Ciss was nervous at the best of times but she was suffering more than usually in the aftermath of Irene's suicide. She was consumed by worry about Amy, sending her regular packages of chocolate biscuits and cakes. Initially Amy responded by trying to carry on as if nothing was the matter: she asked her mother to post her a pillow and eiderdown because she did not like the ones in her lodgings, and when she visited Hull she left walking-socks and ten handkerchieves to be laundered. By January 1930 Ciss was complaining of headaches and Amy's letters to her mother were filled with concern. Will sent Ciss to Bournemouth for a period of recuperation and Amy met her in London and then visited her at the Vale Royal Hotel.

Ciss's illness brought her as close as she had ever been to Amy, who felt responsible for her mother and acted as go-between for her parents. She wrote to her father saying that a word of censure from him could cause Ciss to cry for hours on end. After one visit to Bournemouth Amy told her father that a psychologist had 'adopted' 'Muth' and was talking to her about Irene's death. Ciss also received massages and violet-ray treatments from a Nurse Pitman, whom Amy believed had psychic healing abilities. Glancing at a photo of Amy in Ciss's room, she announced that Amy was afflicted with abdominal problems. The diagnosis prompted Amy to reveal to her father that she had been suffering 'another big trouble in connection with a woman's illness'.[14] She left Ciss to explain the details but merely told him that she had been so worried that she had gone for a clandestine examination last time she was in Hull and that the person she saw had prescribed a monthly tonic that cost three shillings and sixpence per bottle. Nurse Pitman had recommended a course of fifteen electrical treatments (this was not the controversial electroconvulsive therapy or ECT) and massages that she believed would cure Amy. Ciss wrote to Will, recommending that Amy should have them, and felt well enough herself to allow Amy to take her up for her first flight.

At the start of 1930 Amy picked up some work from Major Nathan. This was probably Nice Nathan, as opposed to Nasty Nathan. As well as having a sunnier disposition, Major Nathan had a wooden leg. He was planning to ship his Moth out to the West Indies but asked Jack if one of his men would give it an overhaul before the journey. Although rather startled when Jack suggested that 'Johnnie' could do the job, the Major agreed. Amy described it as one of the hardest week's work ever, but she was paid £3 and was allowed to fly the plane in return for her expertise as an engineer.

Her evenings were spent studying navigation as part of her qualifications to gain her pilot's 'B' licence. Every pilot now had to pass an exam in navigation that was much more technical than the previous lackadaisical qualification, the main component of which was the number of hours flown. Even experienced pilots found the prospect daunting and seasoned flyers, including the London Aero Club's two instructors, were forced to attend lectures held at the De Havilland Technical School. Although navigation was primitive compared to the modern pilot's bank of glowing lights and the constant crackle from the control tower, the new requirement was an attempt to remove some of the more amateurish elements from flying. Candidates had to know Morse, be able to operate a wireless (although few planes had one), be able to forecast the weather and steer by the sun, moon and stars.[15] The syllabus covered the earth's magnetism, use of compasses and international legislation. Dead reckoning, the art of calculating the plane's position by estimating direction and distance travelled, was a key part of the exam.

Amy had two hours of lectures most days and studied until 1.30 a.m. at night. Lady Bailey invited Amy and Miss Wood to her house in Bryanston Square to practise Morse together. Amy was unashamedly impressed by the footmen who attended them and wrote to her mother: 'It was great fun. I made several mistakes at dinner, but Lady Bailey is awfully sweet and has the art of making one feel perfectly at ease. She's got a lovely house.'[16]

On 8 January a reporter from the *Evening News* waded through the mud at Stag Lane to interview an Indian pilot who hoped to beat the record from England to his home country. While he was there the reporter asked Perrin if there were any other interesting pilots and Perrin, despite his earlier qualms, could not resist mentioning Amy. Jack urged her to snatch the opportunity for publicity. Sensing a better story, the reporter discarded the Indian and turned his attention to Amy. By the time his report appeared, she had been transformed into the twenty-two-year-old daughter of a 'wealthy Midlands family' who made a 'comfortable living from aviation'. Outwardly she was furious at the newspaper's errors – particularly the claim that she was well off. Secretly she wallowed in the publicity because it singled her out as special and because she knew its importance in raising money. The piece described her as the first woman engineer and mentioned her plan to fly alone to Australia in a secret plane.

After the story appeared Amy's face looked out from every newspaper window in Fleet Street. She received fifty phone calls about her plans and a cine-film operator and ten reporters arrived at Stag Lane, some representing the Australian press. As a businessman Will was delighted by the 'stir' Amy was causing and recognised that journalists would be all the keener because Amy had not sought the attention. The idea of a lone girl's flight to Australia in a mystery machine fuelled their interest and once she was well known she would be able to ask the press for money. He began counselling her like a business manager or agent, responding to her queries and her requests that he should use his Masonic and Rotary Club contacts to find out more about making the most of publicity. He told her: 'In the first case you have to let the Press off free in order that you can get your standing and publicity and then in your next step forward you can make some demands.'[17]

Will encouraged her to write for newspapers and magazines and was pleased when she earned £4.4.0. for a piece that appeared in the *Chronicle*. He urged her to be very cautious about what she said to the journalists. 'There isn't any such thing as a friendly talk with them – they report it all. If you have anything you don't want to be known then don't even wisper [*sic*] it to a reporter.'[18]

The journalist teased out of Amy her barely formed plans to fly to Australia and his article made the plan reality. After the report appeared there was no going back. If she gave up now she would never be taken seriously again. In her diary she turned to the blank page for 5 May and wrote 'best day'. This was the date that she calculated was likely to provide the kindest weather conditions along the route to Australia; any later and she would meet the monsoon head on. Once that date was in her diary she needed financial backing, and the most obvious source for that was the 'patron saint of aviation' and the head of the company that produced Castrol Oil – Lord Wakefield.

Chapter 9

Jason
(1930)

In the years following the Great War the world was in a hurry and Charles Cheers Wakefield enjoyed being in a position to help a new breed of pioneers to go further and faster. Castrol Oil, developed by Wakefield's company, lubricated Alcock and Brown's plane across the Atlantic and enabled the Smith brothers to become the first pilots to fly from England to Australia in 1919. Malcolm Campbell 'put his trust in Wakefield Castrol', as he was contracted to point out, when he pushed his cigar-shaped car, *Bluebird*, to beat the world land-speed record.

Wakefield was an old-style paternalist who held sway over his staff with a top-hatted, stickler-for-punctuality approach to management. But when it came to marketing he could be bold, even avant-garde. He had just turned seventy when Amy started her campaign for an audience with aviation's greatest benefactor. Wakefield, who was born in Liverpool, the son of a Methodist lay preacher, was a devout Christian who poured money and time into numerous charities; when he died *The Times* likened him to Carnegie and Rockefeller. But his devotion to aviation was not charitable: he believed in its power to cement Britain's imperial roots and as an important marketing tool for his company. His family motto was 'For God and Empire' and his coat of arms bore an aeroplane's propeller.

C. C. Wakefields oils turned the cogs in trains, ships, mines and countless heavy industries throughout the world. In 1909 the company developed a new blend that worked perfectly for the nascent plane and car markets. Castrol, which took its name from its main ingredient of castor oil, was an elixir untroubled by extremes of temperature. But investing in a product that served the highly speculative markets of planes, cars and motorcycles was a huge gamble and one that Wakefield knew had to be supported with imaginative and expensive marketing. In 1922 the company made advertising history when an aeroplane traced the word 'Castrol' in smoke across the London skyline above St Paul's Cathedral. A year later Wakefield was spending a quarter of a million pounds on promoting its oil.

Alonzo Limb, Wakefields inspired head of marketing, was astute enough to spot that the best adverts were driven by a human-interest factor. If Castrol could be linked with a daring feat or tale of endurance the product would stick more firmly in the public's mind. Wakefield recognised the power of celebrity endorsement but knew equally well that if his product were associated with a failure, especially an ignoble one, his oil would be tainted by association. He had yet to back a woman. Supporting a female flyer had its advantages: the publicity would be massive, but if she failed – or even died in the attempt – Castrol would have egg on its face, if not blood on its hands.

Amy first asked Lord Wakefield for an interview shortly after the *Evening News* piece appeared, but he was unwell and not in the mood for bothersome young women. She continued to pester his office throughout January and asked one of his secretaries, who occasionally visited Stag Lane, to sound him out on her behalf. While she waited for Wakefield's health to improve Amy devoted her evenings to systematic 'networking'. At the end of January she attended a lecture at which the Director of Civil Aviation, Sir Sefton Branker, and aircraft manufacturer Frederick Handley Page were both present. Amy's hero George Bernard Shaw, who travelled as often as he could by plane, was also there.

One by one she visited the editors of the aviation magazines in an attempt to win them over. She wrote an article for *Air* magazine and subscribed to a newspaper cuttings service to make sure she was aware of everything being said about female pilots. Amy became a furious scribbler. When the *Dispatch* carried an article entitled 'Why women are not good pilots' she wrote a robust reply, and her efforts paid off in February when the 'Airwaves' page of *The Tatler* showed her climbing into a plane as if she were mounting a horse.

Amy realised that as she was a minor celebrity, interest in her would quickly fade and that if she did not find a major backer soon Fleet Street would turn their attention to someone else. The delivery date for Jimmy's plane had slipped back to March – barely a month before she planned to set off for Australia. She agonised over the pros and cons of buying a plane against waiting for Jimmy's new model. Owning her own machine would give her greater control but a brand-new plane would attract more attention.

'Moths are too well known to excite any interest and De Havillands won't do anything new for publicity, having already made their name,' she wrote to her father.[1] Amy believed that if she flew a new model to

Australia she could claim a directorship of the company when it joined the stock market. She toyed with the idea of taking a seaplane, such as the type that Sir Alan Cobham had used when he flew to Australia in 1926, but that would mean mastering the techniques of taking off and landing on water. In her desperation she considered looking abroad for a suitable machine. She even bought a ticket for a raffle in which the first prize was a plane.

Amy was constantly looking over her shoulder. In January 1930 the bespectacled Francis Chichester, who was to become famous as a round-the-world yachtsman and who had been taught to fly by Travers, flew solo from England to Australia in a journey that took five weeks. There were rumours that at least three other pilots were planning attempts on the route. News leaked out that Bert Hinkler, whose record Amy was hoping to beat, was building a new plane in the barn at the back of his house in Southampton. The press was fascinated by the 'mystery plane' with which Hinkler 'may again astonish the Aviation World'.[2] Hinkler added to Amy's torment by issuing a statement saying that he was considering using the new plane to make an attempt on his own record. 'Each month, almost, it [flying to Australia] is becoming less of an adventure,' Amy wrote in anguish to her father.[3] She was growing suspicious of Miss Wood, the university lecturer who was studying navigation with her and Lady Bailey. Miss Wood told Amy that she was taking the exam for fun, but Amy's paranoia increased when Miss Wood was spotted at Denham.

Despite having no money and no plane, Amy continued to prepare for the journey. She visited Stanfords, the map specialists in London's Covent Garden, and Lillywhite's, a sports shop in Piccadilly Circus, agreed to make her a flying suit in return for her endorsement. Amy chose her favourite colour of the moment, bottle green. The excitement of working towards a huge adventure energised her. 'I'm feeling splendid and full of vim!' she told her father.[4] Distracted by the importance of what she was doing, she relied on her mother to help with the minutiae of life, sending her underwear home and asking Ciss to tighten her knicker elastic for her. Will did his part by dispatching boxes of kippers to anyone of influence whom Amy thought might appreciate the gesture. Her parents' support was uppermost in her mind when she considered what to call the plane that was still no more than a dream. Sitting in a Lyons' Corner House, she wrote to her father to tell him that the aircraft that was to take her to Australia would be called *Jason*, the telegraphic address of her father's fish business and a flying tribute to the Johnson family.

Will and Ciss both fretted constantly about Amy's health but their concern did not stop Will, who had assumed the role of parent/manager, dispensing frank advice:

Your letter says everyone is so apathetic and so slow while you are wearing your nerves down with worry and impatience. I quite understand it dear, but to speak plainly no one troubles themselves that you are impatient and wearing your nerves down, further it's only a few who are REALLY keen in the aviation matters. Have your big ideas by all means, but master the smaller points first; look up to the top of the ladder . . . but you can't jump up there all at one stroke, it has to come step by step and you must use patience in the process.[5]

Will urged caution over Crockers' proposal to retain her as the firm's 'aviator'. Although she used their offices as a base Will advised her not to become too closely tied to them as he felt that such a relationship would rule out more lucrative deals and that she would be at their 'beck and call'. Instead, he advised Amy to encourage the proposal without actually signing anything until a precise format of payment had been worked out that included a fee per trip based either on miles flown or an hourly rate, a limited annual number of flights and a seat on the board. Will's ultimate goal was that a large newspaper would agree to sponsor Amy: 'If the *Daily Mail* takes you up you are made.'

Ciss's nerves were still bad and, even after her convalescence in Bournemouth, Will was worried that she was heading for a 'general breakdown'.[6] The first half of 1930, when Amy's plans for her hoped-for voyage to Australia were at their most feverish, was marked by a series of family crises that left Ciss in a state of permanent anxiety. In January Will's father suffered a seizure that paralysed him down one side, then Will's mother was taken ill and his uncle Niels became unwell; another uncle, Frank, was thought to have cancer of the liver. In February Will was working long hours as the herring season hit its busiest time; the phone, which in the Johnson family could never quite shake off the association with bad news, rang with alarming regularity. Will did his best to think up distractions for Ciss: he chose a golf club for her to join and planned to take her to the Rotary International Convention in Chicago because he thought the ocean crossing would do her good. She began a course of 'violet ray and high frequency electric treatment' which, on Will's suggestion, Amy tried. Will treated himself to 'vapour' baths, probably a type of Turkish bath, at his local swimming pool.

Her parents complained if they did not receive regular letters from Amy but, on the whole, they managed to contain their deepest worries about her ambitious and dangerous plans. It was as if all three of them were so consumed by her efforts to be allowed to fly to Australia that they had lost sight of the fact that it might actually take place one day soon. Will sent her instalments of money – £50 at the beginning of March followed by the same amount on 2 April – and Ciss worked out her anxiety in the kitchen. For Ciss baking was proof of a solid family life and she bombarded Amy with the fruits of her labours, sending her buns, a currant loaf, coconut confections and a chocolate cake over which Amy made 'quite a beast' of herself.

Will sent her a typewriter which she used to pound out letters to people whom she thought might be able to help her. One Sunday evening she typed seventeen letters. On 5 March she wrote an impassioned plea to Sir Thomas Polson, founder of the United Empire Party, in which she laid out her credentials. She told him how, with no money or influence, she had trained herself for a career in aviation; her efforts had made her the 'first – and only – certified woman aircraft engineer'. Flying solo to Australia, which she believed was 'the greatest distance practicable for a land-plane', would raise her profile further.

The United Empire Party embodied her own ideals, 'fighting the very apathy and timidity against which I have been struggling'. Amy said that she wanted between £1000 and £1500 to finance the flight and that she would be able to repay the money in the bonuses she expected to receive from sponsors such as oil companies and the plane's manufacturer:

> I am not out to make money. I merely want to do my bit in spreading Empire Aviation, and incidentally to make a living. It is surely common sense that England cannot keep her lead if she doesn't keep up to date, and she's hopelessly behind hand in this most important mode of transport.

She suggested that, just as Lindbergh's plane had been called *Spirit of Saint Louis*, so a plane called *Spirit of England* could capture the public's imagination and do its bit 'towards Empire Unity by bringing the Mother Country into closer contact with [the dominions]'. Amy offered to carry messages to parts of the Empire, to start campaigns along the way and on her return. She ended her appeal with a veiled threat, saying that if the Empire Party turned her down she would be forced to look abroad:

America respects her women pilots and gives them splendid opportunities and positions, and I have good reason to believe there would be keen competition among certain European countries for an available British woman pilot with such qualifications as I possess.

But the Empire did not heed her call and Amy fired off letters to Lords Beaverbrook and Rothermere and Sir Sefton Brancker. She began her letter to Branks by saying that she agreed with his comments at the Royal Aeronautical Society's lecture of the previous night at which he had said, 'I wish England would wake up.' She added that one of the reasons she wanted to fly to Australia was that such a flight by an 'English girl, solo and in a light 'plane, would do much to engender confidence amongst the public in air travel'. Amy drew his attention to her appeal in *Flight* magazine and told him of her qualifications and included a list of people, including Perrin and Lady Bailey, who would 'vouch' for her 'sincerity and capabilities'. She told him, 'Everyone in Aviation Circles speaks well of you and say [*sic*] how much you would do for Aviation if you only had a free hand.' She begged him to suggest someone who could give her the necessary money or arrange for them to see her letter. In her haste and desperation she forgot to sign the note.

Two days later Amy wrote to Lord Wakefield asking if the company might let her use its oil. Sensing that Wakefield offered her best chance of funds she risked flattering him with her frankness, admitting that she did not have a plane. Her first choice was the new De Havilland Moth III but she feared this might not be ready in time. If she decided to postpone her trip she would have a choice between the Moth and a new design of plane. She was weighing up whether to fly a Gipsy Moth to Australia (and possibly back) without trying to beat the record; or whether it was worth trying to beat Hinkler's time on the outward or return leg of the journey – either in an old Moth or a completely new plane. While urging him to secrecy she asked for his opinion.

The most daring part of her proposal was the route. With the boldness of the uninitiated she planned to fly across Europe in a straight line that would take her through Belgium and Austria-Hungary to Constantinople and then Syria, from where she aimed to pick up Hinkler's flight path. The early stages of his route had followed the more lengthy and less arduous path that went south through Italy, Malta and north Africa. Amy's course saved several hundred miles.

She had now approached all the big names in aviation but so far there had been nothing to give her hope. The date of her navigation exam was set for 24 March, but she was growing more and more

anxious about her chances of passing, especially the paper on meteor-
ology. The shame of her Sheffield failure still burnt in her memory.
Will was concerned at the strain she was placing herself under and was
hugely relieved when she decided at the last minute to postpone the
exam. Amy was convinced the examiners would pass Lady Bailey.
'They daren't do otherwise,' she wrote bitterly to her father. In fact,
Lady Bailey also dropped out. Miss Wood passed with honours and
Winifred Spooner, another pilot who was making a name for herself in
the many flying competitions of the day, also got through.

At the end of March Travers finally allowed her to make her longest
flight so far, from Stag Lane to Hull. She flew over Denham, where she
looped the loop in a triumphant gesture imprinted on the spring sky to
cheer the two engineers working in the primitive huts below. Her aero-
batic prowess was self-taught and she wanted Baker to give her extra
lessons so that she could be 'a bit better than the ordinary woman'. The
trip to Hull took her solo hours up to ninety and gave her invaluable
practice with navigating by compass. But the money her father had
given her had dwindled to £28 and there was no sign of Jimmy's plane.

Despite her lack of success with sponsors Amy continued with her
preparations, sending off cables to various countries asking for permission to fly over their territory and arranging for the Air Ministry
medical she needed to pass every three months to retain her 'B' licence.
She was disappointed at the progress of her new machine at Denham
and cross that she arrived too late at the opening of Selfridges' aeroplane department to meet the sort of influential people who might
have helped her. The weather was too wet to allow her much flying
and, as a distraction, she treated herself to a visit to the cinema and
spent time with Winifred.

Out of the blue she was summoned to Branks' office on 3 April.
Amy's allusion to the article she had written for *Flight* magazine had
given Branks the clue he needed to trace the author of the anonymous
and impassioned letter. He scribbled a note to his secretary, 'I'd like to
see her.' Amy's imminent meeting with Branks brought home to her
parents the fact that their daughter might be setting off for Australia in
six weeks' time. Ciss was reduced to a jangle of nerves and Will urged
Amy to censor the letters she wrote to her. 'I am sorry to say Mother
isn't so well and we are being very careful with her, therefore do not
write anything suggesting complaints or worries or anxieties in your
letter to her.'[7]

Will was also worried about business, describing trade as 'rotten'.
Amy realised that now, more than ever, her parents needed reassurance

and she asked Jack to write and convince them of her abilities as a pilot. His letter, and Will's reply, helped to cement a relationship between the two men that was almost one of father/son-in-law. Jack's letter reads like a formal reference in which he extols Amy's skills both as a pilot and an engineer.[8] In his reply Will breathes a sigh of relief that a third party is willing to endorse Amy's optimism: 'Whatever success she may achieve, a great amount of credit must be due to you for the great interest you have taken in teaching her so well . . . Your assistance has been more creditable by the fact that in these days so many men are ever ready to push the woman down rather than give her a lift up.'[9]

With barely a month to go before the day when she hoped to be setting off for Australia, Amy faced the most important meeting of her life. The Director of Civil Aviation met the prospective pioneering pilot on the afternoon of 3 April in the restrained hush of his Whitehall office, with its background of distantly ticking clocks. Branks was fighting back a mountain of paperwork and concentrating on ways to make planes, not airships, seem the obvious contenders to defend Britain's skies in the same way that her warships stalked the oceans. From behind his monocle Branks turned his unblinking gaze on Amy and demanded to know more. As she spoke with passion of her plans, Branks the reluctant civil servant became once more the adventurer who was happiest riding an elephant through the streets of Calcutta at midnight or flying across Asia with Sir Alan Cobham.

Branks, at fifty-three, still thought of himself as something of a playboy. He was friends with Gertrude Lawrence and Noël Coward and, although married, travelled round the world with his actress lover, Auriol Lee. He liked dancing, drinking and eating and was brimming with energy. It was said of him that he had been 'bitten by a mad aeroplane' and the injury had led to a permanent obsession with flying. Listening to Amy's plans caused his 'affliction' to flare up once more. He was instantly seduced by her enthusiasm and the scale of the adventure she planned. Branks himself was a poor pilot: the same short-sightedness that manufactured his air of severity made it difficult for him to judge the distance from the ground when he was trying to land a plane. Amy offered the vicarious thrill that poor eyesight and the shackles of Whitehall forbade him. He was also susceptible to the novelty of an attractive young woman who enjoyed talking about planes. Amy found him 'absolutely charming'. 'I have certainly found a good friend in him . . . I've taken an immense liking to him,' she wrote to her father, adding that Branks was a Rotarian and a 'brother' (i.e. Freemason).[10]

The two of them discussed her options. Branks immediately quashed any lingering hopes that Jimmy's plane would be ready in time: a quick glance at the official records showed that Denham had not even taken the preliminary step of notifying the Air Ministry about the machine. Branks doubted that she could make the trip in an ordinary Moth but still thought it was worth attempting for the publicity value. He closed their meeting with the promise that if his inquiries at Stag Lane confirmed that she was a good pilot, he would write to Wakefield suggesting that he allowed Amy to put her case. 'I am told that if I can only see Wakefield my battle is won, but the great difficulty is to get into his presence,' Amy told her father.

Amy rushed from her interview to warn Travers that Branks would be in touch but the Director of Civil Aviation had already phoned. An engineer who had overheard the conversation reassured Amy that Travers 'did me real proud';[11] but it was not quite that simple.

Travers had watched with a mixture of annoyance and trepidation as Amy added to her qualifications and her public standing. He was particularly suspicious of her appearances in the press. His loathing of newspapers can be traced back to his beloved elder brother's death as a test pilot at Croydon Airport six years earlier. Travers heard the newspaper boys hawking the tragedy and saw the news vendors' headlines summarising the death before he received official notification of his brother's accident. Eyewitnesses reported seeing the pilot leaping out of the burning plane as it plunged towards the ground. From that day Travers viewed the press as untrustworthy and unpatriotic.

Travers and Branks were old friends. They came from a similar background and got to know each other when Branks and Auriol Lee visited Greece, where Travers was working as a test pilot for seaplanes. Travers' daughter, Eva, remembers well the consternation that the name 'Amy Johnson' caused in their home.[12] Her father was convinced that Amy was not a good enough navigator to fly to Australia alone, that she relied too much on luck and that she had no idea what such a journey involved. Travers repeated these views to Branks but said he would not stand in his way if Branks was prepared to assume responsibility for Amy: indeed Travers was delighted to think that the petulant woman might be taken off his hands.

Wakefield was astute enough to realise that he was not being told the whole story and, according to Eva, Wakefield invited Travers to lunch to discuss Amy without Branks. The night before the meeting Travers paced the floor of his home trying to decide what to say to Wakefield. He was convinced that Amy would fail to make it to Australia and that her failure would be a disaster for the future of civil aviation. Only his young daughter's genuine interest in a woman flying alone to Australia reminded him that, foolhardy though the scheme was, Amy's plan was a pioneering, even heroic one. When he met Wakefield he said she should be allowed to make the flight – so long as she improved her navigational skills.

A week after meeting her Branks wrote a carefully worded letter to Wakefield. It began: 'I write this as a letter of introduction, but not as an appeal for help.' He then went on, very gently, to put her case. He described her skill as a pilot and engineer and her keenness, pointing out that her father had agreed to help her financially. 'She is as reliable as most people who come forward with pioneering propositions. Anyway she has impressed me very favourably. Please forgive me if I have worried you unjustifiably and don't hesitate to turn her down if you do not like the idea of helping her.'[13]

While Amy waited hopefully to hear from Wakefield she continued to explore every possible way of funding the flight. Reluctantly, and guiltily, she wrote to the German plane manufacturers, Junkers and Klemm, 'just to see what they say'.[14] One of the most outlandish schemes that she gave serious consideration to was delivering an Irish setter to the Maharaja of Patula in Allahabad. Amy, who loved dogs, told her mother that the animal was well behaved and had been trained by the same handler who had coached Rin Tin Tin. 'He would certainly make the trip less lonely, and if I had a forced landing anywhere would be invaluable,' she wrote to Ciss.[15]

She continued to 'network', visiting a gliding club in Tring that Wakefield had given £1000 to. The club's opening was attended by Lady Bailey and other flying celebrities. 'I was quite one of the crowd,' Amy wrote to her mother.[16] She even contemplated attempting to become the first person to glide across the Channel – a feat that carried prize money of £1000. When Lady Bailey was unable to give a lecture Amy took her place. Her picture appeared in the *Daily Express* and she was recognised by a member of the public on the train.

On the evening of 9 April Jack took a telephone message from Branks who wanted to speak to Amy. Jack urged her to drive down to the Air Ministry to see Branks in person. 'I'm not the only one who believes you're going to do this,' Jack added.[17]

On 11 April 1930 Wakefield sent Amy a note asking her to visit him in his office on Monday morning. Amy, who rarely left London, had decided to visit Hull where Branks was opening the Air Pageant. She also wanted the chance to see her grandmother, who was gravely ill.

The invitation from Wakefield, for whom punctuality was so important that he gave staff an extra day's holiday if they had been on time during the whole of a calendar year, went unanswered. Amy only discovered the message when she returned to London. In her panic she phoned Wakefield House from King's Cross station but was told Lord Wakefield was about to go away for a few days. She sent him a desperate message asking to be granted an interview, stressing that the matter was 'very urgent'.[18] Eventually he relented and invited her to meet him in his head office in the City.

Wakefield House had a similar bustling atmosphere to Crockers, except that its founder's presence permeated the whole building. At certain times of the day the lift was reserved for his sole use and Wakefield's familiar figure in a high, starched Gladstone collar, walking with a stick and wearing his usual top hat, commanded respect that stopped just short of fear. Wakefield had recently been made a baron and his office had the trappings of a self-made man: a view of the river Thames and a large box of gold-tipped cigars on his desk.

It was an all-or-nothing meeting, but Amy believed she had Branks' backing and the support of Travers. Wakefield's inquiries had confirmed Amy's competence as a pilot; now he wanted to assess her character for himself. Standing in front of him he saw someone who was as ordinary as the girl next door and yet possessed an intangible quality that set her quite apart from most women. Wakefield, who adopted a daughter but had no children of his own, was attracted to her vulnerability and as a publicity vehicle Amy provided endless scope. Wakefield agreed to pay for the petrol, which would be supplied by Shell, and to donate £300 towards the cost of the plane beyond Will's contribution of £500. The practical and psychological support of one of the biggest names in aviation transformed Amy's plans into reality. She was on her way to Australia and she immediately arranged a test flight in a prospective plane.

Will wrote to Wakefield thanking him for his support. 'I would like to assure you, you are helping a straightforward good and clever girl to obtain her ambition and at the same time forward aviation . . .'[19] Although the fish business, like most other industries in 1930, was suffering from a worldwide economic downturn, Will continued to send Amy money at regular intervals. As the pace of her preparations speeded up so did the size of the cheques he wrote. By the time she took off for Australia Will had given Amy £550 (over £17,000 in today's money) towards the expedition. It seems more than coincidence that this was exactly the amount that Irene and Teddy's house had sold for in January 1930. Perhaps he saw his patronage as a way of balancing the books: Irene had been allowed her dream, now Amy should be given her chance.

Less than a week after her successful interview with Wakefield, Will's mother, and two days later, his uncle, died at Bridlington. Once again Amy found herself stepping into the role of head of the family at a time of crisis. She wrote separately to her parents to try to console them. 'It seems a shame to go on talking about my trip to you when you must be feeling very done up,' she wrote to her father, 'but it doesn't do any how to brood over things that can't be undone, does it? I am sure the best thing is to fill up one's mind with other things and try to stop thinking about the painful things. I do hope you're feeling alright [*sic*]. You don't say anything in your letter, but I can guess what you must be feeling.'[20]

As well as the emotional trauma the two deaths added to Will's already crushing workload. All three of Will's brothers were abroad at the time: one lived in Canada and another in Texas; a third was in Greece on business. The responsibility for dealing with the deaths fell squarely on Will, who had himself just returned from a working trip to Germany. He was the trustee for the estates of both his mother and her brother and had to deal with the deluge of letters that arrived when two members of such a well-known family died. Despite the demands on his time he was keen to be involved in every aspect of Amy's plans. He felt the insurance quote she had received was far too high and insisted on sorting it out himself. Amy, who now regularly signed her letters to her parents 'Johnnie', asked him to find a company that would loan her a parachute.

Now that Wakefield was on board, preparations for the trip moved at breakneck speed. Amy started to build up a dossier on the countries she would pass through. From Baghdad onwards she was tackling stretches of land and sea that had rarely been flown over or surveyed. Maps were unreliable and information scarce. Her typed notes describing what she could expect during the 9000-mile journey from Baghdad to Port Darwin portray in starkly matter-of-fact terms the vast array of natural dangers she faced. The several pages of comments are as unsensational as a set of directions designed for someone visiting a rather remote home for the first time rather than a survival guide for an inexperienced pilot:

Down the Ganges to Calcutta – cut off the corners and cross a mt. range. River about a mile wide – full of tidal eddies and dangerous to fall in . . .

At Bali a volcano may be in eruption. People of Bali of Hindu faith. Main
wind from S.E. . . . At Bima native village is liable to malaria. Stay at rest-
house.

From Bima E. to island of Flores, fly S. of it to island of ROTTI to Timor.
Pass over shoals of whales . . .

Such was her confidence about making the return journey that Amy
typed up notes describing the salient features in reverse order. It took
her about a month to prepare her maps, which she carefully pasted
onto strips of paper and rolled up into sections that related to each leg
of the journey. She approached the travel company Thomas Cook, but
since they had yet to embrace flying as a means of travel, they were of
little assistance. The Automobile Association, which had started an aviation department about a year before, were more helpful. As Will was
a member they agreed to organise some of her visas for her, which she
needed in case of forced landings.

The Airscrew Company gave her a free propeller and KLG two new
sets of spark plugs. The Irving Company was at first reluctant to
provide a parachute for free but Will applied enough pressure that they
eventually relented. Amy was fitted for the parachute (which weighed
a stone and a quarter) at Letchworth five days before she was due to
leave. As well as giving Ciss some comfort, sitting on the bulky package
added several extra inches to her height and offered her a better view
over the sides of the plane.

On 23 April, Amy finally acknowledged that Jimmy's prototype
would not be ready in time, and paid £200 as a down-payment for a
plane owned by a Captain Hope. The machine was a De Havilland
Gipsy Moth: by pure chance the exact type of plane that precisely
matched her experience of flying and engineering. *Jason* had much
more experience of the world, and of flying, than his new owner. He
had clocked up 36,000 miles and flown extensively in Africa and
throughout Europe. The plane had spent a total of 400 hours in the air;
roughly four times as long as Amy's solo flights. He was the twelfth
built by De Havilland and carried the registration 'G-AAAH' painted
on his side and lower wings.

In the run-up to 5 May *Jason* was teased and tinkered with as engineers transformed it into a capsule to transport Amy through extremes
of temperature and across parts of the world that were so inadequately
mapped that Bert Hinkler had been forced to use pages torn from *The
Times Atlas* to guide him. Once used, he flung them over the side of the
plane, leaving a paper trail to float down to the citizens of the British

Empire. '*Jason*' was painted in white, swirly letters on the front fuselage above a silver AA badge and next to the De Havilland star with its drawing of a Moth. The plane, which was little more than a thin, wooden crate with a collection of wires, fuel tanks and engine attached, was to be Amy's home, her second skin, for what she hoped would be the next two weeks.

Amy wanted *Jason* to be green like her flying suit but was advised that, as the plane was already red, it would be an extravagance to have it repainted – especially as an extra coating would make the plane heavier. Weight was an important consideration as *Jason* had been adapted to carry as much fuel as possible. Any frivolous ounces made the plane harder to manoeuvre, particularly at take-off when it was carrying the most fuel.

Captain Hope had already made several alterations to *Jason* to make him more suitable for long-distance flying; the most noticeable was the addition of two extra petrol tanks: one in the front cockpit held thirty-five gallons and a second in the rear locker had a capacity of twenty-six gallons. The top gravity tank held nineteen gallons, providing a total of eighty gallons of fuel, compared to the sixty-six gallons that Hinkler took. Cruising at ninety miles per hour, in ideal weather conditions, Amy had enough fuel to keep her in the air for thirteen hours at a time. She carried two gallons of oil.

Arrangements were made to ensure that supplies of petrol and oil would be waiting for her along the way and in Australia itself, but as her route was in a constant state of flux a question-mark always hung over whether the cans would be in the right place at the right time. Shell agreed to be 'well on the safe side' when estimating how much fuel she would need and only to charge her for the petrol she used. Amy drew up endless lists of the distances between the major aerodromes along the route and intermediate stopping-places that she might be forced to use if the weather or her machine turned against her. Knowing the approximate distances between places was also a helpful navigational tool.

She aimed always to land and take off during daylight. She noted the expected sunrise at each point of departure, when sunset was due at each destination and how many hours of daylight this would give her. Sunrise at Baghdad was forecast as 5.03 a.m., for example, and sunset at her destination of Bandar Abbas was at 18.41 – allowing her 13.38 flying hours. At Bandar Abbas the surface was 'undulating'; there was no hangar but the British Consul was very helpful. She was to discover that much of this information was wildly out of date. The company's telegraphic address was 'Cheery', after Wakefield's mother's maiden name, and as a one-word link with home it summed up perfectly the company's role as guardian angel; Amy hoped to cable Wakefield at the end of each day's flying.

All the essential information she needed for the journey was contained in a battered, dark brown Filofax-style leather ringbinder. This included in neatly typed pages details of *Jason's* engine, oil and petrol and a list of what had to be checked at the end of each day's flight. The book included a code that allowed her to let Wakefield know how the journey was going. She could say: 'I am feeling . . .'; 'The last hop was . . .'; or describe the engine, aerodrome, wind and weather. In each case her adjectives were restricted to: 'good', 'fair' or 'rotten', although she had a wide range of expressions to draw on. There was one phrase she hoped never to use: 'No chance of record now.'

Jason's front cockpit was covered in to make the plane more aerodynamic.[21] She estimated that the alteration added five miles per hour to *Jason's* speed, although the spare propeller strapped to the plane's fuselage probably cancelled out this gain. There was only time for her to take *Jason* up for a few minutes' 'test drive' before agreeing to buy him. All her knowledge was drawn from technical manuals and fuel consumption was largely guess-work. Captain Hope, who was a friend of Hinkler's, offered advice about which spare parts Amy should take with her. She was particularly worried about flying in very hot weather as she had no experience whatsoever of anything warmer than an English summer.

Every inch of *Jason's* cockpit was filled with provisions so that it felt to Amy like a village store; she was surrounded by a mosquito net, a tropical flying helmet, boots to protect her from mosquitoes, special goggles to help her avoid sunstroke, inner tubes, a cooking stove, billy cans, flints, a revolver, a first-aid kit and an air-cushion. Like any English person who ventured into the tropical heat, she had a 'spine pad' sewn into her blouse in the belief that this was the part of the body most susceptible to heat.[22] Unlike Hinkler, she did not carry an inflatable rubber dinghy and paddles, although the final stretch of her journey – the 500-mile leg over the Timor Sea – was one she feared more than the rest of the voyage. The engineers at Stag Lane did their bit by teaching her ju-jitsu in case she needed to defend herself.

Incredibly, Jack suggested that once she had navigated her way across 11,000 miles of ocean, jungle and desert to Australia, she should immediately turn round and fly straight back to England. Amy shared his naivety about the task she faced, writing to her father that it would be 'somewhat interesting' to follow the same route home.[23] She could see the advantage, too, of being back in England in time to take part in the King's Cup Race which offered larger financial prizes than flying to Australia.

Her efforts had been concentrated on raising cash and arranging visas to such an extent that the physical effort of flying for over two weeks with few breaks had not sunk in. A fortnight before she was due to leave the Duchess of Bedford landed at Cape Town at the end of a record ten-day flight from England. Even though the Duchess had not made the trip alone it was a timely reminder that this could be Amy's one chance at the Australia record. 'The Old Duchess did very well, didn't she?' Amy wrote to her mother. 'Good thing our flights didn't clash. I bet she'll go to Australia next . . . but I shall get in first!'[24]

Ciss responded by bombarding her with lucky tokens, including a swastika brooch – an ancient symbol of good fortune which, at the time, carried no Fascist undertones. As the day for her departure approached Amy tried frantically to finalise her plans. Severe headaches pounded her skull and at one point she became so tired that she could not remember whether she was due to leave on the Sunday or Monday; she was determined to go to bed at 7 p.m. on the two evenings before her flight.

On Sunday, 4 May Amy flew with Jack to Croydon Airport; they were escorted by four other planes from Stag Lane including aircraft flown by Travers and Matthews. Whim had triumphed over practicality and *Jason* now had a bottle-green body with silver-grey wings which from the ground spelt out 'G-AAAH'. Even the plane's registration seemed to be clenching its teeth in a defiant, determined grimace.

Chapter 10

Journey's Start
(5–7 May 1930)

Today 'Croydon' is one of those English place-names, like 'Dollis Hill', 'Neasden' and 'East Grinstead', that conjure up images of repressed suburbia and formation workers streaming into the metropolis. But in 1930 the words 'Croydon Airport' united to form a heady combination of glamour and adventure. A photo of the building after its opening in May 1928 carried the biblical caption: 'The suburbs shall shake at the sound of the cry of thy pilots', and Croydon proudly boasted it was the 'gateway to the empire' long before Balham was hailed as the gateway to the South.

The airport's Art Deco booking-hall had the hushed ambience of a gentlemen's club; the smell of wood-polish mingled with the atmosphere of calm endeavour. Croydon was the first air terminal in the world built with passengers in mind, but it could not have been further from the modern concept of an airport where passengers are buried in a world of artificial light and deadened sound. Sunshine streamed through the glass dome of its waiting-room onto the highly polished wooden panelling and rows of benches where passengers waited to board their planes. Airline companies displayed magnificent scale models of their aircraft on their reception desks and a large map showed weather conditions on a continent that was now much nearer than ever before. There was a sub-post office, a bookstall and a coffee-room where customers sipped their drinks side-by-side with pilots. In the early days of the airport travellers were allowed to take 200 pounds, including their own body weight, on board. A forbidding set of scales weighed both them and their luggage, and a certain *Daily Mail* reporter gained a reputation for exceeding the limit even before his baggage was weighed.

Amy's arrival at Croydon was a muted affair. Most newspapers believed she had already exhausted her newsworthiness: the 'story' had been her desire to take on the Australia route; very few reporters felt she had the remotest chance of completing even the early stages of the

Amy as a young girl.

Above: Amy and Winifred Irving in the Peak District; typically, Winifred is smoking. Amy's parents thought the photo too revealing to be published.

Left: Amy with her sister Irene.

Opposite page: Amy became the first woman to obtain a Ground Engineers' licence in Britain and for a time was the only female in the world to hold a valid licence.

Amy prepares to leave Croydon Airport for Australia.

Jason was forced to land on a parade ground at the army barracks at
Jhansi in northern India.

Amy after her crash landing at Insein, near Rangoon.
As the weather became unbearably humid she borrowed lighter clothes.

Opposite page top: 'Amy, wonderful Amy' was the most popular of several songs written to celebrate her flight.

Opposite page below: Betty (far left), Molly and their parents listen in with Jimmy Martin and Jack Humphreys (right) to a phone call from Australia.

Right: Once they arrived in Australia Amy was reluctant to be separated from *Jason*, 1930.

Below: Jack Humphreys became Amy's mentor and one of her most devoted fans.

Top: Jack and Amy with General Nagaoka, President of the Imperial Aviation Society, who was said to have the longest and whitest moustache in the world.

Above: Amy with Charlie Chaplin, Lady Astor and George Bernard Shaw, 1931.

Opposite page: Amy and Jim embrace before he sets off on his solo flight from England to South America in 1933.

journey. Amy herself had deliberately started to 'wind down' her press appearances. She was adamant that she did not want any sort of 'send off', although Jack persuaded her to change her mind. She agreed that her father should be at Croydon Airport. 'It isn't right for you not to be there,' she wrote to him.[1]

Will arrived in London on the Saturday and met Amy at Stag Lane where she was going over last-minute preparations with Jimmy and Jack. He returned with her to her lodgings at Roe Green to help her finish a few letters she still had to write and then went to the Strand Palace for dinner. Sunday was a clear, sunny day and Will reached Croydon Airport at 4 p.m. where he waited for Amy and Jack to arrive by plane. Ominously, Amy had difficulty finding her way across London and *Jason* was late arriving. Amy went to bed at eight o'clock in a room at the front of the Aerodrome Hotel. Today the hotel faces the busy, fume-choked A23; in May 1930 it was a much quieter spot but she still found it too noisy to sleep, eventually asking her father to swap rooms. Will went to bed at 11 o'clock but Jimmy and Jack worked through what was left of the night: filling *Jason* up with petrol, fastening the spare propeller to the fuselage, greasing and oiling everything they could find to grease and oil.

Jack woke Will at three in the morning and her father knocked on Amy's door half an hour later. She got up and took breakfast. Winifred and two other friends arrived at four o'clock, by which time the hotel had the buzz of an all-night party or a family holiday that begins in the secret atmosphere of half-light.

Amy was ready to leave at four thirty but fog was reported in the Channel and she was sent back to the hotel to rest. At dawn she climbed into the cockpit but as she fastened her safety harness and secured her parachute straps she began to smell the sickening fumes of petrol. The stench was traced to a broken connection that was causing petrol to drip out at an alarming rate. Amy switched off the engine and was told to rest while Jimmy and Jack tried frantically to repair the leak as morning began to unravel.

Although fog was still lingering over the Channel she climbed back into *Jason*. There was a chill in the air but she was warm in her baggy Sidcot flying suit with its fur collar turned up to protect the lower part of her face. Her parachute straps trailed loosely over her back, the life-saving package itself hung limply behind her legs. Her goggles were pushed onto her forehead on top of her helmet. As she posed for photographs her smile was relaxed. She was relieved that there was no time for further preparations, that this was it. A gaggle of men clustered round *Jason*, Jack fussing right up to the last minute, Will's teeth clenched grimly round his pipe. Winifred hung back at the edge of the group, the only woman among the inner circle of supporters.

At a quarter to eight Amy taxied across the grass of Croydon Airport, a runway that offered ground staff a regular, rich harvest of mushrooms. It was the first time she had ever attempted to lift such a heavily laden plane. She had discussed the technique with Jack and Jimmy and knew that she had to push the throttle forward hard at the start of the run. If this failed her priority was to stop the plane before it crashed into the perimeter fence. At the first attempt *Jason* refused to take to the air and she managed to pull the plane up just in time.

The narrow escape shattered the pretence of calm and as Amy taxied back to the waiting crowd Jimmy and Jack deluged her with advice. She snapped back at them, saying she would do it her way. As she taxied off to try again Jack stood taut, his body following the plane's every move like a football supporter willing the ball into the back of the net. This time *Jason* made it into the air, a heavily pregnant duck with wings rocking slightly as Amy steadied the engine. The crowd watched as the plane turned into a speck and then finally disappeared.

Few newspapers that day recorded Amy's departure in any detail; most were more concerned with the arrest of the Indian nationalist, Mahatma Gandhi, who was accused of exciting his countrymen to break the law. The *Daily Mail* inflated Amy's newsworthiness by feminising her feat: 'Miss Amy Johnson – Lone Flight to Australia – Off To-day – Cupboard Full of Frocks' read the headline on page thirteen. In fact, Amy had not mentioned 'frocks', merely explaining, when asked, that she stored her luggage in a cupboard at the back of the cockpit. The report went on to describe her as 'golden-haired' and to reduce her age by four years to a more girlish 'twenty-two'. The distance to Australia was doubled to a gargantuan 20,000 miles, although the reporter may have justified the inflation by arguing that Amy intended to make a return flight.

The report in *The Times* was measured by comparison: 'Woman to fly alone to Australia', the headline on the one-paragraph story announced. The newspaper was more interested in the fact that *Jason* had previously followed the Prince of Wales on his African tour. The item pointed out, erroneously, that Amy was the first female ground engineer and, more accurately, that she had little experience of long-distance flying.

Bert Hinkler was thirty-five when, in 1928, he became the first person to fly solo from England to Australia. He was nine years older than Amy was when she left Croydon and at five feet three inches tall he was even shorter. He had thick dark eyebrows and a negligible upper lip. Unlike most pioneering airmen, he hated publicity, making him a nightmare to promote. Journalists referred to him as 'No news Hinkler'. He was eccentric in a quiet way, becoming well known for the crumpled, double-breasted suits that he wore over a knitted vest and his preference for a bowler hat or straw boater rather than a flying helmet. Hinkler and his wife lived in a house in Southampton called 'Mon Repos', their craving for respectability matching perfectly the middle-class cliché that their home's name would come to represent. Hinkler was Australian by birth; his father had emigrated from Germany.

It was his record of fifteen and a half days, rather than Hinkler himself, that Amy viewed as her target. A mutual respect existed between the two aviators and Amy wrote to Hinkler asking for advice about the journey. Hinkler had flown an Avro Avian biplane on his solo trip to Australia, a model named after the company's founder A. V. Roe, the husband of birth-control campaigner Marie Stopes. Both Amy and Hinkler set off from Croydon, although it had not been designated an airport when Hinkler started his journey; both flew biplanes with no radio, and both were trained mechanics. But there the similarities end. When he flew to Australia Hinkler already held the record for the longest non-stop flight in a light aeroplane. He set off in February, heading for Rome. Amy was chasing a record but, by delaying her departure until May, she was also fighting to keep one step ahead of the monsoon season which had the power to wreck all her plans.

Day 1 (Monday, 5 May)

It was her first experience of flying *Jason* long distance and provided an initiation into the physical exertion that comes with spending hour upon hour in the air. The most unpleasant aspect was the task of replenishing petrol in the gravity tank. This was done by hand, and transferring one gallon involved pumping up and down forty times. The petrol fumes made her feel sick and the pumping action sent searing pains through her arm. As her journey progressed her muscles developed and she almost welcomed the task as a way of helping to keep herself awake, but she never overcame her dislike of the nauseous smell.

When she left Croydon Amy had wondered what it would feel like to look down on the English Channel, but the water was still shrouded in fog when she left the British coast. Her first sight of foreign soil was the 'trim fields of Belgium'.[2] She landed at Asperne Aerodrome, fifteen miles outside Vienna, just before 6 p.m. It had taken her ten hours to cover the 800 miles from Croydon and she crawled out of the cockpit feeling stiff and battered. The wind pounding on her eardrums left her temporarily deaf and her body ached from the exertion of clutching the joystick for ten hours in a tiny cockpit. *Jason* needed to maintain a cruising speed of ninety miles per hour if Amy was to reach each of her destinations before sunset, but a headwind on her way to Vienna reduced the plane's speed. *Jason*'s performance on this first leg did not bode well.

Jack had made her promise to overhaul the engine every night but she felt too intimidated by the Austrian mechanics to insist on looking after *Jason* herself. Her confidence evaporated as they regaled her with mocking tales of the last female pilot who had tried unsuccessfully to overhaul her own plane. Amy crept away to let them work on *Jason* without her. There was no hotel and a caretaker gave up his bed for her until she rose at four o'clock the next morning.

At the end of his first day Hinkler missed Rome and landed at a military airfield by mistake.[3]

Day 2 (Tuesday, 6 May)

When Amy started the engine she immediately detected a false note. She could not risk setting off with a doubt in her mind and heaved open the cover on the front cockpit to delve around in her luggage until she found the right tool. The rear plug was badly 'oiled up' and she was forced to clean it before setting off in the direction of Constantinople (modern-day Istanbul).

As she headed towards the Black Sea *Jason*'s pump developed another leak that squirted petrol in Amy's face. The fumes made her feel so nauseous that she had to put her face over the side of the plane while she pumped. These enforced encounters with the raging wind of the slipstream outside the relative calm of her cockpit left her feeling even more battered.

Amy arrived at San Stefano Aerodrome, thirty miles from Constantinople, with an hour's daylight to spare. She had left Europe behind. Her adventure began here, at the heart of the old Ottoman Empire.

So far all she had achieved was the equivalent of a weekend jaunt: a trip in moderately fine weather over countries that had no bone to pick with Britain. The remaining 9000 miles stretched over large expanses of poorly mapped terrain in which white men clung to power by virtue of a day ordered around tiffin and tea on the veranda and the support of a few military aircraft. She would be flying over countries where botched settlements cobbled together after the First World War served to increase resentment towards an unwanted foreign presence.

The Ottoman Empire had fought against Britain in the last war and the Treaty of Lausanne in 1923 finally recognised Turkish independence, but much residual resentment existed towards Britain. Turkey was always a problematic country for pilots and Amy had left Croydon without securing the necessary paperwork. All she had was a letter of introduction to two influential Turks written by Branks.

Customs officials kept her waiting for an hour and a half while her papers were checked and by the time she returned to *Jason* it was dark. She asked the local Shell representative to take her letters of introduction to the two men in Constantinople in the hope that their signatures would be sufficient to allow her to continue.

No one spoke English at the aerodrome but she arranged for the driver of a waiting car to direct its headlamps onto *Jason* to give her enough light by which to overhaul the engine. She spent the next three hours changing the plugs and draining the oil. The local mechanics helped her to refuel but were so inexperienced that they over-filled *Jason's* tanks and the petrol sloshed into the front cockpit, drenching Amy's luggage and leaving her clothes reeking. When she had finished she climbed down and, as she had been taught, straightened *Jason's* propeller so that it rested in a horizontal position.

Through a series of gestures she asked whether the plane could be put in one of the spare hangars overnight. The mechanics, impressed by her skills and concern for her plane, were eager to help and grabbed *Jason's* tail. The plane, weighed down by luggage in the front cockpit and the brimming fuel tanks, crunched down onto its nose. Only Amy's discipline in straightening the propeller prevented it from being crushed. The Turks, mortified by the accident, lassoed *Jason's* tail and pulled it back onto the ground before guiding the plane to the hangar while Amy walked to a nearby hotel for the night.

The building was bleak in its newness and her room contained only a bed. A cable was waiting for her: 'Best luck and wishes – Hans.' There is no record of how she responded to this painful echo from her past. Perhaps the reminder of a long and lonely relationship increased her feelings of isolation at a time when her ambitious journey was at its most precarious; more probably the starkly formal words reminded her of Hans's aloofness and strengthened her resolve to prove herself. She sent cables to Jack and to her parents and went to bed wondering if the Shell representative had tracked down the two men who held the key to her fate.

At 85 Park Avenue Will tried to blot out his worries in a flurry of activity. He wrote letters and kept in regular contact with Jack whom he had already phoned to see whether Amy had arrived safely in Vienna. The two men shared a conspiracy of anxiety. While Will had to put on a brave face in front of his wife and two daughters he knew that Jack was realistic about the dangers Amy faced. Will wrote to Jack, 'Keep smiling and hoping . . . Shall be glad to have your further news; what does Stag Lane say about it?'[4] Jack's reply betrayed his deep pride in Amy: 'Stag Lane is going mad with joy . . . one hears everywhere "damn good effort" and it really is.'[5]

When the pressure of waiting, surrounded by well-meant but persistent inquiries, became too much Ciss and Will decided to travel to Edinburgh to attend a Rotary meeting. Before he left Will sent Jack a gift of fish and £10 to cover expenses such as telegrams and phone calls. Jack was under strict instructions to phone Will at his office 'in case of bad news'.

At the end of his second day Hinkler arrived at Malta.

Day 3 (Wednesday, 7 May)

The man from Shell arrived at the hotel at 4 a.m. He had been unable to secure the signatures of the two local dignitaries: one was in jail and the other did not want to be disturbed in his bath. In desperation the Shell rep had sought out another influential man who was at the theatre and who, between acts, agreed to add his signature to her travel documents.

Amy returned to the aerodrome at 4.30 a.m. but was told to wait in an office. As the hours slipped away she knew that her chances of reaching Baghdad that day were fading fast. She tried hard not to let her impatience show, realising that she was caught in a political game of brinkmanship in which logical argument carried no weight and whose rules were unfathomable.

The bureaucrats examined her luggage and when they came to her Sidcot flying suit picked it up so clumsily that peanuts, chewing gum, a penknife, string and assorted tools cascaded across the floor. She turned her back on them while they scrambled to retrieve the contents, unwilling to trust herself to mask her anger. By 7 a.m. she accepted that she had lost a day's flying and that her new goal was Aleppo in Syria. She managed to secure her release when she remembered that Turks were said to have an obsession with photos. Handing out passport shots of her proved the 'open sesame' she had been searching for.

When Amy returned to *Jason* she found that his oil pressure had dropped dramatically. After a thorough investigation she realised that the oil had become so dirty during the last two days' flying that it had silted up parts of the engine. She vowed in future to check the plugs every day and change the oil. When she finally climbed into the cockpit the sickly smell of petrol reminded her of the leak and, since she was no longer hurrying to Baghdad, she climbed out and asked a visiting French mechanic to repair it while she rested. She left at 10 a.m., straining her ears to detect any change in her engine's noise, aware that the next leg of her voyage would provide the greatest challenge so far for both her and *Jason*. She took a thermos flask of tea and some sandwiches as refreshment.

As for a model biplane in an adventure movie that traces out a route on the globe, the journey ahead encompassed mountains, deserts, jungle, erupting volcanoes and shark-infested sea. Amy's main navigational guide as she headed south-east was the railway line that wound its way slowly towards Syria. The first stretch of the journey took her past the Sea of Marmara. Agatha Christie, travelling by train to Palestine a few years later, said its islands were so beautiful that she longed to own one.

Ahead lay the Taurus Mountains that sweep along the coast of south-east Turkey, pushing north to form a rocky barrier with Syria. It is a forbidding mountain range with peaks that reach to nearly 15,000 feet and which remain snow-capped in summer. Waterfalls gush out of the mountainsides at crazy angles, rocks form Gaudiesque spires and towers, and steep-sided canyons lead to patches of pine trees. Nomadic tribespeople, who roam the area oblivious to the notion of central government, live in black goat-hair tents.

The mountains are rarely visited by outsiders today, attracting the sort of travellers who look for the words 'remote' and 'primitive' when booking a holiday. In 1930 very little was known about the region and that ignorance spawned stories as tall as the mountains' rocky sides. Amy was aware that two RAF pilots who had crashed in the area had never been heard of again. She believed she was flying over the home of 'wild bandits' who were 'utterly lawless and without scruple'.[6] They might hold you to ransom but were much more likely to 'cut you up in bits to decorate their caves or flavour their evening soup'.

As she struggled to follow the railway track that slithered through endless tunnels she imagined suspicious eyes following her course. A thick layer of cloud sent a chill through her open cockpit and made her glad of her heavy Sidcot flying suit; the cloud obscured her view of the mountain-tops and she strained her eyes to follow the twisting course of the ravines. In an effort to find clearer skies she tried to push *Jason* higher, from 8000 to 10,000 feet, at which point the engine started to splutter and cough, forcing her to abandon her search for height.

Her worst moment came when she was caught in a narrow ravine with only a few feet separating each wing from the sheer rocky sides and with her compass spinning wildly. Rounding the next corner, she flew straight into a bank of thick cloud that left her disorientated and with no option but to push down *Jason*'s nose to try to dodge below the whiteness. *Jason* emerged at 120 m.p.h. and with one wing down heading straight for a wall of rock; Amy managed to swerve just in time. The near-miss left her shaken and relieved to emerge from the claustrophobia and fairy-tale menace of the mountains into the wide Syrian plain where sunshine replaced the dank clouds.

Chapter 11

Basra to Baluchistan
(7–10 May 1930)

In passing through the Taurus Mountains Amy left behind her everyday life and entered the mystical land of her imagination. *Jason* and
Amy had faced the mountains' challenge and together they had arrived
in a world where biblical images from her childhood collided with
Scheherazade's *Tales of the Arabian Nights* and the adventures of T. E.
Lawrence that had sustained her through her dull days at Crockers. As
she flew south she saw the traces of long-gone civilisations and then
Aleppo, a trading post between desert and arable lands and one of the
oldest cities in the world. The town nestles in a slight depression; a
jumble of alleyways and souks pierced by minarets, its citadel squatting
on a huge, steep mound, a giant upturned cup on its saucer, as
Gertrude Bell described it.

Amy landed just north of Aleppo at Mouslimié aerodrome where
the French air force treated her with kindness and efficiency. France,
more than any country in the world, celebrated flight and cherished its
pilots. Amy was flattered by the respect with which she was treated and
by the small gallantries the officers showed her. There was plenty of
daylight left by which to refuel and overhaul *Jason* and she felt confident enough in their ability to allow the French mechanics to help her.
She discarded her Sidcot suit to pose for photographs in her riding
breeches, over-sized shirt and jumper.

Syria existed nervously under French control, the country's desire
for independence flaring up into regular outbursts of violence. Amy
was baffled by this mixture of cultures; that petrol pumps should exist
in the desert side-by-side with Arabs seated high on camels. She washed
using water drawn from a well in a courtyard, her ablutions studied
with open curiosity by the Arabs, and that night she slept on a rock-
hard bed in a cubicle at the officers' mess protected by windows with
bars and an armed guard patrolling outside. She wrote: 'Here were real
sheiks from the desert – so dirty and smelly that my dreams of
romance were destroyed on the instant – but nevertheless worth

staring at . . . This was my first petetration [sic] into the East and I felt its glamour.'[1]

At the end of his third day Hinkler missed his target of Tobruk on the Libyan coast by forty miles. He spent the night sleeping under the Avro's wing on an upturned inflated rubber boat on a patch of sand surrounded by thorny bushes.

Day 4 (Thursday, 8 May)

Amy left Mouslimié at dawn. The desert was cold in first light and she zipped herself into her Sidcot flying suit before heading off in the direction of Baghdad some 500 miles south-east of Aleppo. She followed the twisting Euphrates river, where white 'beehive' houses made from mud-brick served as granaries, homes and stables. At times the steep, muddy river-banks merged into the surrounding landscape, making the Euphrates difficult to follow. It became harder to concentrate as the temperature increased and Amy, still ensconced in her flying suit, became a simmering pressure cooker jolted around the cockpit as *Jason* bounced through the thermal eddies that turned the sky into a badly surfaced road. She pushed him higher to escape the heat. But at 7000 feet the air was hazy and visibility poor. She had lost sight of the guiding river and wondered whether she would be able to see anything at all in the gloom that lay ahead. Peering at her map, she guessed she was flying through a section marked only as 'unsurveyed desert'. It was impossible to tell in which direction the sand was blowing; she tried to follow faint tracks below her but these inevitably faded into nothingness. Once she spotted a caravan of horses and camels but as soon as she tried to get closer the animals and their riders scattered in panic.

Without any warning *Jason*'s nose dipped, the propeller slowed momentarily and the plane plunged several thousand feet towards the ground.[2] While Amy struggled to steady the machine and recover from the physical shock of being hurled through the air, the same thing happened again. *Jason* lurched towards the ground a total of three times, pausing momentarily on each occasion like a runaway elevator that allows its passengers to regain their heads and stomachs before subjecting them to the next jolt. She felt so disorientated that it was impossible to be sure that she was not flying upside down.

The final plunge left *Jason* a few feet above ground; dust and wind batted the plane from side to side. Amy's goggles were covered with sand and her eyes smarted with the effort of trying to make out what was happening to her. She felt *Jason*'s wheels touch down at around 110 miles per hour and tried to steer into the wind in an effort to slow the machine, fearing that the plane would at any minute flip over or hit some obstacle. When *Jason* finally stopped Amy switched off the engine and struggled out of the cockpit. The howling wind, smarting sand and her bulky parachute made every movement a huge physical effort. She pulled the machine round so that it faced into the wind but the Gipsy Moth, built without brakes, was immediately blown backwards. Amy struggled onto the plane, now flapping about like a cornered bird, and dragged luggage from the front cockpit to put it behind the wheels.

Her priority was to protect *Jason*, her only means of escape from the desert. The dust stung her face as she battled from one side of the plane to the other, trying to cover the engine and protect the carburettor from the sand and dust. Just as she thought she had secured the canvas on one side the wind wrenched it away before she had fixed the opposite side. It took her thirty minutes to lash the cover down. Her next task was to climb onto the engine to tie her hanky over the air-vent hole in the petrol tank to try to keep the sand out.

Having made her plane as safe as possible, she sat with her back to the wind on *Jason*'s tail in a bid to fix him to the ground. She could see barely a few feet in any direction; she had no idea where she was. 'I had never been so frightened in all my life,' she said later.[3] Her only option was to wait, a prisoner in the wind's cacophony, until the storm subsided. Once she heard the eerie sound of barking in the distance and, remembering the stories of the wild desert dogs who tore their prey apart, she retrieved her small pistol and sat with it at the ready.

After three hours the wind began to die down and the air cleared. Fearing that this might be her one chance of escape, Amy darted round *Jason*, uncovering the engine and hurling her luggage back into the front cockpit. In her panic she dropped tools which were immediately covered with sand and lost for ever to the desert.

Jason's engine started at the first swing of the propeller and Amy pointed the engine in an easterly direction, hopeful that this would take her towards Baghdad. If her instinct was wrong she was heading deeper into the desert and towards a slow death from dehydration. This was an end that pilots feared more than any other; the crazed scribblings left by parched airmen revealed the slowest and most torturous of deaths. Amy imagined her bones being found 'many, long years' after her death; a grim flight of fancy that was itself wildly optimistic.

Although visibility was still difficult she soon spotted what she believed to be the river Tigris. She followed this south until it was joined by what she hoped was the river Diyala. This gave her a 'fix' and she saw the flat, palm-fringed sprawl of Baghdad and the Imperial Airways Aerodrome. On landing *Jason* sank down on one wing and Amy discovered that one of his undercarriage struts had snapped during her forced landing in the desert.

She set off to walk to the distant hangars but a lorry sped out to pick her up. Her relief at hearing English voices was immense. She peeled off her Sidcot suit and discussed what to do about *Jason*. At first it seemed she would have to wait for a replacement to be sent from the nearest De Havilland depot 1500 miles away at Karachi in western India (now Pakistan). Amy was devastated by this news which meant she had no chance of beating Hinkler. However, the presence of an RAF aerodrome at nearby Hinaidi provided some hope and the Imperial Airways manager suggested sending the strut to the RAF aerodrome, where ten engineers worked through the night to repair it.

Leaving the Imperial Airways mechanics to overhaul *Jason*, Amy permitted herself a sightseeing tour of Baghdad. Iraq was under a British mandate and, as in Syria, there was persistent opposition to the foreign presence. Seven months before Amy arrived the Prime Minister had shot himself because he could not stand the political in-fighting and claims that he was too sympathetic to the British. Arab and European cultures rarely mixed. The writer Freya Stark, who left Baghdad just before Amy's arrival, horrified her European neighbours by lodging with a local shoemaker's family in the city. She noted that one of the few occasions when the two cultures ventured outside their own customs was when rich Arabs served Peak Frean biscuits behind their wooden shutters.

Amy went for a drive around the city and had dinner at a hotel overlooking the river. Baghdad had one long tarred high street and, unusually for an Arab city, a few lawns, both of which gave it something of the air of an English provincial town. This parochialism was overcome by its position as a trading-post that attracted a broad ethnic mix including Kurds in their bright-red turbans and Christian women wearing colourful silk wraps in contrast to the black-veiled Muslim women. The street sellers hawked hammered copperware that gleamed in the sun, intricate embroidery and baskets bulging with pistachio nuts and chick-peas. It was a city that smelt of coffee and wood fires.

Before going to bed that night Amy wrote a long letter to Jack. She gave him a technical account of how the engine had performed and expressed her frustration that there had been no Castrol XXL waiting for her at either Constantinople or Baghdad. But she also poured out the dramas of being lost in the desert and her narrow escape in the Taurus Mountains. 'Don't tell my people any unpleasant news,' she begged him. 'Am a bit homesick – I'd like to see you especially when I'm frightened.'[4]

Cables were taking longer and longer to reach Britain. Will felt a mixture of anxiety and excitement at Amy's progress. He leant heavily on Jack for emotional support. 'Now will you promise me not to worry again, for I've an idea you were upset because I did not ring up before going to bed last evening?' Jack wrote to Will.[5]

From a more practical point of view, Will was concerned that Amy, unaware of the stir she was starting to cause in Europe, would accept the first business proposal she received when she reached Australia. 'Before Amy left she felt no one seemed to be really interested in her work and got the idea that Australia might be the best place for her, but NOW things are very much altered . . .' he told Jack.[6]

At the end of his fourth day Hinkler spent a second night in the desert sleeping on his rubber boat on the southern Palestine border.

Day 5 (Friday, 9 May)

The sweltering heat of the desert, and perhaps her experience of sitting waiting for the storm to abate, made Amy less concerned with appearances. She set aside her Sidcot flying suit and borrowed a pair of men's baggy, khaki shorts. These shorts, with their hem several inches above the knee, were a daring adaptation of the voluminous pyjamas-cum-trousers that were fashionable in the 1920s. The contrast of the harsh, oversized shorts on the tiny figure with the sun-blistered face made Amy seem more vulnerable and caused a sensation in the British press. They quickly became an essential part of her image.

From Baghdad onwards Amy's knowledge of her route was encapsulated in the typed notes that summarised the terrain and conditions she could expect.[7] The most alarming aspect of the next stage was flying over the area where Sir Alan Cobham's plane had been shot at when he flew from England to Australia in 1926. A sandstorm similar to the one Amy had encountered on her way to Baghdad had forced Cobham to fly low, allowing a Bedouin tribesman to fire on the seaplane. Cobham's friend and engineer, Arthur Elliott, passed the pilot a note saying he was 'bleeding a pot of blood'. He died in hospital later that night.

The Tigris replaced the Euphrates as Amy's guide. According to her notes the air should be 'moderately cool' at 5000 feet, but 'very hot' on the ground where it was only possible to work between dawn and nine o'clock. Approaching Basra close to the Persian Gulf, she would see a 'great swamp area' where a forced landing would only be feasible on the south side of this marshy area. This was thought to be the site of the Garden of Eden, an area where the Marsh Arabs had lived for centuries in intricately crafted reed-houses side by side with kingfishers. Sixty years after Amy flew over the region it was lost to Saddam Hussein's bulldozers.

As she neared the Persian Gulf the scenery grew less remote, as her notes had predicted. 'The broad river at BASRA littered with mass of shipping. Village of KHAMISYAH near swamp where Elliott shot. Towards head of Persian Gulf is flat swamp area, desolate and uninhabited. Maybe GROUND MIST NEAR BUSHIRE.'

On a clear day Abadan provided a good landmark, the smoke from the oil refineries offering a useful indication of wind direction. 'Wonderful rocky coastline down Persian Gulf – weird rock formations, extend for miles with precise regularity. Vivid colours of axide [sic] formation just below BANDAR ABBAS. To the South in deep blue one can see the island of HORMUZ.'

The weather was perfect and Amy felt more comfortable now that she had escaped her flying suit, but she could not quite bring herself to relax and enjoy the shockingly blue sea that was home to pelicans, flamingos, tropical fish, porpoises and lurking sharks and which reflected Jason's image back at her. She was unable to take her eye off the oil gauge which showed worryingly low pressure. Her engine was misfiring and its spluttering noise made her suspect that one of her plugs was playing up.

As the rocky shores offered no landing place, her one option was to continue to the port of Bandar Abbas, a stopping point in Persia that she had chosen simply because it was roughly half-way between Baghdad and Karachi. Bandar Abbas in May was hot and humid. It had grown into something more than a fishing port because of its strategic position on the Persian Gulf. The island of Hormuz opposite made the port easy to spot but Amy was not expected and she could see no sign of an aerodrome or any indication of which way the wind was blowing. She landed near the Gulf on the one open space she could see, which turned out to be the aerodrome. It was a fast and heavy landing and as she touched down she was horrified to see Jason's left wing trailing along the ground. The bolt holding the top of the new strut had sheared. 'I could not see any hope of help in such a God-forsaken place

. . .' Amy wrote later.[8] She almost cried with relief when she spotted a white man approaching her. For a moment she seemed to have been transported back to the Home Counties: the British Consul took her to his bungalow where his wife and daughter made Amy lie down and brought her cups of tea and massaged her head. In reality, this was her remotest stopping point so far. The consul told her that the aerodrome was rarely used, which explained her heavy landing on the bumpy surface. After the heat and noise of the flight she suffered from a pounding headache that made her incapable of overhauling *Jason*. The consul reassured her that a local man known as 'David' who looked after his car would see to *Jason*. Amy was too ill to protest, or to reflect that anyone with such a quintessentially English first name as 'David' in such a remote place might be stretching their credentials a little too far.

Her main concern was convincing the local officials to allow her to proceed. Sir Alan Cobham had been held up at Bandar Abbas for two days and Amy knew she had to keep calm amid what could be hours of pointless questioning. The white-suited officials expressed horror that Amy did not have inoculation certificates but after two hours she managed to convince them that as she would be leaving Persia immediately she posed no health threat to their country.

By dinnertime her headache had faded but the meal itself was a prolonged affair. The lights kept going out as the man in charge of the electricity had run out of petrol and used this as an excuse to go and gawp at the sudden arrival of a plane. It was dark by the time dinner was over but she insisted on working on *Jason* by the light of the huge Persian moon. She was shocked to find him sitting up proudly and with a new bolt fitted by David who explained that he had gathered his knowledge of planes by studying the RAF aircraft that used the aerodrome. He had found the bolt among spares that had been left behind. Amy used a pile of petrol tins to clamber up onto *Jason* to see if she could discover what was causing the machine to splutter. The middle of a plug had been blown out and, swapping places with David, she instructed him from the ground on cleaning the plugs.

The work was slowed by the sand that blew among the tools and the insects attracted to her torch. By midnight she had drained out the old oil and was ready to fill *Jason* up with Castrol XXL. But when she asked David for the oil he looked at her blankly. After a long search some old cans were found. They were Castrol R – a brand that Amy had no experience of. She did not know how *Jason* would respond to the oil and no one had any idea how long it had lain in the aerodrome. Amy felt nervous about using it but there appeared to be no alternative. As she watched what looked like weak tea being poured into *Jason* she shouted for David to stop.

Amy was no longer the compliant girl flyer she had been at Vienna; she was prepared to kick up a fuss if it meant the difference between breaking Hinkler's record or not. She returned to the consul's bungalow to ask him where he thought the stores of Castrol XXL might be. He went with her to the aerodrome to wake the customs officer to demand the key to his shed. By 2 a.m. the weak tea had been drained out of *Jason* and two gallons of Castrol XXL, a thick green pea soup of an oil, were glugging slowly into the sump.

Amy went to bed at 2.30 a.m. The cool, clear air and her relief at finding the oil meant she hardly felt sleepy at all – which was just as well, as she rose again an hour and a half later.

In Britain reports of her forced landing in the desert were starting to filter through. Until then coverage of the 'Girl Aviator's Lone Flight' had been scant. 'To-night's papers will be sensational . . . You have no idea how welcome your voice sounds,' Will wrote to Jack.[9] But there were signs that the tension was starting to affect even the unperturbable Jack, who had broken his arm in the sort of accident that simply does not happen to a man of his experience. A plane, whose engine was being tested, had jumped its chocks and careered towards Jack, its propeller a whirring disc of light. He instinctively put up his arm to shield himself and the blade cut into the limb. He was lucky not to lose his arm or head. His recovery was slow; he spent several weeks in hospital and even a visit to a Harley Street specialist could not prevent the injury leaving him with a permanent crook in this arm.

Jack kept in touch with Will from Redhill Hospital, Edgware, reminding him how much Amy's story was now worth and that they should be careful not to fritter away an exclusive by talking indiscriminately to newspaper reporters. Jimmy arrived in Hull by car to reassure Amy's family but waited a week to tell Amy of Jack's injury.

At the end of his fifth day Hinkler arrived at Ramleh close to the Palestinian port of Jaffa, just south of what is now Tel Aviv. He had only flown for seventy minutes and intended simply to refuel but was forced to waste a whole day due to delays over customs clearance.

Day 6 (Saturday, 10 May)

The next stage of Amy's journey took her across a fantastical landscape that teased and tried to trap her. Leaving Bandar Abbas, she followed the coast of the Persian Gulf. Her notes described the land north of Jask as of 'hideous appearance . . . all carved with pinnacle-like hills forming ranges with serrated summits'. There were no landing places and the mangrove swamps intersected by innumerable creeks that followed were hardly more promising. Seeking to relieve the boredom of the journey, she swooped down to take a closer look at the beautiful sea but immediately she found herself retching at a 'most curious and sickening smell'.[10] She rushed to saturate her handkerchief with eau-de-Cologne to stop herself vomiting. The stench was later attributed to either a vast stretch of decaying spawn or a chemical reaction to the minerals on the seabed.

Later in the journey she decided to fly straight across a bay rather than follow the coastline. The combination of the intense blue of the sea and the pale yellow of the distant shore produced an optical illusion that convinced her that *Jason* was about to plunge into the water. Instinctively she pulled up his nose but when she looked at her air-speed indicator she saw that the plane was close to stalling. After this she forced herself to fly across the bay using instruments, ignoring the temptation to gaze at the mesmerising water. It took an hour to reach the other side.

As Amy flew across the bleak lunar wasteland of Baluchistan towards Karachi she knew she was close to breaking Hinkler's time and establishing a new world record for the trip from England. But *Jason's* spluttering engine cancelled out any feelings of elation: again she was in a position where a forced landing would be fatal. Her notes warned of hills of volcanic mud thrown up into 'fang-like' formations, giving the impression of a 'sharply serrated and precipitous wall'.

Only when she reached the dusty aerodrome at Karachi did she allow herself to succumb to euphoria. She had beaten Hinkler's record by two days and for the first time in her journey was greeted by more than the solitary white official or bemused mechanic. *Jason's* triumphant arrival in India coincided with Mahatma Gandhi's return to the political stage. Although *The Tatler* made light of his campaign to boycott foreign-made goods, joking that 'what's sauce for the goose is sauce for the Gandhi',[11] there was deep concern in the British press. Northern industrial towns were worried that Gandhi's campaign threatened the British textile industry and launched a drive to promote cotton summer dresses.

Amy's arrival in Karachi offered a rare good-news story in India. Excited crowds pressed bouquets of flowers on the strange, grubby creature in the battered shorts and hung garlands round her neck. It was 110 degrees in the shade and she was whisked off to Government House to recover. A long dinner party had been planned in her honour but she pleaded fatigue and lack of clothes and dined alone in her room.

At the end of his sixth day Hinkler arrived at Basra on the Persian Gulf.

Chapter 12

The British Girl Lindbergh
(11–15 May 1930)

Until she touched down at Drigh Road aerodrome reporters had followed Amy's journey in a desultory fashion, impatient for her to fail so that they could move on to the next story. In beating the record to India, she was catapulted, in the space of a weekend, from the headline status of an anonymous 'airwoman' to the 'British Girl Lindbergh . . . Wonderful Miss Johnson . . . The Lone Girl Flyer'.[1] She was now a 'breaking story'.

Newspapers pored over her route and printed tables comparing her stopping points and daily mileage with Hinkler's. Amy's journey was 500 miles shorter but she had covered a daily average of 700 miles compared to Hinkler's 600. Reports concentrated on her stamina, on how it took 3000 strokes of her hand pump to move fifty gallons of petrol from one tank to another and how she survived on three hours' sleep. The word 'pluck' seemed to have been invented for her.

Despite the exotic locations and her superhuman courage, she was quintessentially and reassuringly British. She restored faith in an empire under economic and emotional attack. The people she met in India were, she said, 'nice, but, of course, they were British'.[2] Her supporters at home, though rooted to their humdrum lives, were made to feel they had played a part in her success purely by the nature of their nationality.

Her physical attractiveness sprang from the jumble of toughness and vulnerability she exhibited. Newspapers maintained her age at twenty-two and interspersed stilted family portraits of her looking neat and manicured with shots in which she was unwashed and with matted hair, but vibrant, almost feral. Each day spent in the air allowed her to 'go wild' before returning to the white-uniformed keepers of the Empire at night. Her outfit of patched shirt and oversized shorts ended with a hint of decadence: ankle-socks that, on closer inspection, turned out to be rolled-down silk stockings. She was the demure typist with a

Bachelor of Arts degree who enjoyed sitting astride the engine of a biplane.

The conundrum of the airwoman who possessed neither title nor stately home led to interest in Amy's background. At the Rotary Convention in Edinburgh Will and Ciss were given a standing ovation. Will managed to shield Ciss from most of the press attention, offering his own media scalp in return. As the head of a family of four women who was prepared to let his eldest daughter loose on the worst dangers the world could offer, Will was a curiosity. When he went for a stroll in between Rotary sessions in Edinburgh he was cornered by persistent reporters and, for the rest of Amy's journey, feeding the insatiable press titbits of information became part of his daily routine. 'I have no son and I have put all my faith and reliance in my daughter,' he told a reporter.[3] In public Will brushed aside criticism of the risks Amy faced: 'We think that is a namby-pamby attitude,' he said stoically.[4]

Amy's two younger sisters were unable to escape the media circus and a *Daily Mail* reporter visited 85 Park Avenue while Will and Ciss were away. Molly was now a rather plump, self-conscious eighteen-year-old and Betty a precocious eleven-year-old. They told him how the wireless set had become the focus of their lives, how they gathered anxiously round it hoping that the news bulletin might mention Amy and worrying when it did. The reporter left with a story of how, before setting off from Croydon, Amy had practised firing a revolver at medicine bottles in preparation for the Arabs, wild dogs, hyenas and tigers she fully expected to meet along the way to Australia.

But Amy was finding the physical and mental strain of the journey more taxing than worries about wild animals or natives. Antoine de Saint-Exupéry, pilot and author of *The Little Prince*, wrote of entering another world when he climbed into a plane, but after eleven hours at a time, six days in a row, Amy's open cockpit was a prison rather than a magical kingdom. Boredom was one of her greatest problems when even the strain of listening to an ailing engine was preferable to hours of nothingness. Apart from pumping the fuel tank and keeping an eye on her instruments, she had to check whether the landscape she could glimpse from *Jason* bore any resemblance to her maps. By Karachi the novelty of constantly changing vistas had worn off: Amy, like Francis Chichester before her, found that too much scenery exhausts through excessive stimulation of the mind and eye. It may be true that travel broadens one's horizons, but Amy's style of travel had telescoped her world into the confined space of her cockpit.

Of all the minutiae that were printed about Amy's flight, the one detail not addressed by the press, and the one that was uppermost in many people's minds, was how she relieved herself. Male pilots could use a 'relief tube' but urinating was, of course, much more problematic for women. During her later record-breaking flights Amy appears to have used a closely fitting plastic contraption, but how she coped in 1930 remains open to speculation.[5] She may have relied on bladder control: in one anecdote ground engineers stationed in Baghdad were told to hold back once she had landed, while she leapt out of *Jason* and immediately squatted down. Another suggestion that she kept some sort of chamberpot in the cockpit is just about feasible, although flying a biplane in a crouching position must have been tricky.

The most testing part of Amy's day came at the end when she had nothing left to give. Landing was not her strong point and the airfields became more rudimentary the further east she went. She never knew what the surface would be like until she touched down; she could only guess who would be there to meet her and whether they would speak English or have any mechanical knowledge. After the solitary hours in the cockpit she had to transform herself into an ambassador for aviation and empire; wiping her grimy face and feigning polite interest at the formal dinners that were laid on for her – even though all she wanted to do was to overhaul *Jason*'s engine and then snatch a few hours' sleep. Most importantly, she could never fully relax until she knew that there was good quality petrol and oil for *Jason*.

The strain of worrying about *Jason*'s engine manifested itself in small niggles that grew into obsessions. Amy was constantly irritated by the petrol cap on *Jason*'s front tank. When she left Croydon it would only screw on for a thread and a half; by the time she left Constantinople the thread was completely destroyed. She was convinced that a Turkish mechanic had hammered it when she was not looking. There was no time to fix it properly so that, after a day's flying and sometimes five hours' work on the engine, it took her another hour to fix the cap, standing, drunk with tiredness, twiddling the wretched fitting.

Filling *Jason* up from petrol tins was a slow task that could not be rushed. Amy carried a huge filter with a very small hole in the centre which a friend had found for her. The device was not designed for petrol and was cumbersome to use. Amy also insisted on filtering the petrol through two chamois leathers to reduce the risk of water or dirt contaminating the fuel. There was no fuel gauge for the front or rear tank and the only way of knowing how full they were was to put a finger inside. The tanks and the air vent, which was below the top of the front petrol tank, often overflowed, soaking Amy's luggage –

including her pyjamas. When this happened she had to lay out all her belongings to dry and air, and squander precious hours of sleep by rising early to repack.

Many of her problems arose from the fact that *Jason* bore the bumps and bruises of a previous owner who had customised the plane for his own long-distance purposes. The step up to the engine had been filled in to make the plane more aerodynamic but this made it harder for someone as short as Amy to clamber up. She admitted later that if she had not been so tired and preoccupied with more pressing worries she would have cut a make-shift step into the fuselage.

Brute force was the answer to many of *Jason*'s idiosyncrasies. The engine cowling, or cover, was held in place by a pin that got stuck every time Amy wanted to inspect the engine. She fell off a petrol tin several times trying to dislodge it with a pair of pliers; and each time it was put back it had to be hammered in, making it harder to pull out next time.

At Karachi *Jason*'s engine was overhauled during the night, the mechanics replacing tools that Amy had lost during the journey. She discovered that David had put two washers on one of the plugs instead of one so that the plug jutted out, almost touching the metal cowling that covered the engine. If David had chosen a plug on the opposite side, where the carburettor was, the mistake would probably have started a fire.

Amy went to sleep with the beat of the engine still drumming in her ears, her shoulders and back aching from ten hours confined to a cockpit. A telegram from the Duchess of Bedford on behalf of the Air League, one of several that chased her round Asia, reminded her that she had achieved something remarkable. But the moment was spoilt when she broke the chain of the lucky swastika brooch her mother had given her.

Day 7 (Sunday, 11 May)

The De Havilland agent and an RAF plane accompanied Amy for the first few miles from Karachi. After they had waved goodbye she sensed she was not alone and, looking out of her cockpit, saw the sinister black figures of vultures effortlessly keeping up with *Jason*. If any one of the eerie escort had been sucked into the propeller or wings it would have proved fatal for both her and the bird.

The first few hundred miles from Karachi took Amy over cultivated land until she encountered the featureless, black sand of the Sind desert and its dry salt lakes. It was a shock to discover that India was different from the lions, tigers and vast jungles she had expected.

Just short of the time she expected to see Allahabad she spotted a river sparkling in the sun, and a town. Allahabad's position at the confluence of two great rivers, the Ganges and the Yamuna (Jumna), makes it an important place of pilgrimage, where the waters help to wash away sins, but Amy knew that since she was arriving at the end of the dry season the rivers would appear shrunken. She could also expect to see, squatting on the edge of the Yamuna river, a huge sixteenth-century fort with massive walls and pillars and three grand gateways flanked by towers. She glided down to look for the aerodrome but although she could find no sign of it, she decided to land. *Jason* was immediately engulfed by excited Indians curious about the apparition from the sky. 'I sat tight and waited,' she said later. 'Soon I saw an Englishman and I asked him where I was.'6

It seems remarkable that Amy simply assumed that, in the middle of India, an Englishman would come to her rescue. What is even more remarkable is that her assumption was correct. The man told her that she had landed at Jhansi, a town a few hundred miles west of Allahabad. The town has a fort which may have made her believe it was Allahabad. 'Thanking him, I turned my machine round and took off rapidly before the crowd had time to spread over the open space.' As Amy described it, finding one's bearings in the sub-continent was as simple as winding your window down in the family saloon and asking a passer-by for directions.

After an hour her fuel gauge showed that she had barely sixty minutes' flying time left. Strong headwinds had slowed *Jason* down and the light was fading; Amy reluctantly decided to return to Jhansi. It was the first time she had been forced to turn back. She was determined to look for a better landing place than the one she had used on her previous arrival in Jhansi. The aerodrome was not marked on her map and she could see no sign of it on the ground. Instead she chose a clearing surrounded by houses.

Jhansi was a sleepy place in northern India, made sleepier by the suffocating heat, but it occupied a footnote in the history of India that made it impossible for Britain to ignore – especially at a time when Gandhi was pointing out the inequality of foreign rule. Less than eighty years before Jhansi was ruled by a maharaja. When he died without a male heir the Governor-General of India decided to annex the state of Jhansi. He had not reckoned on the opposition of the maharaja's wife, the Rani, who organised a force of 14,000 rebels to defend the city. The Indians were brutally suppressed after a two-week siege and the Rani escaped, riding over a hundred miles on horseback in twenty-four hours to rally local politicians. Dressed in men's clothing, she fought valiantly against the British and was eventually killed. Sir Hugh Rose, Commander of the British force, described her as 'the most dangerous of all the rebel leaders' and she became a Joan of Arc figure in the fight for independence.

The Rani's spirit returned to Jhansi in the late afternoon of 11 May 1930. It was a busy time for the 3rd and 8th Punjab Regiment: it was unbearably hot in the still air but the raging heat of midday had started to dissipate slightly and officers were preparing to organise guard duty. The colonel was standing on his veranda trying to decide whether he would spend the late afternoon riding his horse or watching hockey. He was spared this dilemma by the grinding sound of an engine struggling overhead; looking up, he watched a plane circle the army base twice. The whirring, out-of-control aircraft bumped down onto the parade ground, its wheels just touching the bushes on one side before it charged a few soldiers and careered towards their barracks. With no wind to slow it, the plane was a bouncing great insect that twisted round trees, just missed an iron telegraph pole and scattered the group of men waiting to mount guard. One wing tore through a notice-board outside the regimental offices before becoming jammed between two barrack buildings close to the colonel's front yard.[7]

The soldiers raced for the plane and watched as a 'girl . . . almost a child' staggered out.[8] She was wearing men's clothing and a helmet. The skin on her arms, face and legs was burnt and blistered by the sun and she was close to tears. She muttered something about being two days ahead of a record and fearing that everything was ruined.

The forced landing could easily have proved fatal but *Jason*'s wing was not as badly damaged as the sickening crunch had suggested. A bearded 'Mystery Man', or carpenter, in the village repaired the wing so that it was in better condition than before the crash and a tailor finished off the repairs using Amy's spare supply of fabric, cotton and 'dope'.

Motor cars were sent to fetch enough petrol from the aerodrome, which was ten miles away, to enable *Jason* to reach Allahabad. Amy overhauled him while servants kept her supplied with long, cool drinks from the colonel's home. When the officers could see that she was too exhausted to carry on herself, they insisted she directed work from a camp-bed until, at 9 p.m., she was taken by car to a nearby bungalow where she was given a bath, a change of clothes and dinner. She delighted the soldiers with her story of the escort of bald-headed vultures just at the moment when the moonlight shone on the pate of the officer sitting opposite her. When she returned to *Jason* a group of Indian women were waiting to touch her hand, believing she had mystical powers.

Amy found it impossible to sleep that night. 'Jhansi was hotter than I had ever imagined a place on earth could be,' she said.[9] She dragged her bed onto the lawn but the open air tricked her subconscious into believing that she was still in the cockpit and had fallen asleep, so that she repeatedly awoke with the awful start of the dreamer convinced they are falling through the sky.

At the end of his seventh day Hinkler arrived at Jask, a few hundred miles east of Bandar Abbas.

Day 8 (Monday, 12 May)

Amy left Jhansi at dawn. She refuelled at Allahabad before following the Ganges, which at times stretched to over a mile wide, to Calcutta where the Dum-Dum Flying Club overhauled the engine while she arranged to borrow clean clothes. For the first time in a week she saw a familiar face. Mrs Carter, a former member of Stag Lane, now lived in Calcutta. A telegram was also waiting for her from her parents and Jack which urged her not to linger in Sydney as the reception in Britain was 'much more valuable'.[10]

At the end of his eighth day Hinkler arrived at Karachi.

Day 9 (Tuesday, 13 May)

Jason set off at 7 a.m. for Rangoon. Dum-Dum Aerodrome was shrouded in fog and Amy was told to expect 'sticky weather' ahead of her: the start of the monsoon. She flew over the marshy land where the Ganges sends countless tendrils into the Bay of Bengal and on to the jungle coastline of Burma. Her plan was to head south until the Arakan Mountains dropped to a height where she might find a pass that would allow her to cross them and reach the Irrawaddy valley and Rangoon. The only aerodrome en route was Akyab near the northern coast of Burma, but when Amy flew over it she saw that it was completely flooded.

The rain was so heavy that she was forced to retrace her steps and head north back to Akyab. But by the time she reached it the aerodrome had disappeared in the thick cloud, leaving her no option but to continue. She plunged into the thick clouds in an attempt to cross the mountains. For half an hour *Jason* droned through the whiteness, Amy expecting at any minute to run into a mountain hidden by cloud. When she calculated that they should have crossed the range she began, very cautiously, her descent. As the skies cleared she spotted the gleam of what could only be the Irrawaddy river. She circled down slowly, taking care not to lose sight of the precious landmark and then followed it south until her map told her she must abandon it to pick up the railway.

By the time she noticed the metal track snaking through the valley the rain was torrential. She was soaked through and the water that stung her eyes made it difficult to see. Anxious not to lose sight of the railway, she flew down so that *Jason* almost touched the rooftops of the railway stations. Waiting passengers sheltering patiently under umbrellas looked up with frightened faces at the rumble that emerged above the deluge of rain.

Amy started to search for the racecourse, a decision more sensible that it sounds. Pilots who were unable to find an aerodrome often sought out racecourses which offered a large, flat piece of grass that was frequently in a better condition than the aerodrome. Amy's map showed that the racecourse should be close to the railway, on the north side of Rangoon. Amy flew right through Rangoon to the coast without spotting anything that appeared big enough. When she started to run out of both daylight and petrol she decided to return to the small space that she had ruled out as being the racecourse. As she descended she saw a large building with people waving to her from a balcony and she took this as encouragement that she was in the right place. In fact they were pointing in the direction of the racecourse rather than the football pitch she was heading for.

As *Jason* started to prepare for landing Amy realised that the space she was approaching was not big enough to be a racecourse. Far too late to do anything about it, she spotted two goalposts surrounded by a ditch and realised that she had mistaken a running track for a racecourse. The sports-ground was hemmed in by trees, making it impossible for her to lift *Jason* out of the trap. The plane careered straight past the goalposts and into the trench, coming to an abrupt halt with a loud crunch and a great shudder. A post had punctured the left lower wing, ripping the tyre open. The shock of the crash after a day of intense concentration and a series of decisions on which her life depended punctured what little resolve she had left and she gave way to great sobs of anguish and disappointment.

Amy had landed at the sports field of the Government Technical

Institute at Insein, some five miles north of Rangoon. The spectators waving her on to the racecourse were students and teachers. Her despair was such that she was unable to pretend to be pleased to see them, envisaging herself 'stranded in this awful place for months to come'.[11] All she wanted to do was to be allowed to go to sleep, but first she had to deal with *Jason*. His propeller was broken, a tyre was ripped, an undercarriage strut had snapped and, most seriously, a wing was badly mangled. Moving him in such a state was tricky. He had to be lifted out of the ditch and carried over the compound to the shelter of a grove of trees. Once this was done Amy went to bed, refusing even dinner. If she had suffered a similar accident in England she knew it would take three weeks to repair the damage.

At the end of his ninth day Hinkler arrived at Cawnpore (now Kanpur) in Uttar Pradesh, north-east India.

Day 10 (Wednesday, 14 May)

If Amy had to crash anywhere in Burma, the Government Technical Institute was probably the best place for her to do it. 'I was at any rate relieved to know I was near an engineering school, and not a dancing academy,' she said later.[12] The staff had the usual 'can-do' attitude that an outpost of the British Empire prided itself on, but returning a badly mangled plane to airworthiness takes more than the optimism of amateurs. Unusually, the staff at Insein had the technical know-how to give *Jason* a fighting chance of returning to the skies.

The damaged wing was carefully removed and carried through the heavy rain into the Institute's workshop where it was laid out like a critically ill patient on the operating table. Once the fabric was peeled back it became evident that several of the ribs that held the wing together were shattered. The chances of continuing the flight seemed hopeless. Then, right on cue, the Englishman who so often came to Amy's rescue appeared. A Forestry Inspector, who was more used to dealing with Burma's valuable stores of teak, picked up the shattered pieces of wood and said he would deal with them if the Institute would try to repair the metal sections of the plane. When he left the students stripped the damaged metal parts and started to weld them back together. They made new bolts and straightened other pieces of metal that had become bent in the crash. While they worked Amy unstrapped the spare propeller and put it in place, cleaning the engine which had become caked with mud from the ditch. But, even supposing that these repairs were reliable, she still needed to find some way of replacing the wing's fabric. Her emergency supplies of linen had been used up in Jhansi and, anyway, this was more than a matter of patching up a small tear.

Just as there seemed no danger of things getting any worse, Amy was assailed by her pet hate: insects. A swarm of flying ants descended in a huge cloud that made work impossible. She watched mesmerised as the insects flew round for an hour before their wings fell off and they stumbled about the furniture until they keeled over in death throes two hours later. The staff tried to speed up the process by switching off the lights and placing large enamel bowls of water with a candle in the middle to drown the insects. When the plague moved on servants appeared with brooms to sweep away the corpses, but their place was taken by black and brown flying beetles and a whole range of other insects that crawled over Amy's food. She fastened her collar down to stop them crawling along her back but she was unable to check her imagination. 'I felt they were on my hair, amongst my clothes and everywhere.'[13]

When told of her crash at Insein, Will maintained his sang-froid, saying: 'It's a bit of rotten luck for her, that's all.' The delay in receiving press reports meant that details of adventures that had happened to her days before were carried side-by-side with 'stop-press' news of her latest progress, so that she appeared to be pressing on breathlessly from one near-miss to the next.

The Times reported her words as she left Dum-Dum Aerodrome. 'This is just an ordinary flight, except that it is longer. Every woman will be doing this in five years' time.'[14] The Daily Mail talked of Amy's 'jungle town landing' and carried a picture of Ciss and Will studying maps.[15]

At the end of his tenth day Hinkler arrived at Calcutta.

Day 11 (Thursday, 15 May)

The Forestry Inspector arrived with new ribs made from wood that was as close a match as he could find. The parts were glued and tacked into the wing which still looked naked and exposed without its fabric cover.

Suddenly someone realised that the solution was on their own backs. After the First World War hundreds of bales of surplus aeroplane fabric had been sold off at knock-down prices around the world. At Insein thirty thrifty housewives had bought the material to make shirts for their husbands, certain that the fabric would take years to wear out. A decade later these scratchy, uncomfortable shirts were gleefully torn into strips and sewn into one big length of material by a team of seamstresses. The last missing ingredient in this 'Airfix' solution was the 'dope' needed to stiffen the fabric. Amy had only a tiny amount of the concoction left and it was sent to a chemist in Rangoon who mixed up a replacement by trying to match the smell of the original. His version proved too thin, so an extra coat was added. The manufacturers' instructions stipulated that the dope should not be applied in temperatures of more than seventy degrees Fahrenheit and humidity of no more than 70 per cent. In Insein it was well over a hundred degrees and the rain was constant. Finally, a representative from the Dunlop Rubber company took the burst tyre to Rangoon to be vulcanised.

The next stage was to move *Jason* the twelve miles to the racecourse where Amy could attempt a take-off. He was carried to the nearest road and his tail was balanced on the local fire engine. A policeman carrying an umbrella in the still torrential rain walked in front to clear the road. Amy and as many people who would fit on the fire engine huddled under raincoats and umbrellas. As the road was full of potholes the fire engine went at a stately three miles per hour, stopping every ten minutes to allow *Jason's* tyres to cool down. The procession had the air of a bizarre ritual, like the funeral of an eccentric character in the deep South of America. By this time Amy and her band of followers could see the funny side of what they were doing and an edge of hysteria had seeped into the party. *Jason* was secured for the night at the racecourse and Amy returned to Insein to sleep.

The crash had taken her newsworthiness one step higher up the celebrity ladder. Jimmy Martin had been trying to sell her story for days but it was not until she arrived in Insein that there was any great interest. He cabled her to say he had provisionally sold the world rights for her story to the *News of the World* for a 'splendid sum' of £500 (nearly £15,500 in today's money) or £1000 if she managed the return flight.[16] Other newspapers in Britain and Australia bombarded her with offers and the Prince of Wales Theatre in London asked her to appear for two weeks. Will immediately stamped on the idea of putting Amy 'on show', saying it would make her look 'cheap'.[17]

Before she left Insein her father and Jimmy had secured a deal in which the *Daily Mail* paid £2000 (nearly £62,000 in today's money) for her exclusive story. At a time when product endorsement and the mass marketing of a 'star' were rudimentary, and when 'multi-media' meant newspaper, wireless or cinema, the fee represented a huge amount.

Will, Ciss and Jimmy went to the Strand Palace Hotel to celebrate.

At the end of his eleventh day Hinkler arrived at Rangoon. Amy had lost her two-day lead and was now neck and neck with Hinkler.

Chapter 13

Beastly Weather
(16–24 May 1930)

Day 12 (Friday, 16 May)

When she returned at dawn Amy fastened her parachute on more securely than ever before. A faulty petrol cap was an irritation, but an untried, botched-together wing could prove fatal. She refuelled and took *Jason* up for a brief test-drive. When her luggage had been reloaded she took off in blinding wind, struggling down the racecourse that was only 100 yards wide and 750 yards long.

She had added a thick belt to her ensemble. It had been donated, together with some maps for the next leg of her journey to Bangkok, by C. W. Scott who had offered his home as a base for her while she was staying at Insein. Scott had obviously become infatuated with her during their short acquaintance: 'May I just say for myself how much it has added to the pleasure and pride in your feat to know that apart from being so successful you are so thoroughly nice!' he wrote later.[1] Scott worried that his maps were useless in the 'beastly' weather. While he waited for her to arrive in Bangkok he 'felt just as one did during the war when a patrol was overdue!'

Describing the weather as 'beastly' was an understatement. When she crossed the Gulf of Martaban that separates Rangoon from Moulmein the conditions were every bit as appalling as the day before. 'My eyes were stinging as if being torn out,' she told the *Daily Mail*[2] and her hunt for a way through the mountains was nightmarishly familiar. The cloud was so thick that she was unable to make out the aerodrome at Moulmein and she fell back on her tactic of climbing to 9000 feet in a bid to escape the peaks that she knew lurked somewhere in the clouds. It took her three hours to cross the mountains, a journey that in fine weather should have taken half an hour. When she emerged above the jungle plains on the other side she discovered she was miles off course. Her strip maps, which extended for only a small area on either side of her intended route, were useless and she had to fall back on her instinct alone. She flew south, knowing that she should eventually reach the sea. After a while she spotted a network of canals that were marked on her map and which made it easier to find Don Muang military aerodrome, twenty miles outside Bangkok.

Yet another day of intense stress and fatigue left her exhausted and with a blinding headache. She landed at the wrong end of the large aerodrome and had to taxi to the hangar, creeping along at walking pace for over a mile behind a man carrying green and red flags. When the official raised the red flag *Jason* was forced to stop. The twenty-minute, stop/go journey in mind-numbing heat placed a strain on an engine that was already at the end of its endurance and increased the woodpecker pounding in Amy's head.

Crowds of Siamese people were waiting to greet her and a special train had been laid on to take her to Bangkok for the night. She declined, permitting herself a short rest and a meal and allowing the Siamese air force to refuel for her. But when she came to inspect their work she decided that the fuel had been contaminated and that it should be drained and filtered. The aerodrome was wet and wrapped in a blanket of heat. Torchlight brought the inevitable insects. Amy's instructions were relayed in a tortuous game of Chinese whispers, the Shell representative passing on her words to someone who spoke French who translated them into Siamese for the eager mechanics. Neither translator knew any technical terms.

When she finally went to her room in the barracks the white mosquito net shrouding her bed was black with insects. Amy opened the door and blew out her candle in the hope that the outside light would lure them away. She undressed in the dark and climbed into bed. By the light of her torch she 'slaughtered' the 'beasts' inside.[3]

In America newspapers continued to refer to Amy as 'The Girl Lindbergh'[4] and 'The Lone Dove', the latter a feminine version of Lindbergh's nickname, 'The Lone Eagle'.

At the end of his twelfth day Hinkler arrived at Victoria Point, at the very southernmost tip of Burma and just ahead of Amy.

Day 13 (Saturday, 17 May)

Amy left Don Muang as dawn was breaking. Minutes after take-off the cowling flew open on her engine and she was forced to return to the aerodrome, the first time she had attempted a landing with full tanks. The delay meant that covering the 900 miles to Singapore in one day was impossible.

The replacement propeller was not performing as well as the original and there was no improvement in the weather. Staying on course required all her concentration. She hugged the coastline's thin strip of sand, at times flying so low that her wings barely cleared the tops of the waves. At one point she noticed that her compass was jumping from north to east to south, and then west. Eventually she realised that the instrument was not at fault but that she had been flying round and round a flooded paddy field in the belief that she was over the sea. The rain was so heavy and the winds so strong that she could see nothing through her goggles. The turbulence jolted her almost out of her seat and her chin struck one of the instruments. A few oranges and precious pieces of chocolate were lost overboard.

It had taken her eight and a half hours to cover 450 miles – half the distance she had expected to make that day. Amy decided to take advantage of a lull in the storm to land at Singora, on the east coast of the Malay Peninsula – some 400 miles from Singapore. As *Jason's* wheels touched down they sank into sand that was so soft that he nearly turned over.

Petrol and oil had been left by a previous pilot but *Jason* was too hot to touch. By the time the sun had gone down he was surrounded by a good-humoured crowd of picnickers and thousands of brightly robed Siamese kept happy by ice-cream carts. Police quickly formed a cordon around *Jason* and a man who had been sent by the Government to interpret for Amy tried to find a burly member of the crowd to help her unscrew the most persistent nuts and help with the heavy work. The strongman he pulled out of the audience was so shy that he darted back into the mass of people after fulfilling each task so that the gaggle of onlookers learnt to shout 'Strong man, strong man' every time she looked up for his help.

In Britain the *Daily Mail* informed its readers that it had secured Amy's account of her 'great flight'.

At the end of his thirteenth day Hinkler arrived at Singapore. There was now no chance of Amy breaking his record, although British papers clung to the hope of her beating his number of flying hours.

Day 14 (Sunday, 18 May)

When Amy arrived at the aerodrome early the next day she was shocked to discover that hundreds of people – adults, children and Buddhist priests in saffron robes – had turned up to watch her departure. She decided that it would be safer to attempt a take-off from the nearby road, rather than the sandy aerodrome, and asked a few members of the crowd to help her lift *Jason*. But, as a runway, the road had its own special problems – not least the fact that people stood eight deep on either side of it. As well as steering a tight course between the columns of bodies, a take-off meant clearing houses and a row of tall trees. Amy managed through frantic gesturing to move the crowds back a few feet but was still attempting a manoeuvre that put hundreds of people, most of whom had never seen an aeroplane take off, at risk. She was aware that she had to stick closely to a straight course; one swerve and she would plough into her fans. In her anxiety she forgot that she should look out to the right, rather than the left, side and just as she started to move she was momentarily blinded by a jet of petrol in her eye. She was so relieved to be airborne that she waved down happily at the crowd who had no idea of the danger they had been in.

Amy abandoned her plans to fly down the west side of the Malay Peninsula after hearing that it had rained there for two weeks without stopping. As she approached Seletar aerodrome, Singapore, several sea-planes from the local club flew out to meet her. Below her a group of men and women waited patiently for their guest of honour to inject some excitement into their otherwise tightly ordered Sunday. The men wore white suits and sola topis; the women sheltered under parasols in muslin frocks trimmed with lace and chiffon. Amy performed a perfect landing and stepped out of *Jason* wearing a pair of man's khaki shorts that assumed music-hall proportions on her slim frame. Her outfit resembled a child's game in which the player has to construct the craziest human possible by assembling the torso, middle and head from three different characters. She had become a photofit hermaphrodite. Her stockings were stained with a light sheen of oil and her clumpy brogues were covered with dust. A purple blouse with long sleeves was just visible under her light-brown, man's jacket that was pulled in brutally at the waist. The blouse was fixed at the throat by a gold-and-enamel brooch and her topi was held in place by a broad, oil-stained strap. Amy's face and hands were burnt brick-red by the sun. As she wiped the oil and sweat from her face the crowd applauded politely as if she had won a prize for the most bizarre outfit available in the tropics. She defied all categories and in doing so instantly broke down the women's natural reserve. They pressed forward to touch her and hold her hand. The men responded by lending her a new wing to replace the school project that had served her so well since Insein, and by fitting a new air-speed indicator to replace the original that was not performing well. Unfortunately, the replacement was designed for a seaplane and recorded the speed in knots rather than miles.[5]

A cable from her father reminded her that to beat Hinkler she had to arrive at Darwin on Tuesday before 6.50 p.m. It ended: 'Don't overdo yourself be careful.' By then Amy's overriding thought was to get to Australia so that she could give in to her yearning for a long night's sleep in a safe bed. An invitation from the Aeroclub of New South Wales offered a tantalising glimpse of just how close her destination was.

At the end of his fourteenth day Hinkler arrived at Kalidjati, fifty miles east of Batavia (Jakarta).

Day 15 (Monday, 19 May)

Amy had hoped to fly directly to Surabaya, a port a thousand miles away in the Dutch East Indies (Java), but the monsoon compelled her to hug the coastline of Sumatra. When she reached the island of Bangka, to the east of Sumatra, she decided to risk a short-cut across the wide open space of the Java Sea. The weather ahead looked fine and *Jason's* engine was ticking over nicely.

After half an hour, and when she was out of sight of land, heavy rain and thick clouds forced her lower and lower until her altimeter registered zero. Although she did not know it at the time, a volcano had erupted on Java, killing fifty villagers and sending meteorological shockwaves across the Java Sea. She was lost and alone in a violent ocean:

> My mind flew to the stories of typhoons, hurricanes, water-spouts and such-like horrors I had read about in my youth . . . I seemed hemmed in by blackness, with black skies overhead, and black angry waves beneath whose salty foam I could almost feel on my face. Unable to go on, equally unable to turn back or to stay still, I circled round and round. I was more than terrified and shrieked aloud for help. I didn't want to die that way – I knew that thousands of hungry sharks were waiting with mouths wide open – and my fingers closed over the knife I had in my pocket.[6]

She began to pray for help and just as she seemed about to give herself over completely to hopelessness, the sun burnt through the glowering sky and a perfect rainbow appeared. She darted for the opening and headed for what she believed to be the direction of the coast. For Amy the sudden gap in the clouds, together with the rainbow, represented an epiphany. She believed that God was offering her a sign when she had reached her lowest point. Although she did not class herself as religious she prayed at the start of every morning's flight and was convinced that her parents' prayers were helping her. She spoke often of the 'guardian angels' who were watching over her throughout her journey to Australia.

The feeling that an unseen presence is offering spiritual sustenance at a moment of utter despair and loneliness is not uncommon among lone pilots and explorers. Amelia Earhart had a similar experience when she was lost in thick cloud and a perfect circle of light appeared through which she spotted a ship that was able to radio her position to her.

Even Charles Lindbergh, the most level-headed of airmen, believed that his plane, the *Spirit of St Louis*, was briefly inhabited by ghostly figures who passed through the aircraft in a wave of benediction and chatted to him after he had been in the air for twenty-two hours and was close to exhaustion. It took thirty years for the phlegmatic hero to admit to the experience.[7]

Polar explorer Sir Ernest Shackleton said that when he and two of his crew left their companions to raise help they were not alone. He fervently believed that a fourth presence went with them during the unimaginably gruelling journey across snowy seas in an open boat followed by a thirty-six-hour march across mountains and glaciers.[8] The admission inspired T. S. Eliot to write in *The Waste Land*:

> Who is the third who walks always beside you?
> When I count, there are only you and I together
> But when I look ahead up the white road
> There is always another one walking beside you.[9]

Having escaped from her mental blackness Amy was desperate to avoid the night. She knew that in the tropics the sun disappeared in an instant, to be replaced by an unrelenting darkness. Even though her notes warned her of volcanoes she headed for the coast, but all she could see were rice-fields and sugar-plantations. She considered landing on the beach but at the last minute spotted a large piece of open land next to what looked like a factory.

As *Jason*'s wheels touched down, Amy saw that he was heading for a ditch and what seemed to be a repeat of the landing at Insein. As she braced herself for the crash he mysteriously slowed down. When she jumped out of the plane she assumed that the muddy ground had acted as a break; it was only later that she discovered that long bamboo stakes plunged into the ground had slowed the aeroplane. They had also ripped great tears in the fabric of the wings.

She had arrived at a sugar estate at Tjomal, Java, around 200 miles west of Batavia (Jakarta). The open space was a plot laid out with bamboo stakes for the manager's new bungalow. While she slept that night the manager had the stakes pulled out and the ditch filled in, to give Amy a better chance of take-off. The wings were fixed with sticky plaster and her luggage was sent on to the nearest emergency landing spot.

At the end of the fifteenth day Hinkler arrived at Bima, on the island of Sumbawa.

Day 16 (Tuesday, 20 May)

Using non-aviation petrol, which was the only available fuel, Amy flew to pick up her luggage and then refuelled at Semarang in central Java. The aerodrome was a stopping-place for the giant three-engined Fokkers of the Dutch air mail service, and the pilot of one of them offered to show Amy the way to Surabaya. Although she struggled to keep up with the plane it was a relief to feel she was not alone.

Surabaya was the setting for Joseph Conrad's novel *Victory*, and when Amy visited the port it was still a community under siege. The Europeans were hemmed in by mysterious, still islands, some of which were believed to be inhabited by cannibals. The settlers were united by their colour but divided by endemic distrust of each other's country of origin.

Amy's arrival gave the Europeans a chance to set aside their suspicions and provide the 'lone girl flyer' with an uproarious welcome. She was greeted with cheers and flowers and taken to the British Consul for lunch. Afterwards she fitted a new propeller that a local Moth-owner had offered and which was more suited to flying in the tropics.

Molly and Betty both sent cables:[10] 'Bravo well done. Love Betty' and 'Women of England proud of you. Your sister Moll proudest of all.' Will and Ciss urged Amy to be cautious: 'Please dont attempt sea passage unless feeling quite fit and your engine dependable no hurry be careful love father mother.' They reassured her that no one was bothered about Hinkler's record and that she should not fly back from Australia, but Will could not resist discussing business arrangements after she arrived in Port Darwin. He warned her that her public appearances must not clash with the *Daily Mail*'s plans for her and said a tour of America was a good idea. The paper was already nagging her for 'copy': 750 to 1000 words, in the first person, that should include 'good description, enthusiasm and a quote'.[11]

Hinkler arrived at Darwin, Australia on 22 February 1928 at 6 p.m. in the afternoon.

Day 17 (Wednesday, 21 May)

Everyone who met Amy at Surabaya spoke of how tired she looked. Her fatigue was more than just the effect of two weeks of the most dangerous flying the world could offer. From what happened later it is obvious that she was suffering from what today would be called pre-menstrual stress or tension. It was fortunate, then, that when she tried to start *Jason*'s engine she discovered a faulty magneto that forced her to spend a second night at Surabaya.

She wrote to her parents that she was 'very tired . . . and a wee bit discouraged because everything seems to be going wrong . . . shall be so glad when the sea crossing is over which I dread. When one gets so tired I find one loses one's courage too.'[12] In her letter she spoke of being 'ashamed' that she had not broken the record and of needing 'Daddy' to advise her on the various offers she was being made. She wanted to make the most of her appeal in Australia before hurrying home to what she feared would be a muted welcome in England.

Day 18 (Thursday, 22 May)

Amy took off for Atamboea, a thousand miles away on the island of Timor. She hoped to be there in the evening and to make the final hop to Australia the following day where, unbeknown to her, elaborate preparations were being made to welcome her. In Sydney milliners were working on a '*Jason*'s Quest' hat that was shaped like a closely fitting pilot's helmet with a wing over each ear.

At noon Amy was spotted flying over Bima on the island of Sumbawa, one of the larger islands that form giant stepping-stones between Java and Timor. Then silence . . .

Jason was due to land at Atamboea at 9.30 a.m., British time. For the next twenty-four hours there was no news. Will and Ciss found the night hardest, when they knew that the arrival of daylight on the other side of the world meant there was most chance of hearing from Amy. There was little to be said and a heavy gloom descended on 85 Park Avenue. Talk of a return flight and newspaper deals now seemed foolish, a sin for which they were about to pay the ultimate price.

Day 19 (Friday, 23 May)

The regular bulletins describing Amy's latest struggle with the monsoon had formed a daily soap opera for the British public, who felt abandoned when the newspapers and radio could report only speculation on her whereabouts. She was suspended in the deepest recesses of their imagination somewhere over the jungle of Indonesia, a place so far removed from British life that she might have been lost in space. Her fate was the main topic of conversation in factories and offices across Britain and many strangers wrote letters of comfort to Ciss and Will; several compared Amy to Joan of Arc. One woman said that she had had a vision of Amy surrounded by light and that she was convinced she was safe. It is doubtful whether such revelations were of any comfort to Ciss, who was ill with worry.

The wireless station at Kupang on Timor stayed open until 11 p.m. on Thursday night and all sub-stations were told to be alert for news of Amy. At Surabaya the Dutch East Indies authorities prepared to send two seaplanes to search for her.

At a quarter to five in the morning the phone rang in the Johnson household. 'For the last three weeks we have lived in extremities of joy and anguish,' Will said.[13] The news was good: Amy had landed near the remote village of Halilulik, twelve miles from Atamboea. 'It is impossible to describe the relief,' Will told the waiting world.[14]

Amy's forced landing had been the most terrifying so far, when the pages of a *Boys' Own* storybook had sprung vividly to life. The journey had started well with fine weather but when Amy faced the final, long sea crossing from the island of Flores to Timor she had been startled by the sudden descent of night. The craggy coastline of Timor appeared just as light was fading and a tiny island enabled her to find her location on the map, but the poor visibility meant she could not spot Atamboea. She took *Jason* lower and lower as she desperately searched for somewhere to land, aware that her fuel was nearly finished. There seemed no choice but to head for a bumpy field. As she touched down she realised that she had chosen a piece of ground pimpled with six-foot-high anthills. *Jason* dodged and weaved round them until the machine came to a standstill, a mound supporting one wing as if the plane were propping up a bar. Incredibly, *Jason* was undamaged.

When the noise of *Jason*'s engine faded Amy heard high-pitched yelling and a group of native men ran from their mud-and-straw huts, 'hair flying in the wind, and knives in their hands or between their

red-stained teeth . . . '15 They surrounded *Jason* and Amy sat cradling
her revolver. The stand-off was brief: the leader stepped forward,
saluted her and then cautiously touched *Jason* and then his pilot. He
returned to the huddle of men who started to talk in excited whispers.
The leader spoke to Amy. The one word she could make out was
'pastor' which gave her the reassurance to take the tribesman's hand
'with the utmost confidence' as he led her through the darkness. The
other men prodded her gently and the women of the tribe moved
forward to take a closer look at *Jason*. They walked through the jungle
for about five miles until they found a large log building. She sat down
on the steps and fell into a deep sleep until she was woken by a bearded
white man whom she assumed was the pastor.

Although he spoke some French Amy found it difficult to make
herself understood. He gestured for her to come inside. The pastor had
obviously broken into his emergency supplies to prepare a meal that
was more lavish than his normal, basic fare and she dined on tinned
cheese and wine. Their quiet dinner was shattered by the sound of a
car's hooter that signalled the arrival of the Portuguese commandant
of the aerodrome at Atamboea. He explained in English that a bush-
fire had recently reduced the aerodrome to a blackened patch that
made it very difficult to find in twilight. The ground staff had watched
as Amy flew straight over it and then followed *Jason* in a trail that led to
the pastor's log cabin.

Amy spent the night at the aerodrome before returning to *Jason*,
accompanied by a donkey with two tins of petrol strapped to its back.
It took a couple of hours to filter enough petrol to keep *Jason* in the air
for ten minutes. Lack of space meant she wanted to take off using a
'flying start'. This involved three people holding the wings down while
she opened the throttle up, but the tribesmen were so alarmed by the
roar of the engine that they ran off at the crucial moment. Instead she
had to resort to a normal take-off, just clipping the tops of the trees.

The aerodrome was one of the most basic she had seen. There were
no hangars or markings and the black dust from the bush-fire irritated
her eyes. The petrol was red with rust and, conscious of the 500-mile
sea crossing ahead of her, she was even more careful to filter it properly. There was no shade and a guard stood by her watching in case a
spark from the engine caused another fire. That night she was so
excited at the prospect of reaching her destination that she found it
very difficult to sleep.

Day 20 (Saturday, 24 May)

Amy left Timor with no weather report to guide her but she knew that Shell had arranged for an oil tanker, *Phorus*, to stand guard half-way across the Timor Sea. She calculated that she should spot it within three hours and that by 2 p.m. she might catch her first glimpse of Australia when the dark cloud of Melville Island would appear on the horizon. Strong winds could delay the island's appearance and she told herself that she would not start to worry until 3.30 p.m.

In Britain the *Daily Mail* had drafted in the veteran airman Sir Alan Cobham as a pundit to give his view on what Amy faced. 'It is a tropical sea, of course, and infested with sharks. Perhaps never before in her flight has it been more essential to start with her engine in perfect fettle,' he told readers.[16]

Every pilot who attempted to fly to Australia dreaded the Timor crossing, coming as it did when they were at their most exhausted. Sharks stalked the area and some airmen reported watching in horror as the still sea bubbled into life as a shark and its prey thrashed around in the water before calmness returned again, a red stain in the blueness the one clue to the life-and-death struggle.

Amy's experience over the Java Sea had left her with a fear of long stretches of water. She was conscious, too, that she must not let her excitement at nearing Australia lead to a slip in concentration. The sea was calm but she could see black clouds on the horizon. She made a wide detour round them, and two further gloomy patches. When the weather improved she started to worry about the engine, which was spluttering. Convinced that a speck of dirt was irritating the carburettor, she drove the engine forward to try to flush it out. Her action was successful but resulted in black smoke pouring out of the exhaust.

With the engine ticking over, she had nothing to worry about except boredom and nothing to look at but the sea and the sky. She forced herself to delay glancing at her watch until she thought two hours had passed but found a mere ten minutes had gone by. She counted as far as she could in French and then German and recited all the poems and nursery rhymes she could remember. She began to sing but gave this up because the sound of the engine drowned out her voice.

Three hours after she had set off the shape of a tanker appeared on the horizon. As she drew closer she saw someone hurrying to the wireless cabin. She was no longer alone; her progress was being flashed back to Hull and the rest of the world in a spider's web of good news. The crewmen on board cheered as *Jason* flew overhead; they were 'good old British cheers', not tribal yells and, in her exuberance, Amy swooped down and hurled a cake at one of the sailors.

As well as a huge confidence boost, sighting the smoke from the *Phorus*'s funnel allowed her to correct her direction. After another three hours the shadow of Melville Island appeared. As it drew closer Amy was unable to contain her excitement at leaving the open sea behind her. She began to rock backwards and forwards in her seat, slapping the sides of *Jason* as if he were a horse about to cross the finishing line. She tossed her notes on how to recognise the island over the side shouting, 'Away, away. I'm safe over Melville Island.'[17] Remembering that Port Darwin was difficult to find, she tried to calm herself, but her excitement was out of control. When Darwin harbour appeared she grabbed the air-cushion that she had been given in case she crashed in water and started pummelling it, finally hurling it over the side with the words: 'You silly old bladder, I want you not.'[18]

Several planes set out from Australia to meet her but each failed to find *Jason* and Amy arrived at Fanny Bay, Port Darwin, alone. As she flew over the mango trees she glanced down at the aerodrome and saw a space between two planes. Amid her euphoria she had the surreally practical thought that this was where 'they' would park *Jason*. Gazing down at the sea of upturned faces, she wondered why the people did not rush through the fences like the other crowds she had encountered. Suddenly all she could think of was her mother. The pent-up emotions of the previous two years, Irene's suicide and Hans's rejection, combined with the struggle of the last three weeks spent in the tiny cockpit. She began to sob, struggling to see through the tears as *Jason* bounced his way down onto the ground.

When the plane came to a standstill Amy threw off her goggles, took off her life-belt and combed her hair before climbing hesitantly out. A doctor in a white coat approached the sun-blistered figure but she seemed startled by his appearance and they both retreated momentarily in a courtly do-si-do. A reporter rushed forward, notebook in hand, and asked, 'Well, what shall I tell the dear old world?' Before Amy, still deaf from the noise of the engine, could answer, a policeman, attempting to restrain the crowds, shouted: 'Get back, get back!' His harsh cry burst the bubble.

It was 3.30 p.m. on Empire Day. After a formal welcome by the Government Resident, a civic reception and a dance, Amy was allowed, finally, to sleep. She awoke eleven hours later.

Will, Ciss and their two daughters were unable to rest and rose at four in the morning to pace round and round the telephone. 'Directly it rang,' Will said, 'we felt instinctively that she was safe. I would not like to go through another such night for a fortune.'[19] In London the newspaper billboards announced simply: 'She's there' and 'Amy's triumph'.

Winifred, who had been collecting cuttings about her friend's progress, stowed away two of the placards, which she kept for the rest of her life.

PART 3

Celebrity

Chapter 14

The Gimme Gimme Girl
(24 May – 7 July 1930)

For nearly three weeks *Jason's* cockpit had been Amy's whole world, a protective womb through which she glimpsed the light below her feet or endured the knocks that buffeted the tiny plane. The scenery that sped by was incidental and unreal; her life began and ended with the wood-and-fabric capsule, the four dials in front of her and the untidy tangle of wires that escaped from them. While she was flying Amy's fate was in her own hands. She was answerable to no one and spoke only to herself, *Jason* or the few possessions, like the 'silly old bladder', that shared the cockpit with her. What she looked like, said or did were of no importance. The steady beat of the engine measured out her day's flight with the precision of a metronome; she lived for the moment and had no thoughts for the future.

When *Jason* landed at Darwin it was as if a diving-bell had shot to the surface of the sea. Amy needed time to adjust to the different pressures of the world she had just re-entered; instead she was confronted by popping flash-bulbs and the sorts of crowds that she had only ever seen at football matches. There was no opportunity to describe to Will or Ciss, or a close friend like Winifred, the terror and anxiety of her journey: the forced desert landing, being lost in the mountains and the sheer loneliness of the long-distance flyer.[1] An unguarded, spontaneous outpouring might have provided the necessary catharsis to put the journey behind her. But Amy was forced to present an authorised account of her adventures that was carefully monitored and filtered by the *Daily Mail*.

Even when she spoke to her family on the telephone five days after her arrival, the conversation's true purpose was a photo opportunity. Will sat holding the main receiver while Ciss, Molly, Betty, Jimmy and Jack listened in on tentacle-like extension lines that formed a giant octopus with Will at the centre. But long-distance phone calls were so rare that what should have been a fond reunion over the air-waves became a music-hall turn in which Molly insisted on shouting down the line and no one was quite sure whom they were talking to.

When Will said, 'I'm glad to hear your voice. Are you very well?' Amy's reply revealed her utter confusion: 'I am very well indeed. Who are you?'[2]

Over the next six weeks she was paraded in front of millions of people who came to gawp and claw at the edges of the dream she represented. Every section of Australian society wanted a piece of her: paraplegic war veterans strained over the side of their cots to catch a glimpse, toned lifeguards in swimming-caps and modest bathing costumes stood to attention as her car passed and women's groups, from the openly feminist to the unashamedly homely, invited her to lunch. A horticulturist named a rose after her and the Royal Automobile Club of Victoria served a menu that took diners through the highs and lows of Amy's flight from a 'crème Croydon' via 'côtelettes d'agneau à la Calcutta' and 'asperges à la Surabaya' to a dessert of 'Glace Johnnie'. Amy's face stared out from shop windows all over Australia next to Union Jack flags and models of *Jason*. Every day except Sunday brimmed with official engagements and endless panegyrics. The official, meandering speeches given in her name became a byword for cliché: a new 'talkie' movie was described as being as 'witless as a mayoral address of welcome to Amy Johnson'.[3]

At first Amy appeared to enjoy the adulation. She was shocked and totally unprepared for her own popularity but the adrenaline of finishing the epic journey sustained her for several days. Until she arrived in Australia she had only ever made one public speech and at university she was too shy to join in debates. Now everyone wanted to hear her voice: in Sydney alone she made forty-seven speeches in four days, speaking in a strange, hybrid tone. Her delivery was slow and she paused after every syllable and line, her voice rising when she came to the end of a sentence with the gaucheness of a Joyce Grenfell character. She frequently stressed words that needed no emphasis while her body remained static and her voice strained to escape. It was as if someone had told her the secrets of public speaking were talking slowly and varying the tone. At home schoolfriends watched cine film of her with amazement, unable to comprehend the strange creature they had known so well.

She chose words that were so quaint and understated that they appeared comical and endearing rather than patronising. 'I say, people! I forgot to say that I landed here on Empire Day, and I am wondering if you will look on that as of any special significance,' she told the crowds at Darwin Town Hall.[4] After each speech Amy smiled a broad smile and stretched her arm straight up in the air to wave her hand at the crowd in a vigorous, athletic movement as if she were reaching up to jerk her propeller into action. She often ran her tongue over her two front dentures in one of several nervous tics but the press had no idea her teeth were false and marvelled at their whiteness.

Australians liked her informality – she interrupted one speaker who referred to her as 'Miss Amy', insisting that she should be called 'Johnnie' – and her obvious delight in their country and its climate. She made *Jason* sound like a pet dog rather than a plane that had transported her across 11,000 miles, leaving it to newspapers to endow the machine with mythical qualities by regularly referring to her journey as *Jason's* Quest. Her oft-repeated understatement, 'But the engine was wonderful,' became a catch-phrase across Australia and her habit of removing her hat before making a speech made headwear infra dig. Hairdressers rushed to master the 'Amy Johnson wave' or the 'Johnnie shingle' that their customers demanded.

Australians were ferocious in their welcome. The independence movement was in its infancy and this visitor who had travelled across the world from the seat of Empire to see them was given an ecstatic reception, although there was always a threat of violence lurking in the crowd. The Australian public took liberties with their heroes that were unheard of in Britain and they could turn nasty if they felt the recipient of their fervour did not return their admiration with equal enthusiasm. When the Prince of Wales, the future Edward VIII, visited in June 1920 a crowd ripped off the folded hood of his official car and wrecked its running-board. He was prodded and slapped on the back and his hands became swollen after too many vigorous greetings.[5] Celebrities were public property to a greater extent than in Britain and when the Prince of Wales was reluctant to appear, an angry crowd counted slowly and menacingly from one to ten in an attempt to flush him out.

Amy was a celebrity before she touched down at Darwin; as soon as she stepped out of the plane she became a commodity traded between different factions. The press wanted as much of her as they could get; Shell and Castrol were in constant competition to be seen as her patron; and manufacturers from spark-plug makers to Waterman pens sought her endorsement. She was physically and mentally at the end of her tether. In the three weeks since leaving Croydon she had cajoled *Jason*, who in most instances was awash with highly flammable petrol, into the air twenty-four times, and twenty-four times she had tried to steer him towards a safe landing – though in practice her struggle amounted to no more than an exercise in damage limitation. Her ordeal had been solitary and self-imposed; overnight her fate was delivered into the hands of a host of local dignitaries, newspaper reporters and company promoters. After her eleven-hour sleep Amy got up, played a game of tennis and answered some of the hundreds of letters awaiting her arrival. Then, a day and a half after touching down at Port Darwin, she embarked on a tour of Australia that was, in its own way, every bit as gruelling as her solo flight from Croydon. The only time during the next three weeks when she appeared totally relaxed was when she fed baby kangaroos bottles of milk in a photo opportunity that her love of animals meant she genuinely enjoyed.

Two planes, representing Shell and Wakefields, accompanied Amy on her tour of the country. Ostensibly they were there to provide a dignified escort and to help her find her way over the difficult Northern Territory. Charles Scott flew one of the aircraft, a fast cabin biplane jointly sponsored by the *Sydney Sun*, and carrying Wakefield's representative Captain Stanley Bird and a reporter as passengers. Scott was a tall, domineering and frustrated man who had flown for both the RAF and Qantas Airways. He longed to become a record-breaking pilot himself and this, together with a dislike of the English and a scornful attitude towards women, meant he found Amy's success intolerable. He was shocked that she had completed the journey from England and determined that, while they flew together, she would be in no doubt about his superiority.

On the morning of Monday, 26 May Scott tore off at a furious pace south from Darwin towards Daly Waters, leaving the rival Shell plane and Amy straining to keep him within their sights. Scott justified his speed by saying that they had a tight schedule to keep to but he was fully aware that Amy, like all pilots new to Australia, would find it difficult to navigate her way through blinding sunshine and across a terrain in which the only landmarks were the occasional well or dirt track.[6] It was a stretch of Western Australia that Scott knew intimately. The next few days followed a pattern in which Amy spent the hours in the air battling to keep up with Scott and the time on the ground fending off braying crowds.

By Tuesday the three planes had reached Queensland, refuelling at Cloncurry before racing on to Longreach – a stretch of the route in which Amy could not resist swooping down to 'buzz' a herd of 'roos' that she spotted lolloping across the dusty plain beneath her.[7] Longreach was the capital of the sheep-farming district of western Queensland and from the air the houses' corrugated iron roofs looked like a pile of empty kerosene cans flashing in the sunshine.[8] As soon as they landed the mob engulfed Amy before four policemen carried her to safety.

De Havilland's Australian sales manager, Ian Grabowsky, who was waiting to greet them, was shocked at the contrast between the bold, smiling woman of the world's newsreel and the figure skulking by her plane, alone and ignored. When he approached Amy with a message of welcome from De Havilland, she appeared overwhelmed by his concern. Grabowsky's suggestion that she have a rest and a wash prompted Amy to confide in him that she was exhausted and experiencing the 'usual feminine problem'.[9] He explained to Scott and Bird the necessity for Amy to have a break, but Bird retorted that Amy should be used to dealing with her 'feminine problem'. Both he and Scott were adamant that their priority was to keep to a busy schedule. Amy had always suffered from the most extreme period pains; she had become used to being laid low every month, but the fact that she struggled with premenstrual symptoms, on top of all the other obstacles, makes her achievement even more staggering. The fact that this physical difficulty – unlike a problem with a magneto or a monsoon – was unmentionable and misunderstood made it harder to bear.

From Longreach the trio of planes raced on to Charleville, another centre of sheep farming, but the mayor and his official welcoming party were crestfallen when there was no sign of Amy. Scott claimed he had looked for her as soon as she had disappeared but had reassured himself that if she could navigate her way to Australia, finding Charleville should not be a problem.[10] Eventually news of her arrived from the small town of Quilpie 125 miles to the west. Later she told Grabowsky that her period pains, fatigue and headache were so oppressive that she could not face another official lunch after her experience with the mob at Longreach. Instead she had followed the railway line away from the pre-planned bustle to a spot where no one was expecting Amy Johnson and where she could rest and catch her breath. She told newspapers that she had simply got lost.

Jason finally arrived at Charleville as dusk was falling; a huge crowd had assembled and car headlamps blazed out in the fading light. The police were again ineffectual and the crowd again crushed in on Amy before she was thrust into a car and driven to a hotel where she burst into hysterical tears. Bird was scathing when she was too upset to speak to her parents on the phone: 'She is afraid of nothing in the world, from a spider or a mouse to a tropical rainstorm – except crowds,' he told the press.[11] After being mobbed two days in a row she felt alone and unprotected; she began to dread the sea of expectant faces waiting for her at each official function. The experience was repeated at Toowoomba, but she still faced the biggest ordeal of all – the huge reception awaiting her at Brisbane.

Jason climbed over the mountain range to the west of the city and started to glide down over the coastal plains. As Amy circled Brisbane's Eagle Farm aerodrome just before half past two *Jason's* engine began to splutter before it cut out altogether and pancaked onto the ground. Twenty thousand people waiting below could not work out what was happening and watched in disbelief as *Jason* ploughed through the fence and into the cornfield beyond, catapulting over onto its back, its propeller crunching and its wings crushing into the ground like a paper plane. A few spectators who were yards from the crash raced over and found Amy sitting blankly upside down in the cockpit. She calmly unclipped her safety harness and was lifted from the wreckage. A cheer went up as the crowd spotted her picking her way out of the debris; the drama of her crash landing merely fuelled their need to see and hear her. Two burly policemen picked her up under the arms and guided her firmly to a raised platform. She looked dazed and shocked, her pullover was ripped and one boot was torn.

In this new world order where even a near-fatal crash was insufficient to deny the crowd their glimpse of celebrity, Amy gave her traditional speech in an unnaturally loud voice as if the drama of her landing meant everything had to be bigger and brasher than usual. In the procession that took her through Brisbane mounted police cantered beside the open car and crowds climbed onto tramcars for a better view. Amy was frozen in a plastic, mannequin-like pose; she felt apart from the rumpus, as if someone else was causing the disturbance. Wakefields' representative held her upright while Bird supported her right arm to help her wave to the crowds; her smile was fixed and unflinching. At Government House, where she was due to stay, she finally allowed herself to unbend into tears. Only a few engagements were cancelled but doctors advised her not to fly *Jason*. Instead Australian National Airways offered to take her to Sydney in one of their airliners and then transfer her to a six-seater Hawk Moth biplane owned by De Havilland's managing director in Australia.

While Amy was in Brisbane news came through that she had been made a Commander of the Order of the British Empire (CBE) in the King's Birthday Honours. Newspapers argued that the award did not do justice to her achievement and demanded that she should be given a more illustrious title or that a special one should be invented to mark her own brand of heroism.[12] Amy's heroic flight made the careers of the two other women who were honoured – the nursery school pioneer Miss Margaret MacMillan and the novelist Annie Burnett – appear plodding. But Amy was too young to assume the title of dame – especially since newspapers regularly referred to her as a 'girl'. Typically, dames were women from the more sedate world of the arts: the Shakespearean actress Ellen Terry and the classical singers Nellie Melba and Clara Butt. The accolade was bestowed when they were well into middle age, if not dotage, by which time they had proved the longevity of their respectability and there was little chance of them causing a scandal. Only marriage to a peer would qualify Amy to become a 'lady'; but British newspapers demanded that Parliament pass an act to grant her a title. It was the sort of very British conundrum that delighted the foreign press. As one New York paper commented: 'The theory seems to be that while a dame can be a lady, not every lady can be a dame – and no reflection intended on Miss Johnson. Quite the contrary, in fact.'[13]

But Amy's appeal lay in the fact that her background and age disqualified her from grand titles; she was simply 'Amy' or 'Johnnie'. At least ten songs and several poems were written to celebrate her flight[14] but by far the most popular was 'Amy, wonderful Amy', a lilting tune performed by Jack Hylton and his orchestra. The chorus, 'Amy, wonderful Amy, How can you blame me for loving you?' casts her as the nation's sweetheart and captures perfectly the languid, cocktail-hour atmosphere of the 1930s. It is impossible not to sway to the tune which became Amy's theme song and which, for many people, still remains so. 'Amy, wonderful Amy' was part of the soundtrack of 1930s Britain. The 'talkies', the wireless and gramophone records made daily life noisier than it had ever been and Amy's name and idiosyncratic voice appeared in all three media.

'The Story of My Flight', which she recorded on 9 June 1930, has a 'Listen with Mother' quality to it in which Amy talks about *Jason* as her co-conspirator in their awfully big adventure, but despite the gung-ho language her voice betrays an immense fatigue:

> *Jason* is a dear; he's behaving splendidly. Look how he's weathering this terrible dust storm just outside Baghdad . . . Here we are in India. How proud my *Jason* was to reach here in six days, but alas his pride was quickly dashed. The monsoon's raced us after all . . . Poor old *Jason* was so upset that he ran his nose right into a ditch in the wrong field when we were trying to find the racecourse at Rangoon.[15]

Amy's brand of heroism suited the moment perfectly. Countries which had been physically and emotionally eviscerated by the Somme and Gallipoli sought an antidote to a war that had turned out to be an inglorious campaign. Ex-servicemen faced a battle to find work in towns and countryside blighted by a worldwide depression; Amy was the ideal inspiration. She represented a masculine struggle against the elements while all the time remaining essentially feminine. Her enemy was not some innocent, anonymous soldier on the other side of a trench but time and the monsoon. She sought direction in a bewildered world; her quest was elemental and uncomplicated.

In the fan mail that poured into the Johnsons' home she was frequently compared to Joan of Arc, that other helmeted female adventurer who had been granted sainthood in 1920 and who featured in films and plays throughout the decade.[16] When young girls visiting Madame Tussaud's in 1932 were asked whom they would most like to be when they grew up, they placed Amy Johnson as their second choice after the wartime nurse Edith Cavell and before Joan of Arc.[17]

Amy was closest to the Joan of Arc described in a Jerome Kern song: the ideal 'it' girl who escapes her parents' desire to keep her washing dishes.[18] Amy, like Joan of Arc, was the sassy out-of-town girl who possessed a virginal purity capable of uniting nations at a time of great uncertainty. As one Australian paper put it, 'We realise how deep the feeling of Australia, the daughter, is through this brave girl's efforts, to dear Mother England . . .'[19]

Although Amy was quintessentially English, her appeal was universal and she received letters, scraps of notepaper and postcards from around the world. The majority came from the Empire or the United States but her fans wrote from countries as diverse as Finland and Greece. She was so well known that many envelopes were addressed in the vaguest terms: 'To Miss Amy Johnson, The World's Wonder Winged Sweetheart, Hull, England'; 'Miss Amy Johnson, The Empire's Idol, Hull, England'; 'Miss Amy Johnson, Queen of the Air, c/o London Post Office, Hull, Europe'; 'Miss Amy Johnson, c/o Aerodrome (flying station), London, England'. The most succinct read: 'Miss Amy Johnson, wat flies in England' and 'Miss Amy Johnson, Famous Airwoman'. They all found their way to 85 Park Avenue and in Australia a secretary worked full time answering her mail.

Amy was the most famous of a group of sportswomen who were fêted in 1930 for their success in male-dominated worlds. 'Bounding' Betty Nuthall won trophies in tennis, Joyce Wethered and Diana Fishwick challenged men at golf, Marjorie Foster was one of the best rifle shots in the British Empire and Jo Carstairs broke speed-boat records. But Amy was different from these other female heroes. She was more accessible and the admirers who wrote to her from around the world felt they knew her personally. When she was in the air she was completely alone, helped by no one and reliant on her own resources. This last trait appealed to a generation who felt they had been cheated by a government who had led them into war and economic depression. Amy also retained her femininity despite the grime and grease of long-distance flying and this was something that newspapers approved of at a time when there was unease about androgyny among women.

The King and Queen and Prime Minister Ramsay MacDonald sent telegrams of congratulations, as did every important person in the world of flying, including Colonel and Mrs Lindbergh. Louis Blériot, who in July 1909 had become the first person to fly across the English Channel in an aeroplane and was now the grand old man of aviation, sent a cable from Paris that said simply, 'Bravo'. When Albert Einstein gave a lecture at Nottingham University the fact that he had never heard of Amy Johnson was reported as the most startling aspect of his visit and proof that cerebrally he inhabited another planet.[20]

Having a daughter who was a CBE was an unimagined honour for Will and Ciss but they were more concerned about the gossip and hints that appeared daily in their newspapers. There were rumours that Amy was about to marry one of the thousand Australians who had proposed to her and that her health was breaking down. Will fired off a cable demanding to know exactly how she was feeling; Amy told him not to worry but cabled Jack a more honest summary: 'Am wearying of too much sugar. For God's sake send salty cable at once.' Jack told her to be strong, adding that he, too, was worried about her health.

Will and Ciss were beginning to feel the strain of their daughter's reflected glory and there were sympathetic letters in The Times complaining of press intrusion that had turned them into a 'music-hall turn'.[21] The Graphic asked whether the world really needed to know where Amy's parents shopped.[22] The whole family was learning that they now had to be careful about what they did and said. Molly, in a throw-away line about Amy's childhood habit of using rooks for gun-target practice, was mortified when bird-lovers denounced Amy as cruel. Will's traditional forms of escape – travel and the Rotary Club – offered no refuge: he was now a world-famous father. During the ocean crossing to an international Rotary Convention in Chicago he, Ciss and Molly were pestered by passengers who wanted to know all about Amy. Will, who was always afraid of being taken advantage of, found it increasingly difficult to distinguish enthusiastic, but harmless, interest in his family from blatant exploitation, and Ciss complained of the count-less begging letters they received. Jimmy and Jack had provided a bedrock of support when dealing with the press, but the triumvirate was starting to crumble, with Jack the one about to be left out in the cold. Will's growing suspicions of his daughter's long-time mentor and the man who had shown most consistent support were encouraged by Jimmy and may have been sparked by an interview that appeared in the *Daily Express* of 20 May 1930. A reporter described how Jack sat up all night, his arm in a splint, awaiting news of Amy, a photo of her in evening dress at his elbow: 'I can hardly tell you how I feel about her,' he gushed, 'so proud, so more than proud . . . she's done even more than I expected of her, and that was enough, I can tell you. And yet, with all she's done, she's still very much a girl. She's best of all in her dirty over-alls. And next time she does a flight like this – don't be surprised if I go with her!'

Will may have feared that Jack's affection was getting out of hand or that he was usurping his role of father. Perhaps he was worried that Jack might demand a financial stake in Amy's success or that his interview with the *Daily Express* would endanger the *Daily Mail* deal. Whatever the reason, Jack's sudden banishment was encouraged by Jimmy, and Will cabled Amy in Sydney just before he left for America: 'Advise you be very careful regarding Jack advise discontinue sending him letters or telegrams if Jack asks to accompany you on lecture tour advise refer him to *Daily Mail* . . . this advice in your interests. Jack not seriously ill.' Amy can only have found her father's terse message bewildering and distressing.

After five days in Brisbane Amy left to fly south to Sydney in the comfort of an eight-seater airliner that had the luxury of three engines. The journey lasted six hours and Amy took the controls briefly from the two pilots, Charles Ulm and Jim Mollison. It was the first time she had flown anything larger than a Gipsy Moth and a plane that had a steering-wheel rather than a joystick. She chatted with Jim during the flight and he managed to extract the promise of two dances at the ball to be held in her honour at Sydney.

Twenty-six planes, six piloted by women, escorted Amy across the city and passed the two sides of the half-built Sydney Harbour Bridge while ships and factories blew shrill whistles in welcome. Around 75,000 fans were waiting at Mascot aerodrome but again there was very little crowd control.[23] Amy attended the ball against doctors' orders and was escorted by the Governor of New South Wales, Sir Philip

Game. The retired Air Vice-Marshal was not prepared to relinquish the trophy on his arm and snubbed Jim when he protested that he had been promised two dances. The incident left a deep impression on him but failed to register with Amy: Jim was just another admirer who refused to take 'no' for an answer. When they met again two years later it was on a much more equal footing.

By the beginning of June there were rumours that Amy was on the verge of a nervous breakdown; doctors said she was so weak that she must avoid shaking hands or standing for too long.[24] She was confused about which parts of the media she could or could not speak to, cabling her father to ask whether she should have anything to do with Fox Movietone: 'I am greatly distressed and present uncertainty contributing largely to my nervous condition . . .'[25]

At a lunch for 1200 people given by a women's organisation in her honour she sat with bowed head, scarcely speaking and toying with a little silver pencil throughout the meal. 'Johnnie at times looked rather a pathetic little figure,' the *Australian Sun* commented.[26] 'We will have to look after Amy Johnson, and Amy will have to do what she is told. Otherwise there will be a broken little heroine among us,' the *Daily Pictorial* warned its readers.[27] But it was Amy's supposed minders who were in danger of crushing their most valuable possession. She was manhandled wherever she went and much of the time there was a representative from Wakefields, Shell or De Havilland at either elbow, subtly but firmly guiding her in the direction they wanted her to go. Mostly Amy gave no inkling that she might find this physical encroachment unbearable. Occasionally, though, the camera caught her gently trying to shake her arms free from the puppeteers who were surreptitiously edging her into the best photo opportunity while she smiled on unflinchingly. Sometimes the pressure became too much and she wept or lashed out: in Perth she punched a man who tried to kiss her. The outburst made headlines around the world; newspapers interpreted it as further proof of her spirit rather than a sign that she was close to exhaustion.[28] In a mischievous gesture Lord Inchcape, chairman of P&O, presented her with a pair of boxing-gloves.

Despite the straitened times everyone wanted to give her something; gifts included a vacuum cleaner, a gold nugget, an umbrella, a portable gramophone player and all sorts of furniture.[29] An Arts Club in Darwin sent her a sealskin fur coat trimmed with natural squirrel and anxiously urged her to make it clear to the press that the skin was seal rather than common rabbit. Dress shops cabled requests for her measurements so that they could design her outfits and send her every possible piece of clothing and jewellery for any time of the day or night. A Chinese woman in Darwin gave her a jade ring and silk pyjamas and another admirer sent her an 'A'-shaped brooch studded with diamonds. When she finally set sail for home a crate bearing some of her most valuable gifts and marked 'Amy Johnson, c/o *Daily Mail*' was steered onto the ship on a wheelbarrow. Only members of the Otago and Southland General Labourers' Union said quietly, but firmly, that a shilling fund was 'altogether unnecessary' as Miss Johnson was not in need of financial help and that any money collected should go to the unemployed.[30]

As Amy's tour of Australia drew to an end newspapers started to run out of things to say about her. *Smith's Weekly* now attacked the weak spot in Joan of Arc's armour: the relish with which she accepted gifts. Amy was now on such a high pedestal that a fall was likely to be painful; *Smith's Weekly* went into battle with all guns blazing. In a stinging front-page attack the newspaper claimed that she had been given a total of £12,675 and described her as the 'Air Digger of the Skyway' and 'The Gimme Gimme Girl'. The newspaper also concocted a fictitious letter from Amy to her parents:

> I didn't get much out of my trip to Newcastle. So I took the mayor's necktie. I had to take something otherwise they wouldn't have known I had been there . . .
>
> I'm sorry there is no Fishmonger's Guild out here, otherwise I'd have been on another £100 as their guest through dad's association with that ancient trade. But I do loathe crowds staring at me for nothing. I don't mind them when they have been counted at the box office. Such as the other night when I attended a theatre and the management gave me £100.
>
> My right palm is all itching. I must rub it on wood, so it's sure to come good, and then on brick, so it's sure to come quick –
>
> Your Johnnie, The Cash and Carry Girl.

The letter was a clever parody of how Amy's image in Australia had become a marketable commodity and it was certainly true that she generated a lot of money, but it was disingenuous to claim that her main concern was cash. She refused to sign autographs, but her reluctance was due to a painful arm, not an itchy palm. The attack by *Smith's Weekly* gave Amy-mania a new boost as publications rushed to her defence, several repeating the allegations and quoting from the letter in a ploy that allowed them to appear simultaneously sensational and sympathetic. The vitriol, which attacked her two psychological blind spots – her family name and her need for financial security – left her feeling crushed. In tears, she hurled *Smith's Weekly* behind a piano.[31] She told *The Truth* that the allegations had made her 'blood boil' and she vehemently denied that she had asked for anything.[32] Amy was especially sensitive to allegations that she had casually accepted £4000 worth of clothes without any full appreciation of their worth. She protested that she had received only two pairs of shoes and one fur coat:[33]

> In fact, I have very carefully avoided and definitely refused many offers made to me to appear for five minutes or so at some place or other, and be paid for it. I have done this so as not to give the slightest handle on which to hang any suggestion of my commercialising my flight and the Australian public, and this is what I get! Oh! it's not a bit fair or sporting! The only time I have gone to anything like that has been when the proceeds were to go to charity or the unemployed.

The Truth argued that the figure of £12,675 quoted by *Smith's Weekly* included the £10,000 fee from the *Daily Mail* and £300 that Amy had given to charities out of the £1000 she had received from exhibiting *Jason*. According to *The Truth* Amy returned to Britain with £1675 (£51,841 in today's money) – a generous, but not outrageous, sum by the standards of the day. Amy was no more or less greedy than other record-breaking pilots and the generosity of fans and patrons was an important way of supplementing an erratic income. The Australian Government gave Ross and Keith Smith a £10,000 prize for their flight from England to Australia and Smithy and Ulm £5000 for crossing the Pacific. Hinkler received £2000 and £150 for his war service, although technically he was ineligible for this payment because he had not returned to live in Australia. The Government also waived the tax due on the £10,000 given to him in Australia.[34] Hinkler left the country weighed down with gifts from admirers, although they were fewer in number than Amy's. It seemed natural to buy her clothes and jewellery; gifts for Hinkler were more problematic and the most lavish were a gold cigarette-case (although he did not smoke) and a diamond watch for his wife. Labour Premier James Scullin turned down a suggestion that Amy should be given money.

When she closed the door on the luxurious ship's cabin specially provided for her by Lord Inchcape she was shutting out a hullabaloo that she and many other people felt had got out of hand. She set sail for England on 7 July firmly resolved to spend the passage as a tourist, but when she reached Cairo she was told that a book about her life written by the journalist Charles Dixon was being rushed out to capitalise on her fame. It was essentially a 'cuttings job', a hagiography of her and other women flyers. There was nothing malicious about it – as Crockers pointed out to Amy when she asked them to try to stop its publication. *The Times* described the work as a travel book, rather than a biography, and noted that the most astonishing aspect was the speed with which it had been turned round: 'If Miss Johnson set a record for women flyers, Mr Dixon must have done so among book producers.'[35]

The long sea journey restored Amy's equilibrium and she arrived in Egypt at the end of July looking relaxed and sun-tanned. But her enthusiastic reception in Cairo reminded her of her harrowing experience in Australia. She was given a state luncheon and the Egyptian Government awarded her the gold medal of merit – the first time the king had conferred the honour on a woman. Even when she was climbing the pyramids by moonlight or visiting the jewels of Tutankhamen she was on display and she told the Egyptian press that she was fearful of the reception that awaited her in London.

She left Egypt in the comparative comfort of an Imperial Airways aeroplane that stopped at Crete, Athens, Salonica, Budapest and Vienna on its way to Croydon. At Vienna Amy spoke to her father who confirmed her worst fears about the welcome that awaited her. She spent the rest of the flight working on a speech for her arrival in London. As she scribbled away, street artists were already sketching her face on pavements for curious members of the public to walk all over.

Chapter 15

Home Again
(4 August – October 1930)

Despite intermittent drizzle, groups of picnickers took up their positions at Croydon Airport from mid afternoon. Amy was due to land at 6 p.m. on a Monday that was, conveniently, a bank holiday. Conveniently, too, the Duke and Duchess of York's second child, whose birth at Glamis Castle in Scotland was eagerly awaited, failed to appear before Amy. Margaret, the future Queen Elizabeth II's younger sister, was born over a fortnight later.

The atmosphere resembled an open-air concert as spectators waited good-humouredly for the arrival of the star performer while the organisers did their best to entertain them with small distractions. Amy was due to leave Vienna at 7 a.m. aboard the *City of Glasgow* but rain and strong winds forced the airmail plane to make several unscheduled stops for refuelling.

The public-address system rattled out bulletins of her progress to a crowd swollen to 200,000.[1] An estimated 150,000 people had greeted Lindbergh when he landed at Croydon from Le Bourget after his transatlantic crossing in 1927 and police were anxious to avoid the same hysterical scenes of fainting women and crushed silk hats. Specially reinforced iron fences were erected and extra police were drafted in.

As afternoon drifted into evening the airfield crackled with anticipation. *Jason*, in gleaming new paintwork, sat like a prize exhibit parked in a space railed off from the crowds. The *Daily Mail* was fully aware that Amy and *Jason* were a double-act and that the presence of the frail biplane reinforced the heroic journey of the girl from Hull. The newspaper appointed William Courtenay, a freelance air correspondent and publicity manager, to organise Amy's homecoming and tour of Britain, and he went personally to supervise *Jason*'s crated arrival by ship at Marseilles.

Will and Ciss were confined to the VIP enclosure with three cabinet ministers and other dignitaries where, as the hours passed, the small talk became strained. There was no consensus about how to dress for a heroine's homecoming: the Mayor of Croydon stood out in his scarlet robes and cocked hat, while the MP for Hull, Lieutenant Commander Kenworthy, looked sombre in a grey morning-coat and a top hat; Branks, Lord Thomson, Secretary of State for Air, and Lord Wakefield played safe in their dark suits. Ciss peeped out from underneath a cloche hat and an extravagant fur-collared coat; Margaret Bondfield, Britain's first woman cabinet minister, hugged a fat parcel of fan mail to her chest that she was determined to present personally to Amy.

Occasionally a song took hold among a section of the crowd and spread throughout the field, fading when someone heard a rumour about Amy's arrival. A brass band settled themselves, tuned up and then relaxed again. People clambered onto the tops of hangars and milled around Croydon's flat-roofed control tower and the roof of the nearby hotel which the *Daily Mail* had rented for the day. A giant searchlight trained its beam on the raised, wooden platform where Amy was due to greet the crowds, but by 8.30 p.m. there were rumours that she would not land that day. Just as the pink sky was turning to night the crowd spotted what might be a cluster of planes; the droning sound of their engines confirmed the sighting.

When the silver plane landed at Croydon Airport the noise from the crowd, together with the planes' buzzing overhead, was deafening. Amy walked down the plane's steps into a thick sea of faces; the control tower was black with people waving hats and handkerchieves. The blazing lights and popping flash-bulbs trapped her on a luminescent stage that made it difficult for her to pick out details in the backdrop gloom of the fading evening. Strangers rushed to shake her hand and kiss her and she struggled to grasp a giant bouquet of flowers; photographers pleaded with her to look at them, while pressmen tripped over the cumbersome news reel cameras.

Amy looked remarkably composed and well-groomed compared to the tousled-haired mechanic that the crowd was most familiar with. Her high-collared, light fawn coat was slightly too big and made her look like a prim head girl; only her sun-tan and hair, which without the restraint of a hat refused to lie flat in the evening breeze, gave any hint of an adventurous spirit. She hugged her mother and kissed Will and Branks before walking along the red carpet laid out for her and bounding onto the platform where the microphone obscured her mouth like an oxygen mask. She apologised for keeping the crowd waiting and said how glad she was to be home – although most of her speech was drowned out by cheering – then she was driven twice round the airport perched high on the back seat of a car so that everyone could see her.

The headlamps from the following vehicle bathed the tiny figure in a halo of light.

The cavalcade wound its way slowly through the anonymous South London suburbs to the opulence of Park Lane and the stately Grosvenor House Hotel. It took two and a half hours to drive through twelve miles of delirious crowds who stood four and five deep along the route, details of which had been published in the newspapers. Nearly every window had a face at it; crowds waved their hats, handkerchieves and newspapers as she passed. Gangs of cyclists tailed the procession and mounted police tried in vain to prevent admirers climbing onto the running-board of Amy's car. At least twelve people fell under one of the cars in the slow-moving procession, but as Courtenay later recorded, 'they were quite cheerful as they were carried off to hospital', adding that the *Daily Mail* met all claims for compensation.[2]

The crowds outside Grosvenor House had been waiting for eight hours and emotions were teetering on hysteria. The hotel's managing director gave Amy another bouquet and guests in evening dress watched with guarded curiosity. Amy and her family were taken to the Empire suite on the seventh floor to meet friends, officials and reporters. After the chill of the long drive in the night air the rooms were over-cooked with too many bodies. Painted scenes of soldiers marched the length of one room, adding to the impression that she had simply moved from an open-air crowd to one contained by walls. Piles of letters and telegrams covered every table and flower-filled baskets pressed their heavy scent among the expectant gathering. Amy waved her handkerchief at the crowd below from a balcony illuminated by a searchlight until her right hand became numb and she changed to the left. When she finally went inside she could hear the strains of 'For she's a jolly good fellow' echoing up from guests several floors below her. It was three o'clock before she got to bed.

Although the *Mail* had originally agreed to give Amy three clear days of rest after her arrival at Croydon, they changed their minds and announced a grand lunch at the Savoy on Wednesday at which she would receive a cheque for £10,000 (£309,500 in today's money) and a gold cup. Nearly 300 well-known people were invited. They included aviation heroes such as Bert Hinkler, Louis Blériot, Sir Arthur Whitten Brown (one of the pair who crossed the Atlantic for the first time), the land and water speed record holder, Malcolm Campbell, Channel swimmers and tennis stars. The arts were represented by John Barbirolli, Evelyn Waugh, J. B. Priestley, Noël Coward, Alfred Hitchcock, Ivor Novello, Cecil Beaton, R. C. Sherriff, author of *Journey's End*, and the conductor Malcolm Sargent.

A doctor studied Amy throughout the ceremony in case her gastric cramps, which may have been period pains, needed medical attention. She was due to broadcast the story of her flight on the radio that evening but felt so ill from a heavy cold and stomach pains that the BBC had to come to her hotel suite. There was a brief panic when no one could remember where Amy had put the £10,000 cheque. A search at the Savoy was called off when Betty pointed out, correctly, that it might be in Amy's gold cup.

Over the next few months Courtenay gradually charmed his way deeper into Amy's life. His role evolved from speech writer and publicity manager into a sort of lady's maid-cum-chaperone. He laid out her clothes and looked after her luggage when they were travelling; he reminded her whom to thank and kept what he described as 'undesirables and bores' away.[3] One of his biggest tasks, which he performed with the help of two typists, was responding to a deluge of fan mail. He saw it as his duty to protect Amy from some of her more corrosive admirers – what Courtenay termed 'perverted females who wished to make clandestine appointments through advertisements' and men who sent 'scurrilous post cards posted in obscure suburbs of London'.[4] Amy continued to receive marriage proposals from strangers; an Australian clergyman wrote her letters of at least sixteen pages in length which arrived with every post. Other suitors expressed themselves in poems – most of them laughably bad:

> They talked about it in theory;
> She did it practical, the dearie.[5]

Admirers made pilgrimages to Grosvenor House and some got as far as her suite of rooms before they were challenged. On one occasion an elderly Czech sculptor with a white, wispy beard was found sitting patiently in her lounge. He was so gentle and unassuming compared to most of Amy's admirers that she agreed to meet him. From then on the artist, who always wore a very long coat, followed her from aerodrome to aerodrome, a benign presence whom Courtenay nicknamed 'Astrakhan Stravinksy'.

Manufacturers of everything from food to cosmetics sent Amy free samples in the hope that their products might be associated with her. Twelve typewriter companies asked her to confirm that she had used their model during her years at Crockers – she finally endorsed the Royal Portable. Amy turned down most of the requests and sent several of the gifts home to Hull. There were so many toiletry bottles that Molly lined them up in a parade that marched down the stairs from the very top of their Park Avenue house. A Mr Hinton patented a new board-game called 'With Amy Round the World' in which small biplanes raced horses in long-distance adventures. He offered Amy a third of the net profits if she allowed him to use her picture on the box.[6]

She was also given two new planes. De Havilland presented her with one of its elegant new monoplanes that she christened *Jason II*. The Puss Moth took flying into a different, more comfortable age. Its enclosed cabin removed the wind, and much of the noise, associated with early aviation. There was no need to wear goggles or heavy leather suits; the cabin, which had upholstered seats for three people, was heated and there was plenty of room for luggage. De Havilland claimed it had all the luxuries of a saloon car: maps could be spread out on the empty seat without fear of being blown away and the new engine sprayed less oil onto the windscreen. Its one set of wings, which sprouted from the top of the cabin, made the plane more aerodynamic and improved visibility. But De Havilland was launching the plane in the darkest economic conditions and it needed the help of a celebrity like Amy to make the Puss the plane to own. Will Hay bought one and the Prince of Wales had his painted in the Brigade of Guards' colours of red and blue. For Amy the new design opened up more possibilities of record-breaking flights.

Her second new plane was a Gipsy Moth, *Jason III*, which readers of the *Daily Sketch* and *Sunday Graphic* bought through a 'shilling fund'. The plane was presented to her one Sunday afternoon in Hyde Park. It was a rite of passage in two ways. Owning a brand-new plane confirmed that she was no longer the untested girl flyer who had to scrimp and plead to find a second-hand machine. The ceremony also put an indelible full-stop at the end of the most painful relationship of her life. Hans Arregger, his mother and one sister were among the 100,000 people who watched the presentation. Amy, accompanied by Branks, knew that there could be no greater confirmation that she had proved her worth. The reunion with the Swiss family she had once dreamt of being part of was warm – and final. She and Hans never met again.

Amy also had a new car, given to her by the motor manufacturer Sir William Morris – an MG saloon with a model of *Jason* on its radiator. Jimmy Martin drove Branks and Amy to Buckingham Palace in the MG to receive her CBE, and the same day she flew *Jason* to Hull on their first cross-country flight since the disaster at Brisbane. She landed at the local aerodrome where her eighty-seven-year-old grandfather was so excited that he jumped up and down despite the effects of a recent stroke. Three hundred thousand people packed round the town hall that Amy's great-grandfather had helped build to cheer her as she swept through the streets.

Amy had still not had a holiday since returning from Australia but it was hard to know where she could go without being recognised. She was mobbed when she popped to the bank, and when she went shopping for a new hat with her mother and sisters there was a scramble to buy anything she had tried on. Will and Ciss were worried that she was heading for a nervous breakdown and that the arduous tour planned by the *Daily Mail* would precipitate her collapse. They arranged for her to spend a few days away with Molly in Wales, naively believing that Amy would find some anonymity there.

The sisters stayed in small hotels using the pseudonyms 'Anne and Moll Jones'; Amy wore glasses and scraped her hair into a dowdy style that she thought would fit her assumed identity of the school teacher she had once aspired to be. It did not occur to them that the shining new MG parked outside might explode their subterfuge. The numberplate became so well known that every time they returned to the car it was surrounded by children clamouring for Amy's autograph. She wrote to her father from Pwllheli in North Wales saying that she was 'utterly wearied of "showing myself off"' and was considering returning to Australia.[7]

She was also discovering that she had to be careful about what she said. She repeatedly urged her audience to reject the motto of 'safety first', adding at the Savoy, 'I do not think it gets us anywhere; but I do believe in taking every precaution you can and then taking risks.'[8] Although Amy seemed unaware of their importance the choice of words was a blatant attack on the Conservative Party leader, Stanley Baldwin, whose slogan 'safety first' had become well known during the last election. Her speeches were almost certainly written by a representative of the *Daily Mail* – probably Courtenay – who was using Amy as a mouthpiece for the views of the paper and its proprietor, Lord Rothermere. The *New York Times* commented that Amy's choice of words showed that she had become a puppet of Rothermere, whose paper was funding Amy, and regretted that her claim to be 'England's Lindbergh' was in danger; their own hero, they argued, would never allow himself to be exploited in such a way.[9] Rothermere had a pathological dislike of Baldwin, blaming his unimaginative election campaign for allowing a Labour Government to come to power in 1924.

The *Daily Mail* waged an unremitting war against Baldwin, describing 'safety first' as a 'euphemism for want of courage'[10] and printing enrolment forms for the United Empire Party, which spluttered into life under the aegis of the two press barons and friends, Lords Beaverbrook and Rothermere. The party demanded free trade within the Empire but tariffs on goods produced everywhere else.

At the end of August 1930 a *Daily Mail* headline announced 'Miss Amy Johnson for Bromley, To help in the Prosperity fight'.[11] The article that followed explained how Amy was to support the United Empire candidate in a by-election at Bromley in South London and how she had been a member of the party before her trip to Australia. Rothermere recognised that an endorsement from Amy could easily sway voters and sent a 'gorgeous bracelet' to try to persuade her to join the hustings.[12] The press reports alarmed Will who immediately cabled her: 'Politics dangerous to your best interests.'[13] He urged her to make it perfectly clear that she was 'non-party' and had only 'Empire interests at heart from general standpoint', reminding her that her speech would be reported in Australia. Amy replied that the 'Bromley affair' had been 'grossly abused' and her offer to speak had been made at Lord Rothermere's personal request.[14] She was definitely not going, she said, but by then it was too late and she had already forfeited her political anonymity.

Courtenay had planned a grand expedition around Britain beginning in Hull on 11 August and ending three months later in the same city. During August the roadshow would concentrate on seaside resorts such as Yarmouth, Clacton, Margate, Folkestone, Eastbourne, Bournemouth and Brighton. In September Amy would zigzag across the country to take in Portsmouth, the Midlands, Bristol, Wales, Liverpool, Morecambe, Plymouth, Glasgow and Edinburgh. October would start in Newcastle and cascade south through the Midlands and East Anglia. The itinerary was designed to give Amy maximum publicity; her visits were timed to coincide with local events – a hospital fête, the inauguration of a new aerodrome or, in Colchester, an oyster festival. In a typical day *Jason* landed at 4.30 p.m. and Amy, wearing a floaty summer dress, stepped out into a field of grass. At times her fleeting descents were as dreamlike as a scene from *Le Grand Meaulnes*, the carnival crowds drunk on the sunshine in their fancy-dress costumes and harlequin outfits, surreal and ghost-like next to Amy's awkward formality. Generally she spoke for twenty minutes before being paraded to the local town hall where she suffered a gala dinner and dance. Occasionally she met someone more interesting than the local mayor: at

Brighton she was introduced to the Australian batsman Don Bradman, who was wreaking havoc among the English cricketers.

After a month on a tour that resembled what Amy had hoped to avoid at all costs – life as a music-hall turn – she was physically and mentally exhausted. The weather had changed dramatically at the end of August when temperatures soared to ninety-two degrees in the shade and there were reports of people walking down the street in bathing costumes; on one day alone there were twenty-one heat-related deaths, before dramatic storms cleared the air.

Will oscillated between hard-nosed businessman and loving father. He worried that she was frittering away her celebrity status and reminded her that she had three important weapons – her financial capital, her brains, and the press – and he urged her to take on a maid and secretary so that she could start work on her autobiography.[15] But she already faced grumbles that she was 'holding back' in her talks so that she could save the best material for her book.[16] On the other hand Will was desperate for Amy to return to Hull, when 'we shall really feel that we have got our girl back again . . .'[17]

At the beginning of September her doctor ordered two months' rest and on 9 September she dictated a letter to her father from Crockers saying she was 'thoroughly run down' and had decided to follow Branks' advice and accept an invitation to stay at the country house of Norton Priory, at Selsey near Chichester. Three days later she wrote to her parents describing how the sea and the beautiful gardens with their thirty peacocks, dogs, parrots and ducks had helped to drag her away from mental collapse: 'I was just afraid for one moment that I was going to have a complete nervous breakdown, but fortunately I have been able to come away in time to prevent this.'[18]

Amy had bolted from her agreement with the *Daily Mail*, leaving two months of her grand tour unfinished, but the paper's executives agreed to cancel the arrangement after seeing for themselves her state of exhaustion. They insisted that their pilot should complete the tour with *Jason*, but Amy threatened to burn the plane if someone else took the controls. Eventually the *Daily Mail* agreed to donate the plane to the nation and it was taken to the Science Museum in Kensington, London, where it hangs suspended from the ceiling, dwarfed by the plane that Alcock and Brown used to fly across the Atlantic. *Jason* is a rather sad exhibit, like a fly caught in a spider's web, looking down at the schoolchildren who gawp up at his undercarriage.

At Selsey Amy rested, replied to her correspondence and mulled over the future. 'It's perfectly obvious to me that I can't settle down quietly for some time to come – I'm much too restless,' she told her father. She pondered going abroad 'to give people a chance to forget me before I do something else to get my name in the limelight', but her father wanted her to make the most of her fame: 'were you to fly to the moon and back, you could never be on a higher pedestal than you are just now . . . don't forget there aren't many bouquets for failures,' he wrote.[19]

The respite from her public duties allowed Amy to tidy up outstanding loose ends from her Australia trip. Her luggage still had not been completely unpacked and two handbags she had been given had already gone missing. Among the gifts were two puppies which she asked her parents to take in while she looked for a permanent home. Finding her own home in London became a priority and she considered asking Molly to live with her. Will and Amy's ideas on the sort of property she should buy differed wildly: he wanted her to have an out-of-town house because it was a better investment but Amy felt the need for a *pied-à-terre*. Vernon Wood and Will were both worried about Amy's mental state and corresponded secretly over how best to alleviate some of the pressure on her. Wood revealed to Will that an anonymous donor had contacted the *Daily Mail* to offer Amy a house near Stag Lane but had withdrawn the gift after it went unacknowledged. Wood was keen to persuade the donor to reconsider without letting Amy know. 'One of the first things we have to do is to get her settled down in some suitable place in London where she can be as quiet as she likes . . .' he wrote to Will.[20] Wood was ecstatic about the transformation that Amy's rest in Selsey had achieved: 'the change in her is very marvellous; just over a week ago she looked very sad and pensive but now she is as bright and cheerful as a bird with two tails.'

Her daughter's homecoming had done little to calm Ciss's nerves. She worried about Amy's health and the fact that she seemed distant from her family; Ciss was also anxious about the poor state of the fishing trade and about the begging letters they received – most of which turned out to be from 'such utter frauds'.[21] Amy did her best to cheer up her mother by arriving with Jimmy Martin and the surprise gift of a new Austin Seven car. The extravagant gesture had an immediate, if temporary, effect. Will reported Ciss's 'great joy . . . it seems to have given her new life . . . talk about a kid with a new toy'.[22]

On 1 October Amy's doctor warned that she needed ten days of complete rest. Amy cancelled her appointments and entered the Mandeville Nursing Home, just north of Wigmore Street and within walking distance of the Marylebone flat that she had shared with

Winifred. It was to be a period of quiet contemplation during which she was allowed no visitors or letters. Afterwards she planned to stay with friends in London; as in Wales she would use a false name – this time she hoped with greater success.

Before Amy left for the nursing home she settled up with her father. Will had received £264 from the *Daily Mail*, the *Daily Mirror*, Gaumont, the *Pictorial* and the Dunlop Tyre Company but had lent Amy around £730 towards the Australia trip. On 1 October she paid him the outstanding £465, leaving her with £7000 in her savings account.[23] Will could not afford to waive the debt, but he still sounded apologetic: 'Of course if you hadn't obtained such a big financial result I should not have expected any repayment from you,' he wrote.[24]

At first Amy enjoyed the nursing home's routine of reading and eating, but what little equilibrium she had managed to regain was shattered on 6 October. Although she had not told her parents, because she did not want to worry them, she had been keen to accompany Branks on the maiden voyage of the *R101*, the world's biggest airship, when it flew from England to India. Branks used all his influence to try to secure a place for her but the voyage was declared an all-male affair. One of the last things Branks did before joining the Government-built airship at Cardington, near Bedford, was to send Amy some roses and a book with the inscription, 'Speedy recovery to you, Johnnie. B.'

In the early hours of the morning of Sunday, 5 October, the great, lumbering *R101* ran into a storm and started to lose height. Just before two o'clock the airship crashed outside Beauvais in northern France and instantly burst into a roaring hydrogen fireball. Only six of the fifty-four people on board survived the inferno; Branks and Lord Thomson, the Secretary of State for Air, were among the dead. The accident was the greatest disaster of the inter-war period and France declared a special day of mourning to honour the victims. Branks' death achieved what he had spent his life working towards: in one horrific incident the aeroplane became the future of air travel. Pictures of the giant, burnt-out skeleton appeared in most national newspapers, creating an indelible image that forced the Government to distance itself from airship production. Most of the airship industry's leading engineers were killed in the crash.

The disaster was a personal tragedy for Amy that set off a morbid train of thought. She had lost several close friends, many of whom had been at Croydon to applaud her good fortune in escaping death on her way to Australia. That they should die in the official, seemingly safe – even luxurious – setting of an airship was shocking. Amy scribbled a note in pencil to her mother as soon as she heard of *R101*'s fate, in which she confessed that she had hoped to be on board the airship. 'I've lost a good friend in him [Branks]. Then there's the awful disaster in Germany today. It is a time of bad luck just now.'[25]

Vernon Wood wrote to Will warning him that Amy was 'cut up after the *R101* tragedy'.[26] In a blatant breach of confidentiality Amy's doctor also wrote to Wood telling him that her blood pressure and weight had both dropped alarmingly and that his twenty-seven-year-old patient needed a 'strong hand on her'.[27] When Wood passed on this advice to Will he agreed but added, 'I have no control whatever.'[28]

Both of Amy's closest friends now lived a long way from London: Winifred was working in Liverpool and Gwyneth was teaching in Durham. Jimmy Martin and Will were still doing their best to keep Jack and Amy apart and at the end of October Jimmy telephoned Jack to ascertain that he had not been in touch with her.[29] Amy's paranoia led to a breach with her parents when she moved out of her nursing home and into two rooms in a house owned by Sir Archibald and Lady Weigall at 39 Hill Street, Berkeley Square. Lady Weigall was a member of the Maple furniture empire and used a wheelchair after falling on an icy pavement two years earlier. Sir Archibald was her second husband and they had spent the early years of their marriage in South Australia where he had been governor. Only Amy's parents and Crockers knew where Amy was and that she would be using the pseudonym of 'Miss Audrey James'. She was furious when Will phoned the Weigalls and inadvertently used his daughter's true name. The slip-up unleashed a stream of invective that startled Will and Ciss who had not realised the extent of her torment. Amy told them how she 'detested' the 'publicity and public life' that had been forced on her. She acknowledged that this was not their fault but berated them for not understanding her better:

> I am seeking hard to lose my identity of 'Amy Johnson' – because that personage has become a nightmare and an abomination for me. My great ideas for a career in aviation have been annulled, for a long time to come, by the wrong kind of publicity and exploitation which followed my return to England (which in reality followed the take over of my career by the *Daily Mail*).[30]

She planned a new flight and would not return to England for a 'long time'. 'There is no way in which mother can help me sweet and willing as she is. Merely being willing doesn't accomplish anything . . .' Perhaps what was even more startling than the outburst was that she wrote the very next day to apologise. Her excuse was that, according to her doctor, she was 'on the edge of insanity', that she was 'not normal at present'. But she compounded her insult by telling them that if Ciss came to London Amy would have to look after her, rather than the other way round. She also gave the impression that Lady Weigall was fulfilling her mother's role by helping her to decorate the new flat she was moving into.

Amy and her parents managed to paper over the disagreement but it was a turning-point in their relationship as significant as Amy's decision to leave home. She was feeling oppressed by the different factions manipulating her life and she needed to find her own way out. Her confusion about her own worth was not helped by the fact that less than a week after the *R101* disaster Charles Kingsford Smith smashed Hinkler's England-to-Australia solo record. His time of nine days, twenty-one hours and forty minutes was ten days faster than Amy's. Suddenly her own flight did not look quite so impressive and there were rumours that she was seriously ill. The need to prove herself again started to gnaw away at her.

Chapter 16

Tokyo
(November 1930 – Autumn 1931)

Spurn Head arcs out into the Humber Estuary, a long claw of sand and scrubland. To the west ships ply backwards and forwards to Hull with their cargoes of people and fish, to the east the North Sea stretches endlessly beyond the horizon. The three-mile track of land attracts rare seabirds, as well as man-made debris washed up on its sloping beaches. Standing on Spurn Head feels like standing on the edge of the world; on a clear day it is possible to see for miles: the column of the Wilberforce monument pricks through the skyline of Hull – a small eruption amid miles of flat countryside that sweeps round to the coast.

Amy faced 'dirty weather' when she set off from Stag Lane in her new Puss Moth, *Jason II*, for Hedon Airport, just east of Hull, on the afternoon of 9 November 1930. She had packed a suitcase full of jewellery and some of the more valuable gifts from Australia. As she approached the Humber Estuary her plane became engulfed in a thick fog and she climbed to 6000 feet to try to escape the blinding whiteness. When she believed she was above Hull, and just as darkness was beginning to fall, she flew down to search for her home town. But Hull remained firmly hidden somewhere in the gloom and for an hour Amy circled the open sea trying to find a bearing. The pinpoints of light from the ships below gave no clue as to whether she was over the estuary or the North Sea; it was too dark to read her compass and she had failed to bring a torch. At last she spotted the lights of a passenger liner; slipping off her shoes, she brought *Jason II* close to the water, intending to ditch the plane and swim through the gloom to the ship.

Just as she was bracing herself for the icy seawater she spotted the lighthouse of Spurn Point.[1] The blinking light guided her towards the strip of land and she managed to land on a thin stretch of sand between two groynes. She clambered over a pile of barbed wire to reach the lighthouse. Two men were sitting studiously cleaning lamps when she pushed open the door. They appeared unmoved by her appearance and consulted a black regulation book about how to deal with her sudden arrival. As there was no protocol for a forced landing they secured the plane and set a man to guard it through the night while Amy was taken to the nearest village of Kilnsea. Will and Ciss were at Bridlington visiting Will's father when Amy phoned Park Avenue. Molly, who had recently passed the newly introduced driving test, set out with Betty along the winding desolate roads east of Hull to meet Amy. They arrived home at nine o'clock just before their parents.

When Amy returned the following day to Spurn Head to retrieve *Jason II* she found schoolchildren from Kilnsea waiting with their parents, both groups mesmerised by the star who had alighted on their remote home. One mother, who admired her thick, fashionable coat with its high collar, was overwhelmed when Amy suggested she try it on. But apart from the local adulation it was a humiliating incident: a near-miss that should never have happened and a warning that her judgement was still impaired by the strain of her homecoming. Asked by reporters about her health, she replied: 'Oh, I'm feeling practically all right now. I knew I was about to have a collapse – and I got it.'[2]

Amy moved into her new home shortly after her visit to Hull. Fifteen Vernon Court was a modern flat in a four-storey, red-brick block situated at the point where the Hendon Way meets the Finchley Road in North London, conveniently placed for Stag Lane and the West End of London. It remains a strikingly neat building today with little balconies and discreet turrets; the only irregularity is a blue plaque commemorating the fact that a famous aviator once lived there.

She immediately asked Ciss to send 'Rough' (a wrinkled Bull Terrier with pink eyes framed by white eyelashes) to London. Until he arrived she made do with 'Mickey', a teddy bear given to her in Australia and which she asked Ciss to post. Rough's arrival helped Amy to settle into a routine. 'He's such good company,' she wrote to her mother.[3] She took him for runs at Stag Lane and he was waiting for her when she arrived home after her evenings out. 'Rough sends his love,' she added at the end of a letter to her mother in early December.[4] The Bull Terrier gave Amy a toehold on domesticity that helped her rein in the peripatetic lifestyle she had led for over six months. She enjoyed turning her flat into a home; she put cutlery at the top of her Christmas-present list and agonised over which of her countless Australian souvenirs should be displayed at Vernon Court. One room became an office where a secretary dealt with the continuous flow of correspondence. Going out became less of a strain once she had a front door to shut behind her – especially when there was a dog waiting on the other side of it. She even started to enjoy semi-formal events, such as dinner at Lady Astor's. 'I seemed to be the star turn. She's awfully nice,' Amy wrote to her mother.[5] But there was another reason why Amy was happier; she was planning a new flight.

Rough, and a Red Setter called Rex whom Amy had flown to collect from Manchester, joined Amy for Christmas in Hull. It should have been a contented family gathering but Will and Ciss were stunned by the news that Amy intended to set off for Peking on 1 January in *Jason III*. She planned to fly to Berlin and then on to Warsaw and Moscow from where she would follow the trans-Siberian railway to China.

It is impossible to exaggerate the foolhardiness of such a scheme. Amy was planning a long-distance flight at a time of year when she would count herself lucky to manage an afternoon's flying in England – let alone the exposed wastes of Russia where temperatures could plunge to one hundred degrees Fahrenheit below freezing. She aimed to travel 8000 miles in an open-cockpit Gipsy Moth – a plane totally unsuited, and untested, for such extremes. It was uncertain whether the engine would even start in these conditions, and snow and freezing fog would put the oil and petrol under tremendous strain. A forced landing would be impossible in the many areas of thick forest and tundra and if she crashed in a remote spot she would freeze to death before she was rescued. When the British embassy in Moscow asked the Soviet authorities for their advice, even they could not think of a convincing reason why Amy should choose to visit their country in mid winter.[6] They were worried that there was insufficient high-grade fuel available and pointed out that all regular Soviet flights had been grounded due to the appalling weather. In the unlikely event that she got as far as Smolensk her plane would need to have special skis fitted for landing.

Amy had started to plan the trip shortly after the *R101* disaster and had managed to keep the project deadly secret, dispatching her friends to various shops to buy maps of the countries she planned to fly over. Will and Ciss were horrified, but offered little resistance. Amy's outburst over the Weigall incident was still fresh in their minds and they dared not risk a second confrontation; perhaps they hoped the weather would limit her to Europe or that the journey would end abruptly due to a lack of a permit to fly over Russia. Will dutifully agreed to send Perrin his usual palliative of smoked salmon to help ease any opposition to the flight at Stag Lane. Jack said he would look after Rex and Rough while Amy was away.

The Russian permit had still not arrived when Amy left England on New Year's Day 1931. As soon as news of the expedition leaked out the press let off a barrage of criticism about the journey's recklessness that ricocheted around the world. Newspapers agreed that the flight was further proof that Amy had yet fully to recover from the ordeal of her Australian trip. The *Daily Express* claimed that she had became a 'neurotic from the strain of her flight to Australia' and quoted a flying friend, George Campkin, who said she was 'overstrung, irritable, depressed and restless and does not realize what a winter flight over the sub-Arctic snowfields involves'.[7] Her parents stressed that Amy had not consulted them about her plans. Ciss told the same paper: 'We approve the flight because we must. After what she has gone through the adventure will be a relief and soothing influence for her. She has shown restlessness at home for months.'[8]

Ciss wrote to her friend Mrs Glass complaining that Amy had been so busy that she still had not had a chance to tell them about her trip to Australia. Ciss resented the fact that Amy seemed unaware of the sacrifices they had made and how Will had neglected AJK for nearly three months to concentrate on the flight. She worried, too, that strangers had misled Amy over 'what really happened with the *Daily Mail*'; 'such a lot of harm is done, which can never be obliterated . . . when one lavished such loving thought and care on their children, one often gets hurt afterwards.'[9]

Will and Ciss turned to Jack for comfort and support in much the same way as they had done during the early stages of Amy's Australia flight. He was in favour again at Park Avenue, Will and Ciss realising that he had no interest whatsoever in cashing in on Amy's success. Amy, too, had made it clear what she thought of Jimmy Martin, who had been spending a lot of time with her parents, even helping Will to choose a new Chrysler Coupé car. 'That man's the biggest mischief-maker I know,' Amy wrote to Will during her stay at the Weigalls, although she failed to explain exactly why.[10] While Jimmy had charmed his way into the Johnsons' inner sanctum, Jack had kept a respectful distance. When Ciss wrote to him about the Soviet trip his reply showed his unswerving belief in Amy but his desire to be no more than a back-room player in her success: 'Apparently some of the Press are against her,' he wrote. 'I fear it's because they are not very brave and she is more than that. The wife and I get every paper for news and I still think she has the public with her.'[11]

Will also recognised Courtenay as an important source of information and the two corresponded regularly and frankly about Amy. Courtenay made sure Will knew of some of the more alarming rumours about her safety in case the reports had not reached the northern editions of the newspapers. Will told him: 'It seems to me the Press have got the wind up about this flight and are anxious to stop it.'[12]

Amy's choice of destination was seen as every bit as foolhardy as her choice of season. Russia was the seat of Bolshevism, a movement as feared in sections of Britain as land taxes or lesbianism. Amy's one-time champion, the *Daily Mail*, viewed the Soviet Union as the scourge of the civilised world – out to destroy everything that its proprietor, Lord Rothermere, held dear, including the upper classes and religion. The paper ran regular stories about the country's dark depravity: how Russia was about to abolish Sundays and that nine-year-old girls were forced to work for a living. In 1931 it was a country that only eccentric intellectuals such as George Bernard Shaw and Lady Astor visited and even they had the sense to make the trip during the summer months – as they did when they travelled there together later that year. Russia was no place for a heroine of the Empire; her route took her far from the colonies and there was no sense in which she could claim to be strengthening ties with old allies. If she crashed there would be no friendly RAF team to help mend a wing or refuel the plane.

Even before she left Europe Amy was harried by driving snowstorms and patches of thick fog that forced her to make several unscheduled stops. She stayed overnight at Liège in Belgium and bad weather forced her to land at Cologne. From there she left for Berlin despite appalling weather forecasts and the pleas of ground staff. Several hundred spectators, members of German aero clubs, Lufthansa staff and the wife of the British ambassador waited for her at Berlin's Tempelhof Aerodrome. Amy was several hours late and when she finally appeared was exhausted by the cold and the strain of trying to find her way through the snow. Over several cups of tea she explained that she had been driven off course trying to avoid the heavy snow until she was forced down at Lübz, a small village in Mecklenburg. Amy stayed with the British embassy that night and set off for Warsaw at noon the following day.

A strong wind blew her north of Warsaw but when she turned the plane to head back for the city she ran into a thick bank of fog. She was long overdue at Warsaw and police throughout Poland were told to look out for her. While they searched Amy sat in a potato field sixty miles north of Warsaw where *Jason III* had been forced to land due to engine trouble. His propeller and undercarriage were damaged and Amy suffered a minor eye injury. The full version of what she believed happened next only became known two years later when it provoked an international incident. At the time she said merely that a car fetched her from Krasnosielc, half-way between Warsaw and Poznan, and that she stayed the night in the house of a Catholic priest.

When it became evident that the plane could not be repaired Amy continued her journey to Moscow by train hoping to garner information for a future attempt to cross Siberia. The visit of the world-famous pilot was a publicity coup for the Russians and Amy was fêted wherever she went. Lenin's widow, Krupskaya, described her as the ideal role model for Soviet women and she met the top officials in the Russian flying world. Amy found the Russians helpful but told her parents that there was not much to see or do in Moscow. She returned to Hanover by train and joined the Glass family for a skiing holiday. The Glasses, who had two daughters, had become good friends of the Johnson family and Amy felt safe in their company.

But she was restless and difficult to please; the excitement of the Australia flight had made thrills difficult to come by and left her highly sensitive to perceived snubs. 'How strange it is that all my life I have longed for winter sports and a fortnight's holiday seemed nothing,' she wrote to her father. 'And now when I can have an illimitable holiday and go anywhere I want, I no longer want these things!! Oh, well, life's a very funny thing.'[13]

The International League of Aviators proclaimed her the greatest woman pilot of 1930, but Amy was more concerned that she had not been invited to Buckingham Palace in a celebration to mark the achievements of that year. Two other female pilots, Winifred Spooner and the Honourable Mrs Victor Bruce, attended. Will was convinced that her invitation had simply gone missing, but she was sure that the *Daily Mail* had used their influence to keep her away.

Amy was acutely aware that she was only as good, or as famous, a pilot as her last flight. Women were regularly setting new records for altitude, speed and distance but Mrs Victor Bruce was a particular threat because of her skill as a self-publicist. She had already snatched speed records at land and sea and had raced in the Monte Carlo rally; then she learnt to fly after spotting a plane that took her fancy in a shopwindow in Burlington Gardens. In September 1930 she set off alone on a round-the-world flight with a mere forty hours of solo flying in her logbook – a figure that made Amy seem like a seasoned flyer at the time of her Australia flight. Mrs Bruce took a primitive radio set with her to allow her to send, but not receive, messages and chose a Dictaphone in preference to a parachute so that she could record her adventures.

Her critics said her plane's registration, 'ABDS', stood for 'A Bloody

Daft Stunt' but her account of the trip shows unlimited reserves of a quality previously synonymous with Amy's name: 'pluck'.[14] She returned home five months later having covered 20,000 miles and three continents. Although she 'cheated' by putting her plane on a ship to cross the Pacific and the Atlantic, she nevertheless became the first person to fly solo from England to Japan and achieved the longest solo flight. She was eight years older than Amy and barely five feet tall, easily qualifying as another 'lone girl flyer'. When she invited Amy to dinner Amy told her mother that she enjoyed being there as 'an ordinary guest', although she could not resist adding that everyone wanted to meet her and ask for her autograph.[15]

Amy and Winifred Spooner were among the famous pilots who escorted Mrs Victor Bruce on the final leg of her journey to Croydon. Mrs Victor Bruce quickly produced a book on her flight using the notes made on her Dictaphone.[16] Amy, too, wanted to publish a book but decided to wait until her next flight provided a blast of publicity.

A photo that appeared in leading national newspapers at the end of February 1931 summed up more than any other just how famous Amy had become.[17] She stands primly clutching her gloves and bag in an ill-fitting suit, a fur around her neck, her hair hidden under the sort of toque favoured by Queen Mary; the ensemble makes her look as though she has raided her mother's wardrobe. Next to her Charlie Chaplin, in a double-breasted suit, links his right arm through Amy's and his left through Nancy Astor's, who appears more poised and chic than Amy. George Bernard Shaw completes the chain of celebrity, half standing, half perching on a giant urn like a bearded and bushy-eyebrowed mischievous garden gnome. The photo delighted both Amy and her parents. 'What a mixture,' Will wrote to her with pride, adding that he would like to hear Shaw and Amy argue.[18]

Amy was exactly the sort of person Shaw liked to collect. He surrounded himself with adventurers and men who had pushed themselves to the edge of their physical ability. Shaw and his wife Charlotte became close friends of T. E. Lawrence and Apsley Cherry-Garrard, one of the youngest members of Scott's last expedition to the Antarctic. Shaw was fascinated by the effect of superhuman journeys undertaken by adventurers still in their twenties, and gave invaluable editorial advice on Lawrence's *Seven Pillars of Wisdom* and Cherry-Garrard's *The Worst Journey in the World*.

Like his heroes, Shaw was addicted to speed, driving a motorbike with gusto until he was nearly seventy and owning a variety of cars.[19] As he grew older and frailer he quenched his thirst for adventure by entertaining those still young enough to enjoy it. Shaw was an early convert to flying, curious about both the physical sensation and the potential of planes. He had flown as a passenger over Hendon aerodrome in 1916 and during his foreign travels in the 1930s took every opportunity to go up in a variety of machines.[20] Cecil Lewis, a wartime flying ace who had won the Military Cross, became a friend and Shaw met Lindbergh at Nancy Astor's home, Cliveden.

The playwright had been a hero of Amy's ever since she had debated *Getting Married* and *Saint Joan* with Hans. She had been thrilled to spot Shaw in the audience at an aviation lecture in January 1930 and when, in the spring of 1931, she was invited to one of Shaw's famous lunches at his flat overlooking the Thames at Adelphi Terrace in Westminster, the invitation was as great an honour as any international trophy, although she was not impressed by the flippancy of the other guest. 'I like him, and also Mrs Shaw, but I've taken a dislike to Charlie Chaplin. One can soon see too much of him!' she wrote to Will.[21]

Amy was gently easing herself back into society; she entertained for the first time at Vernon Court when she invited fourteen people from Stag Lane to a party, and commissioned headed writing-paper with a green picture of *Jason* in the top left-hand corner. Molly came to stay in May to help Amy reply to the fifty or so letters she received each day and Winifred, who was working in Derby, visited. Although Amy had £1800 in her bank account at the end of February 1931, money had become a worry again.[22] She faced a tax bill for the £10,000 the *Daily Mail* had given her, although Amy argued it was a gift. 'The dirty dogs . . . they would take the crust out of the mouth of the widow and orphan,' Will wrote to her when she told him of the demand.[23] The tax bill, which Crockers appealed against, concentrated Amy's mind on her cash-flow. She decided to accept only those invitations that were useful to her career and pushed for an interview with Lord Wakefield to discuss a new record-breaking, long-distance flight. But Wakefield was suffering from flu and still smarting at the *Daily Mail*'s coup in claiming Amy as their own discovery. In the meantime she appointed an agent to negotiate more sponsorship money from Ovaltine and manufacturers of other products such as flying goggles and chocolate.

She planned to tackle the aborted trans-Siberian trip in the summer; much to her parents' relief, Jack was to go with her as co-pilot. In preparation for the flight Amy worked at getting fit: she went horse-riding every morning, swam, played tennis and went to the gym. A few weeks before she was due to leave, Rough died from a leg injury and Amy concentrated her affection on Rex, writing to her mother, 'I love this one as she is obedient and affectionate,' adding, 'I do love my horse.'[24]

Her preparations included adapting the maps she had bought in Moscow so that they could be easily consulted in the cockpit. They were so flimsy that they had to be mounted on thick paper and linen and then cut into small squares to be formed into a folding book. Amy did not trust anyone else with the laborious task and spent hours assembling the booklets. The exercise involved more than twenty sheets of large drawing paper, sixteen yards of linen and ten pots of glue.

Travelling in the summer and with a co-pilot had transformed the journey into a far less risky enterprise, and Amy mulled over ways of making the flight more newsworthy. She looked into the possibility of buying a Segrave Meteor plane that would give her the range to attempt a worldwide odyssey of breathtaking audacity. From Japan she would fly across the Pacific to Alaska, Canada, the United States and then South America. Charles Kingsford Smith had made the first Pacific crossing from America to Australia in June 1928 together with Charles Ulm and a radio operator/navigator – at over 7000 miles the ocean journey was nearly as far as the flight from England to Japan.

Amy was drawn to South America because of its increased trade with Europe. The Prince of Wales was working hard to promote the Puss Moth in Argentina and Aéropostale had established an airmail service between South America and France. Amy discussed the possibility of forming a joint company to take advantage of flying opportunities in the region with a business contact from Stag Lane who offered to invest £5000, and Crockers drew up a joint company naming Amy and the colleague as directors.

Vernon Court would be let while Amy offered joy-riding trips, taught flying and eventually set up her own airline in South America. If the venture failed she would start a flying circus in England, although she viewed this as a last resort that would 'pull down my reputation as a pilot enormously'.[25]

Plans to shift the axis of her life to the other side of the world coincided with a major upheaval for her parents. Will was easing his way into retirement and had decided after twelve years to leave 85 Park Avenue for a house in Bridlington that fitted their elevated status as respected business-people and the parents of a world-famous celebrity. Their new home, 'Brynmawr' in Cardigan Road, stood in a wide street of large, imposing houses which, although within walking distance of the beach and still circled by seagulls, was far enough from the centre of Bridlington to avoid rowdy holidaymakers. It had a full-sized tennis court and two kitchen gardens, and was close to the golf course – a sport that Will and Ciss still occasionally dabbled in.[26]

Much to her parents' relief, Amy avoided – by half an hour – setting off for Japan on the anniversary of Irene's suicide. Amy and Jack left at 12.35 a.m. in brilliant moonlight on 28 July from Lympne aerodrome, near Folkestone in Kent, in *Jason II*. She had abandoned her grandiose schemes of flying to South America; instead the 8000-mile journey was a straightforward attempt on the record from England to Japan. The Puss Moth carried no extra tanks so that the flight would be an example of how far a 'normal' light aircraft could fly.[27] The decision made take-offs and landings easier but meant that they had to refuel three or four times a day.

For Jack the ten days they spent crossing a continent were a blissful holiday of wild flowers and endless sunshine, a stark contrast to his previous visit to Russia during the First World War. In the notes he jotted down about the journey he made no mention of the record they were chasing; it was enough that the flight put him back where he was happiest – as Amy's second in command.[28] Mechanical problems that irritated Amy increased Jack's pleasure at being of some use to his pilot.

From Moscow they flew east to Kazan over huge, rambling collective farms with long barrack-like workers' quarters and gleaming modern machinery, and then on to Kurgan, Tomsk, Irkutsk and Chita, taking it in turns as pilot to hunt for the trans-Siberian railway as it scurried in and out of dense woodland. They watched the moon rise and drank tea from a samovar with the commandant of an aerodrome at Velikiye Luki: a 'very jolly' woman who spoke good English and wore riding-breeches and a revolver at her hip. When they were forced down in the middle of the steppes to correct a faulty oil connection on their way to Kurgan they were greeted by a twelve-year-old herdsman who read Shaw sitting on a pony while he guarded 200 cattle. But they saw nothing of the trainloads of deported peasants on their way to the freezing north, and very little of the crippling poverty of the most rural and remote parts of the country. As they flew further east the landing grounds became more primitive, identifiable from the air as a scattering of stones. They ate stodgy, black bread and at one aerodrome had a 'boiler bath' stoked up with wood that left them 'red, but refreshed'. Jack noted there was just one 'privy' which he found difficult to use, wondering to himself, 'How does one manage these balancing tricks on a single board?'

They flew over miles of unbroken forests of huge trees, once stumbling upon a raging forest fire. The land felt as remote and desolate as the Iraqi desert. Jack spotted a fly that he was sure had entered the cabin at Lympne and was accompanying them across the continent.[29] But apart from this passenger they became lulled into a sense that they were completely alone, so that when a speeding Russian plane roared past them they had to bank suddenly to avoid it. Another time they were startled when an eagle swooped dangerously close to their engine. At the great, inky Lake Baikal they ignored advice to skirt round the water because of the danger of sudden changes in air pressure and quickly found that their instruments were not working properly. When they were half-way across the lake *Jason II* lurched suddenly towards the water and Amy and Jack were startled by a loud bang which they eventually discovered was an exploding flask of tea.

They made their way uneasily through Manchuria, a part of China that Japan was eyeing up greedily. Amy was told to stick to a strict route that avoided all military areas. *Jason II* flew over camps of nomadic tribes and when they landed they were greeted by a White Russian trader dressed in fur who spoke English and gave them their first white bread for days. Local people in pigtails gathered round to stare at Jack, but especially Amy. Mukden, the capital of Manchuria to the west of the Korean border, was a 'first-class aerodrome' where they stayed with the British Consul whose Chinese butler was mesmerised by Amy. The last stage of their journey took them to Seoul and Hiroshima where two planes were waiting to escort them. Between Okayama and Osaka they flew over neat, tightly packed fields that Amy thought looked like a large chocolate cake divided up into squares, although she could not help wondering where they would land if their plane was forced down. As they neared Tokyo on 6 August the air grew bumpy; they spotted Mount Fuji and a swarm of aeroplanes eager to greet them. At ten and a half days they had taken longer than they had hoped but had beaten the record for a light aeroplane from Berlin to Tokyo set by a Japanese pilot, Seipi Yoshahara.

They arrived in a part of the world awash with record-breaking American pilots. Clyde Pangborn and Hugh Hernden touched down at Tokyo as part of an attempt on the round-the-world record on the very same day that *Jason II* landed. Charles Lindbergh and his wife Anne Morrow were on their way to Japan from Alaska and arrived in Tokyo to a welcome that was almost religious in its fervour. Wiley Post, usually described as 'the one-eyed Indian from Oklahoma', and his navigator Harold Gatty had just skirted Japan in a daredevil flight around the northern hemisphere. Post took eight days to fly in a 15,500-mile loop from New York that followed Amy and Jack's route across Russia and which made their crossing of the continent look like a lazy dawdle. The one well-known British pilot, Francis Chichester, was languishing in a Japanese hospital after crashing his seaplane on a solo flight from Australia. When Jack and Amy visited him his goatee beard and intellectual's glasses made him look more like Lenin than an intrepid aviator.

Tokyo in the summer of 1931 was a startlingly modern and culturally confused city. The devastating earthquake that had struck Japan on 1 September 1923 had killed 140,000 people, injured tens of thousands more and turned the capital city into a muddy wreck that contemporaries likened to the Somme. The cost of rebuilding, together with Japan's dearth of raw materials and the collapse in agricultural prices, thrust the country into an economic depression bleaker than the one Amy had left in Europe. In rural areas the threat of starvation forced many farmers to sell their daughters into prostitution and in towns and cities factory workers took to the streets and roofs in protest.

Against this background of Dickensian hardship the new Tokyo sprang up as a monument to the avant-garde. The offices erected after the earthquake contained the paraphernalia of Western business life, such as lifts and telephones, and their workers dressed in European fashions and flirted with lipsticks and Eton crops. They rode to work by streetcar or subway and peered in the windows of department stores that aped Harrods and Bloomingdales. Airwomen like Mrs Victor Bruce and Amy were seen as emissaries of the modern and attracted huge interest.

But there was confusion on both sides as to how far Japan wanted to progress along the path to Western fashions. Photos of Amy's stay in Japan show a topsy-turvy world where neither guest nor host is sure of the right clothes to wear or even the right way to sit. Amy is frequently pictured looking uncomfortable in a kimono that she wears as informally as if it were a Grosvenor House bathrobe; when Jack is forced to attend tea ceremonies he sits on the floor with the resigned anguish of someone awaiting a firing squad. Most bizarrely, the Japanese men who greeted Amy often wore straw boaters and jackets. At a dance given by the Imperial Aviation Society Amy towered over its president, General Nagaoka, whose twenty-inch moustache was reputed to be the longest and whitest in the world and which plumed out from each nostril like a seagull's wings.

Amy's Australian flight ensured that she was already well known when she arrived in Japan and she faced the usual hectic schedule of public engagements. On one Saturday she visited the ministries of communications, foreign affairs, the navy and the army, and the British embassy. The Rotary Club of Tokyo departed from convention by asking a woman to lunch for the first time, but eased the departure from tradition by describing Amy as a 'superman'. She was paid 200 yen to appear at the Mitsukoshi department store for between twenty and thirty minutes. The organisers specified: 'It is desired that Miss Johnson speak her farewell message amidst smiles, etc. to the gathering present . . .'[30]

Jack kept a low profile, watching from a distance and grumbling that the music from a local café kept him awake: they had only three records, 'Land of Hope and Glory', 'Sous les toits de Paris' and a song from *Carmen* which they played incessantly. He joined Amy on an official visit to some hot springs but said the lack of 'real' food left him hungry. He enjoyed a two-day visit to Japan's oldest English residents, a Mr and Mrs Mollison (coincidentally) who lived by the sea.

Once they were back in *Jason II* Jack relaxed into the task of keeping the plane on course for England. He much preferred the down-to-earth hospitality of Russia where tea was drunk from a samovar and entertainment was spontaneous, like the time when they were taken in cars on a bear hunt. At Kazan Amy could not take her eyes off a puppy as it played with its owner; just as they were about to leave its owner thrust the dog at her.[31] When they landed in England a policeman whisked it away for six months' quarantine and it was only later that Amy discovered that 'Dushka' was a wolf cub.[32]

In terms of publicity the expedition to Tokyo was a disaster and Will wrote to the BBC complaining about the lack of coverage.[33] Amy had been pushed off the front page by Jim Mollison – the same pilot who had flown her to Sydney the previous year. In the summer of 1931 he took his Gipsy Moth from Australia to England in slightly more than eight days, making him the fastest solo pilot over that route and wiping nearly two days off Scott's record. Jim's first attempt had ended as he was taking off from Darwin when he crashed into a telegraph pole; he was unhurt but the plane was wrecked. On the night of 13 November 1931 he somersaulted into an Egyptian maize field during an attempt on the England-to-Cape-Town record; again he was unhurt but his machine was destroyed. Jim's flying career, like his private life, was marked by thrills and spills.

PART 4

The Flying Sweethearts

Chapter 17

Jim Mollison
(Winter 1931/2)

By the time Jim Mollison landed among surprised holidaymakers at Pevensey Beach in the summer of 1931 he was giddy with the strain of pushing his body and plane to its limits. When he arrived at Croydon Airport for his official welcome someone had the bright idea of presenting Jim with a kangaroo to mark his historic journey from Australia. The frightened animal's response to the heroic airman was to thump him in the stomach – just one more blow to someone already punch-drunk with fatigue.

In smashing the Australia-to-England record Jim went from the co-pilot who had failed to secure a dance with the world-famous Amy Johnson to a celebrity sought after in his own right. One of Jim's favourite places to relax in was the 43 Club in London's Soho. He lived for the moment and felt instantly at home in the Gerrard Street house, every cranny of which was populated with strange creatures who came out at night to feast on the club's illicit atmosphere of celebrity, drugs, alcohol and sex. Eccentrics and men and women of notoriety rubbed shoulders on each of the building's six rickety floors: drug dealers mingled with murderers, a man who had committed bigamy six times and another guest who always wore a teapot on his head and which was replaced free of charge every time it smashed to the ground. Film stars such as Tallulah Bankhead and Jack Buchanan provided the glamour and writers like J. B. Priestley and Joseph Conrad observed the heady mixture. Arctic explorers and the most daring pilots were welcome. Charles Scott celebrated at the club after his flight from Australia, and Colonel Minchen and Captain Leslie Hamilton were regulars before they disappeared over the Atlantic with their passenger, Princess Löwenstein-Wertheim. Maharajas, European royalty and members of the British nobility spent their evenings with daredevil stars whose next flight might be their last.

The chance to acquaint himself with these rich, well-bred voyeurs was the main reason why Jim offered to help out at the club while its proprietor, an Irish divorcee called Kate Meyrick, spent one of her many spells in Holloway Prison. The club provided Jim with all that he required of life: female company, alcohol and influential people who spent their money freely. Ever since leaving his comfortably off family in Greenock, Scotland to join the RAF shortly after the war Jim had developed a knack of squeezing the most pleasure and least discomfort out of any situation he found himself in. During his training at RAF Duxford, near Cambridge, he made buying a Morgan sportscar a priority and spent every other weekend with friends in London, leaving the capital at two in the morning to be on parade by six o'clock. Often he drove with no lights, an escapade that he later said gave him an insight into 'blind flying'. One of his favourite pastimes was performing steep turns as he flew over the austere, red-brick tower of Girton College on the outskirts of Cambridge, where he imagined the women students gazing up at him in awe. He later wrote in his memoir:

> I am afraid that it is lamentably hedonistic, but one cannot be young for long, and it has always been my practice to live for the moment. What is the use of eternal preparation for the future, for contingencies which may never arise . . . to find when the time for realisation of hopes has come that youth, the corner stone on which all the edifice was built, has gone beyond recall.[1]

Jim became well known for dodging mess bills and for never carrying his own matches. He drank heavily, stopping just short of the alcoholism that ruined his father and led to his parents' divorce when he was ten. His mother, Mrs Bullmore, was a strict Presbyterian who clung to those of her son's exploits of which she could be proud and did her best to ignore the less Calvinistic side to Jim's nature. His years in the RAF made him eminently 'clubbable': 'I have one of those mass-production faces and look quite harmless,' he wrote later, 'but whenever I go to an hotel where I don't know anyone, I always seem to meet some friendly people who are good enough to let me share their amusements.'[2]

After the RAF he drifted round the world, visiting Germany, France, Switzerland and Tahiti before finding work as a lifeguard and then as a commercial pilot in Australia. He stayed in each place just as long as the supply of money and women lasted. The Australian flying scene fitted in perfectly with his own ethos and he admired the 'young, virile, enthusiastic race', commenting, 'every Australian is an individual because each is brought up to look to himself alone.'[3]

Success allowed Jim to indulge his taste for smart clothes; he was proud of his suede shoes and double-breasted suits that quickly became rumpled, giving him a just-got-out-of-bed look reinforced by his languid posture. He wore rather too much eau-de-Cologne so that his fragrance arrived slightly ahead of him and lingered long after he had left. Jim admired men like the Prince of Wales who combined style and indolence.

At five foot seven inches, Jim was short and prone to podginess. He freely admitted that he used alcohol to calm his nerves, earning himself the nickname of 'Brandy Mollison'. He cultivated the impression that flying was just one strand of his sybaritic lifestyle, often wearing a dinner-jacket in the cockpit to show that being a pilot was something he fitted in between cocktail parties and trips to the casino.

When Jim arrived back in England from Australia he had long since stubbed out any trace of a Scottish accent; instead he cultivated a haughty upper-class drawl – an affectation that was badly misplaced since the fashion among the upper echelons of society to which he aspired was a quasi-cockney accent. Languor came easily to him and he made a point of always arriving late. His favourite pose was one hand in his pocket; in the other he held a cigarette between thumb and middle finger. It was as if he had spent so long propping up a bar that he knew no other way of standing. He rarely smiled, preferring to look bored.

He was the sort of trophy pilot that members of the Mayfair set enjoyed having in their midst and he, in turn, did all he could to become part of their clique. If he found himself on a cross-country flight in need of a field to land in, he would seek out a stately home that offered the best chances of a good meal and aristocratic connections. By the time he attempted to beat the solo record from England to Cape Town in the spring of 1932 he was unofficially engaged to Lady Diana Wellesley. The eighteen-year-old debutante and great-granddaughter of the Duke of Wellington towered above Jim both physically and socially. Diana's mother, Clare, Countess of Cowley, did her best to beat out the flames of the ill-suited romance between the deb and the air ace, telling reporters that her daughter was not engaged[4] and insisting that the *Sketch* add a footnote to a piece about the couple that spelt out the fact that they were not betrothed.[5] At the end of 1931 Will Johnson wrote in his diary:

1931 has proved a gloomy year and everyone seems happy that it is over. World situation terrible. Personally I am thankful for 1931. Good health for self and family. Moved to new house in Brid. in July. Fair business year. Betty started boarding school. Moll engaged to Trevor. Amy safe return from Tokio [*sic*] flight. Ciss very good health.[6]

The world situation that Will fretted about had led to a 'national' government with the Labour leader Ramsay MacDonald at its head, backed up by the Conservatives Stanley Baldwin and Neville Chamberlain. An emergency budget cut public-sector pay and unemployment benefits to help the country balance its books, but opposition to swingeing pay cuts, particularly from naval ratings who mutinied at Invergordon in Scotland, caused panic among foreign investors. In three and a half days £43 million worth of gold fled from London.[7] The only answer was for Britain to 'go off the gold standard' so that the Bank of England was no longer legally obliged to sell gold for sterling at a fixed price. Beyond Britain, India still hankered for independence, Japan invaded Manchuria and soaring unemployment hit Germany and the United States.

Will clung to the hopeful aspects of life in 1931 and was relieved that Molly had found a suitable fiancé. Trevor Jones, a solid Welshman with a moustache, was the sort of steady son-in-law he and Ciss had always hoped for. He was senior assistant solicitor to Hull Corporation and in February 1933 was chosen from a field of forty-eight applicants to become deputy town clerk at Blackpool on an annual salary of £700.

During the autumn and winter of 1931/2 Amy toured towns in the North of England giving a lecture entitled 'How *Jason* and I flew to the Land of the Golden Fleece'; Jack acted as assistant and chauffeur. She was on better terms with her parents than she had been for months and they asked to buy her a piece of jewellery to mark her flying achievements. A pair of Cartier diamond ear-rings that she liked carried a shop price of £150 but Cartier agreed to sell them to her for £128. The ear-rings represented a provision against hard times which was as important to Amy as their beauty and status; she wrote to her father that the stones could 'any time realise their value which I think is always a good asset, don't you?'[8] Writing to thank her parents she said: 'You know all these qualities popularly attributed to me, pluck, endurance, common sense, ingenuity etc. etc. are all inherited and I know I couldn't be in the position I am today without you both.'[9]

By January she had resumed plans for her most ambitious expedition yet – a round-the-world flight to challenge the eight-day record set the previous summer by Post and Gatty. She would follow the trans-Siberian route taken on her trip to Tokyo and then cross the Pacific to Canada. Jack would come as her engineer and they would take a twin-engined plane equipped with a wireless. She wrote to the Soviet authorities asking for permission to fly over their country and to carry a gun and camera.[10] She also asked the US Hydrographic Office to send her pilot charts of the 'upper air' over the North Pacific Ocean during the summer months.[11] But her plans were forgotten when she suddenly collapsed at Bolton with severe stomach pains; the lecture tour was abandoned and Jack drove through a foggy night with Amy writhing in agony on the back seat of the car.

At the beginning of February 1932 she took an irrevocable decision that was to alter for ever her view of life and what she wanted from it. Press reports described the operation she underwent as the removal of her appendix;[12] the truth was that she had had a hysterectomy. According to close friends, Amy decided to have what is still today a major operation for two reasons. All her life she had suffered appalling period pains accompanied by violent mood swings; her periods were irregular and tiresome to deal with at the best of times. She believed her future was as a long-distance pilot, and if she was to stand any chance of beating ever more demanding records she could not afford to be 'femininely unwell', as she had been in Australia. Amy was twenty-eight when she had the operation.[13] Although she had had several affairs since Hans, none of them had been serious enough for her to consider marriage. During her relationship with Hans she had made no secret of the fact that she wanted children but when they separated she put the idea to the very back of her mind. According to her friends, Amy enjoyed an active sex life – hardly surprising, given that she was such a physical person.[14] Much of the thrill of flying was that she was exposed to the elements and she became restless and irritable if she was unable to play sport of some kind. The decision to sleep with Hans was so momentous that, once it had been taken, the question of whether or not to have sex with other men could never be as important.

When she moved to London and then owned her own flat it became much easier to conduct discreet relationships; the circles she moved in were less censorious about sex before marriage and her celebrity status made her highly desirable. Once she had given up on the idea of marrying, a hysterectomy provided the answer to the problem of long-distance flying and the risk of an unwanted pregnancy. She would never again feel as unwell as she had done on landing in Australia, or suffer symptoms that were unmentionable – or, if they were alluded to, elicited scant sympathy in the male-dominated world of flying. After the operation Will said it had been a long time since he had seen her looking as 'calm and happy and contented'.[15] Two months after the hysterectomy she started a relationship with the man who was to become her husband.

Amy spent three weeks convalescing in the Duchess Nursing Home in London before moving to a nursing home in Colchester. But she found this last place 'so very shabby . . . fly blown . . . all so gloomy and dingy'; the walls were peeling and it was full of 'ancient ladies', one of whom had a beard.[16] She persuaded the doctors to allow her to take a holiday and, with a nurse to look after her, she boarded the *Winchester Castle* for Madeira. When she reached the island she decided she did not like the hotel or the 'gossipy, catty, society people' who were staying there.[17] It had been raining for six weeks so she returned to the ship and continued to South Africa. On board she took navigation lessons from one of the ship's officers and enjoyed the respite from letters and phone calls so much that she decided to stay on board until Durban. 'I adore this free and easy ship life,' she wrote to her parents.[18]

Jack was left to plan their round-the-world bid; Amy cabled him from the ship every few days to ask for news of the test flights and to update him on her latest strategy.[19] She confided in him that she was likely to be overdrawn at the bank and asked him to secure credit on her behalf. Eventually she decided that they should postpone the flight until next year when they would be better prepared.

Amy stepped off the ship at Cape Town feeling relaxed and well rested. The place was buzzing with excitement about the expected arrival of a pilot on his way from England in an attempt to beat the solo record. For the first time Amy viewed a record-breaking flight from the spectator's side of the aerodrome. It was nearly eight o'clock when Jim Mollison's Puss Moth approached Cape Town; he had barely slept in the four days since he left England and the weight of tiredness made it impossible for him to focus properly. As he circled the aerodrome the beacons and lights of the field below him danced in a nauseous blur that leapt in and out of double vision. Every minute that he wasted trying to decide whether he was capable of landing in the glare threatened to rob him of the record and he decided to head for an unlit strip of beach. The beach turned out to slope more steeply than he had expected and as the Puss Moth touched down it ran into the sea and turned over, leaving Jim in the closed cockpit, the plane in five feet of salty water. The forced landing and the threat of drowning pumped enough adrenaline into him to rouse him from his stupor; he kicked out a window and struggled up the beach feeling sick from the seawater he had swallowed.

A taxi took him to the aerodrome where Amy, as a visiting record-breaker, was the obvious person to welcome him. Jim was bedraggled and catatonic from lack of sleep; of the huge crowd that greeted him only Amy could fully appreciate what he had been through and what the press and public expected of him. She accompanied him to his hotel where she helped him deal with the waiting cables. The next day, after a haircut and a rest, Jim's insouciance was fully restored and he lunched with Amy. The press wanted to know more about his supposed engagement to Lady Diana Wellesley and were too busy criticising Amy for cancelling a number of invitations due to ill health to make any romantic connection between the two flyers. Amy spent the last ten days of her visit to South Africa in the seclusion of a millionaire's country house with its clifftop views over the Indian Ocean where she sunbathed quietly surrounded by nurses and doctors. On the sea journey home she made up her mind to attempt a crossing of the Atlantic.[20]

Chapter 18

Marriage
(1932)

In May 1932 Amy's place in history shifted. The flight to Australia had earned her an enduring spot in the record books and until that date the feat remained the most impressive by any female pilot in the world. But the public wanted more and more from their flying heroes, as Amy discovered when her Tokyo trip disappeared amid the scrum of famous pilots driving their machines further, faster or higher than their rivals.

The transatlantic crossing was still the most prestigious flight path in the world. It took a special kind of pilot to cross thousands of miles of bleak ocean: exceptional navigational skills and endless courage were vital, and few people believed a woman possessed one of those qualities, let alone both. Amy had for a long time wanted to attempt the 'water jump'; she knew that the first woman to make the journey alone would never be forgotten, but her ambition was put on hold when she met Jim again in London. She lost her chance for ever when Amelia Earhart landed amid grazing cows near Londonderry in Northern Ireland in May 1932.

Amy returned home from her cruise on 5 May and four days later she and Jim got engaged over lunch at Quaglino's, a fashionable London restaurant, on what could loosely be described as their second 'date'. She immediately phoned Ciss in Bridlington and Will recorded his daughter's momentous meeting with 'Mr Mollison' in his diary, adding, 'All morning papers on Tuesday made a big stunt of it.'[1] He and Jack went to meet Amy and her fiancé, whom Will now referred to in his diary as 'Mollison', at the Grosvenor House Hotel the day after their engagement. Will noted in his journal that he was suffering from a bad cold but passed no judgement on his daughter's future husband. The couple posed for photographs on the hotel roof, Amy in a dress with a wrap-round, caped top and Jim in his usual double-breasted suit and suede shoes, Amy on one hand, a cigarette in the other.

In one of only two letters and a postcard that Amy sent to her parents that summer she apologised for not writing more often. 'Please believe that I'm <u>very, very</u>, happy,' she wrote to her father on 16 May 1932. 'Jim is a dear, and in spite of newspaper publicity, which seems to point to the engagement being only a business partnership, it is more than that. To begin with I didn't realise it quite so clearly as I do now. I don't think I shall ever regret this big decision in my life.'[2] She went on the defensive, too, when she spoke to the press, claiming that she and Jim had been 'good friends' since their first meeting in Brisbane. 'I should like to correct a mistaken impression that many people seem to have. Naturally our engagement came as a sudden surprise to the public, but it is by no means a sudden affair so far as we are concerned.'[3]

Amy appears genuinely to have fallen in love with Jim and it is easy to see why. He was a dashing, record-breaking pilot, someone who shared a rare insight into the loneliness of the long-distance flyer detached from the world in their tiny capsule. He was fun-loving and lived for the moment; he offered Amy the chance to enjoy herself in a spontaneous, carefree way that she had not experienced since she shared lodgings with Winifred.

Jim was also a 'man of the world' – in both the literal and metaphorical sense. As he travelled round the globe he made a point of sampling every new pleasure he could find and this was exactly the sort of history that Amy required from a lover. Four years earlier she had written to Hans that she preferred to 'pit' her 'experience against the experience of others than to teach the young and innocent';[4] there was obviously no need to 'initiate' Jim 'into the ways of the world'. But the most overriding reason for marrying Jim was that he asked her.

There was no uncertainty about her role or embarrassment among friends about where exactly she stood: he proposed before the world had noticed they were in a relationship (Jim was still unofficially engaged to Diana Wellesley) and their friends were calling to congratulate them within the hour. From Quaglino's the couple took a taxi straight to *The Times* to ensure that the next day's paper carried an announcement of their engagement.

One explanation, written by Jim five years later, of why he proposed to Amy so prematurely is tainted by the passage of time but gives some clue as to what he saw in her:

In Australia she was the ex-typist who had become a famous pilot – a person whose hair becomes windblown; whose nails got dirty; and who often smells of petrol. Amy was attractive then, yes, but not the type to stir the pulse of the sophisticated. Now, across a red-lighted luncheon of the choice foods and white linen, she smiled back at me, a manicured, powdered, waved blonde. It was all pleasantly changed and different.[5]

He was astute enough to spot the publicity value of a romantic alliance between the 'The Flying Scot' and the 'Lone Girl Flyer' but there was more to their relationship than simply a canny marketing ploy. Jim was an all-or-nothing sort of person – which was one of the traits that made him good at breaking records – and at that moment, Amy meant everything to him. When Jim trained his beam of charm on a woman he could make her feel like the only female in the world, and when he proposed to Amy at Quaglino's the romance of the occasion finally matched the dream she had harboured since adolescence.

Will continued to write to Amy but his tone became distant and subdued. He realised that the long-established order had been toppled and his advice was no longer welcome. Shortly after the announcement of their engagement Ciss confided to Jack that she felt 'terrible' about the news. Despite his own misgivings, Jack wrote back saying that he was sure that Jim and Amy loved one another.[6] But after returning with Amy from Antwerp to find Jim waiting at the aerodrome Jack, too, realised that he was no longer welcome and decided to look for work elsewhere. Months earlier Jim had been charged with assaulting a night porter in London's Bayswater after the man told Jim and his two female friends to move on[7] and, although he was acquitted, Jack had good reason to suppose that Jim would not countenance any threat to his position. Will worried that Jack would struggle to find a new job among Britain's three million unemployed. 'I'm very busy at the office but it isn't easy to make money these days,' Will wrote in one of his rare letters to Amy.[8]

Amy paid a dutiful, if stultifying, visit to Jim's family in Scotland in late May but there was no sign of Jim visiting Ciss and Will in Bridlington. At a time when a father could still expect to be asked for his permission before a man proposed to his daughter, Amy's failure to visit her family presented an obvious snub. Will and Ciss were reduced to reading the papers to discover what their daughter was up to. They saw pictures of her and Jim with Amelia Earhart and presenting a cash prize to winners of the *Daily Herald* crossword competition. Amy, urged on by Courtenay, whom she and Jim employed to handle their publicity, was increasingly sensitive about her image. When apologising to her parents for not visiting she gave the excuse that it was important for her profile abroad that she should be seen lunching with Amelia Earhart. She and Jim offered to fly Amelia from Londonderry to Glasgow and to help her while she was in England.

Will and Ciss watched as their daughter's physical appearance changed; under Jim's guidance she became more groomed and tailored. Shortly after their engagement the couple posed for a series of photos by Bassano, a famous studio that had taken pictures of Queen Victoria and the image of Kitchener used in the 'Your Country Needs You' recruiting poster. Jim gave Amy a solitaire engagement ring with a large diamond perched on diamond-encrusted shoulders, while she bought him a gold cigarette case in the hope that he would no longer 'borrow' from other smokers. At the end of July Amy announced to Ciss that from now on she would only wear black and white.[9] She sent her mother, 'Moll' and 'Bee' (Betty) packages of cast-offs: a coat and a dress that had shrunk at the dry-cleaners and woollens she had been given but which she felt unable to wear because of their unfashionable colours.[10]

Vernon Court did not fit in with this new image and its dark, damp walls made Amy feel lonely; having her own flat seemed like less of a sign of independence and more an onerous burden. She moved first to the Dorchester Hotel and then to the luxurious anonymity of the Grosvenor House. The hotel, built in 1927 to a design by Sir Edward Lutyens, sat like a sentinel on the edge of Park Lane. It claimed to be the first hotel to offer running iced water suitable for drinking in its bathrooms; other facilities included a gymnasium, a large swimming-pool and squash courts. Advertisements boasted of the 'social swirl' of the ballroom, shops and an ice-rink used for fancy-dress balls that attracted the Prince of Wales from nearby Buckingham Palace.

At the end of June, Jim and Amy went on holiday to the South of France. Amy found the beach at Juan-les-Pins too much like Brighton but Jim enjoyed the casinos and the excitement of moving in the same sphere as film stars. A picture in The Tatler[11] shows them wearing swimming costumes and standing next to the actress Helen Gilliland, and Carl Brisson, who was about to return to his starring role in The Merry Widow. Amy and Jim look like two little children next to the towering actor; Amy's hair is loose and untamed after a swim.

Her bank overdraft was growing and yet she had no money-making schemes. She had sold both her planes and felt as though she were 'marking time'; a suggestion of accompanying Jim in a transatlantic bid had been squashed and a date had still not been set for their marriage. She told her parents that they did not want a big wedding with a cake and bridesmaids; they were, she said, trying to avoid publicity, but all the London Register Offices were being watched. With no plans of her own, Amy became consumed with anxiety about Jim's bid to become the first person to fly across the Atlantic in the more difficult, westerly direction. For the first time she had a taste of the torment her parents had endured during each of her three long-distance flights. 'I wish I didn't worry so much and take things so deeply and seriously,' she told her father. 'I think it's far better to take life lightly, but I'm not made that way.'[12] She found it difficult to sleep and longed to wake up in a month's time when Jim's flight was over.

At the beginning of the summer she and Jim started work on a short film called *Dual Control* to publicise Jim's Atlantic bid. An eccentric piece of cinema made at Elstree Studios, it has the feel of an Ealing comedy. The story begins with pictures of clouds and stirring music followed by Amy and Jim waving to each other from two planes that are obviously parked in front of an artificial sky. Beneath, passers-by crane their necks to catch a glimpse of the two aeroplanes: a courting couple fall off their tandem and a group of young girls on a cross-country run scamper through a stream to chase after the aircraft. Jim, wearing startlingly white overalls, lands to refuel. The girls, their wet shirts now clinging to their chests, cluster round him as he explains, in a voice that carries some of the affected hesitancy of a modern-day Prince Charles, how the aeroplane works. 'I wish you'd take me up . . . in your plane I mean,' one of the girls sighs. In another part of the field Amy, in a military-style coat, her cheeks powdered smooth and looking shy, talks with much more dignity about her flight to Australia. In a prescient comment she says that solo flying has the advantage that there is no one to quarrel with and that she always wonders if she will be given a cup of tea at the end of a flight.

Eventually an AA scout refuels Jim's plane and they take off again; Amy gives a small boy a ride after she agrees that he can tell his schoolmates that the pilot was a man. Jim's passenger is a young woman. Amy appears much more relaxed in a plane – even if it does not leave the ground. When they return to earth a policeman lands in an auto-gyro to book them for trespassing. The film abruptly cuts to Jim in front of the plane in which he intends to fly to America; a disembodied voice questions him about his forthcoming flight. Jim says he is flying the Atlantic because 'We all know that British aircraft are the best.' 'Deeds, not words, are his motto and he's a hero in the company of Drake and Raleigh, Scott and Shackleton, and while that spirit lives England yet shall stand,' the interviewer concludes.

Amy now mixed almost exclusively with Jim's friends who tended to be the sort of gossipy, society people she had done her best to avoid in

Madeira. Kathleen, Countess of Drogheda, stood out as the most forceful of the Mayfair set and someone who was genuinely interested in flying. A big, bustling divorcee who liked fashion and speed, she was one of the first women to fly as a passenger and to play in the Wimbledon lawn tennis singles. The Countess received the CBE for her efforts in recruiting pilots for the Royal Flying Corps during the Great War and her friends included Sir Alan Cobham and Branks. She grew up in a Scottish castle before marrying a diplomat and moving to Belgravia where she drove a silver Rolls-Royce. By the time she met Jim she had divorced her second husband – a miniature Mexican who spent his time indulging his twin passions of Baccarat and polo.

The last week in July was 'rather a bad week' for Will and Ciss.[13] It was three years since Irene's suicide and Betty was again proving 'difficult'. Things were to get even worse. On the evening of 28 July Amy sent her parents a cable telling them that she was getting married the following morning at ten o'clock: 'we are trying to keep it as quiet as possible. We should have much liked your presence but in the circumstances of Jim's approaching flight have decided to keep it an absolutely private affair between ourselves much love Amy.'[14]

The unexpected telegram wrenched the Johnsons out of their despair and hurled them into a panic of activity. It was unthinkable that they should miss their daughter's wedding and, after discovering that there was no train that would get them from Bridlington to London in time, they decided to drive through the night. While Will pumped up the car's tyres Ciss scrambled to find suitable clothes for a Mayfair wedding. They collected Molly's fiancé, Trevor, at 2.30 a.m. and then called at Will's office in Hull to pick up his coat before driving the 300 or so miles to London in torrential rain.

From the very beginning the wedding had an air of clandestine panic to it. Amy's bridal transport failed to arrive and she and the Countess were forced to drive to Mayfair in a sports car. They abandoned the vehicle with a policeman near Hanover Square and walked to the eighteenth-century church of St George's, a building hidden in a clutter of streets with only the elaborate bell-tower making any impression on the skyline. Crowds had been waiting for hours around the church's six great Corinthian columns that cling precariously to the very edge of a busy street, and a cheer went up when they spotted the famous airwoman.

Amy was a monochrome bride dressed in a black coat-frock, a short eye-veil and white gauntlet gloves. A silver fox fur crouched on her shoulders, the dead animal's glassy eyes peering over her right shoulder. She carried no flowers. Inside Jim waited in a grey lounge suit. The only guests were the Countess (who gave Amy away); the best man and Branks' replacement as Director of Civil Aviation, Lieutenant Colonel Francis Shelmerdine; Jim and Amy's secretary Miss Doreen Pickering and representatives from Wakefields. St George's had long been a fashionable venue for weddings; its marriage register contains names like Percy Bysshe Shelley, Mary Ann Evans (George Eliot), John Buchan, Benjamin Disraeli and Guglielmo Marconi.[15] But despite these distinguished predecessors, the church has a stark simplicity with its heavy wooden pews and white walls relieved by a huge stained-glass window and a gloomy picture of the Last Supper above the altar. None of the wedding party felt comfortable with absolute silence and the distant rush of traffic only made the quiet of the church appear deeper and more troubling. Amy appeared unsettled and at the last moment changed her mind by promising to obey her husband, a decision that went against the trend among modern brides and was remarkable enough to prompt the headline: 'Miss Amy Johnson's Marriage: "Obey".'[16]

The uninvited guests from Bridlington arrived at Golders Green in North London at 9.40 a.m. where they were still a tube and taxi ride away from the West End. Chattering crowds surrounded the church and reporters pounced on the family from Yorkshire telling them they were too late to hear their daughter make her vows. The shame of creeping into a church after the service had started was particularly acute for a group of people whose lives were regulated by weekly chapel meetings. Inside Amy was signing the register. Someone offered to show the late guests into the vestry but they declined and instead huddled together in seats slightly apart from the nave. As Amy walked down the aisle with her new husband she failed to notice them. It was only at Grosvenor House, where numbers were swollen by other guests including Lady and Sir Alan Cobham, and the Marquis of Donegal, that reporters told Amy her parents were in London. She was horrified and asked someone to ring round the major London hotels to try to find them, but the Johnsons were already on their way back to Bridlington. To the public Amy's family were a constant backdrop in her dramatic story and the fact that they had failed to appear in the latest chapter of her life was in itself newsworthy.

Film of the reception shows a joyless and stilted affair, more like a press conference than a wedding breakfast. A waiter with a shock of hair like Stan Laurel's hovers behind the couple clasping a bottle of champagne, its neck cloaked in a napkin; Amy looks subdued and depressed. Jim's speech concentrates on his forthcoming bid to cross the Atlantic; the nearest he comes to paying his new wife a compliment is when he says he would have liked Amy to have gone with him but that all the arrangements had been geared towards a solo flight. Amy's reply makes the wedding sound like a huge ordeal: 'Kathleen, ladies and gentlemen. I can't tell you how glad I am that you've held me up through this morning's work. I think it's all been terribly nice of you and I thank you for being with us today and helping us. That's all I can say at the moment. I thank you very much.' She sat down to polite – rather than rapturous – cheers and cries of 'Happy Landing!'

Their honeymoon began with bride and bridegroom racing each other to Scotland in separate planes – Amy won. They stayed as the guest of Lady Bowden at Kelburn Castle in Fairlie on the west coast of Scotland. The castle itself, the home of the earls of Glasgow, made a rather austere setting for a romantic break although the dourness was relieved by the views of the Firth of Clyde and the nearby spectacular waterfall and glen.

But Amy was unable to relax and on the first day of her honeymoon sent a cable to Bridlington scolding her parents about their behaviour; she was 'very disappointed at their attitude . . . which resulted in much adverse publicity'.[17] When talking to reporters she denied a rift, but privately she traded letters with each of her parents in which the three of them expressed deep hurt and outrage at the other's behaviour. 'I'm not sure what kind of reception you'll give me now,' she wrote on 3 August. 'The whole thing has been a great pity – you seem to regard yourselves as the injured party; whereas it's probably apparent to you by now that your action has done me a lot of harm and was the only thing that prevented the day from being completely happy.'[18]

Her excuses confirmed her parents' suspicions that she was ashamed of them and that they were no longer important to her. She and Jim had 'stacks of relatives', Amy explained, and they had decided that 'rather than offend by only asking one or two' they had chosen to ask none. Hosting a reception, she added, was a last-minute decision after a few friends heard of the wedding. 'I'm so sorry that you felt hurt at not being told, but in the peculiar circumstances, I felt utterly incapable of facing any fuss . . . I shall always love you both and would not willingly hurt you.'

Ciss's reply on 5 August left Amy in no doubt about her parents' feelings: 'We were so terribly grieved, so bitterly hurt, I was ill at the shock. Surely a "mother" and "father" are different to "stacks" of relations? We did not wish to mix with your friends: Duchesses, Lords, Ladies etc.

I have no title except "Mother"; no castle except our home which we have worked hard for . . .' She added that Will would write when 'the terrible blow you have dealt us has worn off a little' and ended her letter, 'Love from Mother now unwanted.'[19]

Amy answered her mother's letter from a hotel in Dublin while she waited for suitable conditions that would allow her new husband to set off across the Atlantic from Portmarnock Strand. Jim was unbearable to live with during the week it took for the right weather to arrive, unable to concentrate on anything – even finishing a cigarette. Their wedding had boosted the publicity surrounding the flight and even the name of Jim's plane, *Heart's Content*, highlighted the romantic subplot of a daring pilot abandoning his new bride to risk his life by flying alone across the Atlantic, turning round and then heading back to her. (In reality the plane was named after a place in Newfoundland where Jim hoped to land.)

Amy continued to harangue her mother about the wedding: 'I have only one comment to offer – are you proud of the fact that after 29 years you do not know or understand your own daughter.'[20] She told her mother that her motto was now, 'nothing really matters' and chided them again for not realising that the press were bound to recognise Amy Johnson's parents outside the church. All they had missed, she wrote, was a 'ten-minute ceremony which may any day now leave your cherished daughter a widow.' To drive home her point she sent them a newspaper cutting headed, 'Treat your children as friends' with a note, 'What about this?'

Immediately after the wedding Will revealed his true feelings in a letter to Mrs Glass. 'Please do not be anxious about us, as we shall pull through. We can only conclude that both Amy and Jim have lost their heads. Meanwhile, they are in God's keeping and we know He will protect and watch over Our Dear Girl.'[21] Writing to Amy, he pointed out that she had only visited them once since Christmas and that that had been to present a gold cup in Hull. He said she had changed since returning from Australia and becoming famous, that she now moved in different circles.

When conditions finally allowed Jim to leave for America, Amy spent the night of 18 August alone in her suite in Grosvenor House high above Hyde Park. The following day Courtenay took Amy and Doreen Pickering to lunch. He had struck a deal that gave the *Daily Express* exclusive rights to the story and a female reporter from the newspaper joined them at the meal. Courtenay was called away to take a telephone call and returned bubbling with the news that a plane fitting the description of *Heart's Content* had been sighted over Halifax. Amy was unmoved by the announcement, muttering that Jim still faced the danger of a return crossing. A second message confirmed that the plane was Jim's and Courtenay cabled a message of welcome: 'Hearty congratulations on your splendid achievement. Thank God you have caught the last edition. BILL.'[22]

On 20 August Jim landed in a field in New Brunswick, Canada, thirty-one hours and twenty minutes after leaving Ireland. His journey in a De Havilland Puss Moth half the size of Lindbergh's *Spirit of St Louis* was the fastest ever west-bound crossing of the Atlantic and the furthest non-stop journey in a light aeroplane. After a long sleep Jim spoke to Amy on the phone. He had accomplished the journey on such a tight budget that one American journalist commented that the call home probably cost more than the flight.[23] Will recorded in his diary: 'Mollison arrived safely New Brunswick. 5.40 p.m.'

New York gave Jim an ecstatic reception. A motorcycle escort accompanied him everywhere he went, blowing its sirens to scatter anyone who stood in the way, and Union Jacks appeared at every hotel or restaurant he entered. Jim met his hero Charles Lindbergh at a secret location in Park Avenue; the kidnapping of Lindbergh's baby boy meant his father shunned publicity as keenly as Jim sought it. The two pilots discussed their preferred transatlantic routes and the future of aviation. Jim continued the discussion with Amelia Earhart, both agreeing that the unpredictability of the weather meant that commercial transatlantic flights were still a long way off. In England Amy told reporters that she wanted to become the first woman to cross the Atlantic alone from east to west, but predicted her husband would object to the plan.

Jim planned to fly home but faced another long wait for the right weather. While he was sitting in New York and Amy was alone in London, two other planes set off from America to cross the Atlantic. Both had two-men teams; one plane was never heard of again; the other crashed before leaving the mainland. On Sunday morning 28 August Jim was given the all-clear to take off but thick fog forced *Heart's Content* down near Harbour Grace. The following day he received a long telegram from Amy urging him not to attempt the crossing. He ignored the plea and carried on through a thunderstorm until he met a plane that had been sent to escort him to Cape Breton Flying Club. That night he stayed with a doctor who secretly sent a cable to England stating that Jim's nerves were in no state to carry him across the Atlantic. Amy responded by sending a message begging him not to carry on and following it up with a telephone call. But it took a cable from Lord Wakefield to tip the balance. His message read: 'In the interests of the nation and of British aviation I most strongly advise you to abandon this flight.'[24] Jim bowed to the pressure of his sponsor and sailed home. Amy met him off the boat at Cherbourg.

After a long silence she cabled her parents to invite them to Jim's welcome-home reception. It would be a 'much more important thing than our wedding and much more time for rejoicing', she wrote to her father.[25] The letter was an act of conciliation in which she conceded that her father's letter had been reasonable. Will and Ciss decided to accept the invitation and, together with Jim's mother, who had also not been invited to the wedding, celebrated Jim's safe return at Grosvenor House.

When Amy and Jim visited Hull in September they stayed with the county sheriff, rather than her parents. Will was now resigned to Jim's indifference towards his in-laws, writing to Amy that she should not 'over-persuade Jim to come to Brid; I dont intend to be nasty Amy, but we do feel Jim has'nt [sic] much use for us and if that's true we dont want any unwilling guests. One can't expect to be liked by everyone so we are'nt [sic] making any worry about it.'[26]

An uneasy truce existed between parents and daughter. They wrote infrequently to each other, imparting inconsequential pieces of information such as Amy's decision to have her ears pierced, until Will told her at the end of October that there was no need to refer to the 'trouble' again. The reconciliation was prompted by a startling piece of news. Amy planned to fly alone from England to Cape Town in a bid to beat her husband's record.

Chapter 19

Solo to Cape Town
(Winter 1932 – Summer 1933)

The easiest way to fly from England to South Africa in 1932 was via the 'all-red', east-coast route. The pilot heading off in this direction could hopscotch down the map's pinky-red crazy-paving path of British territories that started on the Red Sea and ended several thousand miles south at Cape Town. From April 1932 it was possible to shadow the route set by Imperial Airways' weekly passenger service between Croydon and Cape Town. The service, backed up by a network of roads, railways and aerodromes, flew south via Cairo, Khartoum and Lake Victoria. The lone pilot who ran into trouble anywhere close to this route was likely to be swept up in the airline's safety net. Surviving a forced landing in West Africa was much less likely and added another layer of psychological stress to the flight, as Amy said: 'You might as well be crossing an ocean for all the help you would get.'[1]

The forbidding Atlas Mountains, which separate the Mediterranean coastline from North Africa, present an early test for the pilot attempting the west-coast route. If he or she survives the range their next challenge is 1200 miles of unremittingly featureless Sahara desert. From here a few scattered French military bases offer some comfort before the final, barren stretch through Angola and south-west Africa (now Namibia) when the pilot is most tired and the chances of rescue most remote. At this point in the journey it is quite possible to fly for three times the distance from London to Glasgow without seeing so much as a mud hut. The west-coast route to Cape Town had only two advantages: it was 600 miles shorter, and, in 1932, its few scattered outposts of imperialism made it appear much more exotic.

Both aspects appealed to Amy. Her plan was, as one French newspaper described it, a '*raid audacieux*'.[2] In the same way that, when planning her route to Australia, she had simply placed a ruler in a straight line across Europe, she liked the simplicity of following the most direct route. Taking the road less travelled also appealed. A final attraction lay in the fact that Jim had followed a westerly course when he set the London-to-Cape-Town solo record the previous year. Pitting herself against her husband made a better story and she suggested to her parents that if she got lost Jim should lead the hunt for her as a way of securing wider press coverage.3

Moonlight held the key to a successful West African flight, guiding the pilot for six nights every month through its waxing and waning. Amy planned each stage of the journey to take into account moonrise so that she could cram in as many airborne hours as possible, regardless of how much sleep she had managed. She also took a course in blind flying to improve her navigational skills which would be tested to their limits when she set off across the Sahara. The lessons involved flying in a plane with a specially fitted cover that pulled over the cockpit like a pram hood to simulate night-time or thick cloud, leaving the pilot to rely on charts, compass and instruments. Jim passed on his knowledge of conditions in Africa and Amy studied the maps she had secured from the AA's aviation department.

Monday, 14 November

At 6.37 a.m. she stepped into her new Puss Moth, *Desert Cloud*, wearing high-heeled shoes with slim ankle-straps, leather gloves and a spotted scarf round her neck. Both she and Jim wore matching leather coats trimmed with astrakhan. In one hand she carried a sola topi and a stack of maps, in the other a soft overnight bag. A mobile flood-lighting truck illuminated the small crowd who had gathered at Lympne, including Doreen Pickering, the Countess, Courtenay, and a few local dignitaries. The dark-red boundary lights bled a misty glow in the distance.

Amy sat in front of an extra fuel tank specially fitted to increase *Desert Cloud*'s range from 700 to 2000 miles, the fuel adding the equivalent of the weight of six people. At Lympne there was no wind to assist take-off and the plane rose slowly after a long run. Jim, who had lent her the St Christopher token that he had carried across the Atlantic, escorted her as far as the French coast and then waved her goodbye. He and Courtenay went back to Grosvenor House to field the stream of telephone enquiries from around the world before retiring for the night.

She had hoped to make Oran, Algeria, non-stop but was forced to refuel at Barcelona at 2.30 p.m. As she flew over the Mediterranean she began to smell petrol and found that the gravity tanks in the wings were leaking. Scrabbling around in the cabin, Amy found some old newspapers that she shoved into the holes in the vents near her seat in an attempt to stem the loss.

Moonlight guided her to Oran where she landed at 7.30 p.m., having covered 1100 miles in one day. Jim had urged her not to attempt a take-off from the small aerodrome with a full tank but she ignored his warning and barely cleared the trees at 11.30 p.m. After she left Oran there was no news of her for thirty-six hours.

Tuesday, 15 November

Amy flew through the night, taking good care to keep above the 4000-feet peaks of the Atlas Mountains. The range held the same terror for pilots as the Taurus Mountains, a fear heightened by the death in December 1929 of two RAF pilots on their way to the Cape.

She followed the Sahara railway line through the fertile oasis country, scattered with groups of mud huts and green palm trees, until the signs of habitation faded into the biggest challenge of the entire journey – 1200 miles of sand. The French Government deemed the Sahara so difficult to navigate through that it had just introduced a new rule that any pilot wishing to attempt a crossing should deposit 100,000 francs with them to cover the cost of any search. The regulation was waived for Amy because she had started planning her flight before its introduction.

Her only other experience of desert flying was the sandstorm outside Baghdad – one of the most terrifying experiences of her Australia trip. But despite her fear she became mesmerised by the landscape beneath her, the dried-up riverbeds and the sky dimmed by the whirling clouds of sand and dust. For the first 200 miles or so she followed the tracks left by the Trans-Sahara Car Service, peering to see whether she could glimpse any of the five large tin casks that punctuated the route. She was amazed by the 'dry, tonic air' and the 'choppy yellow sea' of dunes, some fifty feet high, 'wave after enormous wave, as though some god had stretched his arm over a restless sea, petrifying its restlessness into waves'.[4]

As the hours passed she settled into her customary routine of long-distance flying: listening to every beat of the engine and trying to push to the back of her mind the image of a slow death from dehydration. Relying solely on her compass, she headed for the shimmering pools of water on the horizon which faded as she approached them. As the day grew hotter the plane bounced through the hot air like a car on a track full of potholes, but after a while even this failed to relieve the boredom.

At last grass and shrub started to poke through the sand and Amy knew she was on the edge of the desert. In the centre of a high plateau of flat, hard earth she passed 'Bidon Cinq' ('Tin Number Five') – which she described as the 'loneliest landing-ground in the world'.[5] A single Arab, who depended on the irregular car service for supplies and human contact, watched over the airfield's petrol pump, aircraft beacon and hut. One keeper had gone mad with loneliness and boredom, another died of thirst after selling his water to some passing travellers. Nearby, petrol tins marked out a street and a railway carriage masqueraded as a hotel.

The broad, muddy Niger with crocodiles half snoozing on its banks appeared suddenly and Amy pounced on it, knowing it would take her to the French military aerodrome of Gao. She had been flying for nearly twenty-four hours continuously but the plane was soon re-fuelled and she took to the air again, quickly jettisoning the water that the French authorities had thrust on her before settling back to gnaw on the whole chicken they had presented her with. *Desert Cloud* felt suspiciously light and, flashing her torch on the instrument panel, Amy realised she had only five gallons of petrol in a tank that held forty-two. After barely an hour in the air she had no option but to return to Gao.

The aerodrome was no more than a ghostly shadow in the fast-disappearing moonlight. Amy revved her engine furiously until the noise roused the commandant, who rushed out and turned on the landing-ground lights. There was no mechanical fault; the problem was much less serious but just as devastating – the petrol tanks had not been filled to capacity.

After refuelling it was nearly midnight and the moon had disap-peared, leaving behind a deep African darkness. Amy rested in a small bungalow until dawn.

Wednesday, 16 November

The ground appeared intermittently through the low cloud and rain, but she kept a steady course at 110 miles per hour, passing over the last stretch of the Sahara and the aerodrome of Niamey towards Nigeria – a rare pink patch on her map of north-west Africa – and playing tag with the river Niger as it darted in and out of the impenetrable forests.

Desert Cloud landed that afternoon at the small aerodrome of Douala on the Gulf of Guinea where the sea leaves a thumb print on the coast of Cameroon. Amy spent one hour and twenty minutes on the ground

– just long enough to refuel and study the weather reports. She had been in the air for more than ten hours. Jim had warned her that Douala was too small an aerodrome for her to risk a take-off with a fully loaded plane; she had also been told that there were thunderstorms ahead. Amy herself was worried that for the first six hours of her journey she would be without moonlight. Despite these concerns she took off early that evening.

She immediately flew into heavy tropical storms. The rain fell in sheets, battering the sides and roof of *Desert Cloud*'s cabin. Amy could see nothing outside; inside she peered at her instruments as the plane lurched up and down. She scribbled her thoughts on scraps of paper in blue ink that quickly became smudged: 'Lightning on all sides – very frightening. Thunderclouds on east forced me at WNW over S. Atlantic when only patch of fairly clear sky was pitch dark.'[6]

The next stage of her journey took her 1400 miles over some of the remotest areas of West Africa. There were very few aerodromes and many were in such a poor state of repair that they offered little shelter. For the next fourteen hours she headed south, mostly flying over the Atlantic Ocean rather than following the circuitous coastline. 'At 200ft. suddenly into cloud. Started climbing immediately but v. bumpy and lost control.' She steered towards the sea; at one point the winds blew her a hundred miles from the coast.[7]

As the plane droned through the night she noticed that her oil pressure was sinking and started to worry that she had not filled up her reserve petrol tank. She poked a pencil into the tank. 'None! What to do? – very worried.' She calmed down when she remembered that she had turned on the reserve tank after four hours and that the fuel would have drained below the level that her pencil could reach. But there was no solution to the problem of the oil pressure and she became transfixed by the gauge, aware that if the oil gave out the engine would seize up, possibly tearing itself free from its mountings.

She began searching for a landing place but she could barely see the ground. As she peered through the side window, a line of white surf gave her a clue as to the position of the coastline, but the beach was too rocky for a landing. 'Very frightened. Cld. not see ahead at all.'

Thursday, 17 November

Amy reached Benguela in Portuguese West Africa (Angola) at 8 a.m. GMT (6 a.m. local time). She expected to land on a sandy aerodrome but instead sank into a morass of mud. The local Reuters agent,

R. V. C. Middleton, discovering that probably the biggest story of his life had just landed, rushed out to greet her and then immediately wired Grosvenor House.

Middleton found a Portuguese mechanic who woke someone in the nearest town to help him find a spanner to undo the plane's oil sump. The long crossing over the Sahara had blown sand into the oil and the engine, and Amy spent the next nine hours fitting a new filter, when all she could think of was sleep. She ended her telegram to Jim: 'Terribly disappointed. Amy.'[8]

After an hour's rest she left at 4.50 p.m. for Mossamedes, just north of the border with South-West Africa (now Namibia). She had thirty-one hours in which to beat Jim's record.

Friday, 18 November

Amy reached Mossamedes at 6.30 p.m. and was back in the air at 1.50 a.m., hoping to cover the final 1200 miles in one final dash. She chewed a few raisins as she flew and maintained her concentration by looking straight ahead for long periods of time and then forcing herself to study every detail of *Desert Cloud*'s cabin as a way of reminding herself that this was the same plane that had left Lympne.

Tumultuous crowds cheered her arrival in Cape Town at 1.31 p.m. (3.31 p.m. GMT). Over the previous four days, six hours and fifty-three minutes she had survived on a total of five hours' sleep – the longest stretch lasting two hours. Her eyes were red and she was deaf from the noise of the engine but she looked 'remarkably spick and span' in a black flying suit, a white silk blouse and a sun helmet.[9] After stepping out of the plane she rested her head momentarily in her hands as if collecting her thoughts before she smiled and waved at the crowds. She wanted a cigarette and, most of all, a bath. She spoke to Jim by radio-telephone from the airfield, their tone a stage-managed banter. It was Jim, rather than Will Johnson, who was asked to comment on Amy's achievements: 'I'm so proud that she has done it but I knew she would. Perhaps the world thought she never could repeat her great flight to Australia, but this shows she has the stuff in her. This is wonderful. For a man it would be fine, but for a woman it is splendid.'[10]

Her time over the 6200 miles was ten hours and twenty-six minutes faster than Jim's – near enough to be described as half a day. They had flown similar planes and covered the same route; the one, tiny difference was in the horsepower of their engines, which gave Amy an advantage of about five miles per hour.

After sleeping for fourteen and a half hours Amy made an appointment with a hairdresser. She broadcast a message via the BBC to which
Jim replied from London. The tone was that of a joshing double act,
but in private Amy was desperately homesick. Once the fuss had died
down she stayed quietly with friends by the ocean, waiting for the
moon to allow her to return to England. Sitting on a balcony with
views of the sea and mountains, she wrote the one letter to her
husband that has survived. She told him she was leading a very quiet
life:

> lots of fresh air, sunshine and exercise. No late nights, no smoking and drink-
> ing . . . I miss you so much that I can't really enjoy the blue sky and sunshine
> because I'm thinking all the time how much nicer it would be if you were
> here (and then I think maybe we'd quarrel about something and spoil it! –
> but then maybe we wouldn't).[11]

The rest of the letter is an account of the flight that could only have
been written from one seasoned flyer to another. She finished the letter
by saying, 'I do love you, Jim.' In return he sent her short, encouraging
and affectionate cables, telling her not to worry about talk of possible
rival flyers and offering to meet her in *Heart's Content*.

The Duchess of Bedford had made the outward journey to the Cape
in April 1930 in under ten days and had taken the same time to get
home; but in both cases she had been accompanied by co-pilot Captain
Barnard and had flown a plane with a range of 1500 miles. Amy was the
first person to attempt the round trip alone. Given that she had taken
less than five days to reach Cape Town, she appeared to have a good
chance of beating the record set by the 'flying duchess'.

Amy left Cape Town at 7 a.m. GMT (5 a.m. local time) on 11 December, but quickly hit thick fog and cloud. On her second day she was
forced to fly so low that she barely cleared the treetops until she
decided that the powerful crosswinds might blow her out to sea and
climbed again, flying 'blind' for hundreds of miles towards Douala.
Without a radio she had no way of knowing whether the aerodrome
was free from fog. If visibility was poor she risked colliding with the
13,000-foot Mount Cameroon that guards the aerodrome but by that
time her fuel would have run out, leaving her no other option but to
attempt a landing. Amy was far out over the Atlantic Ocean when she
calculated that Douala must be close by. She turned east to head for the
coast, its outline guiding her through the 'back door' and into the
safety of the aerodrome.

By Wednesday the Atlas Mountains were lost in a heavy snow-storm and winds of seventy-five miles an hour. As Amy flew through a deep valley she pushed the plane's nose towards the wind until she was flying almost sideways, like a crab. But still the wind drove her nearer and nearer the ravine's rocky sides, eventually forcing her to give up and turn back. When she took off again the weight of the snow settling on *Desert Cloud*'s wings threatened to bring the plane down and Amy was forced to wait until the weather cleared. But the strong coffee and caffeine tablets she had been taking made sleep impossible. By the time she reached Oran she had to hold the machine down to stop the winds blowing it away.

Bad weather meant she did not reach Le Bourget near Paris until 17 December and finally arrived at Croydon the following day, taking seven days, seven hours and five minutes to travel from Cape Town – a record that stood for nearly four years. In London the Crown Perfumery Company in Burlington Arcade created a special fragrance which they called 'Sarcanthus' to mark her achievement.

Amy and Jim were 'Britain's foremost flying family'.[12] When she landed at Croydon Jim fought his way through the crowd to plant a kiss on her lips. 'The only thing that kept me going was the thought of seeing my husband,' she told reporters.[13] In France her triumph contributed to the growing anxiety about the 'masculinisation' of women. One French writer, Henri Falk, was concerned about the decreasing prestige of husbands compared to the 'new woman', expecting a modern bride to remark: 'Leon, I love you and will marry you, but you must realize that I am a passionate parachute jumper. You must let me jump whenever I want. Otherwise, nothing doing.'[14]

Reporters estimated that Amy had flown solo over 22,500 miles and had covered some of the loneliest and most dangerous stretches of the earth.[15] She told reporters in Paris: 'The flight that I want most in the world to make is to America, but there is no immediate prospect of that. All I want to do now is to get home and rest.'[16]

It was during this period of frenetic record-breaking feats that a photographer based in a ramshackle studio near the seafront at Blackpool produced the most striking images of Amy and Jim. John Capstack was already an established landscape painter, miniaturist and fabric designer when he set up his seaside photographic studio. His artistic background gave him an innate sympathy for light and shadow and his photographs have a distant, ethereal atmosphere.[17] His portrait of Amy wearing her flying helmet became her favourite image and shows her face emerging from a high astrakhan collar, her goggles pushed up onto her forehead. It combines the smooth-skinned, high-cheekboned look of Greta Garbo or Marlene Dietrich with the far-away gaze of a pioneering pilot constantly scanning the horizon; her luminous eyes are perfectly framed by pencil-line brows that trail off into the harsh leather of her flying paraphernalia. A second photograph entitled 'Speed' captures her in a very different pose. Her bare shoulders and hair flowing loose behind her form a figurehead in profile; her face is expressionless as she clasps her forehead with one arm so that her elbow forms the apex of a triangle. The image, reminiscent of the statuette on a Rolls-Royce, appeared on the motoring page of The Tatler of 1 March 1933.

In December 1932 Amy spent her first ever Christmas away from her parents. It was a departure from tradition that both sides were acutely aware of and Amy, writing from the Place Vendôme in Paris, tried to reassure them that she was very fit and 'as happy as I can remember ever being'.[18] She wrote again from the Palace Hotel at St Moritz where fellow guests included a Hollywood producer and the cupid-faced Clara Bow who had starred in Wings, the film that had inspired Amy and helped to convert her father to flying, and – Amy's favourite of the celebrities – the comedian Harold Lloyd. Bow had failed to make the transition to 'talkies' and retired in 1931; by the time Amy met her she was physically and mentally frail.

Amy confided to her parents that she missed the routine of a family Christmas and found France very expensive where 'everyone is out to rob you'.[19] There were compensations for being famous, though, and on her way home to London she visited Chanel who gave her the 'most marvellous evening dress' and offered to supply her with clothes at cost price.[20] Will's news was mundane by comparison: he had managed to sell a cargo of herrings.

Amy and Jim returned to Grosvenor House, from where Jim finalised plans for his next endeavour – an attempt to fly solo from England to Brazil in three and a half days. The journey included a 2000-mile crossing of the South Atlantic – a stretch of water that only one other airman had traversed alone. That airman was Bert Hinkler who, weeks before Jim set off for South America on Monday, 6 February, had been reported missing over Italy in an attempt to regain his solo record from England to Australia. Amy offered to take part in an aerial search for Hinkler but his body was eventually discovered in the Tuscan alps by a group of charcoal burners. It appears that his plane crashed in freezing weather and he managed to stagger forty yards from the wreckage. His left hand was missing and had probably been eaten by wild animals.

Hinkler was unaccounted for when Amy and Courtenay arrived at Lympne aerodrome to wave Jim goodbye. The *Daily Express* had agreed to pay a fat fee for Jim's exclusive story when he arrived at Port Natal in Brazil. Over the next forty-eight hours Amy waited as Jim flew to Barcelona and skirted the west coast of northern Africa until Senegal provided a jumping-off point for the South Atlantic.

Jim was due to arrive at Port Natal on Thursday night and Courtenay and Amy went to the offices of the *Daily Express* hoping to speak to him. News came through that he had landed but, as there was no telephone at the aerodrome, they were unable to contact him. When Jim's 'exclusive' failed to appear, the editor ran a story about how Amy had been with her husband in spirit as he crossed the South Atlantic. Reporters knew that with Amy and Jim they got twice as much story for their money.

Amy finally spoke to Jim on Saturday afternoon when he had reached Rio. The conversation was filmed by Paramount who set up a studio at Grosvenor House to record it for newsreel. The conversation also provided an exclusive news story for the *Evening Standard* and a full-page photo of Jim appeared on the front of *The Tatler* three years after Amy's photo had featured there. Capstack's photo depicts Jim in a *Boys' Own*-style companion portrait to his image of Amy, goggles pushed onto the top of his flying helmet as he gazes heavenwards. A striped, tightly knotted scarf adds to the comic-book image. The muffler is probably one knitted by his friend Princess Arthur of Connaught, which allowed him to boast that 'few men can go out to fly dressed in clothes made by British royalty.'[21]

While Jim was away Courtenay and Amy visited the Crufts' Dog Show. Mr and Mrs Cruft gave them a guided tour and Amy was required to have her photo taken holding the paw of countless animals. A group of fans trailed behind her as she went from dog to dog. The following day Amy and the Countess visited one of the exhibitors' kennels in Surrey and returned with a kitten for Courtenay and a golden spaniel for herself, which she called 'Rio' to mark Jim's arrival in the city. Dogs had always been part of her life; in the cine film that Will made using the camera Amy bought him there are usually two or three small dogs in the background, snapping at each other in the garden or bounding across the sand at Bridlington. Animals were a good leveller and Amy made several friends through encounters that began with 'dog talk'. It so happened that dogs in the 1930s were a fashion accessory. *The Tatler* ran a regular page called 'Ladies' Kennel Association Notes'. The Prince of Wales loved his dogs, as did the Mitford sisters, and in the book *Whose Dog Are You?* Amy and her Dachshund, Teena, appear next to Lloyd George, Gracie Fields, A. J. Cronin and Sir Malcolm Campbell.

Amy travelled to Madeira to meet Jim's ship on its way home from South America. The close proximity of her African flight and Jim's flight had left her 'nervy' and she needed a break. Waiting for Jim had brought her closer to his mother who saw Amy as a steadying influence on her son. 'I like the frank way you admit your love for him,' Mrs Bullmore wrote to her. 'His ideals and mine have often clashed and he has sometimes hurt me terribly, but though he has a good streak of his father in him he has a lot of me too, and we are bound to be fundamentally alike in many ways.' But she worried about the effect of record-breaking flights on their relationship: 'both of you have been living at high tension since you were married.'[22]

Aviation journalists were starting to wonder out loud about the value of long-distance flights and the huge amounts of money and fame being lavished on pilots. Aeroplanes were in danger of becoming a curiosity as ineffectual as the biplanes that buzzed round King Kong while he swung from the top of the Empire State Building in that year's hit movie. But record-breaking was a way of life for Jim and Amy, a trade that financed their expensive lifestyle of grand hotels, fast cars and holidays in the South of France. Part of their appeal sprang from their ability to scoop huge amounts of money in one burst of daring that pushed them to the very edge of physical endurance, unlike the rest of the population who trudged daily into work or who subsisted on the dole.

Each flight brought in money from media deals and endorsements. In 1932 Wakefield 'gave' Jim a total of £8500 (£288,745 in today's money) in return for the right to make his successful Cape Town and Atlantic flights the focus of advertising campaigns.[23] Wakefield gave Amy £6000 (£203,820) in December 1932 after her South African triumph, for which she cabled her thanks in a form that lent itself perfectly to advertisement: 'I owe another record to your absolutely reliable and peerless lubricant.'[24] Success usually sparked a plague of generosity so that an Australian businessman felt compelled to give Amy £1000 after she landed in Cape Town to match the sum he had given Jim when he broke the record to Australia.[25]

She also made money from journalism. Sometimes she wrote her own pieces; other times she dictated them to a reporter who knocked her account into a publication's particular style. The articles offered a vicarious thrill that the reader could enjoy from the safety of their own sitting-room and worked well when Amy was describing tribesmen from far-flung outposts of the Empire, such as the 'savages' who surrounded her at Atamboea on her way to Australia. Problems arose, however, when the local people she wrote about read her account.

Like the child who believes that putting a paper bag over their head makes them invisible to the people they cannot see, Amy believed that local people who did not speak her language lived in a parallel universe that ceased to exist for her once she had left it. Her profession made her a visitor who was always glancing at her watch, rather than a traveller. This approach, together with an imagination that often ran out of control when she was on exhausting, long-distance flights, proved a volatile combination. That combination finally caught light in an article which appeared under her name in the *Sunday Dispatch* of 22 January 1933; the piece produced a legacy of ill feeling that rumbled on for the rest of the year.

In describing her forced landing in Poland in January 1931 Amy reached back into the stuff of childhood nightmares to paint a picture of being lost in a thick forest inhabited by ogres. In this stygian world, which she compared to one of Grimm's fairy tales, she was confronted by a dozen 'peasants' from a collection of 'mean dwellings'. They were all men and only one, 'a dirty, bearded, evil-looking man' who looked at her 'greedily', spoke a few American words. He gesticulated 'in a menacing way', repeating the word 'money'. Eventually a horse and sleigh arrived to whisk her to safety, but just as they were leaving the edge of the forest the 'awful ruffian' who had demanded money rushed forward and tried to pull her into a hut. 'My life has often hung by a thread, but never before nor since have I felt such terror as at that moment when I struggled with this brute, with succour miles away over the lonely snows,' Amy wrote in the *Sunday Dispatch*.

The article made an exciting, breathless read; the only trouble was that its contents were widely circulated in Poland where investigations and research by the Polish Aero Club, police and journalists discovered that Amy's Grimm-like description was rather too close to a fairy tale. A letter from the Polish Aero Club to its British counterpart detailed, point by point, the many errors in her account. The most glaring were that her reception party was not all-male – one of the first people to meet Amy was a female school-teacher; the area where she landed is not surrounded by woods; the 'dirty, bearded, evil-looking man' was the well-respected and clean-shaven local mayor and Amy was taken to the nearest town in a carriage, not a sleigh. The letter also pointed out that the cost of repairing the plane had been met locally and that the money Amy offered to the villagers was used to erect a cross to mark her landing-place, the residue being donated to the local library. The Aero Club produced a letter of thanks sent by Amy to the people who had helped her, which earned her the local title of the 'charming girl from heaven'.

Although Amy told her mother it was a 'silly fuss about nothing'[26] she sent a placatory letter to Perrin that she asked to be forwarded to Poland. In it she put the blame firmly on the *Sunday Dispatch* reporter who 'badgered' her for 'exciting incidents'. But this was not sufficient for the Royal Aero Club or for British and Polish journalists who had got wind of a good story. Under pressure from Lord Shelmerdine the club sent Amy an official letter of reprimand which placated the Polish Aero Club.[27] Amy was stung by the telling-off which she regarded as an insult and considered suing the club. She visited the editor of the *Sunday Dispatch* in a state of 'considerable agitation' but he was not prepared to allow one of his reporters to assume blame for the story.[28] In a letter to Courtenay the editor pointed out that Courtenay had 'passed' the article before publication and that the reporter had actually 'toned down' parts of her account.[29] But Amy could not let the matter rest and she and Jim exacerbated the situation through articles in the *Daily Express*, the *Evening News* and the *Evening Standard* in which they accused the Poles of lacking a sense of humour.[30]

The 'Polish Affair' was a distraction at a time when Amy and Jim were concentrating on their next big flight: plans to cross the Atlantic together in the more difficult westerly direction. In May Amy stayed at the Abbey Hotel, a grand ivy-covered building in Malvern where she went riding and relaxed before the Atlantic flight. The ideal day to leave was 5 June because of the full moon. 'This flight means a tremendous lot to Jim and me,' Amy wrote to her father, 'and without unduly stressing matters, there is always the risk that this may be the last you see of us.'[31] She and Jim made their will, in which they left everything to Jim's mother.

Chapter 20

The Water Jump

(1933)

The appearance of the great, black, lumbering biplane in the clear evening sky drove the 8000 people waiting on the beach below into a frenzy.[1] At first the machine was just a smudge on the horizon, but as it drew closer its distinct outline took shape and the noise of its throaty twin engines rumbled down to the sand below.

Amy and Jim peered anxiously at the four miles of upturned faces squinting at them through the July sunshine. *Seafarer*, which was travelling at a steady 100 miles per hour, swept low over the wide, open sands of Pendine Beach, scattering the crowds as they tried to guess where the plane might land. A solitary policeman and an AA scout did their best to keep order but were unable to prevent several people from being injured in the stampede to greet the pilots when they landed. The plane taxied along the beach for nearly a mile, chased by a posse of cars, vans, bikes and tourists in summer clothes and bathing costumes, with pressmen, photographers and cine-operators in the lead.

Amy, who had just celebrated her thirtieth birthday, emerged from *Seafarer* in brilliant white overalls that made her look ghostly and overexposed in the countless photos taken of her. She waved at the crowd and said in her strange, almost royal voice: 'We are very grateful for your marvellous welcome.'[2]

As the masses pressed in on her and *Seafarer*, her composure faltered and she added: 'I have nothing else to say, except that I would ask you to keep away from the plane as our lives depend on it.'[3]

The couple were slapped heartily on the back and good-luck charms were pressed into their hands. The Beach Hotel where they were staying offered scant refuge: the dining-room was invaded by fans who had missed *Seafarer*'s landing, and Amy and Jim were forced to make a dash for their bedroom. Amy was later called down to the front door to shake hands with a group of women who refused to leave until they had met her. At 11 p.m. Jim was summoned to check that *Seafarer*, now roped off and guarded on the beach, was safe from the incoming tide.

In 1933 Pendine Beach in Carmarthen Bay, South Wales, was strongly associated with speed. The same seven-mile stretch of firm, golden sand that attracted tourists drew men like Sir Malcolm Campbell for attempts on the world land-speed records. Amy and Jim were the first transatlantic hopefuls to see the beach's potential as a natural runway. It was wide and straight and conveniently placed on the west coast of Britain. Moreover, the beach's length gave them a greater chance of lifting *Seafarer* off the ground. The plane, specially adapted to carry extra fuel, had been nicknamed 'the Flying Petrol Tank' by the press. In private, Jim referred to *Seafarer* as 'The Flying Coffin', commenting to Courtenay that the plane only needed brass handles to complete the effect.[4]

Seafarer was a De Havilland 84 Dragon, a new model that was already proving popular with the flying set. The Prince of Wales, the future Edward VIII, had recently bought one and the royal version was an 'air liner in miniature' with a six-seater cabin for his guests. In *Seafarer* the cabin space was taken up by three 200-gallon petrol tanks so that the pilot had to lie on his or her back and shuffle through the darkness to reach their seat. The feeling of claustrophobia was compounded by the fact that the only windows were the triplex windscreens. The blackness of the plane's fuselage was briefly relieved by the white swirl of its name and the Union Jack on its tail added to its sombre character.

'The King and Queen of the Air' arrived at Pendine on Monday, 3 July 1933 hoping to use the small Welsh resort as their starting point for a series of aviation records. Jim aimed to become the first person to make the crossing twice and together they wanted to be the first husband-and-wife team to conquer the Atlantic. After flying 2700 miles to New York, they planned to continue straight to Baghdad in a 5994-mile journey that would secure them the world non-stop record.

Pendine marked their second attempt to make the Atlantic crossing. Only a few weeks earlier they had left Grosvenor House at 4 a.m. for Croydon Airport. Their arrival, just before dawn, was in sharp contrast to the chaos that greeted them in Wales. At Croydon 300 well-wishers waited patiently for them to appear; many had come straight from London parties and were still in evening dress. They cheered politely as the chocks that held *Seafarer* in place were removed and the plane began to trundle uneasily down the runway. Jim opened the throttles and *Seafarer* managed 200 yards along the ground before it clipped a drainage gutter that Jim had overlooked. The plane tipped over onto one wing before slumping onto its wheels. Ambulance bells clanged loudly as the crew rushed to extricate the couple from what was effectively a powder keg threatening to blow up at any minute. Amy cried all the way back to Grosvenor House.

From the moment *Seafarer's* wheels touched down on the golden sands of Pendine Beach a waiting game began. Amy and Jim lived on tenterhooks until they heard the weather report for the following day that was phoned through to the village's post office at 6.30 each evening from the Air Ministry. Every day the crowd grew more impatient, failing to appreciate that while the sunshine made the beach ideal for a seaside holiday the weather several hundred miles out in the Atlantic might be quite different.

The delay meant that Jim and Amy were able to attend Molly and Trevor's wedding. Amy enjoyed the visit home to Bridlington which gave her a chance to see at first hand how much Will was enjoying the expensive motorboat she had bought him. Molly's joy at having her big sister present at her wedding cancelled out any feelings that the two celebrity guests had edged her out of the limelight.

Pendine quickly assumed a carnival atmosphere that local people still remember today. Crowds continued to flock to the beach, taking numbers up to 10,000.[5] Amy and Jim were a cheap spectacle and the heatwave allowed tourists to camp out in the dunes overnight or sleep in their cars.

A small funfair arrived and stall-holders sold coffee and fruit; shops and pubs had never been so busy and took £3000 (over £105,000 in today's money) in the first three days after the couple's arrival.[6] When Amy and Jim marched out to inspect the sand they were tailed – at a respectable distance – by a line of tourists chattering among themselves as if the two celebrities inhabited a different world and were thus impervious to the presence of so many strangers. Amy wore the style of flimsy floral dress that *Vogue* was recommending that summer and kept her blonde, shingled hair closely pinned to her neat head. Jim strode ahead in his flannels and short-sleeved shirts; Rio scampered along at their heels.

They tried to relieve the boredom by motoring out for lunch at country hotels; Amy went on brief shopping trips and attended a Kennel Association event. They made the most of the fine weather by playing golf and going for early morning swims and tried to please the crowd by visiting a local school; Jim even took a ride on a donkey. But even if they had not been famous in their own right, they were too well groomed and well dressed to blend into a remote part of Wales. Amy's clothes combined the fashionable nonchalance of the era's new-found interest in leisure and the outdoors with its obsession with clean lines and neatness. When the couple visited Chepstow races she wore a grey, tailored flannel suit, a blue beret and a blue-and-white scarf tied casually at the neck.

At Pendine it was becoming impossible to ignore the inquisitive band of tourists who waited outside Amy and Jim's hotel window. One member of the crowd gave a running commentary on what was going on inside their bedroom and the couple were forced to make an impromptu speech sitting on the windowsill of their room before the group of fans would agree to leave.[7]

Other guests at the Beach Hotel complained about the noise and about the man who was caught climbing up the hotel's drainpipe. When the cine-film operators asked Jim and Amy to pose for shots beside *Seafarer* and to give speeches as if they were about to take off, the spectators refused to believe that this was not the real thing. They burst through the ropes protecting *Seafarer* and extra police had to be drafted in. Amy and Jim eventually took up a local schoolmaster's offer to stay at his isolated hillside home.

A few days into their visit the weather became squally. *Seafarer* was threatened by the incoming tide and had to be hurriedly moved further up the beach. Even then it was not safe. A family, following the instinct of any British holidaymaker, decided to brew up a cup of tea near the plane.[8] The grass in the dunes caught fire and the flames came close to engulfing *Seafarer*. That afternoon the plane was flown to Cardiff Airport where, in one day, 2000 people paid to see it. A week after their arrival Amy and Jim decided to retreat with *Seafarer* back to London to wait in the comparative anonymity of the capital.

The east-to-west route is by far the most difficult direction in which to cross the Atlantic. Setting off from Europe, pilots face headwinds that slow the machine down dramatically, forcing them to carry dangerously large supplies of fuel. The journey's toughest test – the disorientating fog-banks of Newfoundland and the insidious icicles that can creep up on an engine – occurs when the pilot is most tired, nearly thirty hours after taking off. Jim had experienced the Atlantic in this direction before, but the knowledge of what he was about to put himself through only added to his anxiety. Showing fear, though, was not part of the job description of a record-breaking aviator. 'I have always felt that my destiny was in some way connected with water,' he told a newspaper. 'I have faith in it – in its solitude, its loneliness. I suppose the essential spirit of such a flight must be faith – faith in oneself, one's companion in the aeroplane and in the engine.'[9]

Jim had complete confidence in his wife's skills as co-pilot. Four years later, when their relationship was less happy, Amy's professionalism in the air was one of the few aspects of her character he was unable to find fault with: 'As a flying companion I would still choose Amy as above reproach,' he said.[10]

Amy dreaded the thought of a long journey over water and still remembered vividly her terror at flying over the Java and Timor Seas. She became contemplative and withdrawn. 'It is not death I fear, but partial failure,' she told a newspaper. 'Both Jim and I would rather die than face that. After all, we should be together, and that makes the possibility of death easier to bear for both of us. It is my fate to make this flight with my husband. I want to do it, and that is the end of it.'[11]

Apart from the effect on their nerves, the waiting gave others the opportunity to knock them off the front page of newspapers eager for aviation news. As the Mollisons' delay dragged into weeks, the Lindberghs flew to Greenland on a survey for Pan-American Airways of the best transatlantic route for passenger and mail services by seaplane. Italy's extravagantly bearded Air Minister, General Balbo, led a procession of twenty-four seaplanes known as the 'Bachelor Armada' from Rome to Chicago in a macho show of air muscle whose progress the Pope plotted on an easel outside his papal office, and Wiley Post attempted to become the first solo pilot to fly round the world.

On the evening of Friday, 21 July weather reports showed that the headwinds on the Atlantic's surface were blowing at less than 15 miles per hour and that at 2000 feet above the ocean they were 25 miles per hour or lower. These were the speeds they had been waiting for. But the realisation that they would soon be off on their epic journey filled Amy with foreboding, and she found it difficult to conceal her nerves from Courtenay and Jim when they dined together.

News that Shell Mex and BP had been told to send fuel to Pendine caused a ripple of excitement at the beach, although there was some scepticism after so many false rumours. On the morning of Saturday, 22 July Amy and Jim woke up to an Air Ministry report that was slightly better than usual. The winds 800 miles west of Ireland were westerly to south-westerly up to a height of about 500 feet. It was foggy and there was some drizzle. Beyond that, to Newfoundland, the winds were 15 miles per hour up to 500 feet. Visibility on the other side of the Atlantic was good, although there might be some showers and fog. From there to New York the winds were variable at about 10 to 15 miles per hour. 'Weather conditions are reasonable, though not particularly good, but they are good enough for us to take a chance,' Jim told a local reporter.[12] He and Amy knew they couldn't afford to wait any longer and they left Stag Lane at 7.45 a.m. on Saturday. 'I have never been so excited in all my life,' Amy told a reporter. 'The strain of waiting is terrible, but it will be all right when we get into the air.'[13]

Courtenay was with them when they returned to Pendine, crouching in the back of *Seafarer*.[14] Throughout the journey the little man hunched over his typewriter composing a fictitious account of the crossing in which the couple displayed all their courage and skills as pilots in their epic battle against the Atlantic Ocean. He later gave the swashbuckling tale to Amy because he thought it might provide an amusing distraction during the flight.

Seafarer landed at Pendine on a drowsy summer morning. Jim and Amy walked over the sands to make sure that it was firm enough for take-off and then asked a local paper to position one of its vans to mark a stretch of soft sand. Jim held a white handkerchief in his right hand to test the breeze. It hardly moved. He examined *Seafarer's* engine while Amy, blithely ignoring the risk of fire, stood by his side, her mouth clenched grimly on a cigarette. It took two hours to refuel *Seafarer* with 428 gallons of petrol. At Croydon they had taken on board 450 gallons, but Jim hoped that by carrying a smaller quantity they would now avoid a repetition of the earlier take-off fiasco.

At about 11.30 a.m., Amy, who had discarded her flying overalls to reveal her orange jumper and grey skirt, walked to the post office for the last time to phone Will and Ciss. A final call was made to the Air Ministry to confirm that the weather conditions had not altered since they had left London. In fact, there was now drizzle over less of the route.

As noon approached Amy and Jim made their way down to the beach in a borrowed car. The atmosphere was eerily subdued. They shook hands solemnly with their friends as the wind whipped Amy's hair into a candy-floss cone that made her look even more apprehensive. Jim swung *Seafarer's* propeller into action with an awkward sideways twist of his body and, looking like modern-day astronauts in their white suits, they clambered onto the plane to sit side by side at the dual controls. At the last minute Amy thrust a bag at Courtenay containing her gold cigarette-case, her money and other valuables. Her only luggage was a tube of lipstick, a comb, some face powder and some eau-de-Cologne, which she slipped into her overall pocket. She shouted above the noise of the engine: 'Now for the greatest adventure of my life.'[15]

Jim taxied to the end of the beach to make the most of its seven miles. Clouds of sand sprayed the crowds as the plane raced at 70 miles per hour down the make-shift runway. Amy began counting to calm her nerves. She reached 60 before, 500 yards along the beach, Jim managed to get the 'flying petrol pump' airborne. Amid cheers from the crowd it rose gracefully and then doubled back over the beach, heading for the Atlantic. It was followed at a safe distance by four light aeroplanes which escorted *Seafarer* until it left the British coast.

By the time *Seafarer* had reached Ireland the weather had closed in. They were surrounded by thick, low cloud; fog and drizzle obscured the craggy coastline and their heavy fuel load made it impossible to climb above the cliff-tops. Jim was still at the controls and Amy strained her eyes in search of the obscured rocks that they knew were lurking in the fog. She screamed at him to bear left as a cliff suddenly loomed up in front of them. 'We climbed carefully and prayerfully,' she recalled later, 'and at last emerged above the clouds into a new world, a wilderness of blue sky staring at a marble floor.'[16]

They passed Mizen Head, the southernmost tip of Ireland, at 2.20 p.m. and from then on *Seafarer* became a capsule of sensory deprivation. The ocean was visible for just three out of the next twenty-two hours; they were suspended in a sea of whiteness that robbed them of the feeling of movement. It was only their furtive glances at the airspeed indicator, which showed they were travelling at one hundred miles per hour, and the constant rumble of the plane that proved to each of them that they were actually moving.

Courtenay waited an hour at Pendine in case they were forced to return and then flew back to London where he could not resist passing on Amy's pre-flight fears to the editor of the *Sunday Express*. In the morning the paper's readers woke up to a front page 'splash' in which Courtenay described Amy's feelings of foreboding on the eve of the flight.

Amy and Jim's provisions were two thermos flasks of coffee, two of iced water, a bag of boiled sweets, tomatoes, sandwiches and some barley-sugar which Amy had raided during the weeks of waiting, and, officially, two bottles of beer for Jim. They took it in turns to fly the plane for an hour each, whoever was not on duty scrambling to the rear of *Seafarer* to rest on a camp bed. Jim maintained his bravura by pretending to read a novel during his breaks, although in reality he spent time peeping through the hole in the plane's floor for signs of the waves below or gazing at the back of Amy's head as she leant against the wall of the cockpit. It was too noisy to talk and communication was kept to a minimum; they wrote notes to each other or used hand signals. They were no longer celebrity husband and wife; instead they had become detached professionals treating each other with a reserved politeness. Amy wrote later:

> And so it went on, hour after hour after monotonous hour . . . Nothing happened to break the awful monotony. Our imaginations ran riot. Were our instruments lying? Were we really many hundred miles out to sea? What was below us? The urge to go down and see became well nigh unconquerable, but commonsense came to the rescue and saved us this waste of time and fuel.[17]

They were 'flying blind': relying on their instruments, without the help of landmarks or waves to show them the direction of the wind. They carried three compasses: the second to check the veracity of the first and the third to confirm that the second was true. *Seafarer* flew with the sun, making the longest of long days even longer; twilight lasted until midnight, British Summer Time. Amy watched as 'wisps of cloud materialised in front of us and were cut, like so much paper, by our propellers.'[18]

Whoever was navigating had to make sure the plane was sticking to its compass course and was on an even keel. Their eyes began to smart through staring at *Seafarer's* instruments: compasses, oil-pressure gauge, rev counter and petrol gauge each assumed a mystical role. These dials alone proved that they were moving and only they held the secret, unlocked by a map and a protractor, of their position.

Despite the pervasive, nauseating smell of petrol they struggled constantly against tiredness and 'utter boredom'.[19] Amy found that if she relaxed for a second her head dropped, jerking her awake in panic as she tried to remember where she was. 'Oh yes, of course, you are somewhere in the middle of the North Atlantic,' she told herself, 'with hungry waves below you like vultures impatiently waiting for the end.'[20]

Twilight lingered an unnaturally long time until the plane's luminous dials started to glimmer and the exhaust left an effervescent trail behind them. As night-time descended so the temperature dropped and Jim climbed to the back of the plane to put on his warm black flying suit and wool-lined boots, at first struggling to get into Amy's by mistake. Both of them shook out their arms and legs as far as they could in the confined conditions to try to keep cramp and the creeping cold and damp at bay. Black coffee helped them to fight sleep and the barley-sugar relieved their dry lips.

They began to long for morning light and when it did, finally, arrive Amy realised how dishevelled she looked and felt. When it was her turn to rest she took the opportunity to comb her hair and to apply some face powder and eau-de-Cologne. Jim was so impressed with the results that he combed his hair, although he could do nothing about the day's growth of beard.

When they at last descended through the cloud they found themselves in a new, white world, which Amy described as 'like a giant's pudding basin clapped upside on a layer of dough'. They were a fly caught inside it, 'there seemed no escape, no beginning and no end'. Without warning the floor disappeared; 'we had a funny feeling we were going over the edge of the world'.[21] They had plunged into the feared Newfoundland fog-banks which engulfed them for the next three hours.

They had worked out in advance that the earliest possible time, under ideal conditions, at which they could expect to spot land was 10 a.m. British Summer Time (BST); but Amy started to search for signs of land long before this. Peering through the peephole in the plane's floor, she saw, for the first time since they had left Ireland, the occasional glint of water and then what she thought were small white islands. She handed Jim a scrap of paper with 'icebergs' written on it. 'Soon the water was littered with lumps of drift-ice, like a huge bath strewn with soap-flakes.'[22] The icebergs broke the monotony and allowed her spirits to soar: 'We had a glorious sensation of speed and movement, now that we had objects to flash past our wings and leave behind.'

But the stately, yellow-white mountains that drifted in and out of the fog filled Jim with despair. He was convinced that they meant *Seafarer* was too far north and he was about to turn the plane onto a southerly course when they both spotted birds, a sure sign that they were near the coast. At noon BST Jim shouted 'land'. As the rocky coast of Newfoundland started to take shape, the couple shook hands solemnly.

It might be bleak and barren land that offered small comfort if they were forced to put down, but it was still land. *Seafarer* had conquered the Atlantic and was heading for New York. They discussed whether they were over the Bay of Fundy, on the western coast of Nova Scotia, or whether their navigation had been faulty and they were several hundred miles further north, off the coast of Labrador. As more of the coastline emerged it became evident that they were in the United States, rather than Canada, and that their navigation had been accurate. Although they still had 1100 miles ahead of them, they felt

Left: Jim Mollison.

Below: Crowds welcome Amy home after her record-breaking flight to Cape Town and back, 1932.

Opposite page top: Amy and Jim study their charts before setting off across the Atlantic in 1933.

Opposite page below: The couple recover in hospital after crashing on their way to New York.

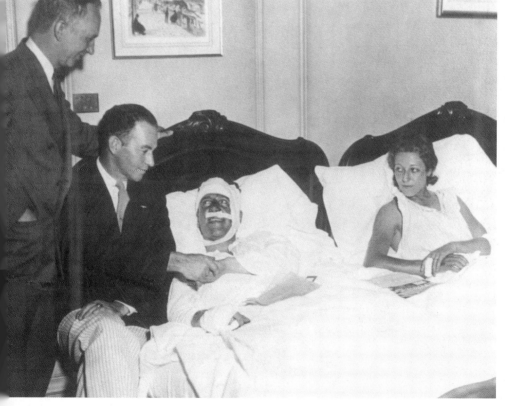

Above: President Rooseve
and his wife, Eleanor
spend Sunday afternoon
with Amy, Jim and Ameli
Earhart.

Left: Amy holds a young
fan at the opening of a
new pool at Butlin's
Holiday camp in
Skegness, May 1936.

Opposite page: Schiaparel
designed this woollen su
for Amy to mark her flig
to Cape Town in 1936.

First solo flight from
England to New Zealand
October 5/16th

JEAN

First Woman to fly
the North Atlantic solo
east to west
September 4/5th

BERYL

Record flight London
to Cape Town and back
May 4/15th

AMY

LET'S JOIN THE LADIES —
AND USE WAKEFIELD PATENT
Castrol XXL

Above: Anna Neagle and Amy at the opening of the speed boat season at the Welsh Harp in north London, 1931. The actress was to play Amy in the film *They Flew Alone*.

Left: Beryl Markham and Jean Batten became Amy's rivals for publicity.

Opposite page top: Amy after one of her many court appearances, 1935.

Opposite page bottom: François Dupré with his second wife, Anna Nagy.

Amy with her friend, Amelia Earhart in the summer of 1933.
Both died in mysterious circumstances.

confident that the only thing that would prevent them making their goal was lack of petrol. The headwinds had forced them to use more fuel than they had planned for, so they cut back their cruising speed to seventy-five miles per hour to conserve petrol.

Their confidence grew as the weather cleared over Portland, Maine, and the American coast emerged to guide them on their way. As they neared Boston, Amy, who was at the controls, protested that they should refuel while it was still light, but Jim was adamant that they should press on for New York. They saw two planes which appeared to be taking pictures of them.

In London, Courtenay was at the offices of the *Daily Mail* with the Countess and the paper's air correspondent, Roger Fuller, watching the wires for news of *Seafarer*. At 5 p.m., BST, on Sunday the plane was spotted at Robinson's, St George's Bay, on the west coast of New-foundland and, five and a half hours later, at Bar Harbor in Maine. Reuters confirmed a sighting over Revere in Massachusetts at 6.47 p.m., Eastern Standard Time (12.47 a.m. on Monday morning, BST). By 8 p.m. (2 a.m., BST) they were over Rhode Island. Courtenay calculated that the tanks would run dry in about one hour's time, when they had been in the air for thirty-nine hours.

Some forty miles north of New York *Seafarer*'s engines began to splutter; a sure sign that fuel was running dangerously low. Each time Jim tried to ease its nose higher the remaining fuel trickled to the back of the last tank and the engines started to fade. Their only hope was to land at the small aerodrome of Bridgeport on Long Island Sound in Connecticut, but after a day and two nights without proper sleep they were unable to make even the most basic judgements about the landing site. The aerodrome was hemmed in by marshes and both Amy and Jim found it impossible to see where the airfield ended and the swamp began. To make matters worse, the airport manager had ordered that all the lights should be switched on in an attempt to ease their descent. The sudden blaze of illumination added to Jim's feelings of disorientation. Amy, too, misread the manager's efforts to help them as they circled for the sixth time. He had sent up an aeroplane to try to guide them down and trained a searchlight on a windsock to alert them to the direction of the wind. But both Amy and Jim failed to spot the windsock and saw the other plane when it was returning. They assumed it was taxiing for take-off and, as a result, they misjudged the wind direction. Five times they prepared to land and five times Jim thought better of it, until they both knew there was no alternative. A final surge of adrenaline, prompted by the knowledge that they faced the most crucial moment of their journey, overtook their exhaustion. Their bodies assumed the taut position of two pilots braced for descent into whatever lay beneath the blur of light. Their eyes burnt with tiredness and their heads pounded with the noise of *Seafarer*'s labouring engines, but they knew that their reactions in the split seconds as the plane touched down were all that mattered.

Instead of being sucked back into their seats as the plane slowed they were jolted forward. Too late to do anything about it, Amy realised that they were landing with the wind – rather than against it – and closed her eyes. The extra force sent them hurtling down towards the lights at breakneck speed. A runway appeared and just as quickly vanished. Jim struggled to control *Seafarer* while the plane groaned in protest, barely clearing a line of telegraph poles. A menacing darkness momentarily replaced the unbearable brightness before the plane slumped onto the heavy marshland with a sickening crunch. It continued to wheeze along the ground for a few metres before flipping upside down into a ditch. Amy, held firmly in her seat by a safety harness, watched helplessly as Jim was flung through the windscreens before bouncing partly in again.

She hung suspended in her harness from the roof of the upturned plane in the deathly quiet and darkness. Next to her Jim was slumped over the shattered windscreen. As she fumbled to escape she felt what she assumed was petrol trickling through her hair. Uppermost in her mind was the thought that the plane might explode at any moment; she knew that she must get them both as far away from *Seafarer* as quickly as possible.

Rescuers fought their way through the tall meadowgrass and then began to wade, almost waist-deep, in the swamp. A woman's low whimpering voice guided them through the darkness to the scene of the crash, where the wrecked plane lay like a disembowelled creature staked out ready for dissection. They found the pilots in a ditch partly hidden by long grass; Amy was cradling Jim's body in her lap. When she heard the rescue team she shouted: 'Hurry, please, we're over here . . . my God, hurry, please.'[23] The desperate phrase was one that Amy used only when she thought she was about to die.

Chapter 21

Looking for Work

(1933–4)

Amelia Earhart and her husband were enjoying a quiet Sunday supper by the pool at a friend's house. America's most famous airwoman was distracted by a live radio broadcast from Roosevelt Airfield on Long Island where 700 policemen were struggling to keep a crowd of 20,000 under control as they waited for the Mollisons. The commentator was nervously running out of small talk as the expected time of their arrival came and went. It was almost with relief that he announced that they had crashed attempting a landing at Bridgeport. 'They deserved better luck,' Amelia told her friends before hurriedly gathering up pieces of clothing to take to Amy.[1]

At the offices of the *Daily Mail* news came through that Jim was dead and Amy seriously injured. Courtenay could not help regretting that the story had broken too late for Monday's paper. He was concerned, too, that if his typewritten, fictitious account of their crossing was discovered amid the wreckage it might appear that he had planned to pass this off as the 'true story'. In the wrong hands the manuscript could jeopardise the deal he had struck with the *Daily Mail* for the exclusive rights to their tale.

When the rescuers arrived at the scene of the crash they found Jim alive, although barely conscious. Wreckage from one of *Seafarer's* wings was converted into make-shift stretchers to carry Jim and Amy to waiting cars. By the time they arrived at the local hospital Jim was laughing and joking with nurses, telling them he looked 'a bit of a mess'.[2] He was given thirty stitches in his head – a figure which more than tripled when he came to write his autobiography. Amy suffered minor cuts and bruises, mainly to her legs. Her chief concern was that her parents should know that they were safe. 'Tell them,' she urged local reporters, 'that we are OK, and are not much injured, but we are terribly disappointed.' She added, 'Jim's injuries are only slight, thank God. We are both terribly tired, and just want to fall asleep. We are very upset and distressed, but we have done our best, and got safely across.

I do hope everyone in England will not be too disappointed with us.'[3]

Within two hours of the crash 7000 cars had arrived at the road nearest the wreck. Souvenir hunters swarmed over every inch of *Seafarer*'s wooden frame, stripping it of anything that could be lifted – bits of canvas, instruments, even nuts and bolts – and scribbling messages on immovable objects. A copy of Saturday's *Daily Mail* was discovered, sodden but still readable, among the wreckage.[4] It was posted onto billboards outside a cinema in Bridgeport where people came to read it by torchlight throughout the night. It was the first time many people had seen a British newspaper and the fact that the news was barely a day old added to its mystique. To the people of Bridgeport the Mollisons were more than transatlantic pilots: they were time travellers. Such was their fame that a baby girl born locally at midnight on Sunday was named Amy Mollison Stafford.

By Monday morning the hospital was under siege. Newspapers carried artists' impressions of Amy and Jim lying side by side in their hospital beds like the tomb of a medieval king and queen, their arms neatly folded, their eyes closed. Soon this image was superseded by a more dynamic press photo showing Jim with his head swathed in bandages and with a bad cut on the left side of his face, above his lip. Amy had already seen the hospital's manicurist and hairdresser and by the time she was photographed she looked as though she were resting before going out to a London nightclub, rather than recovering from the worst crash of her life. She sat upright in a stiff, white hospital nightdress, studiously applying lipstick she had borrowed from a female reporter. President and Mrs Roosevelt sent white roses, which helped to give the hospital the air of a movie star's dressing-room, and the arrival of Amelia Earhart, who brought a change of clothes for her friends, boosted their celebrity status still further. Wiley Post, who, barely three hours after *Seafarer* crashed, became the first person to fly solo round the world, left a dinner given in his honour to drive fifty miles to visit the injured couple.

Glamour quickly restored Amy's spirits and she began to enjoy the attention; Jim took longer to recover. She had immediately sent her clothes to be dry-cleaned and was able to change into the red jumper, grey flannel skirt and silk stockings she had worn for the transatlantic crossing. She looked fit and animated during an interview on the hospital balcony for a 'talkie' news item; Jim was a brooding presence in the background, lolling in a long chair, his pain and ill temper obvious.

Fourteen hours after they were admitted, Amy and Jim left hospital. At the airport Amy continued to take the lead, giving a brief speech and helping police to lift Jim into a waiting plane where she was seen waving gaily from the window. *Seafarer* had arrived shortly before its owners; its front section was completely missing, the cabin was bent and twisted and the wheels had been removed. To Courtenay's relief, what was described as the typewritten 'log' of the voyage had been found that morning and returned to Amy, who had promised an auto-graphed copy of the story once it was published.[5]

As they arrived at Floyd Bennett Aerodrome in New York, police formed a cordon around the plane to protect it from the crowds. Jim made a feeble attempt to point out the landmarks to Amy before exhaustion forced him to ask the doctor accompanying them to take over. Amy's wide, uninhibited smile beamed out at the crowds, fresh-faced and demanding to be liked. Although she was the most well-travelled woman in the world, she had yet to see anything like Manhattan. The city had only recently started to push its Art Deco fingers into the sky: the Empire State Building, the Rockefeller Center and the Chrysler Building were new landmarks that protested a confi-dence that was only skin-deep in a country in the midst of a deep depression.

Amy and Jim stayed in the hushed opulence of the Plaza Hotel and arrived to a stack of telegrams six inches high and flowers from well-wishers, including Amelia Earhart. In their Imperial Suite they were given anti-tetanus jabs by the three doctors and one nurse looking after them. They were then left to sleep until late Tuesday morning, while their two police guards kept away all visitors. On waking they ate a large lunch and Amy went shopping for new clothes and another man-icure.

Jim took a back seat at their tickertape reception. He had seen it all before after his solo Atlantic crossing and his heavily bandaged head and arm gave him a slightly ridiculous air. While Amy laughed and waved her handkerchief through the paper snowstorm, Jim occasion-ally shook a fist at the 300,000-strong crowd, like an out-of-sorts Egyptian mummy. He was unsettled by this daylight, wholesome face of Manhattan, preferring the more seedy nightclubs and late-night drinking joints. At a dinner given in their honour at the Plaza by the Federation of Scottish Societies, Jim vomited when the third course, 'Chicken Glasgow', arrived. His illness was attributed to 'serum sick-ness' following his recent tetanus jab.[6]

Amelia Earhart, who invited them to stay with her and her husband, George Palmer Putnam, puzzled Jim. He described her as 'that strange, charming woman' and never quite knew how to handle her.[7] Amelia, with her short, tousled hair and freckled face, had a tomboyish energy that Jim had not encountered before. The light, bias-cut dresses and tailored trousers of the 1930s sat comfortably on her long, lean body. Jim respected her for her flying skills, but was uncertain how to treat a woman who was obviously not in the least bit susceptible to his charms and who was teetotal. Jim had much more in common with Amelia's husband, the divorced, wheeler-dealer publisher whom journalists nicknamed the 'lens louse' due to his eagerness to appear in photographs with his wife.

Jim's wariness of Amelia was heightened by her friendship with Amy. He liked to control the people his wife saw, and this was the first time in their marriage that Amy had forged a strong relationship with someone whom Jim was not equally close to. Amelia, who was five years older, appealed to Amy's intellectual side. Her work nursing veterans of the First World War had turned her into a pacifist and before taking up flying she had been a social worker among immigrant children in Boston. She liked to write poetry, but had a cynical, matter-of-fact view of marriage. On the eve of her wedding she wrote what must be one of the least romantic letters ever received by a bridegroom: 'You must know again my reluctance to marry, my feeling that I shatter thereby chances in work which means most to me. I feel the move just now as foolish as anything I can do . . . I know there may be compensations but have no heart to look ahead.'[8]

Over the next few days Jim and Amy gradually unwound at Amelia and George's extravagant, Spanish-style mansion in Rye, New York State. It was a comfortable house with six bathrooms, banisters of imported wood and blue tiles in the front hall brought from China by an explorer friend of George's. Books lined the sitting-room and a large bay window looked out onto the garden that Amelia enjoyed working in. The open hearth lay unused during the Mollisons' visits as temperatures rose into the high nineties.

Amelia and George took their guests to their swimming club and to the beach. Jim and Amelia discussed forming the North Atlantic Solo Flight Club; Wiley Post thought it a good idea. The two other eligible members, Charles Lindbergh and the tall Texan Jimmie Mattern, were to be consulted. Then, out of the blue, the two couples were asked to join the President and Mrs Roosevelt for lunch. Amelia and Eleanor Roosevelt were already good friends and the President's wife was fascinated by flying; even so the invitation was a startling compliment – much more so than the tickertape processions that were bestowed indiscriminately on most aviators.

Later, Jim said grandly in his memoirs that he had taken his wife to lunch with the President of the United States,[9] but a more accurate description was that Amy's reputation had allowed her husband to meet the Roosevelts. FDR had been in office for less than five months and was struggling to keep together a country eviscerated by hardship: 12.8 million people – a quarter of the workforce – were unemployed, those who still had jobs saw their wages fall by over 42 per cent and prices plummeted to such levels that many farmers became destitute. There was not much good news around.

On the last weekend in July the President announced he was too busy to receive visitors, but suddenly changed his mind. 'The Flying Sweethearts', who had crossed the Atlantic the hard way, had come close to losing their lives and still wanted to continue on their long-distance marathon, were a living example of FDR's battle cry that 'the only thing we have to fear is fear itself'.

So it was that the two couples found themselves driving behind a motorcycle escort on its way to the President's country retreat and boyhood home of Hyde Park, New York State. Each of the three pilots had met British royalty before but these occasions had not been as intimate as a private lunch with the most powerful man in the world.

Hyde Park is set in several acres of woodland and has impressive views of the Hudson river. Amy and Jim were driven up a gravel driveway that ran between cornfields, then round a large lawn dotted with tall, spreading trees, finally ending up at the front door of the mansion. The President's father and his first wife bought the house in 1867 and the original clapboards were later removed and covered in stucco. A porch with a sweeping balustrade and small colonnaded portico completed the conversion to a grand mansion. The avuncular President greeted Amy and Jim, who looked like two wayward children next to his impressive bulk. 'Well, well, you're both looking fine in spite of your accident,' he said.[10]

The interior of the house was dominated by heavy, dark furniture, naval prints and rows of stuffed birds collected by FDR as a boy. Amy sat on FDR's right-hand side; Eleanor and FDR's powerful mother, Sara, were also present at a meal that lasted an hour and a half. Jim said later that he liked the President, although he 'detested' his politics.[11] As someone used to pushing his body to its limits, Jim was fascinated to see how the President coped with his physical disability in the swimming-pool. 'The crippled President is completely at home in the water, swims entirely with his arms,' Jim wrote.[12]

Sunday lunch with the President had increased the Mollisons' social standing and they were invited to a string of dinners and lunches in their honour. The Ninety-Nine Club, an organisation launched by Amelia and other leading women flyers to promote female pilots, held a lunch at the Aviation Country Club in Hicksville, Long Island, to celebrate Amy's achievements. The meeting was a revelation for Amy. It was the first time that she had found herself the centre of attention based purely on her flying expertise, rather than the fact that she happened to be a woman. She was amazed to discover that the USA had 600 women pilots compared to Britain's thirty.

Forty-three pilots attended the event, driving by car or appearing on the horizon in a motley collection of different planes that they had flown from around the country. They were young, attractive women bubbling with confidence; enjoying what they did and proud of it. The *Ninety-Niner* newsletter reported that 'the girls' flew a total of 3675 miles to join Amy for lunch, while Amy had covered a mere 3600 miles to be there. 'And the gals had to fly home again too.'[13]

They sat at tables placed on the lawn in front of the clubhouse and listened to Amy talking about her experience of flying in Australia, Africa and across the Atlantic. She told them of the limited variety of planes in Britain, how there was a huge gulf between the light planes and the big transport 'ships' and how she wanted to try her hand at faster planes. The afternoon's swimming was cancelled so that the 'hangar talk' could continue.

When Jim sailed for Britain to make arrangements for a replacement for *Seafarer* Amy remained in America, living in the Plaza Hotel and spending much of her spare time with Amelia who was planning to start a new airline, Boston–Maine Airways. Her partners in the scheme were Sam Solomon, a former army officer and amateur basketball star; Eugene Vidal, father of Gore; and Paul F. Collins. Amy helped Amelia to publicise the new venture by talking at women's social clubs in New England. Amelia, in turn, arranged for her to fly one of Boston–Maine's ten-passenger Stinsons. Amy also co-piloted a twelve-passenger Ford flown by Transcontinental and Western Airline (TWA) from Newark to Los Angeles. She was impressed by the American pilots' expertise in night and instrument flying, and the slick operation of ground controls.

In LA Amy, wearing her TWA uniform and beret, autographed the flying helmets of adoring Ninety-Niners who had turned out to greet her, and she was given the chance to 'talk in a normal voice' in one of TWA's quiet, new high-speed planes. She visited the Douglas and Lockheed factories and flew a new Douglas plane. In the development of commercial aviation America was years ahead of Britain.[14]

When Jim returned from Britain, ready to re-start their trip to Baghdad, he found a changed Amy. She was more confident and less committed to the idea of record-breaking flights. Their bid to take off from Wasaga Beach on the Canadian Lakes felt like a tired re-run of the Pendine experience, and after three attempts they decided that the overloaded plane would not leave the ground. While they were in Canada Amy fell off her horse, and a routine check-up in a New York hospital on their way to a holiday in Bermuda revealed a stomach ulcer. She stayed in hospital for three weeks and was told that she needed to rest for six to eight months. The manager of the Plaza allowed Amy to stay at the hotel free of charge while she recovered; Jim continued on his way to Bermuda.

The crash at Bridgeport was a turning point in their relationship. Sharing a near-death experience had driven a wedge between them rather than bringing them closer; Amy saw just how selfish and driven Jim could be, and the aftermath, when she became the star, made her realise how much he resented taking a back seat. During their stay at Pendine Amy had confided to her mother that she and Jim frequently quarrelled but the life or death argument about whether or not to refuel showed that their differences went deeper than petty squabbles.

When she joined Jim in Bermuda she was unable to muster the patience to deal with his heavy drinking and in November she went alone to Florida to continue her convalescence while he returned to Britain. By November 1933 speculation about their separation and the possibility of divorce had started to appear in a few British newspapers; Jim denied both suggestions indignantly.

Amy's reception in America gave her a new confidence and independence. Driving back in her Mercedes from Miami to Palm Beach in the early hours of the morning after a party, she was stopped for speeding by two plain-clothes policemen. It was a time when gangster movies were popular and when John Dillinger, the original Public Enemy Number One, was at large. Amy's vivid imagination, which had transformed the mayor of a remote Polish town into a savage rapist, instantly assumed that the two men on the lonely stretch of road were about to rob her. She tried to escape and in the ensuing struggle hit one of them in the face. A court appearance followed at which she was fined $50 and asked to pay $20 costs.

Her marriage, which was barely a year old, appeared to be foundering and she turned to her career for ballast. Amy could not decide where her future lay: whether she should stay in America or Britain, continue to make daring flights or seek some Lindbergh-style role as an aviation ambassador or consultant. Whenever her career appeared to hit the buffers – as it had when she could not find backing to fly to Australia – Amy resorted to lists. Now was one of those moments and she jotted down eleven options, giving each a suitability rating.[15] Becoming an aviation editor was top of the list; writing fiction and journalism on topics such as playing tennis, living in the country and horse-riding came in at number ten. Her second and third choices were politics and 'Government work . . . (experimental flying). Stratosphere.' Amy was also considering jobs in commercial flying: demonstrating for the manufacturing firm of Blackburn; working for an air-taxi service run by the entrepreneur Edward Hillman; joining a foreign airline such as KLM or Lufthansa; and taking *Seafarer* joy-riding in India. The only possible long-distance flights were crossing the South Atlantic in *Seafarer* and then flying on to California, where she would study at Boeings and do some film and radio work; or attempting to fly non-stop to Cape Town.

She returned to Britain in February 1934 to put the eleven-point plan into action; she was immediately successful. The *Daily Mail* offered her a six-month contract as Aviation Editor for fifteen guineas a week; she had to deliver a weekly feature and was not allowed to write for another publication. The Conservative Party were keen for her to stand as a parliamentary candidate in the West London constituency of Hammersmith, but she quickly decided a rural seat would be preferable, allowing her to fan interest in her candidacy by swooping down on voters in a plane. Hammersmith, she wrote to her father, was a 'poor slum district, very tough' that harboured 'a great deal of dissatisfaction with the Government'.[16] As it seemed certain that a Socialist would be elected, Amy felt it was a waste of time 'and possibly prestige' for her to stand.

Her foray into politics lead to a tiff with Courtenay who was desperate for money to pay for his wife's doctor's bills; Greta was ill and he needed £500 for treatment. In a confidential letter to Jim, Courtenay complained that he had advised Amy on a career in politics and even accompanied her to Conservative Central Office, but he was hurt that she had not discussed Hammersmith with him and had approached the *Daily Mail* by herself.[17] Amy wrote back that she was willing to discuss a retainer and spelt out the terms of his role as agent: if he found a home for an article he would receive 20 per cent, or half the fee if he also wrote it.[18]

Amy became a tireless 'networker', writing to influential men such as Lords Rothermere and Londonderry, Sir Josiah Stamp and Brigadier

General Sir Harold Hartley CBE. Most agreed to meet her – who could turn down an invitation from Amy Johnson? – but each told the same story: they would love to help but the work was just not there. Hillman's response was typical, but more direct – business was 'none too good'.[19]

She appealed to Shelmerdine's patriotic side when she wrote, ostensibly asking for advice, but in reality sounding him out about possible jobs.[20] She told him there was no future in 'stunt flights' but that there was 'still plenty of scope for what might seem to be spectacular flights but which are really of some scientific and technical value'. She wanted a 'serious' job and had been offered several in America but could 'hardly forsake England'.

Amy also had a vision of what politicians now call an 'integrated transport network'. She wanted to help the Air Ministry choose sites for aerodromes, to draw up contracts with municipal authorities and to advise the railway and shipping companies on links with airlines. The job she envisaged for herself included inspecting existing aerodromes for safety and introducing the level of lighting and markings that she had seen in American airports. She was prepared to waive a salary until she had proved herself.

Lord Londonderry, Secretary of State for Air since 1931, agreed to see her and then put her in touch with his wife who was secretly planning a Women's Legion Reserve to help defend Britain in an emergency. Edith Londonderry had played an active part in the suffragette movement and had founded the Women's Legion during the Great War, initially to recruit female cooks to the army. After the war she gave glittering receptions at her home in Londonderry House to which she invited her close friends: Ramsay MacDonald, Nancy Astor, Winston Churchill and Sir Samuel Hoare. Her revamped Women's Legion would include a flying section to be controlled by the RAF which would count female pilots, wireless operators, mechanics and 'riggers' among its numbers. According to correspondence held at the RAF Museum in Hendon, the idea appears to have had Government approval, although it is unclear whom Lady Londonderry saw as the major threat. Lord and Lady Londonderry became friendly with top Nazis and attended the Munich Olympics, where they had private talks with Goering and Hitler. As late as 1938 Lord Londonderry published a book in favour of detente with Germany; the couple's enthusiasm for Nazism finally disintegrated in March 1939 when Hitler invaded Prague.

In May Amy and Jim rented a country cottage, 'Belfairs', in the tiny village of Lurgashall, between Guildford and Chichester in West Sussex. Amy was relieved to leave London and Grosvenor House; the cottage, which was six miles from a railway station, was the 'next best thing to having your own house'.[21] They had reluctantly sold *Seafarer* to De Havilland and Amy drove an old, borrowed Delage as her Mercedes was in America. There were signs that the break from London might be just what they needed to settle down into some sort of routine; Amy even asked her father to send some of her books to the cottage. They cycled daily across the Sussex Downs in a, for Jim, unprecedented fitness regime to prepare themselves for their next big flight. Then, after less than a month in the cottage, Amy suddenly decided to sail for America in search of work.

After visiting the Beechcraft factory in Wichita she signed a contract to sell their planes in Britain and applied to her friend, Eugene Vidal, now director of Air Commerce, for a US transport pilot's licence, but this proved impossible so long as she remained a British citizen. Much as she admired America, changing nationalities was a step too far.

On her second trip to America she became a true tourist: in her *Daily Mail* column she wrote excitedly of the romance of cowboys, of visiting the Grand Canyon and a native American village. But she was also fascinated by the Americans' scientific approach to flying, and her journalism conveyed complex issues clearly and enthusiastically, showing a prophetic grasp of the future of aviation. She predicted that high-altitude flying would one day be the normal way for air passengers to travel, allowing the pilot to climb above storms and strong winds; she explained how this could only be possible when a variable-pitch propeller capable of cutting through the thinner high-altitude air was developed.

During a lecture on her Australian flight she explained why she continued to tackle long-distance records: 'I can't help myself. It is the kind of a gamble which appeals to me more than any other. After all, the whole world gambles – marriage is a gamble, children are a gamble, business is a gamble; the greatest gamble of all is the gamble with life and that is the fascination which attracts all who love adventure.'[22] In the autumn of 1934 Amy threw the dice again. This time she planned to fly 12,000 miles in a brand-new, high-speed plane that had barely been tested. Her co-pilot was someone whose skill and character she now severely doubted.

Chapter 22

Mildenhall Madness
(October 1934)

Mildenhall's first ever moment of glory came just four days after the RAF airbase was officially opened on 20 October 1934 when it played host to the start of the most spectacular air race the world had seen.[1] For almost a week a searchlight was trained on the desolate Suffolk airfield. Today RAF Mildenhall is a US airbase, a bastion of Americana in the middle of the East Anglian countryside. Towards the end of the twentieth century it seemed merely a relic of the Cold War, a safari park for eager plane spotters who peered through the perimeter fence for glimpses of the giant, grey C135 aircraft that sat broodingly on the distant tarmac. At the beginning of the twenty-first century the base sprang into life again, sending its huge refuelling planes off to service fighter aircraft in search of Al Qaida targets.

Mildenhall's remoteness was also its main attraction in 1934. When the organisers of a prestigious air race from Britain to Australia were looking for a suitable starting point, Mildenhall was the newest venue under consideration. It had the space to house what was expected to be a large number of competitors and if the unthinkable happened and a plane crashed on take-off, it was more likely to plunge into the heavy Suffolk soil than a cluster of houses.

The air race, funded by the wealthy Australian chocolate baron, Sir MacPherson Robertson, was designed to celebrate the centenary of the city of Melbourne. In reality the event was all about patriotism. Three years earlier MacRobertson, as he preferred to be known, had sponsored a joint Australian / New Zealand expedition to the Antarctic. In recognition of his generosity a region of ice was named after him. Now MacRobertson was worried that the economic slump, which was hitting his beloved Melbourne so badly, meant the city was losing out to Sydney and Canberra. MacRobertson, who was brought up in Scotland, was concerned, too, that Australia was growing apart from Britain and that British aviation was falling behind its American rivals. He believed a high-profile air race would convince the aviation world

to consider establishing faster air links between Australia and its imperial homeland, and in so doing would give the British aviation industry
the fillip it badly needed.

MacRobertson's patriotism was catching and his race quickly
became a contest to see which world power was capable of dominat-
ing the skies. Throughout 1934 debate raged in the press and in
Parliament over Britain's strength in the skies.[2] Winston Churchill bel-
lowed about Germany's secret drive to rearm and described in vivid
detail the destruction of London at the hands of the Luftwaffe.

When the air race was first announced the press grew anxious about
the lack of a British-built entrant that had any hope of winning. Geoffrey De Havilland, spotting the opportunity for worldwide publicity,
announced, nine months before the race's start, that his company
would design and produce a plane especially for the event. The costs of
developing a prototype ran to £50,000 but he recognised that this was
beyond the reach of most pilots and offered the planes at a nominal
£5000 each. Amy was still in America when De Havilland announced its
plan to build a plane specifically for the race. Jim cabled her to see what
she thought and she agreed that they should place an order. He put
down a £1000 deposit on a make of aircraft they had never seen and
which they later found out was to be called the Comet.[3]

There were two parts to the race: one based purely on who reached
Melbourne first, the other a handicap contest. The winner of the speed
race took £10,000 and a gold cup; the handicap prize, which was calculated using a complicated formula that included the plane's weight and
the power of its engine, was £2000. No one could win both prizes.
There were smaller cash prizes for the runners-up, but not enough to
cover the cost of competing.

Amy and Jim were strong favourites because they had both flown
the route before (although Jim's record had been in the opposite direction); the race even followed the route Jim had taken in 1931. But the
disaster at Bridgeport had left a question-mark over their ability to
work together as a team. They were also handicapped by their decision
to avoid night landings at all costs, a strategy they adopted partly
because there was so little time to accustom themselves to landing the
Comet and partly because of their experience in America.

As the difficulty of finding the right plane for the right crew became
evident, the list of possible entrants began to dwindle. The man who
had hatched the idea in the first place was concerned that there was no
Australian entry. In particular, he could not understand why Australia's
greatest airman, Sir Charles Kingsford Smith, was not on his way to

England for the race. Smithy had flown the route before and most Australians believed he could win. MacRobertson, a white-haired man of seventy-four who had started his candy empire in his parents' bathroom, even offered to buy Smithy a plane – so long as it was made in Britain. But Smithy travelled to America to find what he wanted, a single-engined Lockheed Altair that he named *Lady Southern Cross* after his previous, record-breaking plane.

To reach England in time for the race he had to leave Australia in September, but documents for his plane were slow to arrive and the Turkish Government, whom Smithy had criticised in the past, were reluctant to grant him permission to fly over their country. Realising that the race would not be quite the same without their friend, Amy and Jim publicly urged Smithy to hurry to Mildenhall. But at the last moment he discovered cracks in his engine that could not be repaired in time and he was forced to withdraw. The Australian public felt so cheated that he received white feathers in the post.

Amy's main rival for newspaper column inches, Jean Batten, did not have time to return from Australia to enter the race. The ruthless and glamorous New Zealand pilot, who was six years Amy's junior, had tried to beat Amy's England-to-Australia solo record in April 1934. The attempt ended in a spectacular crash in Italy, but she succeeded the following month, earning her the title of 'try-again-Jean'.

As would-be contestants weighed up the pros and cons of taking part and tried to find backing, De Havilland's team worked round the clock, and in absolute secrecy, to build a winning plane at their new factory at Hatfield in Hertfordshire.[4] De Havilland knew he had to produce a racing plane – something capable of travelling at over 200 miles per hour and of covering between 2600 and 3000 miles in one flight. Such velocity demanded a highly streamlined machine with slim, wooden wings; wings that were too flimsy to hold the extra fuel tanks needed to carry the plane through 3000 miles. De Havilland solved this problem by placing the tanks in the fuselage, the smallest positioned just behind the cockpit. Every bolt and nut sat flush with the plane's surface to ensure a smooth finish. But even such an aerodynamic plane needed something extra to help its twin engines to push their speed up to and beyond 200 miles per hour. The answer lay in the sort of variable-pitch propeller that Amy had written about in her *Daily Mail* column. The device allowed the pilot to alter the angle of the blades so that once the plane was cruising at a steady rate, they would slice deeper into the air, adding another 10 per cent to its speed.

The Comet's other innovation was a retractable undercarriage which improved the plane's streamlined appearance still further. The device was operated manually by a wheel and its crudeness became evident during trials when the test pilot grew confused as to whether the undercarriage was safely tucked away or left dangling. An observer on the ground was forced to run to his car to fetch a spare wheel which he held in the air to remind the pilot that the undercarriage needed to be retracted. Had there been more time for trials, the device might not have proved such a problem.

When Amy and Jim finally took possession of their Comet in September 1934 it had been through just four short test flights and had spent a total of one hour and twenty minutes in the air. Amy was over-awed by her sleek new plane which was capable of flying at over twice the speed of the Gipsy Moth that had taken her to Australia four years earlier. The Comet was long and slender with a cigar-shaped fuselage and its humming twin propellers gave the machine the urgency of the waiting plane in the closing frames of *Casablanca*. It had a wingspan of 44 feet and was just under 9 feet tall. Amy was to sit behind Jim in the narrow cockpit enclosed in a transparent canopy that lifted open by sliding a bolt fitted along its length. Jim, with his unfailing knack of choosing the most unfortunate analogy, compared it to a coffin lid. They christened their Comet *Black Magic* and painted it black and gold. Amy wrote to her mother that the plane was 'beautiful and fast, but very difficult to fly'.[5]

De Havilland sold two other Comets. Amy's old adversary, Charles Scott, and Tom Campbell Black bought one and called it *Grosvenor House*[6] after the hotel owned by A. O. Edwards, who was backing their bid. They painted it a brash, pillar-box red. Flying instructor Ken Waller and racing driver Bernard Rubin took the third plane. Writing in the *Daily Mail*, Amy said *Black Magic* was 'sleek and sophisticated beside its more brilliant-looking rivals'. She added, in an aside that betrayed her anxiety, that Rubin and Waller's Comet, which they had painted green but failed to name, would be difficult to find if it crashed in the jungle.

After much debate Mildenhall was chosen from a short-list of four aerodromes as the starting point for the race. It had three grass runways and plenty of hangar space, but not everyone was happy with the decision; many people had not even heard of the Suffolk village. A poem sent in to the magazine *Aeroplane* summed up the disgust felt by many aviation enthusiasts: 'With England at their beck and call/They choose that dust-heap Mildenhall.'[7]

There was very little accommodation available and Jim and Amy were forced to stay with friends of Courtenay's. Will and Ciss agreed to look after Rio and a St Bernard that Amy had been given as a present. 'Christopher' was only two years old but already weighed more than Amy, who sent her parents detailed notes about his diet and temperament. She was keen that the big dog should not be spoilt in the way that Courtenay had pampered Rio. Christopher must not be fed sweets or scraps and should have regular mealtimes. He should not be exercised for more than a mile at a time, as this was bad for his legs, in the same way that encouraging a baby to walk before she is ready could impair her physical development.

Facilities at the aerodrome were primitive: a potato sack became a make-shift windsock, to be replaced later by two pillows sewn together. There were no Very pistols (a device that shot a sort of firework to alert pilots to wind direction or danger) or signalling lamps, and competitors were told to avoid low flying in case they upset the valuable racehorses at nearby Newmarket.

Then, with less than a week to go, Amy and Jim announced that they might take their Comet off in a completely different direction.[8] On 9 October a thirty-four-year-old Croat leapt onto the running-board of the car carrying King Alexander of Yugoslavia as he travelled along the crowd-lined streets of Marseilles. The King was on his way to Paris for important talks with the French Government about Italy's position in the Adriatic. Both the King and the French Foreign Minister were shot dead in an act of terrorism that shocked the world. Interest in the assassination grew when it became known that the murder had been captured on film. British cinema-goers had seen the newsreel and the film company guessed that American audiences would flock to watch the footage – but so long as it appeared in movie-houses before their brief attention-span had been diverted to some new, home-grown tragedy. Five days before the MacRobertson Race was due to start, Amy and Jim were in negotiations about delivering the film in an 'Atlantic dash' of ten hours and for a cool £30,000 (£1.04 million in today's money).

But eventually Amy and Jim decided not to risk an untested plane over several thousand miles of ocean. Instead, they turned their attention to a bleak airfield in the middle of East Anglia. Jim approached Mildenhall three times in a forty-mile-per-hour wind before finally risking a landing in *Black Magic*, one of twelve planes to arrive at the start of the week. By Monday the 'Mildenhall Madness' had started to ferment. The sound of each new plane buzzing in the sky brought crowds out to greet its arrival. Cars crawled past the airfield to catch a glimpse of the competitors, their planes and their teams of mechanics.

Local farm labourers made a point of visiting the airfield on their way to and from work to gaze at each new aircraft and the exotic people they brought with them. Amy described the 'canvas town' of different tents that sprang up overnight to feed the pilots and their engineers. The organisers' one telephone was constantly engaged as drunken Cambridge undergraduates rang the race headquarters to offer their views on the event. The loudspeaker played the same ten or so gramophone records over and over, adding to the feeling of institutionalised panic. At one point 3000 curious spectators burst through the enclosure to have a closer look at the planes and several mechanics complained that the crowds had damaged their machines.

Tuesday was taken up by a grand weigh-in: the planes, their pilots, their passengers and their other 'baggage' were all weighed to make sure they met the race's strict rules. At dusk on Tuesday night the race's other female pilot arrived just in time to check in. Smoke from a glowing brazier helped to give the pilot some indication of the wind direction, but even so the Granville monoplane almost stalled at 200 feet before bouncing onto the grass. Rather than leap out of her plane to greet the waiting reporters, the pilot kept them waiting while she changed shoes, replaced her flying helmet with a neat hat, smoothed down her hair and touched up her make-up. When she finally emerged she handed the expectant pressmen a typed statement from her lawyer and refused to comment further.

Jacqueline Cochran was quickly dubbed 'the New York beautician'. She weighed just over eight stone but was tougher than most of the male pilots. Cochran grew up in a North Florida sawmill town where her foster family was so poor that they could not afford to buy her a pair of shoes until she was eight. She never knew her true parents and claimed she did not own a birth certificate, although she was probably no more than five years younger than Amy. She picked the surname 'Cochran' out of the telephone directory as a way of breaking with her foster parents. Her work as a beautician enabled her to travel to New York where she met the millionaire lawyer Floyd Odlum who persuaded her to learn to fly. Cochran, who later became the first woman to fly supersonic, wrote in her memoirs: 'Women pilots in the thirties were a very special breed. I hadn't been born to such surroundings, but if I had to push my way in, push my way to the top, I knew I'd do it. Winning such a race [the MacRobertson] would offer me an entry.'[9] Cochran was so well organised, and so optimistic about arriving at Australia, that she had arranged for spare parts and changes of clothes to be stationed at regular points along the route. It was said that a bath had been specially plumbed in for her use at Allahabad.

Amy, by comparison, kept a low profile. She appeared at the aerodrome when there was work to do on *Black Magic* or, as the *Daily Mail* said pointedly, when she needed luncheon. She wore a grey-blue silk flying suit with a beaver collar and a 'magnificent mink coat and golf socks' as protection against the winds that whipped in from the North Sea.[10] Her own thoughts were also kept wrapped firmly beneath the thick coat: 'She fetches and carries for herself, works hard on their machine, going up and down tirelessly for practice landings, talks to almost nobody,' a female reporter noted.

The press were also intrigued by a young woman passenger,[11] 'broad shouldered, blonde and genial, expansive, cheerful and good company', who carried a huge pigskin satchel and was one of three passengers on board the Douglas DC2 which was piloted by two Dutchmen: K. D. Parmentier and J. J. Moll. The plane was a mini airliner with fourteen adjustable seats and a wide corridor.

The only other female contestant was Miss E. M. Lay, the 'most elusive of the air race women',[12] who dressed 'inconspicuously' and wore her hair in an old-fashioned 'cartwheel' style. Miss Lay was twenty-eight, from Bognor Regis and of 'independent means'. She had learnt to fly at Brooklands and was paying H. L. Brook to take her to Australia 'for interest and adventure'. It was not a happy combination and he became infuriated by her silent presence behind him punctuated by the click-clacking of her knitting needles – a pastime Brook believed was unlucky.

Amy found it difficult to hide her worries about the route for the MacRobertson Race which, she told *Daily Mail* readers, included 'mountain, sea and desert hazards'. She complained that the rules stipulating that competitors had to check in at various designated points increased the dangers by making it more problematic to land and take off in daylight. One of the hazards she did not mention to the press was her husband, whose preparation for the race was to drink heavily. Scott and Campbell Black, in contrast, had given up alcohol and their abstemiousness lent them an air of determined calmness. Scott held the record for the route and his experience as a pilot with Qantas meant he knew Australia well, which would stand him in good stead for the final leg of the marathon from Darwin to Melbourne.

The two men had met in the bar of the Royal Aero Club in London and made a pact not to compete in the MacRobertson Air Race without each other.[13] They later bumped into Edwards in the gents after their original backer had pulled out of the race. Campbell Black was a popular thirty-five-year-old from Brighton who had set up Wilson Airways in East Africa and piloted the Prince of Wales around Kenya on his visit in 1931. That same year he became a hero by rescuing Ernst Udet, the First World War German flying ace, when he lost his way in the desert. Campbell Black had also taught Beryl Markham, who later became a record-breaking pilot, to fly and, as was the case with most of her male acquaintances, they had become lovers.

At the time of the MacRobertson Air Race Campbell Black was in love with the actress Florence Desmond. 'Dessie', as she was known, was an archly beautiful revue artiste who included impersonations in her stage act. One of her acts featured a British airwoman who became the first woman to fly upside-down to the North Pole with her baby, who was dressed in a matching flying suit.[14] The parody's main joke was the woman's insistence, despite repeated warnings from the BBC announcer, on advertising the oil, carburettor and everything else she had used on the flight. The sketch ended with the woman holding her baby over the side of the plane and saying: 'You will be able to tell your children that you were the first baby to be sick over the Arctic Circle.' Although it was never made explicit that Dessie was impersonating Amy, her clipped speech was instantly recognisable to anyone who saw the stage act or heard the record. While Dessie's other victims, such as Tallulah Bankhead, were flattered by the impersonations, Amy did not enjoy being made fun of.

Dessie added another dimension to the antipathy between the two Comet teams. There was still considerable ill-feeling between Amy and Scott, and Jim and Scott were too similar to be anything other than bitter rivals. They had known each other during their early flying days in Australia and each thought he was the other's superior as both a womaniser and a pilot. When Scott heard that Jim and Amy were to marry he commented tersely: 'They deserve each other.'[15] Scott was much taller than Jim and at Mildenhall he reinforced his size by dressing in a flat cap, a huge RAF scarf and plus-fours, making him look as outlandishly heroic as Roy of the Rovers.

The tension between the two Comet teams was palpable and threatened to turn the whole event into an unrelentingly serious business. But the strange assortment of planes and teams ensured that the competition was more like a *Wacky Races* cartoon than a Grand Prix of the Skies. Colonel Roscoe Turner was largely responsible for introducing a carnival atmosphere. A film stuntman and aviation adviser to Warner Brothers, he added a '7' after his official entry number, '5', so that his plane bore the digits '57', in the style of his sponsors, Heinz. He strode round the aerodrome in knee-length boots and breeches like an early Hollywood director, his teeth gleaming beneath a Valentino moustache. Turner designed his own Ruritanian uniforms and claimed that his swagger-stick was made from a favourite lion's tail dating back to his days as a lion-tamer.

Although Turner was happy to present himself as light relief, he and his co-pilot, Clyde Pangborn, were strong contenders and Turner took the event very seriously. The previous September he had flown across the United States in ten hours, breaking the record for the easterly route by thirteen and a half minutes. He frequently suffered from nightmares before the start of any major flight and once tried to jump out of a window in his sleep, believing he was bailing out of a foundering plane.[16]

On Wednesday Amy and Jim took *Black Magic* up to practise landing, despite the squall that had blown up over Mildenhall. They needed to adjust to the Comet's landing speed of ninety miles per hour, its retractable undercarriage and its sloping front that made visibility poor. Jim achieved two good landings. Their rivals were hardly better off and, before arriving in Suffolk, Scott had landed *Grosvenor House* five times and Black twice. The third Comet team was shattered when Bernard Rubin fell ill and nominated Owen Cathcart Jones to take his place. When it arrived on Thursday at 5 p.m. the Comet crashed on landing, leaving the engineers with just over twenty-four hours to fetch new spares and repair the plane.

Friday, the day before the race's start, was one of feverish activity so that the unexpected arrival of King George V, Queen Mary and the Prince of Wales from their home in nearby Sandringham proved an irritating diversion for the mechanics. The hangars were strewn with spare parts, clothes and rations for the race. Jim described the King as 'a bearded, bowler-hatted, black-coated old gentleman';[17] Queen Mary walked grimly behind him; and their son, in a checked coat, chatted with evident enthusiasm to Scott and Campbell Black. George V commented to Jim that Amy seemed to have overcome the nerves that had struck when she received her CBE at Buckingham Palace. She jokingly asked the King if he would come with them to Australia.

The American competitors were less reverential. Turner welcomed George V with the words, 'Hello, King' and brushed protocol aside by urging the monarch (who, unlike his eldest son, abhorred anything to do with planes) to step on board his Boeing Transport.[18] Captain John Wright, a former professional footballer who had the bulbous neck and shoulders characteristic of his sport, went up in his Lambert

Monocoupé to perform a few stunts for the royal visitors, adding: 'Say, listen. I'm only flying this ship on condition that if I violate any parts of the Air Code you give me absolution.'[19]

Dessie arrived at lunchtime, in one of hundreds of cars on their way from London to the remote airfield. She joined the pilots, relatives, backers, pressmen and aircraft designers in the large refreshment tent. It was an uneasy gathering; champagne flowed but Scott and Campbell Black remained abstemious. Dessie did not want to stay for the race's start and Campbell Black walked her to her car, climbing into the passenger's seat to ask her to marry him. She said she would give him an answer on his return.

Two hundred charabancs arrived with yet more spectators. Extra police were drafted in at the last minute and ambulances commandeered. The Chief Constable of Suffolk announced that a young Dutchman was on the run and might be trying to hide as a stowaway on one of the Dutch planes. Johannes van Leswollen, aged twenty, had escaped from a detention cell at Croydon Airport after his passport was found not to be in order. He had told officials he had come to England to see the famous air race and was last spotted hiring a cab to take him from nearby Ely to Mildenhall.

By nightfall the hangars were lit up like West End stages as mechanics crawled over the machines to make last-minute checks. When the pilots finally went to bed, the Dutch pilots sleeping in their cockpit, the planes were guarded 'like racehorses on the eve of the Derby'.[20] A ballot had placed *Black Magic* first to take off; the other competitors were to follow at forty-five-second intervals. In Australia gamblers had placed a total of £25,000 on the race.

Saturday dawned cold and overcast. Some 60,000 people, many abandoning their cars in the narrow Suffolk lanes, trudged over the muddy fields to see the 6.30 a.m. start. Men in evening jackets and women in satin bias-cut gowns and flimsy shoes drove through the night from London. Amy's former flying instructor Major Travers arrived with his wife Hermione to see if the Comet lived up to its reputation. Tea and coffee, toast, eggs and bacon were on offer for the mechanics who had worked through the night and for any of the competitors who could face breakfast. The public-address system droned out the latest weather reports and thirteen selected photographers were allowed to move close to the starting line. But, just as they did so, a crowd of between 10,000 and 15,000 people surged forward, and the PA crackled out an urgent request for extra police and fire engines to keep them at bay.

Amy heaved on her parachute and climbed into the cockpit behind Jim. The coffin-lid was bolted shut. Sir Alfred Bower, the acting Lord Mayor of London, dropped the starter flag. *Black Magic* moved slowly down the runway for what seemed like an interminable time and then slowly lifted off. Turner, dressed in a particularly garish uniform, followed. Cathcart Jones and Waller were forced to abandon their first attempt after white flames shot out of their Comet. Two other planes took off before a second attempt saw Cathcart Jones and Waller airborne. One by one the assortment of planes with their various crews and passengers followed in an orderly procession.

A local schoolboy, Frederick Ashby, found a prehistoric mound among the flat landscape from which to view the race's start: 'It was dawn and we could hear the engines warming up and as the light grew the first plane took off, followed by the rest at regular intervals . . . Especially, I remember one of the three De Havilland Comets, a red one, flying just over our heads and disappearing into a scarlet sunrise.'[21] *Grosvenor House* was the sixth plane to leave, Scott's head almost touching the top of the canopy roof, the two men looking like brothers with their twin bristly moustaches.

A total of twenty planes left that grey October morning, out of an original field of sixty-four. The race was less cosmopolitan than Mac-Robertson had hoped but there were still representatives from Britain, America, the Netherlands, Australia, Denmark, New Zealand and New Guinea. Competitors were obliged to stop at five aerodromes, although several optional checking places had been made ready in case of accidents. If everything went to plan, Amy and Jim were heading for their first control point – 2053 miles away in Baghdad.

The planes sped out over the dark fen soil. A rainbow welcomed them at Southend and as they droned over Herne Bay people ran into the streets to wave their caps at the cavalcade on its way to Australia. Even as they were crossing the Channel the Comets began to leave the rest of the field far behind. *Black Magic* cruised at just short of 200 miles per hour at 10,000 feet, occasionally rising to 16,000 if Amy needed to see the sun to help her navigate. *Grosvenor House* was not faring so well; Scott and Campbell Black caught the bad weather that *Black Magic* managed to dodge. In Turkey heavy thunderclouds rocked the plane. 'I had the unhappy impression that we were barging through an inferno,' Scott said later.[22]

It was noon before there was any news of the competitors and it was not good. One plane had struck engine problems over the Channel and was forced to land at a small village south of Boulogne. The KLM

Douglas plane was the first to arrive at Rome, one of the optional stop-ping places, but there was no sign of *Black Magic*. By the time Brook reached Cyprus, Miss Lay had completed her second jumper.[23]

Two New Zealand airmen, Gilman and Baines, developed engine trouble over Foggia in southern Italy; they lost control of their Fairey Fox plane which hit the ground and burst into flames. Both men were killed. Cochran and her co-pilot, Wesley Smith, also ran into difficul-ties. Over the Carpathian Mountains Cochran tried frantically to switch to her second tank of petrol, but nothing happened. As the engine continued to struggle there seemed no option but to bail out. The latch on Cochran's side of the cockpit jammed, trapping her in her stumbling plane. Smith refused to abandon her in the plane but just as they seemed to be sitting waiting for death, Cochran tried flicking the switch in the opposite direction. The tank coughed into life: the plane's manufacturer had marked the on/off switch the wrong way round.

There was no word from any of the Comets until the evening, when *Black Magic* roared over the intense heat of the Iraqi plains and on to the floodlit aerodrome at Baghdad, where Amy and Jim were met by members of the cabinet. Jim's first question was to ask whether Scott and Campbell Black had arrived; nothing had been heard of them for eleven hours. Jim and Amy headed for the aerodrome hotel where Amy had a tomato juice and a bath and Jim had an alcoholic drink. They had travelled 2530 miles in under thirteen hours, at an average speed of 199.77 miles per hour, and had arrived with two hours' fuel to spare. They were received as visiting dignitaries, the crowds demanding a speech from Amy and presenting her with a bouquet of flowers.

Cochran withdrew from the race after her plane was damaged on landing. After reapplying her make-up, she 'bequeathed' all the resources she had carefully organised along the way to Amy – the sole woman pilot left in the race. Although Jim and Amy did not know it at the time, the *Grosvenor House* crew were lost over Syria, finding their way at the last moment when the clouds parted to reveal the moon and allowing them to put down at an RAF station in the desert. This unscheduled stop meant Amy and Jim were the only competitors to have flown to Baghdad non-stop.

Black Magic left Baghdad at 8.45 p.m. Campbell Black and Scott arrived fifteen minutes later, the dust kicked up from the departing Comet still hanging in the air. Thirty-three minutes later they were back in their plane. Amy and Jim's next stop was Karachi, which they reached at 4.53 a.m. (GMT), twenty-two hours and thirteen minutes after leaving Mildenhall, a time that smashed the previous five-year

England-to-India record of fifty hours. They were greeted by the bright tents and awnings of the maharajas who had come to watch the race and who were disappointed when *Black Magic* touched down safely, robbing them of the chance to see a dramatic crash.

Amy and Jim were in the air again at 5.49 a.m. but returned to Karachi because Jim felt that the undercarriage had retracted so well that there must be some fault.[24] Departing for a second time, Amy took the controls while Jim slept. At 14,000 feet a thick ground haze made it impossible for her to spot any landmarks; a strong north wind started to blow them off course and at dawn she woke Jim to help her navigate. Still half asleep, Jim realised he had brought the wrong maps: the scale was too small and they were unable to distinguish the myriad rivers below them. They made a second undignified return to Karachi, where they waited until 9.50 p.m. to avoid a night landing at Allahabad, where the confluence of rivers often led to confusion.

When they finally set off fierce thunderstorms sent their two compasses spinning and they were unable to agree on their position. Jim, who had a deep mistrust of compasses and preferred to carry three, yelled back over his shoulder and gesticulated wildly to Amy sitting behind him. Each was convinced the other was wrong, Jim's frustration fuelled by the level of alcohol coursing through his system. Strong winds blew them further off course and they circled the small town of Jabalpur, 175 miles south-east of Allahabad, until dawn allowed them to risk a landing. The only fuel they could find was from a bus depot; Amy's training as a mechanic convinced her that its poor grade would damage the engines but Jim said they had no alternative.

The effect of the low-octane fuel was immediately evident in the noise of the engines and the flickering pressure gauge, but Jim insisted on driving *Black Magic* to its limits, admitting later: 'Our hotted up engines couldn't stand the pace.'[25] Amy pleaded with him to slow down and not to push the engines so hard in such a low altitude. Then, 150 miles from Allahabad, the Comet's right engine failed. Amy, who was at the controls, noticed a trail of white smoke coming from the engine. Fearing that they would have to jump, she struggled to strap her parachute on; but they managed to limp to Allahabad.

There was no movement from the plane's cockpit for some time after they landed. Race officials approached gingerly and retired when they realised the cockpit had become a capsule of pent-up fury. When Amy and Jim had finished screaming at each other they finally lifted the coffin lid. A tractor towed the Comet, with its three empty whisky bottles lying next to Jim's seat, to the De Havilland office. Amy, now unable to restrain her tears, was comforted by one of the race officials. She lit a cigarette and drank several glasses of lime juice. The Comet had a worn cylinder and three cracked pistons. Parts would take four days to arrive from Baghdad, but Amy and Jim had not yet given up hope of continuing the race.

Scott and Campbell Black had swept past Karachi and on to Allahabad, which they reached on Sunday morning (GMT); Scott's first question on arrival was to ask whether *Black Magic* had arrived. After refuelling they were off again. There was a possible sighting of *Grosvenor House* at Alor Setar in Malaysia. By Sunday evening they were at Singapore; tiredness or mechanical fault were the only things that would prevent them from winning the race now.

Amy and Jim had no option but to sit back and watch the Dutchmen, Parmentier and Moll, take off for Singapore. Over the next few hours and days a stream of competitors soared triumphantly through Allahabad. *Grosvenor House* touched down in Melbourne very early on Tuesday morning after crossing the Timor Sea on one engine. Scott and Campbell Black had covered the 11,300 miles in two days, twenty-three hours, and demonstrated that Britain and Australia were now separated by little more than a long weekend. India was a hop away and Europe was no longer a necessary stepping stone to the East. They had won both the speed prize and the handicap prize, although, under the rules of the competition, they were not allowed to keep both trophies.[26] Moll and Parmentier, who on the way had been forced to land at Arbury racecourse in New South Wales, where cars switched on their headlamps to help guide them down, were awarded the handicap prize. Their success in an airliner stressed the possibility that 'ordinary' passengers could make the trip in a short time. During the flight the sole woman aboard the plane had served pastries and tea and sandwiches like an air hostess on a jaunt to Paris or Le Touquet.

Of the twenty planes which set off from Mildenhall twelve made it to Melbourne. Turner came third in the speed race and at the official reception he sought out the winners to tell them: 'I certainly do congratulate you. It sure was an honour to take the fumes from your exhaust.'[27] One plane, flown by Hemsworth and Parer, did not arrive until the spring – 116 days after the race had begun and long after the event had been officially closed. H. L. Brook and Miss Lay arrived twenty-seven days after the end of the contest, but MacRobertson decided Brook still deserved a medal. Miss Lay immediately disappeared to stay with Australian relatives while Brook turned his machine around and flew back to Croydon minus his in-flight knitter. He arrived home seven days, nineteen hours and fifty minutes later, breaking Jim's 1931 record.

The race was hailed as a resoundingly British victory: the winning planes, engines, fuel, plugs, instruments and tyres were all made in Britain. The pilots' watches and underwear, even the tomato juice and grapenut cereal that had kept them going, were British. The race demonstrated the importance of speed in air travel and spurred the Government to work hard at improving the England-to-Australia air route. Lord Londonderry announced plans to introduce flying boats capable of travelling at 200 miles per hour and wireless stations along the route. The first airmail left Croydon Airport for Australia on Saturday, 8 December 1934.

As MacRobertson had hoped, the race acted as a spur for aircraft development. The Comet's aerodynamic design, its retractable undercarriage and its new propeller gave it a speed that might otherwise have taken years to evolve. Names like Douglas, KLM and Boeing were now recognised around the world.

Repairs to *Black Magic* took three weeks and Amy and Jim, still barely speaking to each other, sat in the heat and dust watching the remaining competitors pass through Allahabad. Humiliatingly, they were still there at the end of October when Cathcart Jones and Waller arrived on their way back, carrying film of *Grosvenor House*'s arrival, and themselves attempting to break Jim's 1931 record from Australia to England.

When it became obvious they were not going to winter in Australia, Amy cabled Wakefield to ask him for a £100 loan to allow them to return home. They managed the pretence of a happily married couple for a few days, appearing together at a banquet given by the King of Iraq at which Jim looked ridiculous in an oversized tailcoat borrowed from the Foreign Minister. Asked what had impressed him most about the race, Jim said, 'the tremendous difference in temperature between Mildenhall and India'.

By the time they arrived at Athens the strain of being in each other's company was too great and Amy left Jim to fly *Black Magic* home while she took a seat on a Dutch airliner. The significance of the separation was not lost on the press: 'The Mollisons come home separately. Amy tired', the *Daily Mail* headline told its readers.[28] When she arrived in Amsterdam alone, while Jim remained in Rome, she explained that the De Havilland engineer was flying with Jim to help him sort out the engine problems but that a faulty magneto had forced them to wait in Rome. Amy confessed that she wallowed in the luxury of the capacious cabin and longed for a change of clothes. 'What woman can enjoy being stranded without clothes?' she appealed to the *Daily Mail's* readers.[29] The following day, though, she was forced to deny that the reason they were travelling apart was that they had quarrelled: 'Jim and I are still the happiest of couples and I hope we shall always be . . .'[30]

Amy arrived at Croydon Airport with little luggage except a coat she had borrowed from an army officer. Courtenay and the actress Dorothy Ward were there to meet her. Scott and Campbell Black returned to a well-publicised reception which acted as a constant reminder of Amy and Jim's failure. 'Hail, Scott and Black, the world's most famous airmen!' the papers cheered.[31] The winners embarked on a round of after-dinner speeches, and Scott's autobiography, *Scott's Book*, was rushed out later that year to capitalise on the huge interest in the two pilots. Dessie accepted Campbell Black's offer of marriage, making him a modern knight who had won his fair maiden by meeting her impossible challenge. *Grosvenor House* was shipped home, arriving, to Amy's chagrin, at Hull before touring Lewis's department stores in the North.

The race had cost Amy and Jim between £6000 and £7000 and they immediately put *Black Magic* up for sale. It was bought by the Portuguese Government in February 1935 and renamed *Salazar*.[32] Jim told a reporter:

> In my opinion the need for record-breaking flights is still as great as ever, for the simple reason that they serve to test the stability of the machines and provide the necessary basis on which designers and manufacturers can improve their aerial craft. Perhaps another reason why there is little glory to be got out of record-breaking flying is that the pioneering element is disappearing. Long-distance flights are becoming so commonplace that the heroes of one day are forgotten the next.[33]

But the Mollisons' comments sounded a sour note in a year when there was enough good news around for people to allow themselves the first taste of optimism in a long time. The Chancellor knocked sixpence off income tax and the Prime Minister dared to turn away a delegation of the unemployed simply by dismissing them as 'Communists'. Britain had notable successes in sport: Henry Cotton won the Open Golf championship and Fred Perry took the Wimbledon men's title. At the end of November Princess Marina married the Duke of Kent in an orgy of royal celebrations. People felt free to indulge their fantasies, whether of a fairy-tale wedding, a Loch Ness monster or the latest Dennis Wheatley novel. Even notorious villains were on the wane. In

America Clyde Barrow and his nineteen-year-old girlfriend Bonnie Parker were shot dead and John Dillinger, Public Enemy Number One, was gunned down by police. It had yet to dawn on many people that the Nuremberg rallies of September had displayed a more dangerous villain much nearer to home.

PART 5

Alone Again

Chapter 23

In Search of an Image

(1935–6)

Edward Windsor began his affair with Wallis Simpson in 1934 but, while much of the world gossiped freely about the couple, all except a very few British subjects remained oblivious to the scandal that threatened the very core of their royal family. English newspapers averted their eyes as the heir to the throne cavorted with an American divorcee; Amy's love life, by comparison, was exposed to the full glare of publicity. As early as November 1933 Will noticed rumours in the 'unimportant press' that Jim and Amy were considering separation or even divorce.[1]

After returning from their enforced stay in India they experienced a miserable visit to Scotland; the weather was bitterly cold and boredom drove Amy to eat more than she felt she should. A three-week stay at Champneys health farm, during which she lived off fruit and massages, raised her spirits slightly. She longed to come home to Bridlington for Christmas but Jim preferred cocktails to cosiness and so they headed, instead, for Switzerland. The winter break together proved as disastrous as their time in the cockpit of *Black Magic* and Jim left abruptly for America. Amy put her possessions into storage and moved out of Grosvenor House before taking a horse-riding break in Malvern with her youngest sister. Betty was an unhappy teenager who hated school and had few friends. Will and Ciss worried endlessly about their last daughter who still lived at home; 'she seems like a bird in a cage,' Will wrote to Amy.[2] On their holiday Amy recognised in Betty a kindred spirit and confided to her that she felt desperately lonely.

Publicly Amy and Jim were able to cover up their separation: it was expected that the busy schedules of two celebrities would force them to spend time apart. But to anyone observing them in private it was obvious that their marriage had descended into a squabbling match: Jim seemed always impatient to be somewhere else and Amy's eagerness to snatch brief moments with him made her appear like a nagging wife. Cine film of the Johnson family shows Amy and Molly linking arms to dance together in a larky, carefree moment in someone's back garden. Ciss gently tries to persuade Jim to join in but he remains a distant figure unwilling to take part in the silliness.

Jim treated marriage like his time in the RAF: he left someone else to pick up the bills and put in as little service as he could get away with. He turned out when he was required 'on parade' but disappeared soon afterwards. Their arguments became more frequent, sometimes escalating into a physical tussle that stopped short of violence but which demonstrated their mutual frustration. As Jim felt increasingly trapped he became less guarded in his behaviour towards Amy. Lack of alcohol made him morose and he settled into drinking sessions which began with three 'white ladies' (a cocktail with a refreshing citron tang that conceals a powerful kick: half dry gin and a quarter each of Cointreau and lemon juice with a teaspoonful of egg white to give it a slight frothiness). His sensibilities anaesthetised, Jim hurled insults at anyone who stood in the way of his enjoyment; he abused Amy's friends and called her a 'horse-faced hag' in front of them.[3]

Although Amy had 'vague suspicions' that Jim was cheating on her, she had no hard evidence of infidelity and chose not to find any.[4] Their relationship had from the start been tempestuous; now it fell into the pattern of their flight across the Atlantic: short periods of calm followed by turbulence that finally ended in a dramatic crash fuelled by alcohol and overwrought emotions, before the whole process started again with high hopes and replenished supplies of good will. Amy refused to believe that the marriage could not be rescued. At the beginning of the summer of 1935 they were still living apart: Amy at the Savoy and Jim, insisting that he preferred the life of a bachelor, at the Grosvenor. Amy begged him to move back in with her and Jim conceded, prompting her to dream up outlandish flying schemes to keep them together.[5] They discussed setting up a new private company, Atlantic Airways, to offer the first commercial freight service between America and Britain in which they would take it in turns to fly a twin-engined plane equipped with a wireless across the Atlantic and back, making an estimated weekly profit of £6000. The idea failed to materialise.

The crisis in their marriage pushed Amy back towards the security of her family. She and Will had been cautiously circling each other for some months, anxious to return to the former intimacy that had given them both so much support. By the end of 1934 Will began to open up to his daughter again; his father had died and Will was troubled by business worries caused by especially difficult trading conditions in

America. Just before Christmas 1934 he confessed to Amy that he had been close to a nervous breakdown and Betty's report on Amy's mental health made Will suggest a 'quiet talk'. Amy agreed that this would be a good idea but said it would be best to wait until she returned from her holiday in Madeira as she suspected she might have a 'prejudiced mind' on some of her problems.[6]

Will was back in his old position as counsellor-in-chief, urging her to draw up a balance sheet and telling her to pay for goods in cash as a way of curbing her spending. At first his assessment of her marriage was based on Jim's financial probity. 'If you did happen to find all your money gone and did have some unpaid accounts to meet, do you think Jim would help you with it? If not then it's certainly time you looked well into your own affairs and faced the facts.'[7] But the institution of marriage was too important to Will to base a decision purely on money, and by the end of March 1935 he praised Amy for her confidence in Jim.

She lacked stability in every aspect of her life and it seemed that the whole world was conspiring against her. On Good Friday (19 April) 1935 she took Trevor and Will for a drive to show off her new Mercedes, with her father sitting next to her in the passenger seat. Just before 3.30 p.m., as they approached Fraisthorpe on the coastal road south from Bridlington, a motorbike travelling in the opposite direction crashed into the back of a car that had braked sharply to avoid two cyclists. The impact sent the motorcyclist careering out of control. Amy, who, by her standards, was driving unusually slowly at under thirty miles per hour, struggled to avoid him. Her Mercedes swerved violently onto the grass verge where one of her wheels crushed the motorbike and pinned the young man within the wreckage. The pillion passenger was killed instantly; but the motorcyclist lay on the road with severe damage to his spine.[8]

It was clearly not her fault but she was badly shaken by the accident and waited in a state of deep shock until an AA scout, the police and an ambulance arrived. The whole incident was deeply distressing, made worse by the fact that Jim, who was in New York, was not there to comfort her. She reacted, as she had done after the violent deaths of Irene and Branks, and as she would in the future following a series of flying tragedies, by blanking out the event to concentrate on the practicalities of day-to-day living – as if the fatal crash had been just another forced landing that was bound to happen occasionally. Amy concentrated her worries on whether the survivor would sue her: 'I feel very distressed, of course, but I cannot feel responsible,' she wrote to

Vernon Wood.[9] Her fear of litigation was probably displaced guilt. The motorcyclist's family had no intention of suing her and the young man's uncle reported that in the week that he had owned the motorbike he had had an accident on each of the three occasions he had driven it. Locally, there was nothing but admiration and sympathy for Amy. The dead man's sister shook hands with her at the inquest and expressed her regret that Amy had been involved. After delivering a verdict of death by misadventure the coroner went out of his way to comfort Amy. But there was no getting away from the fact that she had killed someone. The accident came a few months after she appeared at Bow Street Magistrates' Court accused of dangerous driving on Victoria Embankment, and it coincided with agitation in the press about the number of cars on the road.[10]

Up until this point Amy's affinity with engines had been a cause for wonder, now it was a liability; her fame lay in her willingness to risk her own life, not others'. In court she was portrayed as the sort of inconsiderate and selfish road-hog that the press liked to vilify. She had hooted a car driving at thirty miles per hour and virtually pushed the vehicle off the road in her haste to overtake it. When the two cars collided she failed to stop and did not bother to report the accident. The press had not seen this side of Amy before; from now on they were on the look-out for further evidence of her latent aggression.

A few weeks after the fatal motorbike accident Amy crashed the new Beechcraft that she had just bought from America in her role as British agent for the plane. 'What a lot of fuss about my accident yesterday,' Amy wrote to her father. 'It was my own fault but it could not be helped.'[11] She took the incident in her stride, reassuring herself that it had helped her to understand how the undercarriage worked. It cost her dear, though, as she was uninsured and the bent propeller ruined her plans to take the aircraft to flying meetings. She was disappointed by the lack of interest in the plane, which high import taxes had made prohibitively expensive to British customers. She considered having extra fuel tanks fitted so that she or Jim could fly it either alone, or together, back to America. Eventually a businessman called Stanley Spiro chartered the plane.[12]

Amy's 'vague suspicions' about Jim's adultery became harsh reality when she returned home from the theatre earlier than expected to find him drunk and sprawled on the bed with a woman whom she did not recognise. Jim claimed that they were simply sleeping off their inebriation and that he had never been unfaithful to Amy. Soon afterwards Amy went to stay with a female friend in the country. The tableau imposed a new and indelible image of their relationship in her mind. It was no longer possible to suppress her suspicions and from that point on, in July 1935, she measured their marriage against that seedy low-point in a gilded room in the Savoy. The humiliation and hurt increased her feelings of loneliness. She had no close female intimates and her friendships with the flying fraternity, despite the outward joviality, were distant and shallow.

Diana Caldwell, who later became infamous when her lover was shot dead in Kenya in the 'White Mischief' murder, was typical of Amy and Jim's acquaintances. She was a coldly beautiful woman constantly struggling to secure her position in the upper classes through friendships with European royalty and celebrities such as Amy. She liked to hunt and fly, and, with a friend, she ran the Blue Goose cocktail club near Bond Street. The message that appears in Amy's logbook almost certainly refers to her after she and a friend had borrowed Amy's plane in July 1935 for a jaunt to Austria: 'P.S. Diana says blow you a raspberry for being so forgetful and overloading our aeroplane with your literature!!'

The constant threat of death and the inevitable rivalry meant that deep friendships between pilots were rare. Neither Kingsford Smith nor Courtenay had any idea that Amy was unable to bear children, and both urged her to have a baby as a way of steadying an obviously unstable marriage. Smithy, whose son was born the year Amy and Jim married, sent the couple a telegram that simply stated the biblical reference: 'Luke X, verse 37'. Looking up the passage, they found the command: 'Go and do as I did'[13] – a comment that must have seemed smug, if not patronising. After his wife died Courtenay urged them to abandon hotel living and to try to find the domestic harmony he had just lost: 'Take a nice home somewhere where you can be together more . . . you should both have a babe and get Wakefield as godfather before the old man dies! Don't leave it too late. It will make a lot of difference to your joint happiness.'[14]

At the end of August 1935 Amy was considering working for a photo news agency in Abyssinia (Ethiopia); it was another ill-timed and ill-conceived pipedream. On 3 October 1935 a terrifying convoy of Mussolini's military hardware, planes droning overhead, crossed from Eritrea into Ethiopia. Despite fine-sounding rhetoric, Britain did nothing to stop Italy's invasion of Emperor Haile Selassie's kingdom. Reluctance was partly due to fear of Italian reprisals; the Admiralty in particular were anxious about the possibility of an attack by a group of young Italian pilots calling themselves the 'Suicide Club' who threatened to fly their planes into British ships[15] – a Kamikaze tactic that eerily foreshadowed the terrorist attacks of 11 September 2001. Planes played a decisive part in Mussolini's victory in Ethiopia. Just before Christmas 1936 the Italians started to spray mustard gas on the enemy below, who were barefoot and armed with little more than knives, while continuing to mow them down like hunters chasing wild boar in the forest. In February 1936, 170 planes bombarded the Ethiopians' rocky stronghold of Amba Aradam. Abyssinia was a turning point in the history of the plane: an heroic, empire-embracing object had become a harbinger of mass destruction.

Confusion over the role of the plane left Amy searching for an identity. In early 1935 the Women's Engineering Society arranged for Jim and Amy to take opposing sides in a debate on the question of whether record-breaking flights still served a purpose.[16] Although Amy argued that such flights were no longer useful *per se*, she used her speech to put forward a serious plan about how to place air travel within the grasp of the ordinary passenger. She argued for fast links between the airport and the nearest city and for multi-engined planes flown by two pilots. Airports, she said, must be bigger and have wireless equipment, night-flying facilities and emergency landing sites. Jim's response was flippant by comparison. When discussing the importance of new forms of fast transport he noted how marriage had been hampered by the introduction of the bicycle, which made adultery easier. Eventually he destroyed his own platform by admitting that he agreed with Amy. Jim did not enjoy being pitted against his wife and the whole occasion was far too earnest for him.

There was no obvious role for a veteran record-breaker like Amy. Other women pilots, particularly Jean Batten and Beryl Markham, had grabbed the headlines; they were untitled and glamorous, two characteristics that until then had been associated almost exclusively with Amy. While she had moved on from being the 'lone girl flyer', Amy's position as one half of the 'flying sweethearts' was now under threat. She needed a new image.[17]

Various ways of making money exploded in her mind; some were practical, others purely fanciful, most were highly inventive.[18] The familiar options of journalism, writing fiction, lecturing and what would now be called 'consultancy' work cropped up on her wish list. She was tempted to join Dorothy Spicer and Pauline Gower, two joy-riding pilots she had known at Stag Lane, but concluded: 'nice girls but little money to be made'.[19] The other ideas on the list reflected her more sophisticated and cosmopolitan image. The head dress-designer at Fortnum and Mason's wanted Amy to join her in opening a shop that specialised in women's leisurewear: clothes for the seaside, holidays and cruise liners. Courtenay suggested that Amy should use her Beechcraft to fly the latest Paris fashions to shops and designers in London.[20] It was a typical Courtenay solution that met several business needs in one fell swoop: it helped to publicise the Beechcraft and made use of her skills as a pilot and her position as a fashion icon.

Amy also designed a travelling case for the cosmetics company of Elizabeth Arden.[21] Neat pieces of luggage with countless compart-ments, some hidden, were highly fashionable in the mid 1930s. Their compactness and clean lines mirrored the clothes worn by Garbo, Dietrich and Wallis Simpson; the very idea that a particular 'look' could be packed away and transported summed up the escapism of the time. In 1933 Elizabeth Arden launched its 'harmony boxes' that helped women to co-ordinate make-up with clothes at a moment's notice. Amy's luggage design addressed the same fear of being trapped in the wrong outfit or, much worse, appearing dishevelled.

Her pencil drawings show a pigskin case, rigid on one side to carry a battery of beauty products, and soft on the other to store evening and day clothes. She envisaged three types of cases: the smallest for an overnight trip and larger versions for a weekend or a fortnight away from home. She believed the case's unique selling points were its weight, strength and ability to withstand vibration. A pocket held slip-pers and passport and the bottom unzipped to expose scissors, nailbrush, soap and toothbrush, five bottles (including eye lotion, mouthwash and astringent) and five jars (containing cleansing and night creams and face powder). The bigger cases provided more room for clothes – particularly complete changes for the evening – and high-heeled shoes. There was extra space for more shades of eyeshadow and powder, in addition to the essential eye-liner and rouge.

As well as being pulled in different directions as far as her career, she could not decide where to make her home. In late 1935 Amy lived for four months in a furnished house, Belgrave Cottage in Upper Belgrave Street, just north of the King's Road. Jim visited occasionally but she found it impossible to believe his protestations of fidelity. She wanted a divorce but Jim persuaded her to use the following six months – when he would be in America and Australia – to think things over. She was still tempted to move to America – either North or South – and could not quite shake off her dreams of an outdoor, solitary life that she had read about in books such as *My Reminiscences as a Cowboy*[22] and *Sun up: Tales of the Cow Camps*. She fantasised about owning a ranch although she realised such a venture was an improbable money-spinner. Ever since her work with Hillman, when she flew passengers to Paris, she had begun to spend more time in France. The country's long love affair with flying was just as intense and Amy was treated with a respectful adoration that she rarely experienced at home. On a practical level, Paris boasted a fashionable American dentist whom she visited frequently while staying with Winifred's sister, Isabel.

Amy first met Peter Reiss, an aviation underwriter, at a dance at Leicestershire Flying Club in 1931 where she was guest of honour. He was a keen pilot and Amy's logbook shows that she gave him lessons in April of that year. Peter had a puppy-dog enthusiasm and adored Amy with an unquestioning devotion. Jack Humphreys viewed his unlimited optimism as the perfect antidote to Amy's black moods and hoped that they might marry. Other friends, though, believed that Amy felt swamped by his over-protectiveness.

Peter was some seven years older than Amy but, even when he entered his forties, retained a big, innocent schoolboyish face sprinkled with freckles; his hair was thin and sandy-coloured. He stayed in touch after she married Jim, sending her a polite telegram when she broke the solo record to Cape Town: 'Best congratulations – Reiss', and gave her squash lessons when she took up the game in March 1934. By 1936 he was one of many admirers vying for Amy's attention. The other contender was a Frenchman called François Dupré.

Perhaps one of Amy's most ambitious and imaginative schemes was Air Cruises – a sort of 'packaged tour' company for the very wealthy which gave the aeroplane its first major role in the tourist industry. Amy planned to buy a second-hand Dragon Rapide airliner, similar to *Seafarer*, which she would personally pilot around the capitals of Europe, dropping her passengers off at luxury hotels. A firm of Mayfair car dealers that she used in Bruton Street were interested in investing in the company but, while Amy acknowledged that their offices offered a 'good address', she worried that they were 'nevertheless motor salesmen'.[23]

By February 1936 Amy wrote excitedly to her father about a new backer for Air Cruises. She had become 'great friends' with François Dupré, who owned a string of hotels, including the magnificent Georges V in Paris. Dupré was extremely 'airminded'; he was also, Amy told her father, 'young [actually, he was forty-eight years old], wealthy and likes me . . .' He offered to invest £5000 in the company and to promote the idea in America and Canada, where he had business interests, and at the Georges V. The one downside was that Amy was uncertain whether she could 'entirely trust a Frenchman'.[24]

Will was excited at the thought of her new business venture, offering to invest £100 of his own money. His sole reservation was that Amy should avoid using her name – either 'Johnson' or 'Mollison' – in the title of the company, presumably in case the scheme flopped. He was all too well aware that her profile could not withstand further bad publicity.

Her enthusiasm for Air Cruises persuaded Amy to consider something that had not appeared on her shopping list of possible career moves for several years: another record-breaking flight. As she mused over a second solo trip to Cape Town, Smithy unwittingly provided a timely reminder that long-distance flights were still a matter of life and death. Jim's closest flying friend disappeared somewhere over the Bay of Bengal in an attempt to set a new record from Britain to Australia in November 1935; a possible sighting of the exhaust flames from his plane was the last anyone ever saw of him.

Will told Amy the flight would 'really put you right back again at the top of the tree and would be fine publicity for your new company'.[25] Courtenay's assessment was blunter. Writing to Will, he said: 'I have told Amy that if the flight were undertaken only as a shop window to get background [information for possible trips] and publicity for Air Cruises it is worth while as it is bound to bring her business and wake up all those who think she is finished.'[26]

The proposed flight was kept deadly secret to avoid clashing with Air Cruises' launch which was publicised in March 1936. Newspapers portrayed the new venture as a luxurious, flying gin palace for the very rich but were curious about why Jim was not involved and why Amy was so adamant about not using his surname.[27] The company's two planes were modelled on the king's private aircraft where passengers sank into deep armchairs made of Moroccan leather or lounged at bridge tables or propped up the cocktail bar. Air Cruises' guests would tour Paris, Berlin, Rome, Vienna, Budapest and Madrid. There were plans to extend the itinerary to the Far East, to fly tourists over the pyramids or to whisk them off to the Scottish isles, Biarritz or the vineyards of France. But Amy's vision of carefree holidays did not tally with the mood in North America, and Dupré cabled her from Montreal to suggest that they postpone the launch of Air Cruises because of 'war talk'. He added, 'all my thoughts are with you always.'[28] Despite his pessimism, Amy was determined to go ahead with the African flight.

She was desperate to keep her plans secret from the press, who

always 'drove' her 'cuckoo' just before the start of a flight, and she
urged Courtenay to 'tell them any old story to put them off'.[29] Courtenay, now remarried, was again acting as her publicity manager; Amy
did her best to keep his fees as low as possible, arguing that he could
only take 10 per cent if he was directly responsible for tying up a newspaper deal. Courtenay encouraged Amy to tell Jim about the proposed
flight in case his obvious ignorance of her plans alerted the press to
their estrangement. On hearing the news, Jim phoned from Australia
to tell her that he would take the first airmail plane to be with her.
Since neither the fatal motorbike accident nor Amy's various plane
crashes had prompted his return to England, Jim must have been
drawn home by the lure of publicity.

The process of meticulous planning started once more. Amy
wanted to take a Beechcraft but Colonel R. V. Jellicoe, a friend who
knew the Sahara well, persuaded her to switch to an enclosed cabin
monoplane, the Percival Gull, a goofy-looking, inelegant aircraft with
a high propeller, but which at least had the advantage of being
British.[30] It also carried special 'blind flying' instruments and – a first
for Amy on a long-distance flight – a radio. She was specific about the
provisions she required: a flask each of black coffee, orange juice,
brandy, and water; sandwiches made from Ryvita bread heavily laden
with butter, and roast beef, rare and without condiments; some
almonds and raisins and chewing gum. She hoped that a prototype of
her travelling case would be ready in time; its contents would include
a French dictionary, a gun and ammunition, field glasses, a notebook
and pencils, caffeine tablets, several changes of clothes, eau-de-
Cologne, smelling salts, eye-lotion and an eye-bath, mouthwash and
cosmetics. A good masseuse was told to be on stand-by for her arrival
in Cape Town.

Weather reports supplied by the AA suggested that Amy would be
buffeted by strong winds during the early stages of the journey: the
mistral in Europe and then 'very pronounced bumpiness' when she
reached the heights of Oran. She carried sandbags and a rope to tie
down the plane if she landed in the Sahara and to avoid a repetition of
her experience in the Iraqi desert.

Insurance cover, at £500 for a plane which was worth £2000, was
much higher than usual, and at the end of March 1936 Amy was slightly
overdrawn at the Midland Bank in Park Lane. She also needed to find a
deposit to fund a search for her if she disappeared over the Sahara. She
approached the *News of the World* about an exclusive deal but long-
distance flights no longer commanded the huge sums they had once

earned. The only story big enough to fund a search for her plane would be her death, a fact she was fully aware of: 'It would amuse me to make them pay for the story of my end.'[31] Her father gave her £200 towards the insurance and her shareholdings were used as a guarantee against the cost of a search.[32] Her customs documentation for the French authorities stated the purpose of her trip as 'pleasure'.

Courtenay and Amy drew up a draft statement to be issued solely to the Press Association news agency once she was on her way. Courtenay hoped that the timing would make Amy front-page news in Friday's newspapers, and that the momentum would continue through the entire weekend. In the draft 'Mollison' has been replaced with 'Johnson' and a postscript added in Amy's handwriting: 'Make personal note of pride in keeping fresh and neat . . .'

A phalanx of Amy's most loyal supporters gathered at Gravesend airport to see her off on 3 April, a date chosen so that she had the benefit of moonlight for as many nights as possible. As well as local dignitaries, Will, Molly and Trevor represented her family, and Jack, whom Amy had barely seen since her marriage, appeared, although Peter Reiss had assumed the protective role Jack had taken in the past. Everything about the expedition was constructed to give the illusion of a routine business trip by the most chic of businesswomen, and her specially made clothes reinforced this image. Elsa Schiaparelli had chosen Amy as an inspirational mannequin for her new collection of 'flight clothes' which included a lightweight suit for crossing the equator. Coco Chanel was now old hat, while Schiaparelli preferred avant-garde headgear in the shape of television sets or shoes. Her style was international and topical: one evening outfit was based on an Ethiopian warrior's tunic in honour of Haile Selassie; a woollen suit designed for Amy included a flamboyant scarf covered with newspaper print. Schiaparelli was fascinated by planes and her designs included details such as wing-shaped collars and sleeves made to look like parachutes. On her flight to Cape Town Amy wore a navy-blue suit and a warm overcoat especially made for her by Schiaparelli – both designed to contrast with the duck-egg blue of the plane. The skirt was 'divided' (culotte style) to combine, as Amy noted in her press release, 'smartness with utility'.[33]

Amy flew directly to the northern edge of the Sahara where she landed at the French military post of Colomb Bechar at 3.45 p.m. to refuel for a night-time flight across the desert. It was a quick and efficient pit-stop: the plane was ready within an hour; Amy's coffee and water flasks had been replenished and she had changed into a cooler, cream silk suit. The next leg stretched 1500 miles in front of her and, to be on the safe side, the fuel tanks were filled to capacity – giving the plane a range of 2300 miles.

The heavily laden Gull waddled down a runway encrusted with large stones; as it gathered speed the plane suddenly lurched to the left. Amy tried desperately to control it but by now the Gull was bouncing uncontrollably towards the very rough ground near the airfield's boundary. The French soldiers watched as the strong winds buffeted the plane from side to side, spinning it round like a crazed puppet until a loud tearing noise put an end to the dance and the Gull lurched forward one final time.

Amy scrambled out of the plane to escape the brimming petrol tanks. The reason for the accident remains a mystery: the tail wheel may have burst or a large stone might have become trapped in the wheels' metal fairings; or perhaps the wind was just too gusty for an already unstable plane to take off safely. She was furious that her plans had been wrecked, not by pilot error or lack of sleep, but by a 'stupid accident', but there was never any doubt in her mind that the mishap was simply a temporary setback. The Gull must be repaired and flown back to Gravesend in time for the next full moon. For six days she waited impatiently for the spares to arrive, unwilling to accept any excuse for the delay. As she was dressing early one morning she heard the hum of a plane's engine and discovered a Sabena passenger plane en route from the Belgian Congo to Brussels. Amy persuaded the captain to wait for her and she hitched a lift back to Europe just as Peter was about to fly to Colomb Béchar with spares and a Percival mechanic. He met her at Brussels in a Leopard Moth and flew her home. Amy left for Africa a week later in an Air Cruises' Dragon Rapide carrying spares for the Gull and with a Percival mechanic to fit them.34 Peter and Molly accompanied them in a trial-run of the exotic flights promised to Air Cruises' customers.

Amy took off again from Gravesend in the Gull on 4 May – the last day that the moon would be of any use to her. It was a very different send-off from her early departure. The aborted flight had given Jim a chance to return home and he appeared on her doorstep to plead with her to give him a second chance. She was quick to relent to his pleas for them to start over, but made him promise to remain faithful. At the time she was living at the Gate House, 59a Ennismore Gardens, with her housekeeper Jessamine James, her secretary Nancy Mudie and a Dachshund called Teena. The house was tucked away just off Kensington Road between the Royal Albert Hall and Knightsbridge tube station; coincidentally less than a five-minute walk from *Jason*'s final resting place in the Science Museum. It was a luxurious and comfortable home: the ground floor had a dining-room with pine furniture and a sixty-two-piece Wedgwood dinner set, a kitchen, an entrance hall and a toilet. A staircase led to a drawing-room, a bathroom that shone with chromium fittings, a maid's room and a stylish double bedroom of sycamore wood and Lloyd Loom furniture. She also had the use of a garage.

When Amy set off again for Africa, photographers captured a fond embrace between husband and wife. The false start at Colomb Béchar had transformed the flight from a trip that interested few people into an inspirational battle against adversity. Amy arrived in Cape Town three days and six hours later, beating the record set by Tommy Rose in February 1936 by eleven hours and setting a new record for the return and round trip. More importantly, she had become, once more, a pilot worth watching.

Breaking records was now so commonplace that the public needed an extra element to provide the essential ingredient of 'pluck' so obvious in the very early flights; bouncing back after failure met this requirement. Jean Batten, who worked hard at her image, which – coincidentally or not – made her look very much like Amy with her plucked eyebrows and high cheekbones, owed much of her appeal to her determination not to give in. During the mid thirties she notched up solo records for both sexes from England to Brazil, England to Australia and Australia to England; but she was known most for her tenacity. She was already 'Try-Again Jean' and now even 'Third-Time-Lucky Jean'. Amy had shown that, despite her hedonistic lifestyle, she had lost none of her perseverance and her success produced an avalanche of fan letters, many from women. The writer Rebecca West wrote from a sanatorium in Austria where she confessed that she had an 'elder sister feeling' towards Amy, recognising in her a fellow spirit who loves her work but 'hates the racket of public life and gets the jitters through it, and often seems to herself like a puppy-dog that's got tangled up in its lead'.[35]

The *Daily Express* bought the rights to Amy's story and *Paris-soir* purchased the French version. Amy told the world that 'My constant habit of drinking Ovaltine is fully justified as I am feeling 100 per cent fit even after my strenuous flight', although, in truth, she had relied on caffeine hits rather than the soporific night-time drink. She was just as tactful about the radio she carried on her trip, writing in strict confidence to the head of the Signals Department at Croydon Airport that it had been 'practically no help whatsoever' due to 'atmospherics' and one of the worst storms for years in the Sahara that had snapped a key radio mast in half.[36] A resounding endorsement of Castrol earned her a £2000 cheque from Wakefields and allowed her to give Will back the £200 he had lent her to pay for the insurance.

Amy cabled Jim from South Africa, 'relying on your promise but hope not necessary', before setting off for home. There were times during her journey through East Africa when she managed to recapture the thrill of the lone pilot flying over landscape rarely seen from the air: the magnificent Mount Kilimanjaro and the vast expanse of Lake Victoria. She was fascinated by the animals and trying to spot perfectly camouflaged creatures helped to relieve the tedium of a long-distance flight. The Rift Valley teemed with game that scattered at the unfamiliar sound emanating from a beast they could not see, and she spied on crocodiles and hippos in their desolate swamp homes.

But her description of parts of the journey contains elements depressingly familiar to any modern-day air passenger. 'Nothing could have demonstrated to me more clearly that flying is now a commonplace than to find comfortable hotels along the route, where I was charged to the hilt for my flask of coffee, packet of sandwiches, or cold drinks on landing.'[37] Whereas it took two months to obtain the necessary authority to cross the Sahara, three cables secured her permits to fly through the Sudan, Tripoli and Greece. It helped that she knew the King of Greece and General Balbo, but she was still flying through highly sensitive areas that, in the case of Italian territories, Mussolini was convinced offered foreigners irresistible opportunities for espionage. Oil and petrol were easy to find and, although a plane could still turn heads, it was not worshipped in the same way that it was on the west coast. Nor were its pilots: 'I could not quite shake off the feeling that I was a trespasser, and a nuisance at that . . .' Amy wrote later.[38]

Chapter 24

France
(1936–7)

Whenever François Dupré needed a break from his business affairs and the excesses of a demanding social life, he flew his private plane from Paris to Normandy, landing in a farmer's field near the small town of Falaise where his chauffeur met him and drove him through the gently rolling Calvados countryside to his stud-farm at Pont D'Ouilly. The stables were still no more than an interesting diversion for a very wealthy man and had yet to produce any of the champion horses that, in the 1950s and 1960s, made the ivy-covered stables the most successful equine breeding-ground in the world.

François' staff remember him today with affection that borders on reverence, as a kind, if largely absentee, employer. Jean Baudouin, now in his eighties, recalls that in the forty-three years that he knew him, he never saw Monsieur Dupré lose his temper – although this is probably more an indication that Dupré's rule was never challenged than of a naturally kind disposition. He was almost fifty when Amy first met him and already divorced from an heiress of the Singer sewing-machine empire. He spoke impeccable English and dressed with an unswerving 'Prince de Galles' sense of style. François was never without a tie; even while walking round his stud-farm he wore a hat and a waistcoat and made sure that just the right amount of handkerchief peeped out of the breast-pocket of his jacket.

He came from an aristocratic family that had had various brushes with both fame and notoriety. His mother enjoyed a long and tumultuous affair with the French Finance Minister, Joseph Caillaux, whom she finally married. After their divorce and his remarriage his new wife stormed into the offices of *Le Figaro* and shot the editor dead because he had threatened to publish love letters between François' mother and Caillaux. The incident became a *cause célèbre* and François' mother was called as the chief prosecution witness in the trial that followed.[1] François' grandfather, Jules Dupré, took a more gentle route to fame, becoming well known as a nineteenth-century painter of pastoral scenes. Turner and Constable inspired him and he became fascinated by stormy weather, sunsets and changes in light. Art experts defined his style as somewhere between realism and romanticism; his grandson's approach veered closer to the former.

Amy got to know François during one of her increasingly frequent trips to Paris and first mentioned him to her father in February 1936 in connection with Air Cruises. 'D.P.', or 'F.D.', as she referred to him in letters, had won the Croix de Guerre and the Légion d'Honneur for his flying exploits during the First World War and, as Amy pointed out to her father, was 'airminded', owning his own plane and employing a pilot/mechanic. Inherited wealth and a career in banking, which included a three-year stint in London, allowed him to invest in a string of luxury hotels. When it was built in 1928, close to the Champs-Elysées and off l'Etoile, the Georges V represented a shocking blast of Art Deco mixed with neo-classicism among the staid nineteenth-century Haussmann-style buildings, but by the mid 1930s the hotel had lost some of its sheen. François hand-picked furniture and paintings to restore its glamour and measured his success by the hotel's increasingly glamorous guest-list, which came to include Hollywood stars such as Marlene Dietrich, Greta Garbo, Gene Kelly, Gary Cooper and Vivien Leigh. Amy joined the list in 1936 when a suite was put permanently at her disposal.

Until the early summer of 1936 Amy was still unable to relinquish the illusion that her professional and emotional future lay with Jim. They planned a round-the-world flight together and discussed buying back *Black Magic* from the Portuguese Government or borrowing a Comet from the Air Ministry.[2] Press photographs showed them at Skegness where they opened a bathing pool for Butlins – at the time a novel new type of holiday camp – and touring Seagers' gin distillery where bottles of egg flip jostled along the production line. But on a holiday in Juan-les-Pins Amy finally faced the fact that their marriage was beyond salvation and started to lead her own life. She appeared in *Vogue* perched on the seat of a small boat in the South of France wearing a swimming costume with her hair hidden by a spotted scarf, and next to a bare-chested Randolph Churchill and the bikini-clad actress Claire Luce.[3] In another photo she stands gazing into the distance on the wing of a plane as it sits on the tarmac; the magazine commented admiringly: 'She dresses for record-breaking as if for a lunch date.'[4]

The marriage of two famous flyers had, in the early days, presented a strong brand that was easily marketed around the world, but by 1936

Jim had become a liability. One publication compared the couple to Little Lord Fauntleroy and Boadicea: Amy was the strong, almost stern partner, Jim the effete and spoilt child.[5] He was accused of drink-driving in Los Angeles and his patriotism was called into question when it emerged that he had flown home from Singapore with the Dutch airline KLM rather than Imperial Airways because the foreign company offered him a bigger discount.[6]

Jim had been seeing a lot of Beryl Markham, the tall, angular Kenyan pilot whose lovers had included the Duke of Gloucester and Tom Campbell Black. Apart from the difference in height, Beryl was a perfect match for Jim. She had led a childhood that was more African than Edwardian; while her mother stayed behind in Europe tribesmen taught her to hunt on the farm where her father bred racehorses. Her upbringing gave her a rugged independence and when it came to men her approach was feral: she was at least their equal and viewed romance as an unwelcome distraction from sex. She saw no reason to remain loyal to one man and juggled several liaisons at the same time.

Tom Campbell Black taught her to fly in Kenya, where she ferried passengers, goods and mail around East Africa. She came to England almost on a whim after a friend challenged her to fly the Atlantic solo in the westerly direction – something a woman had yet to accomplish. By the time she arrived in London she had been married and divorced twice and fitted easily into the celebrity flying set. Jim enjoyed her company – she drank heavily and made no emotional demands on him – and together they visited the most fashionable nightclubs.

Beryl had long coveted the privileges that accompanied a world-famous flyer. At Grosvenor House Hotel in 1930 she had watched the waiting cars and sumptuous gifts that arrived for Amy on her triumphant return from Australia while Beryl's lover, the Duke of Gloucester, slunk past Amy on the hotel's backstairs, each – for different reasons – avoiding the fans waiting at the front entrance.[7] Amy could not help but be aware of Beryl.

When she resigned in June 1936 as managing director of Air Cruises, Beryl took her place as pilot and the press locked the two, together with Jean Batten, in a triumvirate of high-cheekboned, sparkling female flyers. Wakefields gave Batten and Beryl equal billing in their adverts when they urged customers: 'Let's join the ladies – and use Wakefield Patent Castrol XXL'. Courtenay, too, spotted a rising star and offered to work for Beryl.

But Beryl had one major advantage over her rivals – she was a mother; her son, Gervase, was a sickly child whom Beryl rarely visited, but the fact of her motherhood gave her another dimension: she became the 'beautiful fair-haired mother of a seven-year-old son'.[8] Not everyone approved of her motherhood but the venom with which some newspapers attacked her selfishness in combining the role with flying gave her an extra hold on the headlines.

On 4 September 1936 Beryl proved that she was more than a well-connected blonde when she took off from Abingdon in England to attempt to cross the Atlantic alone. Just before she climbed into her Percival Vega Gull, Jim, who had flown her to the aerodrome, handed her the wristwatch he had worn during his own 1932 east-to-west crossing. Beryl later recorded his words in her memoir, *West with the Night*: 'This is not a gift. I wouldn't part with it for anything. It got me across the North Atlantic and the South Atlantic too. Don't lose it – and, for God's sake, don't get it wet. Salt water would ruin the works.'[9] It was an intimate gesture at a time when the wristwatch was still seen as a highly personal accessory rather than an everyday necessity; its significance was even greater for a long-distance pilot since an accurate timepiece was vital for precision navigation. Aviators attempting dangerous flights set great store by tokens that had already helped their owners through treacherous journeys, and by lending Beryl his watch Jim was anointing her with his good luck in exactly the same way that he had Amy four years earlier. Then he had lent his wife the St Christopher that had seen him safely across the Atlantic and which he hoped would guide her in her solo journey to South Africa in 1932.

Just over twenty-one hours after leaving England Beryl's plane landed nose first in the mud of Nova Scotia, making her the first person to cross the Atlantic alone from England (as opposed to Ireland). The very public friendship between her husband and her greatest professional rival was too much for Amy to bear, and she instructed Crockers to start divorce proceedings. But she kept her decision deadly secret. Jim moved out of the Gate House and agreed to provide her with evidence for a divorce before he sailed for America in a month's time. A week later he left the country without a word to Amy, who read about his departure in a French newspaper. He had failed to keep his promise to sort out his affairs and settle his £6000 tax bill.[10]

Once he was gone Amy uncovered enough about his business and personal life to extinguish any lingering trust between them. She discovered that he had been secretly opening her mail and had even bought a plane based on particulars that Amy had requested and which he had kept to himself. Most worryingly, Amy could not find the will that she had made in Jim's favour and which she now wanted to destroy. From that point on they became rivals; instead of consulting Jim about possible flying ventures she started to look over her shoulder in case he was there to snatch an opportunity from her. When she bumped into the head of Fox Movietone News, who mentioned that the company was looking for a pilot to fly a Technicolor film of the coronation to Hollywood, her immediate reaction was to hope he did not mention the idea to Jim.[11] Her husband's betrayal also severed the strongest emotional tie keeping her in London and she spent more and more time in Paris. To her parents she put on a brave face: 'I'm quite happy and contented and looking forward to my future – I've heaps of ideas and plans,' she wrote to Will.[12] But without a fellow pilot to consult, her schemes became more and more impractical and out-landish.

In September Tom Campbell Black was killed in circumstances made all the more horrific by their banality. He was taxiing for take-off at Speke Aerodrome in Liverpool, travelling at between ten and fifteen miles per hour, when the propeller of an out-of-control plane sliced clean through the bubble canopy of his plane. Amy was genuinely upset about the gruesome accident, writing to her father: 'Wasn't it ter-rible about Campbell Black? I knew him well.'[13] But she appeared to have lost any sense of what was normal behaviour when she added, in a breath-taking lapse of taste, that she had phoned Courtenay to see whether, as a 'sentimental gesture', the dissected plane could be repaired in time for her to fly in the England-to-Johannesburg Air Race.[14]

Amy suffered grave aberrations in concentration as well as taste. On 20 October she broke her nose and dislocated a shoulder during a forced landing in fog at Chelsfield in Kent whilst flying her Beechcraft from Paris to London. She was already feeling physically run down: an Indian doctor had given her treatment for her 'nerves' and she had received an injection to ward off colds. Her injuries, which were painful and slow to heal, robbed her of the will to continue the public pretence of a happy marriage; when reporters camped outside the Gate House, Amy announced that she and Jim had separated. She claimed the glare of publicity as the cause of their break-up, but Jim, who was on the other side of the Atlantic waiting to attempt a solo crossing, denied all knowledge of a rift and exploited the situation to his benefit: 'I am very sorry indeed that Amy has made such state-ments,' he told the *Daily Mirror*, 'especially when I am starting on my flight within the next few days. I feel that if only she had waited such words from her would not have been necessary. I am quite in the dark about the whole matter.'[15] He told another newspaper that he had not discussed separation and had no idea what was in Amy's mind.[16] The timing was ideal for Jim, allowing him to act the errant knight who hoped to persuade his wife to change her mind in the unlikely event that he survived the Atlantic crossing.[17]

When Jim returned to Britain he did so in a staggering thirteen and a half hours and in a plane that he christened *Miss Dorothy* after the actress Dorothy Ward. He and Dorothy may have been no more than good friends but Jim was fully aware that flying was symbolic of his life with Amy and that naming a record-breaking machine after another woman represented the ultimate humiliation for his wife. Newspapers played on the connection by clever juxtaposition of stories covering their separation with items about the actress. As Jim finally conceded that their marriage was over, reporters moved in to relay each parry in the couple's boxing-match of insults. On hearing that Amy planned to enter the transatlantic race being organised to mark the tenth anniversary of Lindbergh's crossing, Jim commented; 'She's only joking,'[18] while Amy retorted: 'He probably doesn't even know that there is a transatlantic race.' She tried to go about her social life as if nothing had changed but the world of flying was so claustrophobic that she frequently found herself in excruciatingly awkward situations. Two months after announcing their separation Amy attended the opening of a new darts 'parlour' at Millbank on the Thames in central London.[19] Her opponents in the 'friendly' match were Florence Desmond and Beryl – who had slept with both their husbands.

François offered a respite from painful reminders of Jim and of Amy's life in London. When she visited his stud-farm in the autumn the stables glowed with red ivy and the air was shockingly crisp compared to the polluted London streets. Jean Baudouin and the other farm workers were astonished by their first sight of the *'aviatrice glorieuse'* whom they expected to be a big, imposing woman but who appeared as a shy, 'fragile' figure at François' side whom he referred to as *'ma petite chose'*.

François' lifestyle offered everything that Amy required. She loved striding out in the remote countryside where she could wander unnoticed with François and his black-and-white terrier Pom-Pom, or go horse-riding, returning to meals prepared by a chef flown in especially for their visits. Despite her university studies and her seven-year relationship with Hans, Amy still spoke only basic schoolgirl French and a book she owned in the early 1930s called *France on Ten Words a Day*[20] shows that she was far from fluent. François' perfect English meant there was no urgency to improve her French, but by July 1936 she had started to take language lessons and her copy of Antoine de Saint-Exupéry's *Courrier sud* is battered enough to suggest that it has been read.[21]

Paris provided the glamorous flipside to this rural existence; Amy ventured out from her suite in the Georges V to order new clothes, take skin treatments, or visit her dentist. François seemed – to Amy – surprisingly anxious to please and they talked of going big-game hunting together in Kenya. He even promised to replace Air Cruises' Dragon Rapide with a new French Caudron plane and took her to *haute couturiers*. Will also gave her money (£100 in October) as well as cash to buy jewellery such as the diamond choker that she eventually exchanged for a platinum ring set with rubies.

There was just one thing missing in Amy's relationship with François – passion. When he finally declared his hand it came as a complete revelation to her. 'This man Dupré is a strange man,' she wrote to Will in October 1936. 'He is generous and kind to me in the extreme, so much so that I was worried and had a long talk with him one day. He told me he was "madly in love with me and wanted to marry me when I was free!!!"' But try as she might, and fully aware of what she stood to lose, Amy could not make herself fall in love with him. 'You've no idea what a joke it is,' Amy told Will. 'I can't stand him at any price and I told him I would never marry again . . . what is a girl to do! If I throw him over I'd lose a great many advantages beside. He seems quite content with the situation . . . What would you do if you were me? He admits I've never encouraged him and he says I'm to regard myself as under no obligation whatsoever.'

Amy squared her conscience by arguing that she did 'a lot for him indirectly' through the publicity she brought to his various businesses, but she knew he wanted more. Whether François got more is debatable. Molly was adamant that he did not, and decades later she scribbled an addendum to a letter in which Will and Amy discussed her relationship with François. 'I was with Amy most times during her friendship with F.D.,' Molly wrote in May 1973. 'She did not like him and she did not have an affair with him.'[22] But a younger sister with an unquestioning devotion is hardly the ideal person to judge the nature of a relationship. The rambling farmhouse offered plenty of opportunity for François and Amy to conduct a discreet affair without anyone knowing. The one obstacle was not logistical but whether Amy found François attractive enough to allow their friendship to escalate into a romance. It seems naive to imagine that he, a divorcee, would not have contemplated – even expected – their relationship to graduate to a physical level. Amy may have slept with him for their mutual pleasure and comfort, assuming that it was an arrangement that came with no strings attached and certainly out of earshot of wedding bells.

Perhaps François' devotion made him less attractive. The two greatest loves of her life so far – Hans and Jim – had been unwilling to commit themselves exclusively to her; although she liked the idea of devotion, the reality made her uneasy. While François' infatuation lasted she made use of his willingness to fetch and carry in the same way that she had happily indulged the eagerness with which Jack Humphreys and Peter Reiss had trailed after her. The main difference was that François fetched designer dresses rather than replacement parts for damaged aeroplanes. François, too, had the means to attend to more distant errands. When he sailed to America in the autumn of 1936 Amy sent him a memo asking him to sort out various business concerns.[23] She wanted him to discuss with Movietone the possibility of her flying film of the coronation to Hollywood and to find a replacement for her sextant in New York. She confided in him that she was considering a flight from Britain to Montreal and then on to Los Angeles, and asked him to collect as much data on the Canadian airport as possible. Under the heading of 'Finance' she added, 'Please do not forget that I am hoping you are going to give me the tip for anything good to buy.' But François was too used to getting his own way to settle for this role as stockbroker-cum-messenger boy. He also had good reason to believe that he was being welcomed into the Johnson family: Will met him in February 1937 and liked him, and Molly accompanied Amy, François and a second Frenchman on several skiing holidays.

This second Frenchman may have been the 'Pierre' whom Amy mentioned in letters to her father later that year. Ever since she had started to make regular trips to Paris in late 1935 she had attracted admirers. Winifred's sister remembered bouquets of flowers arriving regularly for her when she stayed at their home and believed she was involved with a film actor; Peter Reiss was convinced that Amy was seeing someone who worked for the French Caudron aircraft company.[24] Amy enjoyed life in the higher echelons of French society whereas she often felt 'used' by the Mayfair set, although she still made forays into it when she returned to London. Revelations about her marriage increased Amy's value on the guest list, but not everyone took her side in the rift. In some quarters the expression: 'Is she any

Amy Johnson?'[25] was asked of anyone thought to be a prude. Without full knowledge of the extent of Jim's indiscretions, newspaper readers were sometimes made to view Amy as bitter and graceless in the face of divorce. The *Daily Express*, for example, reported that Amy had dispatched six of Jim's treasured silver flying trophies from the Gate House to his hotel with nothing more affectionate than an inventory.[26]

In December she attended a 'shop warming' party for a new boutique in Mayfair where guests such as Mrs Anthony Eden listened to the shim-sham band over chatter from the oyster bar.[27] Cowan Dobson,[28] a forty-year-old balding and moustached Scottish artist who was working on Amy's portrait, accompanied her to the Rainbow Ball at the Grosvenor House in aid of the Marie Curie Hospital. Amy wore a low-backed white gown with a gold belt and danced frequently with Cowan. The 600 guests, who included Viscount Wakefield and various ambassadors, fished for bottles of wine and ale in the 'bootleggers' den', but the main topic of conversation was whether or not Edward VIII should be allowed to marry the twice-divorced Wallis Simpson. Details of the scandal had only recently burst onto newspaper pages and a matter of days after the ball, on 11 December, Edward abdicated for the woman he loved.

Despite the distractions of two European capitals, Amy could not shake off her deep-seated resentment and anger. Her gums had become infected, forcing her to visit her Paris dentist, and her shoulder injury was causing her so much pain that she consulted a Harley Street specialist just before Christmas. In January she spent a month in a Swiss clinic with Molly. It was during this period of mental anguish and ill health that she planned a series of articles for D. C. Thompson newspapers. The outlines for the pieces reflect her disillusionment and rage:

> It wasn't worth it. I'd have been happier if I had never been up in an aeroplane . . . Fame in a night and what it meant. Next morning exploiters get busy, I become public property. People who wanted to use my name, people with axes to grind. No more private life . . . I was a machine, not a person . . . No peace. Seeing through Mayfair [underlined in red] . . . What I want in future . . . a real home, children . . . If I had not been born Amy Johnson I would have been happier.[29]

The articles which appeared were toned-down versions of Amy's angry outburst but they nevertheless revealed a less carefree side to the flyer. She described Will's ultimatum to either give up Hans (she did not name him) or leave home, and walking from King's Cross to a hostel with her suitcase of belongings. Amy used the articles to put the record straight, as she saw it. She spoke of the 'unfortunate misunderstanding' that led to 'my people' missing her wedding. 'During my life I have been hurt by many things, but of all the hurts I have suffered, none has brought me more downright misery than the dazzling glare of publicity.'[30]

In March 1937 Amy changed her name by deed poll back to Johnson and started divorce proceedings in earnest. Jim told the *Daily Express* that her interests lay mainly in France while his varied between England and America. He added: 'It baffles me how Amy has put up with my many imperfections as a husband for so long.'[31] At the time the only permissible grounds for divorce were adultery but Jim was determined not to make it easy for Amy to end their marriage.[32] Crockers employed the Mayfair private detectives, Jacks International Bureau, based in Upper Berkeley Street, to procure the necessary evidence but Jim was not easy to pin down. The valet responsible for Jim's rooms in the Hyde Park Hotel agreed that he had witnessed enough proof of 'Mr Mollison's infidelities to satisfy half a dozen Divorce Court Judges' but did not like to tell tales against someone who had offered to find him a new job.[33] Indeed, the valet was so well disposed towards Jim that he intended to warn him that he was being stalked.

With chaos reigning in most areas of her life Amy sailed for America. Despite her sudden decision, she still had time to pack several new outfits especially designed for her by the couturier Mainbocher.[34] She left Cherbourg wearing a tailored chocolate-brown two-piece suit with a matching felt hat trimmed with a short quill. Her luggage included a sporty outfit consisting of a slightly flared grey jersey skirt teamed with a short-sleeved hand-knitted navy-blue sweater and a grey three-quarters-length wool coat. In the evening she wore a gown made from black Moroccan crêpe; a short bolero jacket covered a neckline that plunged southwards at the front and back.

The purpose of her visit was two-fold: to brush up her navigational skills and to have her teeth fixed.[35] She had met Lieutenant Commander Philip van Horn Weems, a retired American naval instructor and world expert in aerial navigation, at a function at the Mansion House in the City of London the previous autumn.[36] He suggested that she spent a fortnight at the Naval Academy at Annapolis in Maryland where he taught celestial navigation; he offered to put a car and a stenographer at her disposal. Amy was always keen to keep her skills fresh and visiting the academy seemed even more propitious once she decided to enter the transatlantic contest.[37] The prize money was $75,000 and Amy planned to fly François' six-seater Caudron Goeland, which had a top speed of 180 miles per hour. Amy was also considering a round-the-world flight for either 1937 or the following year. She was hopeful, too, that if her Fifth Avenue dentist could improve her smile it would increase her chances of work. 'We [she and François] shall probably take a trip over to Hollywood with my new teeth, where I might get a nice fat film contract,' she wrote to her father.[38]

As she scurried to prepare for the trip she gave Kathleen Waller, François' personal assistant from Air Cruises, power of attorney over her affairs, asking her to try to sublet the Gate House and to find jobs for Nancy and Jessamine. Amy suggested that one of François' clients might want to rent it for the coronation. Shortly after she left, Kathleen had to deal with Amy's speeding fine and a related offence of an unsigned driving licence.

In New York Amy stayed with a friend and beauty specialist, Gloria Bristol, who had an apartment on Park Avenue. Amy enjoyed the intellectual challenge of the navigational course that included ten hours of lectures every day in classrooms overlooking the River Severn followed by evening sessions in the planetarium. Weems used a 'bubble sextant' and his system, which pilots found particularly useful for night-flying or 'blind flying', relied on intricate mathematical calculations. A warm, paternalistic relationship developed between Amy and Weems and he sent her father American stamps for his collection. Although Weems received one letter of complaint from a man who resented Amy's presence in an all-male institution, her fellow students hero-worshipped her, sending her photos and letters after she returned to Britain. Weems himself admitted he missed Amy when she was gone and proposed that Longines should name a new model of lady's watch that would carry an aviation motif after her. He remained a well-connected link with the American flying scene, offering to send her maps, interviewing a radio operator for one of her proposed flights and in March 1938 proposing her as a navigator for an expedition to the South Pacific islands, if the leader did not object to her on grounds of gender.

While she was in America Amy bought the latest model of Beechcraft and the manufacturer accepted her damaged plane in part-exchange. Although Amy felt she had not received a good deal she was relieved to be rid of the old plane which had lain untouched since her accident in October. She felt the need to tackle a long-distance flight and complained that the lack of such a challenge had contributed to her weight gain (she had put on 4 pounds and now weighed 120 pounds). But she was dismayed to hear that the transatlantic race that she had been working towards had been cancelled. Amy, like many other pilots, believed that Pan-American Airways had put pressure on the US Department of Commerce to ban the event in case the inevitable fatalities deterred cautious air passengers. 'Many of us spent weeks and considerable sums of money in this country preparing for the race,' she told a reporter as she was leaving America. 'To say I disagree with the ruling of this Commissioner Roper [Secretary of Commerce Daniel Roper] is a brutal understatement.'[39]

Just as Amy was about to return home she received a cable from Crockers saying that a witness had finally identified a woman who could be used to bring divorce proceedings against Jim. She was not Beryl Markham or Dorothy Ward but Florence Desmond, the actress who had for years earned a living from her impersonations of Amy and whose husband had snatched the MacRobertson Race from Amy and Jim. Crockers stressed that it was essential to include Dessie's name when filing for divorce.[40] As rumours of Dessie's entanglement leaked out some people assumed that Amy wanted to name her as a way of hitting back at the years of stage parody. But Amy went against Crockers' advice and Dessie, who was about to marry a stiffly respectable aviation insurer, was pathetically grateful for the chance to avoid a scandal that threatened both her career and her impending marriage. She wrote to Amy:

> I need not tell you how relieved I am that the awful nightmare of the past few weeks is ended. How I was ever involved in the first place I shall never understand because Jim isn't even a friend of mine . . . I have never even been out with Jim in my life. My only meetings with him have been when I have met him at parties mostly in aviation circles. So you can imagine what a dreadful shock it was to me.[41]

Amy had planned to fly home on the German airship *Hindenburg* but on 6 May the airship exploded into a fireball that killed thirty-six people. Instead, Amy sailed for Britain; she left America looking more confident than she had for a long time. She was happy with her new, straight white teeth and had bought twenty-four pairs of shoes and dozens of stockings in America. A New York reporter remembered that 'a couple of years ago the girl was every which way' and concluded that Amy had 'just decided to slick up'.[42]

Her return to England meant Amy had to confront major decisions that she had been putting off for months. By the end of June she had moved out of the Georges V because her relationship with François, who had withdrawn his offer to lend her his plane and had taken it

touring in Europe, was making life there 'a little difficult'.[43] Amy decided
she had had enough of hotel life and found an apartment in Paris.

In letters to both Ciss and Weems she wrote that her career in
record-flying was over. To Will she wrote, 'to keep up my present standard of living something drastic must be done, and pretty quickly.'[44]
She had no money in the bank and was unable to let the Gate House;
a move to the suburbs of London would 'lead to much talk' and
besides, she found it cheaper to live in Paris. Even flying for pleasure
was beyond her means. 'I am afraid I have been feeling rather depressed
these last few days as I can't see daylight anywhere at the moment.' She
wanted to escape from her relationship with François but felt so desperate at the state of her finances that she could not bring herself to
abandon the comfort blanket that he represented, and toyed with
the idea of asking him to relaunch Air Cruises. 'Shall I drop him
altogether, don't you think?' she asked her father. 'I feel better without
him anyway and am not at all sure that I want to do anything in co-
operation with him even if it is a business.'

Amy considered her options: she could write a book, or apply for a
job as a pilot, but this would earn her about £10 a week and would be
'rather a come down'. Working in Australia or the USA were possibilities, and she had requested an interview with Wakefield to ask his
advice. Selling her car and furniture would allow her to escape on a
round-the-world cruise. Or she could set up a Flying School, although
she felt this was too much of a responsibility. The main problem with
all of these plans was that they involved 'exile', from which, if she ever
managed to return, it would be impossible to regain her contacts or her
public recognition.

Even Will's patience was wearing thin and he wrote back that it was
difficult to give advice to 'one who for the last seven years has been
living on an entirely different plane to my own'.[45] He agreed that she
was right to let Dupré go. Her choice was 'affluence (for a time) and
either dishonour or unhappiness while the other alternative was possibly poverty (comparative) and hard work'. He urged her to 'lie low'
while her divorce went through and suggested a number of economy
measures, including travelling by train and not using agents. A fortnight later, perhaps after considering Amy's straitened circumstances
and her past failure at financial prudence, Will modified his stance
slightly. He urged Amy to be more accommodating:

You won't find it easy to get anyone to come up with big money therefore
when you are in touch with a man like F.D. who is really willing to spend

generously then you ought to, at least, try and make the atmosphere as smooth as possible rather than make it more and more irritable, which no man can stand . . . F.D. would be willing to do a lot for you and be satisfied with your pleasant company and society.[46]

Will met Amy in Lowestoft on one of his business trips to East Anglia and together they drafted a carefully worded letter to François asking whether he would help Amy climb out of her financial hole. Amy was astonished by the 'extremely nice' telegram she received in return. She wrote to Will:

> The funny thing is that, away from F.D. I can more easily see his good points which when I am with him get lost in my quite inexplicable dislike of him. I've probably let my dislike colour my judgement, but it's awfully difficult constantly forcing oneself to be nice to someone who irritates one. Sooner or later something is bound to blow up.[47]

The explosion came at the end of July in the sumptuous calm of the Georges V. François blamed Amy for an ill-advised purchase of a plane, but she refused to make a contribution towards the loss. They managed to patch up the disagreement but Amy admitted to her father that F.D. was 'getting on her nerves':

> Really the only reason I am going through with it is on an absolute business basis because I need help to get myself established in something or other and if he can help, he might as well try . . . I have a feeling that no matter how I try with F.D. it will always end in disaster as he has this most peculiar effect on me of irritating me almost to the point of madness.[48]

She had become aware of what she called his 'tactics' in luring her to the countryside. First he would ask her to lunch, then suggest they ate at Pont D'Ouilly and, once they had gone to the bother of flying there, convince her to stay the weekend. The atmosphere at the stud-farm, designed with the sole purpose of breeding, was saturated with François' desire for Amy. He flew her to his kingdom and then laid out before her everything that would be hers if she agreed to marry him: he showed her pictures of the girlfriends he had taken to Venice, Budapest and Rome, tantalised her with his plans to buy a new plane and told her how neglected she looked in her clothes and car – both of which had slipped out of the category of 'latest model'. Fully aware of the temptation, Amy took her sister with her (hence Molly's note written in 1973) and told her father that she had 'with difficulty avoided the purpose for which I had quite obviously been asked . . . I now have no illusion whatever as to what he wanted in return and again all the help was just so much bait.'[49]

It gradually dawned on Amy that most of F.D.'s suggestions carried the ulterior motive of keeping her within his orbit. He told her that she might find work in Canada and it was only later that she discovered that he planned to spend half his time there. F.D. finally gave up his pursuit when it became blindingly – and embarrassingly – obvious that Amy's affections lay elsewhere. He was having lunch with 'Pierre' when Amy arrived unexpectedly. F.D. suggested that Amy join him for a break in the South of France but it emerged that she had already agreed to go with Pierre who was aware of the 'difficult position with F.D.' If Amy altered her original plan it would have meant committing herself forever to F.D. 'There is no doubt at all that I have missed a life of luxury as F.D.'s mistress (which wouldn't matter much if I liked him but I can't bear the idea of sleeping with someone for the sake of what I can get),' she wrote to Will. 'So that's that. I am living in a cheap hotel counting every penny when I might have been having everything I wanted.' After months of shilly-shallying she was happy that the situation had finally been resolved, claiming it was 'rather nice being hard up again'.[50]

About a year after their final separation François found the wife he was looking for, a twenty-eight-year-old Hungarian called Anci, or 'Anna', Nagy. When Amy heard that he had sailed for America with a 'beautiful Hungarian girl', her reaction was 'Thank God it's not me!'[51] When François died in 1966 on the estate in Jamaica that he visited during the French winter, he left his wife £15 million.

The year 1937 ended with a surfeit of villains and a dwindling supply of heroes. Prince Charming had deserted his throne and Adolf Hitler – not yet typecast as the ultimate villain – had sent his troops into the Rhineland. Aviation lost two of its most heroic women. In March 1937 the seventy-two-year-old Duchess of Bedford set off in her Gipsy Moth from her home at Woburn Abbey to fly over the bleak fen landscape in blinding snow. She was never seen again and it was assumed by many that she had had enough of old age and the tinnitus that blighted it, deciding to end her life by soaring over the inky North Sea until her fuel ran out.

Amelia Earhart, Amy's friend and mentor, was lost in July 1937 when she disappeared with her navigator over the Pacific in an attempt to circumnavigate the world. Amy's reaction was similar to her deep shock over Branks' death: 'No more flights so no need to worry! Poor Amelia!' she scribbled in the corner of a letter to her mother. [52]

Europe in the second half of the 1930s was a difficult place in which to be 'hard up'. As quickly as business opportunities arose, international tensions appeared to dash them. The previous summer of 1936 Colonel Jellicoe had confidently told Amy that touring Spain was possible 'without the slightest molestation' and that the country was 'thoroughly settling down' after Franco's revolt against the Republican Government.[53] Less than a year after his comforting words a flock of German Heinkel bombers swooped down on Guernica at the heart of the Basque country in northern Spain. The town was bustling with people flocking into the centre on market day. Wave after wave of planes strafed Guernica and its surrounding countryside, dropping bombs and firing rounds of bullets until the sky glowed with the flames of burning buildings and the air hung heavy with the stench of incinerated human flesh. Awareness of a conflict raging so fiercely in a not-so-distant Europe added to feelings of unease in Britain and a reluctance to take risks.

Chapter 25

Speed

(1938–9)

Amy craved the sensation of speed, but, by the late 1930s, the pleasure had become harder to find. Aeroplanes were no longer the open-cockpit, exposed biplanes that she had learnt to fly in and she was forced to look elsewhere for her thrills. Even at the height of her success she had sought out new forms of danger. On the first day of her visit to St Moritz in 1932 she rose early to put on thick knee-pads and a hefty helmet and, disguised as a man, hurled her toboggan at speeds of around eighty miles an hour down the Cresta Run. Officially females were banned from the bobsleigh track on the grounds that travelling at high speed, face down, put too great a strain on the chest and might lead to breast cancer. But Amy felt so strongly that women should be allowed to enjoy this unique thrill that she spoke at the 1932 annual general meeting of the toboggan club arguing in favour of lifting the ban, pointing out that women competed on an equal basis with men in many other sports.[1]

Her passion for gliding developed gradually over several years until, by the end of the 1930s, she confessed that she enjoyed it more than flying, finding it 'peaceful, cheap and much more interesting than "power flying"'.[2] Gliding had taken off as a sport in 1930 and quickly became a source of international tension. The Germans, prevented after the Great War from building up a fleet of aeroplanes, had turned to gliding as a way of flexing their muscles and teaching potential pilots the rudiments of flying. Branks and Lord Wakefield were among those who saw gliding as another way of promoting 'airmindedness'. In 1932 Amy lent her name to the British Gliding Association, becoming its vice-president and donating £5 to the organisation. But she did so out of a sense of duty rather than conviction. 'To be perfectly candid I do not consider that there is any great future for Gliding in this country,' she wrote to the Association's president, Lieutenant Colonel Shelmerdine, on 7 June 1932.

By 1937, though, her attitude to 'soaring' – as gliding was referred to

– had changed dramatically. She sold her Beechcraft plane and bought her own 'Kite', which she towed behind her car on a trailer to various meetings around the country. On 10 September 1937 she passed her pilot's test at Dunstable Downs in Bedfordshire; as part of the exam she had to 'soar' for five minutes – Amy managed eighteen. Between 12 September and 21 November she went up fifteen times, the longest flight lasting thirty minutes.

Gliding offered a similar release to flying a Gipsy Moth: nothing could compete for a feeling of still solitude and the tiny, claustrophobic cabin gave one the impression that one was floating on a cloud. The sport also gave her a sense of inclusion that she had not experienced since her days at Stag Lane; the esoteric discussion of 'thermals' and 'barographs' was similar to the hangar talk that she had eventually mastered under Jack's tutelage. Even some of the faces were the same – Captain Rattray, an anthropologist and dog-lover whom she had kept in touch with since they had learnt to fly at Stag Lane – was a keen glider pilot.

Gliding offered the chance to escape into the countryside with Teena and to take part in a sport that was as 'hands-on' and physical as flying had once been. The endless waiting for the right weather also restored her equilibrium at a time when she was short of patience. She traded in designer clothes for wide flannel trousers and flat suede shoes so that she could lie prone on the ground to grip the feet of the person in front who held the machine about to be launched. People who took part in the sport were fanatics, so immersed in their hobby that it did not occur to them to treat Amy as an international celebrity. Tourists flocked to see her whenever she took part in a public contest but, rather than resenting the distraction, club members were grateful for the cash that her fame could generate. Fans paid £20 in admission fees and £6 for autographed pictures of her. She was back in a familiar role: 'She is a "Joan of Arc" of Gliding!' the Midland Gliding Club's magazine eulogised.[3]

Cars had always fascinated Amy. She could no longer afford to own a fast motor (although she was still stopped for speeding several times)[4] and instead found ways of persuading other people to allow her to drive theirs. She entered the Monte Carlo rally in December 1937 and was confident that she and two other women could push a French Talbot to victory in the 'Coupe des Dames', giving them a chance to drive the car for themselves and to earn a commission on sales. But it was not until 1939 that she actually took part in the race with Dorothy McEvoy in a Ford V8; the manufacturer paid her £50 for her appearance. Malcolm Campbell, the famous world land and water speed-record holder and a long-term friend of Amy's, waved them off. The pair wore wind-proof ski suits and handkerchieves tied over their heads. 'And skip heavy make-up,' Amy told a woman's magazine. 'Use cold cream instead. You may look like a comic imitation of Joan Crawford, but you'll come out a lot handsomer afterwards.'[5] They arrived seventy-sixth out of a hundred entrants, thirty-three of them British, who finished the race. The weather was unusually mild, leading to the assumption that this was the easiest rally for years.

Amy entered two RAC rallies. In 1938 she drove a Bentley in a thousand-mile race around Britain which ended, conveniently for Amy, near Molly and Trevor's home in Blackpool. The following year she drove a Ford in a shorter rally across England and Wales to a finishing line in Brighton. Amy took the same car round the Royal Scottish Automobile Club Rally in 1938; one reporter, rather patronisingly, praised her 'very neat' driving and ability to pick the right gear when negotiating hairpin bends and steep hills.[6]

These rallies[7] were full of rich, titled women who drove sleek, shiny cars similar to the models that had drawn up outside Stag Lane; Amy was new to the sport and could not afford to put in the hours of practice in a borrowed car that were necessary to win prizes. She did best in events that required short bursts of speed and unwavering nerves; the Shelsley Walsh Hill Climb, which took place along a muddy, twisting, thousand-yard track just outside Worcester, was ideal and she came third in the race in just under fifty seconds. 'Going up there at that speed was, in fact, far more exciting in its way than flying at 250 m.p.h. through space,' she told a waiting reporter.[8]

The French press were ecstatic when she arrived in the spring of 1938 to compete in the women's Paris to Saint Raphael race with her chic co-driver Mademoiselle Lamberjac, who liked to wear stockings decorated with harlequin diamonds. Amy looked drawn and frumpy in her fur coat, her hair pinned tightly to her head in a middle parting and her cheekbones hidden beneath puffy skin. The French press were quick to point out that Amy was returning to France at a difficult stage in her life: '*La célèbre aviatrice Amy Johnson, dont le divorce avec James Mollison a défrayé la chronique . . .*' (The famous flyer Amy Johnson, whose divorce from James Mollison hit the headlines). Nevertheless, it was an unusually successful event: the pair were placed sixth and awarded the Prix d'Honneur and the Prix Concours.

Amy was retreating further from the metropolis – further even than the suburbs of London, a decision which she had once feared would 'lead to much talk'. In the autumn of 1937 she moved to Dragontail Cottage in Haddenham and then, with Jessamine as housekeeper to a furnished house called Monks Staithe in Princes Risborough, both just outside Aylesbury in Buckinghamshire.9 The second house was an old, fairy-tale, timbered, lattice-windowed cottage close to the church; it even had a wishing well in the garden. Each morning she cycled to the local stables where she went riding and often trotted off with the Old Berkeley hunt. Occasionally she drove her Ford motor car to London where she dined at the Ivy, the Savoy and Claridges or took 'voice production' (elocution) lessons. Occasionally she bumped into her former rivals. She told Dupré's secretary that when she met Beryl Markham, 'We rather carefully avoided looking at each other – and no wonder! If you only knew everything!'10

Monks Staithe was a good place to lie low following the publication of Jim's autobiography, *Playboy of the Air*. The book painted Jim in the worst possible light: as a boorish, drunken, selfish philanderer. He boasted of his appeal to women ('I have always worked on the principle that there is no such thing as rape in this World . . .'),11 his visit to a Hollywood brothel (he limited his consumption to alcohol) and his experiment with marijuana, which he found had no effect on him. He dismissed his marriage to Amy in a patronising, but hardly vicious, way and dedicated the book to Dorothy Ward. He even named the wrong Scottish castle when mentioning their honeymoon. Amy was furious and considered suing him. Crockers told her to underline any parts of the book that were either untrue or which represented unfair comment, but advised her that legal action would be expensive. Wood told her gently that the autobiography portrayed Jim in such a poor light that it would increase sympathy for Amy, rather than the reverse: 'it will be held universally that you have done the decent and courageous thing in severing your unfortunate connection with a rotter.'12

Amy certainly could not afford an expensive lawsuit. Will sent her £150 and she concentrated on 'a great deal of spade work to build up for myself a really serious career'.13 She decided to sell her stock-market holdings but the world economy and concern about international tensions meant she was unable to secure a good price; the sale fetched £100 – a negligible return on the stock that she had owned for seven years.

Journalism, including writing for the *Graphic*, brought in some money; she wrote the introduction for Pauline Gower's book *Women with Wings* and contributed an article to *Myself when Young*, as well as receiving just over £10 for a television appearance in early 1938. *Myself when Young* is a collection of essays written by famous women including Sylvia Pankhurst, the Marchioness of Londonderry and Ellen Wilkinson, the Labour Party's first woman MP, who was to become famous for her part in the Jarrow hunger march of 1936. Amy's contribution was honest and thoughtful and many reviewers singled it out as one of the most insightful.

Amy was also working on a book to be called *Sky Roads of the World*, which appeared in 1939. It begins as a rather bland history of flight before bursting into a travelogue of Amy's experiences in Africa and across the Atlantic. She discusses the future of flying and uses the book to vent some of her frustration, talking of America as 'the land of opportunities, a country where a woman is given a job according to her qualifications and not her sex, where new ideas are tried out and not just pigeon-holed'.[14]

In November 1938 a motor news agency in Birmingham asked Amy to edit a new magazine called *The Lady Driver*. Motoring was no longer the exclusive domain of the wealthy; by 1939 there were around two million private cars on the road and one in five families either owned a car or had access to one.[15] About 12 per cent of driving licences were held by women but there was still a lot of prejudice against female motorists.[16] Specialist car magazines urged women to concentrate on map-reading and ensuring that there were sufficient supplies of cigarettes and matches. Even Mrs Victor Bruce could not resist retelling the story of the woman who sent her pullover to Rover, asking them to supply a car in a matching colour.[17] In her career as a motoring journalist Amy concentrated on articles that compared flying with driving and on subjects such as 'Shopping made easy with a Standard Eight'.

Jim offered to lend her his plane and maps so that she could attempt a flight, but she wrote to Will that 'life seems too good to waste it that way'.[18] The nearest she came to a flying job was when Sir Francis Shelmerdine, Director General of Civil Aviation, arranged for her to be interviewed at the Air Ministry. But when she was finally offered a post as a Junior Operations Officer she was disgusted to find out that the pay was a mere £5 a week (her weekly rent alone was £20) and that the top salary for a woman was £100 less than for a man in the same position. 'My two main assets, being Amy Johnson and a woman, are disadvantages at the Air Ministry, and unfortunately nowadays I've lost so much enthusiasm for flying that I can't take on such a job for the pure love of it,' she wrote to her parents.[19] As much as the low pay, she could not face returning to office work, commuting on the train and spending eight hours at a desk. 'I suppose I have got spoilt, but I can't bear the idea of being tied up again,' she told her parents.

By the end of April she had been in the air so little that she had to cram in ten flying hours before June if she was to retain her licence. In the summer of 1938 Amy even considered resurrecting Air Cruises. The idea was a desperate one; if Dupré had thought international tensions made it a hopeless proposition in 1936, wealthy tourists were unlikely to risk luxury tours after Hitler's annexation of Austria two years later. She tried to convince herself that stage work – which she had ruled out in the past because of the risk of devaluing her name – had its merits: 'I'm supposed to have dramatic talent and if there was a suitable avia-tion film or play there's no earthly reason why I shouldn't act in it so long as I don't make a fool of myself,' she told Will.[20]

Her self-esteem was dealt a further blow when Jean Batten flew from Australia to England in just over five days and attracted much more publicity than Amy thought was left in long-distance flying. She was peeved when 'an awful woman', London club-owner Betty Kirby-Green, knocked four days off Amy's return record to Cape Town. Generally, though, the flying stories that took the headlines were quirky tales such as the story of Douglas 'Wrong-Way' Corrigan who set off from New York for California but got lost and landed in Ireland. Crossing the Atlantic 'by accident' suddenly made long-distance flying look a great deal less heroic.

Jim was still capable of making life difficult for Amy. His tax appeal was heard in January and he threatened to claim some of it from his wife. She was forced to pay Crockers to represent her and also suffered the humiliation of attending a hearing with her (nearly) ex-husband. Amy found the experience 'very embarrassing', especially as Wake-field's representative was there, causing Amy's reputation to 'drop to rock bottom'.[21] Just before Amy and Jim received their decree absolute at the end of August 1938, Jim managed to embarrass his wife one last time when French magistrates accused him of causing havoc at Le Touquet Airport by borrowing a plane to perform drunken aerobatics. Jim remarried two and a half months after his divorce from Amy was finalised; his new wife was a wealthy divorcee, Phyllis Hussey, who came from an influential Jamaican family. The marriage lasted a decade before Jim found his third and final wife.[22]

Amy was relieved to be single again and desperate to get the name on her passport – the symbol of all that she had achieved – changed back to 'Johnson'. She also used the opportunity to trim three years off her age. 'Well, I'm free now,' she told a *Daily Sketch* reporter, laughing. 'I've got an open mind on the subject of marriage after the last adventure.' She dismissed rumours of a romance with a 'wealthy French nobleman', saying that she had not been to Paris for over a year.[23]

London attracted her less and less but she attended the première of *Men with Wings* in early November 1938. The film starred Fred Mac-Murray and Ray Milland in 'the whole stirring story of aviation . . . told in TECHNICOLOR through the heart-pounding adventures of men with wings and a woman who waited . . . with her eyes on the sky, a smile on her lips and an ache in her heart'.[24] The cinema on the first night must have produced an atmosphere every bit as tense as that promised by the poster. The King of Greece, Lord Mountbatten and America's new ambassador in London, Joseph Kennedy, who firmly believed in appeasement with Germany, helped to make it a glittering occasion. However, it was an awkward evening for Amy, since the audience included Jim, shortly to be married, and Charles Scott. But rubbing shoulders with royalty was rare for Amy; she was more likely to appear as guest of honour at the Reading Aero Club or to judge a beauty contest at the Combined Laundries Ball at Cheltenham Town Hall. Her friends were once more people who were serious about flying rather than the fame and riches it brought. William Earle Johns, the creator of 'Biggles' and an early advocate of women pilots, took her to lunch and told readers in *Modern Boy* magazine about her new interests of horseriding, gliding and motor-racing.[25]

Amy had kept in touch with Pauline Gower and Dorothy Spicer since their games of snowball at Stag Lane.[26] They were the 'nice girls' whom she had considered joining in their air-taxi work and joy-riding before deciding that there was 'little money to be made'. Both were 'have a go' women – jolly, practical types who loved flying but felt no need to mix with the Mayfair set. Pauline was seven years younger than Amy and on the surface appeared to benefit from the trappings of a traditionally privileged background: her father was a former mayor of Tunbridge Wells who served as a Conservative MP for over twenty years. He was chairman of the Royal Society for the Prevention of Cruelty to Animals and became known in the press as the 'Dogs' MP' for his campaigns against canine vivisection and to improve working conditions in circuses and on film sets.

But Pauline's early years had not been without challenges: she had contracted pleurisy at the age of seventeen and received the last rites. She recovered to claim a season as a debutante before becoming obsessed with planes after a joy-rider took her up for her first flight. Her father immediately cut off her allowance, forcing her to teach the violin as a way of paying for flying lessons. At Stag Lane she met

Dorothy Spicer, a tall, equally bubbly young woman who wore her blonde hair in two plaits and disguised her lanky frame in dungarees. Together they formed a flying double act that darted across Europe in their dual-control plane. Whichever one of them sat in the front held their luggage, raising it at the point of take-off to avoid jamming the throttle. When they flew across France their maps blew out of the cockpit and Pauline comforted herself by playing 'Show me the way to go home' on the mouth organ.

Amy spent a weekend with them at Pauline's father's country house near Tunbridge Wells in October 1937. The family was still coming to terms with the death of Pauline's mother who, believing she had cancer, had committed suicide by locking herself in her bedroom and turning the gas on. One of the letters she left to her two daughters ended with the words, 'Your utterly bewildered and terrified but loving Ma.'[27] Pauline remained cheerful in the face of so raw a tragedy. She was reconciled with her father who had given up hope of her abandoning flying, and when Amy visited their home they went horseriding with Dorothy in the grounds of his house. During the day they motored to Hastings in Pauline's car where they walked along the seafront and discussed the changing politics of continental Europe. They played on the slot-machines before returning home and in the evening Amy listened while Dorothy sang songs composed by Pauline, who accompanied her on a ukulele and a piano-accordion.

By 1938 Amy was so desperate for money that she considered the sort of joy-riding work that Pauline and Dorothy used to scrape a living by. She talked to Trevor about offering flights in a Dragon Rapide[28] from Blackpool beach, but the weather and a lingering fear that it might exclude her from more prestigious work held her back. She asked the AA if she could work as a 'propagandist'[29] for them and was hopeful that Imperial Airways would offer her a job. She was so short of cash that she asked Will for a loan so that she could visit her New York dentist who had been waiting for her gums to shrink back so that he could finish the root work begun two years earlier. Amy assured her father that the work would last twenty-five years.

Casting around for ways of raising money, Amy considered selling her jewellery. Just as she had once sent her mother and sisters packages of clothes that were no longer the fashionable colour, now she suggested that Trevor might like to buy a pair of ear-rings that Dupré had given her and which were worth £30 (£931 in today's money).[30] Peter Reiss later claimed that he took some of Amy's jewellery to a pawnbroker's for her in case she was recognised, but that she had to return in disguise to sign forms at the shop.

Her life seemed to be rewinding in other ways, too. By 1939 she was back in touch with Jack after a very long time; their correspondence leaves a lot of details unsaid but it seems that Amy had asked Jack to try to find her a job – either as a pilot for Mrs Victor Bruce, whose company, Air Dispatch, made deliveries between Paris and London, or by helping Amy to raise money for some business scheme. Jack reverted to her old pet-name of 'Johnnie', asked how 'her people' were and whether she still saw Winifred. He grumbled that whenever he bumped into Amy she was 'always in company' and that he did not even know where she lived. He managed to raise £50 for Amy's business scheme although he told her bluntly that many people had said it was a 'damn cheek' to be asked. 'Of course you're the damn limit,' Jack went on. 'I have to wait until I see Jay [probably Jay Hofer, an old friend from Stag Lane] or read it in the papers to know if you're even alive and the years roll away, the boy's ten tomorrow, but he's a fine kid, Johnnie.' It had been a long time since anyone had dared to be this blunt to Amy. Jack knew she was taking liberties with his endless reserves of good will but he could not disguise his affection and ended his note with the touching comment, 'Your handwriting always does me good.'[31]

Amy's frustration at the lack of a well-paid, high-profile job made her more outspoken in public – although her message was often confused and open to misinterpretation. She was one of nine well-known figures invited to a luncheon at Foyles bookshop. The theme, 'What Shall I Be?', was aimed at children but Amy, wearing a hat that looked like a stunted fez, sounded sarcastic when she announced, 'Well, here I am without a job . . . Women should stick to the jobs they're suited for. We're no good as engineers in greasy overalls – let's design the interiors of aeroplanes – take over the catering arrangements.'[32] A week later she told the National Union of Women Teachers: 'I regard it as a national disgrace that brilliant women have still to meet on occasions like this to ask for obvious justice to be given them.'[33] Amid cries of 'Shame!' she told the packed meeting at Lewisham in South London of the £100 difference in pay between men and women at the Air Ministry and urged the teachers to strike if they did not receive the increase they wanted.

She reserved her strongest criticism for the Civil Air Guard – an idea launched in October 1938 in a frantic attempt to train civilians as pilots and claw back some ground in the race to re-arm. As part of the scheme the Government offered subsidised flying lessons to anyone between the ages of eighteen and fifty so that, in theory, it should be possible to obtain a licence for £2.2.6., rather than the prohibitive £20 to £50. In return these 'shilling a week flyers', as the press dubbed them, had to agree to offer their skills in a national emergency. The wife of an aircraft designer, Mrs F. G. Miles, was chosen to represent women pilots – it was clearly a position Amy had her eye on. 'I think I am the obvious person to have it, but apparently I don't cut much ice in high circles. A handle to your name, influence and "something to grease the palm" seem still to be essential to social and Government success,' she told her father.[34]

Instead, the *Daily Graphic* made her their Civil Air Guard reporter and she toured aerodromes to study the recruitment process at first hand. Her assessment of the scheme appeared in various newspapers and in speeches that she made in the autumn of 1938.[35] The idea was basically a good one, she believed, in that it fostered airmindedness and provided a fourth line of defence, but she felt it could have been better organised and was hampered by snobbery and profiteering. She criticised the CAG's uniform and its lack of discipline. She wanted to see the introduction of proper ranks and rigorous training that included lectures, exams and advanced lessons that covered cross-country flying. Encouraging owners of light aeroplanes through subsidies and petrol tax rebates was as important, she felt, as fostering this new breed of 'ten-hour' flyers. Her comments made a lot of sense but they were partly driven by her profound disappointment that she had not been given a top job in the CAG.

As tension mounted in Europe, Amy became for many people a reassuring symbol of Britain's power in the air. A reader's letter in the *Sketch* suggested her as the obvious face to peer out of an Air Raid Precautions (ARP) poster and she was photographed taking tea at the Forum Club next to Neville Chamberlain's niece, Valerie Cole. Amy is leaning forward intently, listening to what the young woman who went home to Number 10 Downing Street, has to say.[36]

The club was established for women in 1919 but men were allowed beyond its marbled entrance hallway, and its billiard table and liveried servants aped the oldest male clubs. The Forum also offered its pearl and fur-bedecked members a cocktail bar and a beauty parlour that, by 1939, doubled as an air-raid shelter. The establishment mixed the frivolous with the serious: some members played bridge for most of the day, whilst others learnt French. Amy, Dorothy and Pauline sat on the committee of the club's thriving aviation section and arranged lectures and social events. By January 1939 members were discussing how women might be trained for a 'national emergency'. The consensus was that their most important role would be ferrying planes and military staff around Britain. 'National emergency', of course, was a euphemism for war. But the Forum Club brought out Amy's worst insecurities about wealth and class. 'I haven't heard a word from the Forum Club for ages,' she wrote to Pauline. 'Have they decided to put me completely out of the picture? . . . Please tell me the awful truth, if there is anything, won't you?'[37]

By the middle of 1938 many British politicians had come to the conclusion that Hitler's ambitions had tipped him over into mental instability. Having annexed Austria on the pretence that it was part of a Germanic whole, he was slavering over Czechoslovakia. As the summer drew to an end, anxiety about Hitler's ambitions reached a crescendo; his speech at a rally in mid September appeared to present the perfect launching pad for an invasion of Czechoslovakia. It was followed by what the papers called 'Crisis Weekend'. The *Sunday Referee* asked twelve famous people, including the motoring magnate Lord Austin, the conductor Sir Henry Wood, Lord Londonderry, the cricketer Len Hutton, the Roman Catholic archbishop of Liverpool and the entertainers Gracie Fields and Sir Harry Lauder how they intended to survive the high tension. Amy was gliding in a remote part of England when she told the reporter: 'If only Hitler could likewise relax for two days and forget himself.'[38] The suggestion made the German Chancellor sound like an overworked businessman who simply needed a short break to make him realise that world domination was not such a good idea.

The common image of Hitler as a blustering buffoon was a comforting one, but seemed less realistic as he prepared to launch a major military offensive based on the argument that the Germans of Czechoslovakia's Sudetenland should be reunited with the Fatherland. The British Prime Minister, Neville Chamberlain, snatched a last-ditch chance to reason with him and requested a meeting. For the first time in history two world leaders separated by hundreds of miles were able to sit down face to face within hours of agreeing to meet. Chamberlain left Croydon Airport in a twin-engined Lockheed looking as gaunt and humourless as a bank manager. He had never travelled in an aeroplane before and he was anxious about the flight, the first ordeal in a very trying day. At Berchtesgaden, Hitler's alpine retreat, the two leaders spent three hours alone except for an interpreter, arguing over Czechoslovakia.

A week later Chamberlain flew back to Germany to continue the discussions. But Hitler's stance was hardening. At a mass rally he whipped his audience of 20,000 into a frenzy over the Sudetenland. By the time Chamberlain sat down with Mussolini, the French premier Edouard Daladier and Hitler, their task was to divide up Czechoslovakia in what became the basis for the Munich Agreement. These weeks of what today would be called 'shuttle diplomacy' ended with Chamberlain flying back to Heston Airport to a hero's welcome; he offered 'peace with honour' and 'peace for our time'. Behind the public façade of appeasement the RAF was shaking itself awake from years of torpor.

In February 1939 Amy had a 'narrow escape' when she crashed her car near Witney on the road between Oxford and Cheltenham.[39] It was by far the worst car accident she had experienced and it left her with injuries to the head, ankle and fingers and with a broken right knee. The one helpful aspect of the accident was that her insurance policy for the Monte Carlo rally paid out £25 a week while she was unable to walk. She received massage and electrical treatment for her knee and the need for rest provided the ideal reason for her to sail to America for her long-delayed dentist's appointment. As she told Crockers at the end of the month when she queried their bill for fees, she had 'no funds at all'.[40]

Amy viewed money as a benchmark for affection, and relationships that were muddied by a business dimension frequently ended in bitterness; if someone was slow to give her money she saw it as a personal slight. When Crockers, quite reasonably, asked her to settle her account, she wrote them an emotional letter that quoted 'moral responsibility' as the main reason why she felt she should not pay in full.

Her falling out with Gloria Bristol, her Park Avenue beautician friend, was based on a similar perceived slight in which business and pleasure became blurred. Gloria claimed Amy owed her $300 for 'work and preparations' – including some lotions that she had given Dupré to take back with him to Europe for Amy, a gramophone record, telephone calls and 'incidentals'. Amy claimed that the only cosmetics she had received were a bottle of 'acne lotion' and a set of preparations that Will had brought home and which Amy expected him to pay for. She assumed Dupré would pick up the tab for the telephone as most calls were made in connection with his business. But what really rankled was that Gloria had shown Dupré the letters in which Amy told her that Dupré would pay. 'You broke faith with me . . .' Amy wrote to Gloria. 'This is not friendship and I do not number amongst my friends, people who are so disloyal. You will therefore understand why I do not wish to have anything more to do with you.'[41]

In May 1939 Amy got her first 'proper job' since working as a typist for Crockers. She joined the Portsmouth, Southsea and Isle of Wight Aviation Company as a pilot earning a pound a day plus ten shillings for each hour's flying. The company's main work was to provide a ferry service between the three centres but it had also won army co-operation contracts which meant pilots worked extra hours – usually at night (when their hourly pay was double). Anti-aircraft batteries and searchlight operators practised spotting planes flown by Amy and her colleagues who appeared out of the night sky as surprise targets. On one occasion Amy took a wireless operator up with her to give him experience of communicating from the air. Jennie Broad, a qualified ground engineer with both 'A' and 'C' licences, ensured that Amy's plane was kept in good working condition during these manoeuvres.

Amy's new job caused great excitement in the press who pointed out that now anyone could fly with a world-class pilot for just five shillings and that Amy, who had previously raced across the globe, was now making short hops to the Isle of Wight.[42] It all seemed part of the unreal, topsy-turvy world of 1939 when everyone was waiting for something to happen, but at the same time dreading what it might be.

Although Amy never stopped looking for other work, she enjoyed her ferry job. She liked being paid to fly and she got on well with her colleagues. 'I have resigned myself to the fact that they [the companies she had applied to for work] just won't accept the women pilots on the same basis as the men . . .' she told Will. 'It's lovely having a job and having a legitimate reason for turning down bazaars etc.!'[43] She also relished the feeling of 'independence and security' that earning a wage gave her.[44] In her spare time she was drawn to the sea that she flew over on every trip. She became friendly with Bill Long, a yachtsman who had spent five years sailing round the world and who taught her about boats. Sailing in the unpredictable water, exposed to the wind and rain as she had once been in the open cockpit of a Gipsy Moth, was more thrilling than flying and she dreamt of buying a boat that she and Bill would sail round the world in.

When Will wrote to Amy on 21 August 1939 he was still offering her advice about work, money, whether or not she should keep a car and where she should live.[45] He was convinced that Britain would avoid war. Three days later he had changed his mind: 'Now it seems we are in for a terrible mess; it seems war is certain this weekend and God alone knows what will happen once it has started.'[46] Amy shared his pessimism: 'I don't know whether I am taking a particularly gloomy view of things, but everyone at the airport seems to think war is as good as declared,' Amy told Will. 'It's terrible isn't it, and so criminally stupid . . . The weather seems to fit in with the general tension – it is heavy and dull.'[47]

Will's business was barely able to keep going with the few staff who had not left to join the war effort. Ciss had put up black-outs at Brynmawr and started to plan an air-raid shelter. Molly, who earlier in the year had given birth to their first daughter, Susan, tried to persuade her parents to leave Brid and move in with them at Blackpool.

In Portsmouth the waiting was driving Amy mad. Even the interesting moments, such as flying a Squadron Leader to France, increased the sense that they were on the cusp of something momentous. The town was sand-bagged and bristling with gun defences on every corner. Night descended with a blanket darkness unrelieved by lights and Amy's suitcase sat permanently packed ready for the pilots' evacuation to Cardiff that could happen at two hours' notice. 'As regards the war it is a terrible business,' Will wrote to Amy, 'but we don't know much about it yet; I'm very much afraid many terrible things have to happen before it is over.'[48]

On Friday, 1 September 1939 Hitler invaded Poland; on Sunday morning Chamberlain told families huddled round their Bakelite wireless sets that Britain was at war. Shortly after his broadcast an air-raid siren sounded; it was a false alarm that rang out like an anguished howl at the enormity of what had just happened.

Chapter 26

War

(1939–40)

Amy was not good at waiting. She had always found hanging around hotels hoping for the right weather, nerves strained at the thought of trying to lift a 'flying petrol pump' into the air, the worst part of record-breaking flights. The declaration of hostilities in September 1939 marked the start of the ultimate waiting game. As the 'Phoney War' of rumours and planning seeped into the spring of 1940, Amy felt more and more boxed in. Flying no longer offered its usual sense of release, as barrage balloons that bobbed in the sky above London, giving her a sense of security from the ground, constricted her passage through the air to narrow corridors of safety. She became as nervous of the darkened trains that sped through unmarked railway stations as she had been of travelling on the crowded, unhealthy underground when she first moved to London.

When Amy started her flying career in 1929 aeroplanes were making the world smaller, bringing news of relatives and friends from around the Empire via air mail and making it theoretically possible to cross the Atlantic in just over a day. Now the race to build up Britain's air capability superseded everything. The Luftwaffe had pinned non-military flying back to within Britain's shores, back to the very factories where planes were built and which now became the focus of a vital supply line at the heart of the conflict. Whereas women pilots had been an interesting adornment in the early years of flying, no one quite knew what to do with them at the beginning of the war.

Amy found herself pushed around like one of the markers used to plot enemy planes. First her army co-operation work sent her to Heston and then she was moved to Cardiff which she described as a 'detestable place'.[1] She shared lodgings in a house with two other pilots until they were transferred. In October 1939 a policeman felt the full force of her boredom and frustration when he stopped her car and admonished her for driving with undipped headlights. Her reaction, according to the policeman, was to lash out at him with a string of expletives and sharp nails that scratched his face. Amy's defence was that her nails were not long enough to injure anyone and that if she used the word 'damn', it was because she worked in an industry where the word was a common adjective. *Aeroplane* magazine complained that, while this may have been the case, such language 'most certainly is not a pilot's prerogative'.[2]

By the end of November 1939 she was flying for no more than two hours a week. She was 'up against the "woman prejudice" again' and furious that male pilots with much less experience were carrying out work she wanted to do, including flights to France.[3] She played squash and saw *Goodbye Mr Chips* at the cinema. A few weeks before Christmas she decided to sell her mink coat, comforting herself with the knowledge that she still had several silver fox furs in cold storage. There was a sense that things were coming full circle. In November Will suffered a fall that confined him to bed. Amy wrote to him rather too breezily: 'It's funny you started the last war in bed too!', reminding him of the debilitating skin condition that kept him at home wrapped in bandages like an Egyptian mummy.[4]

The (all-male) Air Transport Auxiliary (ATA) was formed in the first month of the war to ferry planes from the factories where they were built to safer parts of the country since the factories had now become targets for enemy bombs. A few weeks later the Director General of Civil Aviation, Sir Francis Shelmerdine, who had been best man at Jim and Amy's wedding, agreed in principle that a few women should be taken on as ferry pilots. But there were two major obstacles to the plan. A residual fear of unemployment – which still stood at just under one million – after a decade of dole queues caused anger that women were apparently taking well-paid jobs from men. C. G. Grey, the outspoken but respected editor of *The Aeroplane*, wrote: 'The menace is the woman who thinks that she ought to be flying a high-speed bomber when she really has not the intelligence to scrub the floor of a hospital properly, or who wants to nose round as an Air Raid Warden and yet can't cook her husband's dinner.'[5]

An organisation called the National Men's Defence League wanted MPs to debate why women were allowed to fly planes in the ATA, compelling Edith Londonderry to write to the *Daily Telegraph* in defence of their role. There was also great reluctance to put females centre stage in a theatre of war – although, of course, these women would not be fighter pilots. In Russia attitudes were quite different and women pilots were to fight at Stalingrad and other major battles.[6] But in Britain the image of the female pilot did not fit in with the traditional role of wartime women, which had always been to keep the home fires burning.

In September 1939 Shelmerdine discussed the idea of women ferry pilots with Gerard d'Erlanger, a director of British Airways who was co-ordinating the ATA. They chose Pauline – who was not yet thirty – to head the women's section, which would start with around a dozen pilots. Amy, the most experienced and famous woman pilot in the world, who had written and lectured on the role of female pilots in wartime and who, for many people, was the face of flying, had been passed over for the top job. The reason why appears in the memo written by Shelmerdine to the director of Civil Aviation Finance, in which he outlines Pauline's qualifications for the job; despite her joy-riding work she had 'never been a stunt pilot with all the publicity which is attached to that role'.[7] The taint of publicity was probably the reason why Jean Batten, Amy's record-breaking rival, was never accepted in the ATA.[8]

When Amy discovered that Pauline had been offered the job she commented that, had she 'played her cards right and cultivated the right people', the title could have been hers. 'But honestly I wouldn't like to have it,' she told Will. 'I'd much rather work in a proper commercial aviation company with men pilots than be one of a team of women sort of being given the crumbs to keep them quiet.'[9] In November 1939 Pauline sent her a standard letter asking her to join the ATA but Amy was holding out for a more interesting job that made full use of her exceptional flying skills. She was dismissive of the ATA's work and of the fact that they were transporting the old-fashioned Tiger Moths that the RAF used for training.

But there were no openings in commercial aviation and the longer Amy left it, the harder it became for her to swallow her pride and join the ATA. In January 1940 Pauline took on her first eight recruits; all were qualified flying instructors and most had several years' flying experience. Amy, who was living in a hotel near Reading, watched from the sidelines, asking her mother to forward any newspaper cuttings she spotted about Pauline or women pilots. For her part, Pauline coaxed and praised Amy, knowing that drawing attention to her absence from the ATA could only strengthen her case to increase its numbers and lure Amy on board.

In March the Women's Engineering Society hosted a luncheon at Park Lane Hotel to celebrate its twenty-fifth anniversary; speakers took as their theme 'Women Aviators in Wartime'. The WES had always treated Amy with uncritical adoration but on this occasion the spotlight was trained on Pauline who bristled with authority in her ATA uniform. Her speech aimed to put right the press's depiction of the ATA as 'menacing the RAF'; rather, she said, the female pilots' aim was to free up their male colleagues who would soon be 'very busy indeed'. The best way to answer the criticism was by 'quietly getting on with the job' – at which point she neatly focused on Amy. 'In this connection the example of Miss Amy Johnson in quiet efficiency is a shining light. She had shown what women could do and the ATA are not going to be beaten by criticism. We do not believe that we are taking the bread out of the mouths of children, one of the other foolish criticisms; eleven women could not do all this damage.' The speech succeeded simultaneously in praising Amy while voicing the unspoken question of why space could not be made in the ATA for such an obviously talented pilot.[10]

In March 1940 the Air Ministry requisitioned Portsmouth, Southsea and the Isle of Wight's entire fleet of planes and gave its pilots a month's notice. This compulsory purchase, which extended to other airlines and civil flying companies, left a hundred pilots and fifty engineers, mechanics and wireless operators without a job. Amy was desperate for work but her pride made it difficult for her to join the ATA while Pauline was head of the women's section. When she finally filled in her application form later that month she did so as a 'last resort' to allow her to continue flying. She had watched Lady Bailey, now fifty, join the ATA in February and leave within a week – her appointment had caused outrage in the press, where it was claimed she had been allowed to dodge the upper age limit of forty-five because she was married to a millionaire. 'There is so much bad feeling against the only women's organisation that I should much prefer to get a job outside it if possible, but I can probably always get into it eventually . . .' Amy told Will.[11] But the idea of a women's ferry pool was so radical that its numbers were allowed to increase only at a snail's pace and she was put on a waiting list.

In the meantime she fired off letters to every possible contact. She wrote to the Finnish embassy to offer to fly repaired ferry planes, equipment, supplies and passengers to Finland, and also considered working in Kenya.[12] She asked Allied Airways and the BBC for a job and trawled through her contacts book – writing to Lords Londonderry and Nuffield (previously William Morris) and Sir Alan Cobham. The latter told her that she could not work as a flight refueller because the task was 'too heavy and too arduous'.[13] Unaware of the constraints on numbers, he joined the growing number of people who urged Amy to sign up with Pauline's 'crowd'.

Lady Astor promised to see Amy and to put her in touch with the Under Secretary of State for Air, Captain Harold Balfour and Lord Nuffield. But Balfour's letter infuriated Amy: he persisted in using her married name (Lady Astor admitted he was merely repeating a mistake she had made) and seemed unaware that Amy had applied to the ATA. Amy wrote to Lady Astor:

> My whole point is this: Were I a man, there is no doubt at all that my particular kind of experience could be used in various ways to good effect, but because I am a woman all these avenues are closed to me. At the moment, this doesn't matter to anyone else except myself, because there is such a surplus of pilots that there are barely enough jobs to go round. If, however, the future calls for more pilots of an experience which today it is impossible to acquire, I am afraid the Government may find that the unemployed have become unemployable, or unobtainable.[14]

Pauline appears to have felt guilty that Amy was left kicking her heels and forwarded a letter from Lady Hoare which outlined a job flying airmail from Toulouse to Dakar, including stops at Alicante and Casablanca.[15] While Amy waited to hear if this job might develop into anything more than an exotic pipedream, she contacted Dupré's office to see whether he could offer any introductions for her.[16] But his secretary wrote back saying that he was in North America.

Wherever she went in her search for a job she was told she was taking work from men. 'I feel like retorting that isn't the boot on the other leg? Why should amateur pilots who ought by rights to join up hide themselves in screened commercial companies thus depriving several qualified women of jobs they could do equally well?'[17] She raised the issue over lunch with Lady Astor, who had already spoken out about the need for women to be given more responsible jobs, and she promised to mention the issue in Parliament.[18]

During the next few months Amy hummed and hawed about whether or not to join the ATA – although Pauline was still waiting for permission to expand her numbers. During April 1940 several newspapers were convinced she was about to take up a job driving an ambulance in the French army.[19] So it was a coup for Pauline when Amy finally agreed to take her flying test and interview on 6 May. Pauline had assured her that it was just a formality but when Amy arrived at the aerodrome car park she spotted another applicant, 'all dolled up in full Sidcot suit, furlined helmet and goggles, fluffing up her

hair etc. – the typical C.A.G. [Civil Air Guard] Lyons waitress type',
Amy wrote to Will. 'I suddenly realised I could not go in and sit in line
with these girls (who all more or less look up to me as God!), so I
turned tail and ran.'[20] In truth, Amy may have been nervous about how
she would fare in a formal flying test in the same way that a motor-
racing driver might struggle to conform to the speed limit and other
constraints of a driving exam. Amy was well known for her rather
abrupt landings and one ATA woman who flew with Amy found her
'very hesitant'.[21] She was above all a solo flyer.

She comforted herself with the thought that the ATA was a 'dead
end'[22] and that she might find a job at Cowley where Lord Nuffield was
masterminding a scheme to patch up bedraggled planes that limped
home after their skirmishes with the Luftwaffe. Amy was even prepared to return to office work if she could find a job connected with
flying and asked Ciss to look out her old shorthand books. Ever
mindful of her image, she also urged her mother to discourage people
from using outdated photos of her.

A week after Amy phoned with the excuse that flu had prevented her
from attending her flying test, the Germans invaded Holland and
Belgium. 'Isn't the news terrible! Things are happening now so rapidly,'
Amy wrote to Ciss after she had been to the cinema to see *Gone with
the Wind* and adding that she would join the ATA 'for the time being'.[23]
Chamberlain resigned and Churchill took over as head of the National
Coalition Government. Churchill had for years been bellowing that
Britain was falling behind in the skies; now he recognised that if Britain
was to stand a chance of holding its own against Germany, it needed a
reliable supply of planes. He placed his old friend Lord Beaverbrook in
charge of aircraft supply as part of the newly formed Ministry of Aircraft Production. As the Battle of Britain unravelled that summer it
became even more crucial that planes were flown away from factories
as quickly as possible and that RAF pilots were freed from ferry duties
to confront a steady stream of German aircraft.

By the summer the number of women in the ATA had increased to
twenty; a further six joined by the end of the year. Amy's old friend
Mabel Glass and her engineer at Southampton, Jennie Broad, were
among the newcomers, but Amy always remained an outsider. She was
older than most of the women – the youngest was twenty – and only a
handful were married. Although many were experienced pilots, very
few had anything close to Amy's 2300 hours in the air. Several came
from privileged backgrounds such as Margie Fairweather, who was the
daughter of a lord, or Lettice Curtis, who had graduated from Oxford

University; others had left behind careers in ballet, beauty pageants and skiing.

Everything about Amy set her apart. The most famous woman flyer in the world had flown over fifty different planes and her logbook (which, like her passport, trimmed three years off her age) included a range of exotic planes, including one Russian aircraft. Amy was divorced and wore clothes that, although not quite up to the minute, had once been and which she wore with unrivalled panache. The controversy that surrounded the women's section of the ATA meant that Pauline had to run it with a sort of lights-out, dormitory style of discipline that Amy loathed. 'It's so like a girls' school, with the same favouritisms, jealousies, cattiness etc.,' she told Will.[24] To Ciss she wrote: 'I dislike intensely being with the ATA; although I know that most of us at present are having to do jobs we don't like. I'm too much of an individualist to work as a cog in a wheel . . .'[25] Amy hated being the 'new girl' and said it reminded her of the paralysing feelings of exclusion she felt when she worked at Morison's Advertising Agency. She contacted Number One Civilian Repair Unit again, asking to be taken on as a test pilot or assistant test pilot but there were no vacancies.[26] She lunched with Lieutenant Colonel Moore-Brabazon, at the time Minister for Transport, and offered to act as secretary to the Civil Aviation Committee.[27]

As she wrote home to her mother she watched the ATA 'boys' soaring overhead in Hurricanes – the powerful monoplane fighters which carried eight machine-guns mounted like teeth on their wings. The Hurricane played a key part in the Battle of Britain – 1300 took part compared to 950 Spitfires – and it had a top speed of over 300 miles per hour. But women pilots were not permitted to sample its power; instead they were wedged in a much older age of flying and Amy found the open-cockpit Tiger Moths both tedious and tiring, especially when she had to lug her kit around with her (her parachute alone weighed forty pounds).

She lived in a slow-moving world that lacked glamour and excitement. The male ATA pilots had been excluded from the RAF because they were too old or infirm. Some had learnt to fly in the Great War and still bore the scars – most famously, Stewart Keith-Jopp, who had lost an eye and his left arm but who still managed to fly some of the ATA's larger planes. Unlike the younger fighter pilots, they had already established themselves in a wide range of careers outside flying – one was a conjuror, another a company director; there was also an antiques dealer and an aviation journalist. Their age and backgrounds left them open to persistent ridicule by the young 'Brylcreem Boys' of the RAF. The ATA, it was said, stood for 'Ancient and Tattered Airmen', 'All Types Accepted' or, in the case of Pauline's 'girls', 'Always Terrified Women'. But the women were too bored to be terrified. RAF pilots resented the apparent freedom that ATA pilots of both sexes enjoyed and – erroneously – believed that they were much better paid. There were rumours that women pilots earned £600 a year (the basic pay for a Squadron Leader or the equivalent of £16,020 today), and Lord Haw Haw, the Nazi propagandist, played on this resentment when he broadcast from Germany that they were receiving £8 a week.

Once the Phoney War burst into reality that perfect summer of 1940, boredom became an emotion to long for. In the space of one month Britain went from a state of mild unease to a position where it appeared to be clinging onto freedom by its fingernails. British forces were evacuated from Norway after an ignominious and ill-planned sea operation; German troops swept through Europe; Holland and then Belgium surrendered. The dying days of May witnessed the astonishing heroism of the evacuation of Dunkirk, when captains of all manner of small vessels heaved troops onto their decks and chugged their way through seas awash with dead bodies back to England, where the boats regrouped and returned in the hope of snatching more lives from the beach battleground of France.

The staccato rhythm of bad news continued into June: Mussolini declared war on France and Britain, and Germany occupied northern France. At the height of summer the skies blossomed with the most perfect of English weather, the ideal backdrop for the feature presentation of 'Luftwaffe versus RAF'. Heads tilted upwards to watch the dogfights played out against the very essence of an England about to be overrun. The Germans were expected at any minute: surging up the beaches now framed with barbed wire, alighting from the railway stations denuded of their signposts or fluttering down from the skies in parachutes.

The threat of invasion shook Amy out of her depression. Suddenly the value of the work carried out by the ATA was obvious; Italy's entry into the war meant that the RAF faced a conflict on two fronts – in Europe and North Africa. The steady flow of aircraft production was vital and the ATA women pilots were at last allowed to get their hands on more interesting planes. Amy swooped low over Molly's house in a big, yellow Airspeed Oxford that she was delivering to Scotland. The desperate situation gave her a sense of purpose that she had been lacking for years: 'I think there's going to be hell let loose here,' she wrote to her mother, suggesting that her parents and Molly left for Canada.[28] Events on the other side of the Channel, where she had made her home on and off for several years, shocked her: 'I can't understand the French packing up. I feel they lack leaders and any real sort of inspiring ideals.'

Amy was feeling less of a loner and more of a respected pilot who enjoyed special privileges and attention. She still did not mix easily with the younger ATA women but she found a close friend in Winnie Crossley, a strong-willed doctor's daughter from Huntingdon who had spent five years towing aerial advertising banners and working in a flying circus before becoming one of the first women to join the ATA. Pauline, whom Amy described to her mother as 'grand', allowed her to commute daily to the women's 'pool' in Hatfield, north of London, from her lodgings in White Waltham, Berkshire. Usually she flew to work in an Anson borrowed from the ATA. The Anson was a difficult plane to fly because its undercarriage had to be retracted by hand using an awkwardly placed handle underneath the pilot's seat.

Her landlords, who charged her a nominal rent, were the Hofers, a couple she had known since Stag Lane. Amy had invested in their engineering business and entrusted them with Christopher, her St Bernard dog. Their home was a haven where she could relax after a day with the ATA and she lavished presents on them, buying their son a train set from Hamleys toy shop and an Elizabeth Arden beauty case for his mother.

Amy sent her jewellery home for safe keeping but badgered her mother with constant requests to post items of clothing from the eight trunks she had deposited with her parents at Bridlington. Ciss erected a rod-and-curtain cubicle in their attic to accommodate the designer clothes and rows of smart shoes, like an upmarket jumble sale. Amy used the birthday money from her parents to buy a more reliable watch to replace her Marks and Spencer's model.

At work she wore a sexless, RAF-style uniform whose heavy material crushed and flattened the natural contours of her body and made her look about as glamorous as an ironing board. Four large pockets and a massive belt with a big brass buckle added to the navy-blue tunic's considerable bulk and a black tie and blue shirt struggled to make an appearance beneath. The RAF tailors were unused to fitting the female form and went to great lengths to keep it at arm's length by lassoing new recruits from a distance with a tape-measure and reading off the figure whilst studiously avoiding any eye-contact with the chest they were trying to measure. When Amy was promoted to first officer

around the time of her thirty-sixth birthday, in July 1940, she was able
to sew two gold stripes on the shoulder of her tunic. Trousers were not
meant to be worn outside the aerodrome; before leaving it the women
were supposed to change into a skirt accompanied by black stockings
and shoes. In very cold weather the pilots put on an even heavier overcoat and a forage cap.

Unless she happened to be waiting to fly back to base, Amy's day
started at Hatfield aerodrome where she was given instructions for her
next flight. She was always disappointed if she was told to fly a Tiger
Moth. Britain was under siege and the measures taken to expel the
invader also made life difficult for the ferry pilots. In peacetime a
railway line proved a useful landmark to follow; in war it usually ended
in a cluster of barrage balloons. As soon as Amy knew where she was
flying she memorised the groups of barrage balloons that she must
avoid and pored over the secret map that showed where aircraft risked
being shot down by anti-aircraft guns. The 'colours of the day' were
locked away in a safe and these, too, had to be committed to memory.
If her plane was challenged by a friendly aircraft, ship or ground
station, she had to be able to respond by firing a series of Very car-
tridges in the correct order and colour for that day. She telephoned for
a weather forecast and permission from Fighter Command Head Quarters to proceed and then collected the outer skins of her flying apparel:
parachute, Sidcot (a cumbersome quasi-boiler suit that helped keep out
the cold), boots, gloves, helmet and goggles. Every ATA pilot packed an
overnight bag in case foul weather or the need to wait for the right
plane left them stranded away from base.

Wherever Amy went, people recognised her. RAF pilots who risked
their lives daily crowded round her plane to ask this seasoned flyer
about her solo trip to Australia and her other record-breaking journeys.
If the weather was bad Amy played darts in the mess, drank execrable
coffee or knitted, listening to the younger women competing with one
another to see who could clock up the most time in the air. Occasionally Amy went to the pub but there was no time, and precious little
petrol, to look further afield for entertainment.

By mid September Amy was flying four hours a day and helping the
women pilots to tread a thin line between making a noticeable contribution to the supply of planes and taking too many risks. In July a
highly experienced flyer, Joy Muntz, whom Amy had known at
Portsmouth, became the first female pilot to die in the war when her
plane crashed, killing her and her instructor; the accident was later
blamed on carbon monoxide poisoning.[29]

At the beginning of December Amy was allowed to fly one of the larger planes whose wheels were almost as tall as she. 'Heaps of people were watching its arrival as a four-engined machine is always rather a sensation,' she told her mother, 'and then they saw a woman pilot get out of it!'[30]

In late September Amy's ATA uniform was blown up.[31] Hitler had started to bomb central London at the end of August and the capital suffered the first mass daylight raid on 7 September. A bustling capital became sandbagged and edged with barbed wire, everyday life existing side by side with the reality of imminent invasion. Children played in parks scored with trenches and motorists peered at traffic lights whose changing colours peeped through slits. Amy had sent her uniform to a Savile Row tailor for alterations but the shop had received a direct hit: 'Eighteen guineas gone west, together with all the time and trouble spent on fitting and alterations,' she wrote to her mother.[32] At a time when London was being pounded by the Blitz, it was the personal inconveniences of the bombing that hit home. Amy was relieved to discover that her trousers had been saved and she wrote to her father that the only way to cope with the bombing was to be 'fatalistic'.

She was more agitated by the fact that Jim had joined the ATA and was stationed at White Waltham airfield. Amy felt he always made a 'beeline' for her. 'Honestly, he bores me stiff!!!' she wrote to her father.[33] The press tried to rekindle the romance but Amy was – very discreetly – involved with a senior ATA member based in Scotland. Her friends believed that the relationship was one-sided: Amy treated the affair very seriously while the airman vacillated from appearing keen to cooling off.[34] One ATA pilot said later that she believed Amy missed 'being married to Jim Mollison, or any way being married to someone – because she frequently took up with somewhat caddish and elementary types of men who treated her rather cavalierly as that type sometimes does when they find a woman who is more enthusiastic'.

Amy was also exercised by the discrepancy between the pay of male and female pilots. She found it particularly galling that Jim earned £700 a year compared to her £450. Although she tried to work up an agitation about the injustice, there were more compelling aspects to the war. The coincidence of tide and moon meant that the middle of September was widely believed to be the date when Hitler, whose forces were poised on the other side of the Channel, would invade. When the nation felt it could breathe again, bombing, rather than invasion, became the main preoccupation.

Amy saw more of Betty, who was working as a typist for the ATA, and who suddenly married a Scotsman in the Green Howards in November. Blackpool seemed more dangerous than the east coast and Will and Ciss had decided to stay in Brid. Amy spent her spare time knitting for Molly's daughter, Susan, and was disappointed not to be with her family at Christmas. Instead she was stuck in Scotland for six days as the fog closed in and prevented her from leaving Prestwick.

Chapter 27

The Final Weekend
(4–5 January 1941)

'I've had the lousiest Christmas stuck up here,' Amy wrote to her parents from the Orangefield Hotel at Prestwick on Boxing Day.[1] She had not been expecting much from the holiday that year – war meant that the ferrying work went on with no concession to the festive season – but she was disappointed not to be able to spend time with her parents whom she had not seen since July. Eventually Amy's patience snapped and she decided to take the long and uncomfortable night train south rather than wait for weather conditions to allow her to fly back to England. Trains were stuffy, overcrowded vehicles in wartime Britain; passengers could expect long delays and Amy would probably have been forced to sit on her parachute in the blacked-out corridor while servicemen pushed passed her, nudging each other as they recognised the famous pilot. Trains, over which she had no control and which were painfully slow, were Amy's least favourite form of transport.

Back at Hatfield, on Sunday, 29 December, Amy wrote what was to be her last letter to 'Dearest Mother and Daddy'. She thanked them for the £5 they had sent her for Christmas and finished the brief note, 'Dearest love, Amy xxx'.

On Friday, 3 January Pauline told Amy to deliver a plane from Hatfield to Prestwick where she would pick up another machine to fly it to RAF Kidlington, just north of Oxford. Although a return to Scotland in mid winter held the risk of another long exile if the weather turned against her, Amy was keen to make the flight.[2] But conditions quickly deteriorated and she decided to land her Airspeed Oxford at Ternhill near Birmingham and spend the night at the Hawkstone Park Hotel in Weston-under-Redcastle near Shrewsbury. It was a rather grand hotel with an eighteen-hole golf course that also offered its guests the chance of fishing.

At Prestwick the next day Amy bumped into Jennie Broad, the engineer who had serviced her planes during her army co-operation night-flying exercises and who had joined the ATA at the end of July. Jennie was an experienced pilot who had taken her first lessons at a flying circus in 1936 and then worked as a sales pilot.[3] She was relieved to see Amy, as it meant she could hitch a lift south, rather than endure the train journey. In the canteen they drank what passed for coffee and then, just as they were opening the door from the Operations Room to walk towards the Oxford, Jennie was called back to take a call from Pauline who told her to return to Hatfield urgently. Jennie was needed to pick up a 'Priority One' plane and Pauline was worried that bad weather would delay Amy's flight south. Instead, Jennie headed for the train station and Amy set off alone. She planned to break the journey by staying overnight with Molly and Trevor at Blackpool.

Her passage from the west coast of Scotland down through the desolate lowlands to the Lake District was a difficult one; mist reduced visibility and Amy had a nagging suspicion that her compass was slightly 'out'.[4] She was relieved to reach Squire's Gate aerodrome; the fact that she would be spending the night with her sister, rather than in a hotel, added to the pleasure of her arrival. Trevor and Molly were out when she arrived in the afternoon and Amy let herself into the solid, respectable house in Newton Drive.

The two sisters had a lot of catching up to do. They exchanged Christmas presents; Molly gave Amy a set of satin underclothes and a large oval mirror decorated with an edge of flowers that Amy packed in her overnight bag still in its wrapping paper. Amy told them about her difficult journey from Prestwick and her concern that the compass was faulty. Trevor offered to phone Squire's Gate to tell the ground staff to check it but Amy brushed aside his concern. She did not want to be held up and was confident she could 'smell her way' to Kidlington.[5]

Amy left her sister at 10 a.m. on Sunday morning; Molly said later that she had never seen Amy looking 'so well and happy'.[6] At Squire's Gate her arrival caused the usual ripple of excitement; before she climbed into the big, cumbersome Airspeed Oxford she discussed the weather with a handful of RAF pilots in an earnest downloading of information rather than a banal exchange of pleasantries. She started the engines and waited for the machine to warm up; there was no sign of the mist dispersing and Harry Banks, a refueller, climbed into the plane to sit and chat with her. Amy was wearing a parachute over her ATA uniform; a brown pigskin overnight bag and handbag were the only noticeable pieces of luggage in the plane. As they sat engrossed in their cigarettes and conversation, a rigger approached to tell Amy that the Duty Pilot advised her not to leave in such bad weather. She appeared unmoved by this warning, telling the two men that once off the ground she would 'go over the top' (meaning she would fly above the cloud level). Visibility was extremely poor when Banks slid out of the Airspeed Oxford. As the door closed behind him he was confident that Amy was alone in the plane. The signal book at Squire's Gate recorded Amy's time of departure as 11.49 hours; her tanks were full.[7]

What happened to Amy, and what thoughts went through her head, during the next three hours and forty minutes will probably always remain a mystery. Some details, though, are indisputable. She was flying an Airspeed Oxford, serial number V3540, a brand-new machine built by De Havilland and delivered to Kinloss in Morayshire for safe keeping just two months previously where it sat waiting to be picked up by the ATA. The Oxford was a stately twin-engined plane, painted in earthy dark green and brown on its top and sides as camouflage against the Luftwaffe but with a bright yellow belly to remind ground defences of its friendly status and to make it easily identifiable to trainee pilots in other planes; RAF roundels adorned its upper wings and the side of the fuselage. The Oxford was used primarily for training; it carried no armaments and its life should have been the most peaceful of any wartime plane. It had no IFF device to allow ground defences to identify the plane as 'Friend' rather than 'Foe'; it was also without a radio set – this was fitted when it arrived at the training unit. Amy had flown Oxfords several times and probably would not even have needed to glance at the booklet of Ferry Pilots' Notes that detailed the main features of the wide range of planes that the ATA pilots transported.

Even on a clear day, the route from Squire's Gate through Britain's industrial heartland was a tricky one that required constant vigilance; obstacles popped up in front of the pilot like hurdles in a modern-day computer game. For ATA pilots the main danger was not attack by the Luftwaffe but the bulbous barrage balloons designed to push enemy aircraft high above areas that were densely populated or which harboured vital factories. Flying into one of the floating monsters, or becoming ensnared in a wire that tethered it to the ground, would almost certainly prove fatal.

Approaching the Mersey, Amy was careful to stick to a four-mile-wide corridor of safety dividing the balloons protecting Liverpool to the west and Widnes to the east. From here she skirted round the industrial sprawl of Birmingham and the outlying radio masts. Once free of the barrage balloons, the pilot approaching RAF Kidlington still needed to be wary of the pylons and masts and the deceptively high ground that makes the final descent as problematic as the journey's start. Cruising at a speed of between 130 and 140 miles per hour, as recommended by the Pilots' Notes, Amy should have reached Kidlington just over an hour after leaving Squire's Gate.

At Hatfield something of the festive spirit lingered on as the airfield prepared for a 'birthday' party to mark the first anniversary of the women's section of the ATA. The ferry work continued and Philippa Bennett took off in an Oxford similar to the one Amy was flying.[8] She was heading for Scotland, keeping below the cloud and, as ATA rules stipulated, in full view of the ground to allow defences to identify her as friendly. At 800 feet she noticed ice crystals forming on her windscreen. The Oxford had carburettor heaters but there was nothing to prevent ice clinging to its wings; continuing in such weather seemed reckless and after ten minutes she turned for home.

Over the Midlands and the South-East of England it was a bitterly cold day. The earth was packed into an icy hardness, snow flurried across parts of the country and barrage balloons over London had to be pulled down and wiped clean. A thin layer of cloud hung over the ground and above this the winter's sun blazed out a belt of warm air. Amy was trapped in this brilliant, heavenly world searching for a gap in the clouds, a trapdoor that would lead her safely through the billowing denseness to the ground below. If she took her chances and plunged down through the cloud she risked hitting one of the many obstacles that made flying in wartime Britain so difficult. As she became increasingly lost she could not be sure that a descent would not take her careering into the side of a hill; Amy was alone in the Oxford with only her compass to guide her and even this may have been faulty.

While the dank winter's afternoon dragged on Convoy CE21 sailed warily along the Thames Estuary towards London. The convoy edged forward in a cluster with seventeen merchant vessels at its centre protected by an outer shell of two destroyers, HMS *Fernie* and HMS *Berkeley*, and a French submarine chaser. Britain was desperately short of warships and the rest of the convoy consisted of vessels that had been converted to offer some resistance in attack: two trawlers, five ships carrying barrage balloons, four minesweepers and four motor launches. Each of the escort carried anti-aircraft guns and the minesweepers flew smaller balloons closer to the water's surface.

Lieutenant-Commander Walter Fletcher, wearing a scarf round his neck and a duffel coat, his hair cut with naval precision close to the scalp above his ears but growing thick on top, captained one of the barrage balloon vessels, a cross-Channel steamer called HMS *Hasle-*

mere. Among the group of people who converged at that desolate spot in the Thames Estuary, Fletcher alone could claim to have experienced anything like Amy's adventurous life and to have a natural penchant for unthinking heroism. In 1934 he was seconded as navigator from the Royal Navy to follow in Amundsen's footsteps in an expedition across the North-West Passage of Baffin Land in Canada, and in September 1940 he stood resolutely at his station while heavy fire killed a sub-lieutenant and injured a first lieutenant next to him on the ship's bridge off Cap Gris-Nez in northern France. Fletcher was thirty-four in 1941, the son of a vicar whose widowed mother lived on a farm in Princes Risborough – incredibly, the same quiet Buckinghamshire village where Amy moved to after her divorce. At one time Amy and Fletcher lived within a mile of each other; they may even have met before their lives and deaths became inextricably entangled that Sunday afternoon.[9]

The atmosphere on board the ships was one of tense boredom. The war had started much earlier for the Navy, which faced the vital task of ensuring that Britain's island status, which offered so much protection, did not also ensure that she was starved to death. Seamen lived under constant threat from attack, unlike the RAF whose life-or-death dog-fights could be played out in minutes. The one out-of-the-ordinary aspect of that Sunday afternoon was that the convoy carried a passen-ger: an American journalist called Drew Middleton who was observing Britain under war so that he could report back to a country that still basked in peace.

At its widest the Thames Estuary feels like the open sea but to a wartime convoy it offered much greater protection than the vast expanses of the Atlantic, or the North Sea. While there was still the danger of attack by a fast German 'E-boat', or a collision with a mine, the Kent shore seemed to the crew on deck comfortably close com-pared to the prospect of floating helplessly in the middle of an ocean, waiting to be picked up by a passing ship. For engineers, though, the distance from land was immaterial; if their ship went down they would drown before they could stagger to the foot of the engine-room steps.

Further west along the Thames at Iwade, just north of Sitting-bourne, and sheltered from the estuary by the Isle of Sheppey, Tom Mitchell, a gunner with the 58th (Kent) Heavy Anti-Aircraft Regiment, settled in for an afternoon of waiting in the cold and damp.

At around 3.30 p.m. Amy was two hours overdue at RAF Kidlington; her tanks were running dry and the winter's daylight was ebbing away. By now her eyes were burning with the strain of peering at the mes-merising whiteness as she wondered what lay beneath. The conditions

were similar to the long hours of flying the Atlantic without knowing
exactly what lurked beneath the blanket of cloud, except that she had
not been alone then. With Jim as co-pilot they had been able to divide
the tasks; one scanning the whiteness, the other flying the plane. If
either lost their nerve and started to mistrust the compass, the other
was there to offer reassurance and sound argument.

It seems most likely that in her growing panic Amy headed east
searching for a break in the clouds near the coast. This is exactly what
she did when she was engulfed in thick cloud after leaving Rangoon in
1930; then it took her three hours to cross a mountain range in a
journey that should have lasted thirty minutes, and when she emerged
on the other side she was miles off course and headed south in search
of the sea. On her flight to Cape Town in 1932 the white surf of the
West African coast gave her confirmation of her position.

But in the fading daylight of a winter's afternoon no clue leapt out
of the blankness; without windscreen wipers the snow flurried gently
in front of her before being swept aside by the force of the plane as if
the Oxford was parting its hair in an effort to see better. Every time she
dipped into the cloud the snow turned to ice, freezing in front of her
and leaving her to worry about its effect on the Oxford's wings. As the
temperature dropped, conditions became more like Amy's disastrous
crossing of Poland when she was forced down in a desolate forest.

The Thames Estuary that Amy found herself flying over in desperation and with her fuel almost spent was unrecognisable from the
stretch of water that she and Jim had soared over in their sleek new
Comet on their way to Baghdad in October 1934. The chances are that
Amy was not even aware that she was over the broad stretch of water
that acted as a convenient guide for German bombers flying from
Holland to Britain's capital. Silver-grey barrage balloons that bobbed
up out of the gloom would have confirmed her suspicion that she was
over ground, rather than stranded above a busy shipping lane. At the
start of the war a line of small fishing boats was positioned from Shoe-
buryness on the north shore of the estuary in an attempt to throw the
German bombers off course; the boats lowered or raised their balloons
depending on the cloud cover and the threat of attack. Aviation historian Roy Nesbit has shown that on 17 December a mine blew up one of
the drifters and the other boats were abandoned with their balloons
still raised; five of them poked through the cloud near to Amy's position over the Thames.[10]

The closest Amy had ever came to baling out was in November 1930
when she was lost over another estuary – this time the Humber. On

that occasion she got as far as taking her shoes off; the terror of that moment never left her. In the summer of 1938 a reporter asked her whether there was anything she feared. She replied: 'The one and only thing I am simply terrified of is a parachute descent. Even if the wing falls off an aeroplane it still feels like solid earth to me, but altho' I have to wear a parachute when gliding, I know inside me that I could never, never pull the cord and trust myself to the air.'[11]

We can only guess what must have been going through her mind as she 'trimmed' the plane so that it circled gently while she clambered to the rear of the Oxford. Perhaps she felt a twinge of embarrassment that she was about to wreck a valuable plane, or maybe all-consuming terror left no room for other thoughts. It seems most likely that she was too concerned with the practicalities of baling out to feel afraid. Instructions on how to jettison the door were stencilled on its interior and as she pushed at it a great blast of freezing air hit her before she jumped into the icy blankness. Survivors of parachute jumps have reported varying emotions – from calmness to exhilaration; fear is rarely one of them. Amy may have wondered whether the parachute packer had done her job properly and whether the package would burst into flower or plummet like a tightly furled umbrella. The shock of what Amy saw as she floated down must have been far greater than the actual fear of her first parachute jump, especially if she caught sight of the strange straggle of ships, some adorned with barrage balloons. But most surprising of all was the steely swell of the sea that she plunged into and the instant iciness whose intensity made it difficult to distinguish between the sensation of being wet or bitterly cold.

Convoy CE21 was approaching Knock John Buoy on Tizard Bank, an area dotted with sandbanks some eleven miles north of Herne Bay. Welshman Lieutenant Henry O'Dea stood on the bridge of HMS *Haslemere* with Fletcher at 3.30 p.m. when, through the flakes of snow, he saw a plane emerging from the clouds to the starboard of his bow and, about a mile and a half away and 500 feet up in the sky, a parachute. The plane seemed under control and made three complete circles of the parachutist. O'Dea alerted Fletcher who immediately took control; the *Haslemere*, a motor launch and an escort vessel pushed full steam ahead to try to reach the body as it hit the water. News spread quickly through the ship that a plane had crashed; resting crew members leapt out of their bunks while others waited for orders. As they approached, the plane hit a wave, settled momentarily on the surface and sank nose first.[12] Fletcher barked orders to try to manoeuvre the ship away from the wreckage but towards what O'Dea believed were two bodies in the water, but the ship ran aground, robbing them of precious seconds.

Raymond Dean, a seaman from Worthing, was on gunnery watch with O'Dea. He, too, noticed two bodies drifting past the ship and ran with Fletcher to the stern. The first wore a helmet and, having a high voice and fresh complexion, appeared to be a boy, who raised one arm in a calm act of supplication. When the voice called out, 'Hurry, please, hurry!' (the same phrase that Amy called to rescuers after she and Jim crashed *Seafarer* at Bridgeport), an expression of amazement, 'It's a woman!' ricocheted round the ship.[13] The crew tried to reach her by throwing lines but each time the current swept them beyond her reach. Dean climbed over the bulwarks and lay on the ship's outer, rubber board in a desperate attempt to catch her. But, exhausted from the effort and by the numbing cold, the woman slipped away from his pleading fingers, the stern rising up before crashing down on top of her.[14]

Drowning is said to be a peaceful way to die, like drifting off to sleep, but if, as seems likely, Amy was mangled by the boat's propeller blades, we can only hope that she was quickly knocked unconscious or that the cold had already robbed her of any awareness of what was happening. Of all the times she had imagined her death, these horrible final moments must surely never have been among them.

Fletcher yelled at Dean to get back on board and then, when he started to strip off, ordered him to stop. Instead, Fletcher began to tear off his own boots and duffel coat before climbing onto the ship's side and jumping into the icy water, heading for the second body which one crewman believed was a German airman because of what he thought was a leather flying helmet. One sailor described the sea as 'confused with a heavy swell' and the crew watched as their captain reached the figure, appeared to support it for two or three minutes before the freezing water took its toll.[15] He released the 'body' and fought his way through the sea towards a lifeboat, shouting in desperation, 'For God's sake, lad, tell them to pull,' as it lurched in and out of view.[16] Eventually a motor launch reached him; one man leant over the side towards Fletcher but the waves were too strong, and the crew used a boat-hook and a second person in the water to drag him on board. By the time he was hauled onto the deck Fletcher had been in the freezing water for about twenty minutes and had drifted into an unconsciousness from which he never emerged. Neither Amy's nor a second body were ever recovered.

Fletcher died at the Royal Naval Hospital at Gillingham from exposure and shock and is buried in Woodlands Cemetery, Gillingham, on a hill that looks out over the Thames Estuary that claimed his life. His battleship-grey gravestone stands in line with countless other naval casualties of two world wars, and, like countless others, gives no clue as to the bravery that led to his death.[17] Ironically, if his rescuers had been slower to pluck him out of the water, Fletcher might well have survived, as it is now believed that the best way to limit the effects of hypothermia is to lift the victim out of the water in a horizontal position.

Just as the crew of the *Haslemere* were recovering from the drama of losing their captain and the unknown pilot who disappeared beneath their ship, the Luftwaffe attacked. The Junkers JU88 plane swooped down on a vessel taking up the rear of the convoy and HMS *Berkeley* replied with anti-aircraft fire; when the attack was over the convoy emerged unscathed and with no casualties. Once calm had returned the *Berkeley* searched the area for survivors. They recovered two pieces of luggage: a pigskin bag with the initials 'AJ' in black on one side and a second bag with 'Amy Johnson' printed on it. Amy's logbook was also recovered and is preserved at the RAF Museum in North London where its catalogue entry is followed by the poignant note, 'Some water damage'.

Later that day a drifter, HMS *Young Jacob*, scooped up two bits of plywood out of the Thames Estuary; the longest piece was ten feet by four feet. Both were covered with bright yellow fabric and one piece bore the numbers '35'. In one of the many strange coincidences that cling to Amy's death, the skipper, Thomas Williamson, was from Hessle, near Hull, and claimed to have known 'Miss Johnson' 'very well indeed'.[18] Pauline later identified the piece of fabric as part of Amy's Airspeed Oxford that carried the serial number V3540.

At about 6 p.m. that afternoon Tom Mitchell and the 58th (Kent) Heavy Anti-Aircraft Regiment sprang into life, blasting wave upon wave of heavy artillery shells at the bombers who flew under cover of darkness through the night to London.

Pauline received a message from ATA headquarters at White Waltham in Berkshire to say that a plane had crashed in the Thames Estuary and that Amy's papers had been recovered. All aerodromes were contacted to see whether Amy had landed; the answer was negative. With no time to mourn the loss of a close friend, Pauline switched into official mode; she sent a 'priority' telegram to Amy's parents at Brynmawr on Monday afternoon with the words that every household dreaded: 'Missing believed killed'. She also spoke to them on the phone and wrote them a letter in which she added: 'We at the ferry pool have not only lost a brilliant pilot but many of us have lost in Amy a great friend.'[19]

There is no record of how Will and Ciss responded to the news, although they had enough presence of mind to send a wreath to Fletcher's mother. Over the past decade they had endured periods of intense worry about their daughter, the longest of which had lasted for nearly three weeks when she flew alone to Australia. At these times they had been braced for a telephone call that would bring devastating news; their anxiety was very public, captured on cine film and reported in newspaper columns. When the blow finally fell there was no time to prepare for it. As far as they were concerned Amy's job of flying round Britain under the aegis of a well-ordered and well-disciplined organisation represented the safest aviation work she had ever attempted.

When Tom Mitchell read that Amy Johnson had died over the Thames Estuary on Sunday afternoon, he assumed the worst: that he had been responsible for shooting down one of the country's best-loved heroines. Urged on by officers, he kept this secret for sixty years, until the death of his sister prompted him to unburden himself.

Will and Ciss barely had time to take in the fact of Amy's death before they were bombarded with a sensationalist account of her last minutes.[20] In the sort of blunder that occurred in wartime when resources were stretched so tightly that they frequently snapped, the Admiralty issued a statement on Tuesday evening that mentioned two bodies. The second figure quickly became 'Mr X', and even a formal correction by the Ministry of Aircraft Production was incapable of expunging the mystery man. By the end of the week the Daily Express was speculating about where Amy had picked up her passenger, and Bill Courtenay felt compelled to defend her reputation by writing a piece for the *Daily Sketch*. As the rumour-mill spun out of control, a friend of Will's wrote to tell him that it was now 'common talk in the RAF' that Amy had been on some sort of clandestine mission and was heading for the Continent when she was forced to bale out.

A week later her cheque-book, wrapped in a waterproof cover, turned up on the Isle of Grain, a promontory that juts out into the estuary further west from where Amy's plane crashed. But her salvaged handbag mysteriously disappeared in what was probably another administrative error, but which added to Will's growing feeling that the truth about his daughter's death should be settled once and for all.

Will instructed Crockers to obtain a death certificate, but in the spring of 1941 proving a death without the benefit of a body was a difficult task: the courts were congested with matrimonial and 'missing presumed dead' cases similar to Amy's. The other major problem was that the eyewitnesses from the convoy were serving men who were difficult to pin down for long enough to give evidence. It was not until December 1943 that the case came to court, almost three years after Amy's death and long enough for memories to fade or become distorted by rumours, idle chat or sensationalist newspaper accounts.

Until then Amy's family had to deal with the many rumours that grew in intensity following her death and which they could not resist listening to.[21] A man whom Will met in Bridlington told him that RAF pilots had described to him how Amy had made several trips to the Continent – many of them secret. Someone else passed on a rumour that Amy was very friendly with a German who had lived in Britain for several years and whom Amy had been helping to return home. Will dismissed this theory but still felt it worthy of a well-thought-out rebuttal – that if Amy had been heading for Germany she would have gone there straight from Squire's Gate and would have crossed the North Sea rather than risk the busy Thames Estuary. The deeper Will delved into Amy's death, the more questions he found: if the Oxford had sunk, why were parts discovered floating in the water and why had Amy's handbag mysteriously disappeared? He wanted a Government inquiry and suspected Pauline may have known more than she was prepared to tell Amy's family. Fletcher's inquest in May 1941 merely added to the mystery.

Will was also troubled by a mysterious telegram and letter sent to him in the months before Amy's death and which he referred to as 'the Wolverhampton affair' or the 'Wolverhampton matter'. The messages were sent from the Midlands by a man who said he had ordered Scotland Yard to arrest 'your daughter'. Unwisely, Will took the matter seriously enough to write and ask him which daughter he was referring to. The man's response was that 'Jim Mollison knew all about it'. Amy laughed the matter off and Vernon Wood tried to reassure Will that the man was mentally ill, but Amy's death and the string of rumours and counter-rumours re-ignited Will's gnawing concern about the episode. To add insult to injury, the hotel where Amy spent the night on her way to Prestwick demanded payment of £1.0.6.

The statements and signed affidavits collected by Crockers for the probate case fulfilled their purpose in proving Amy's death, but instead of extinguishing the controversy about how she died, they merely stoked up discussion that continues to simmer. At least seven witnesses reported seeing her at Squire's Gate; two confirmed that she had full tanks and all but one witness (who was too far off to see) stated that Amy left between 11.00 and 11.49 a.m. The official Signal Log Book recorded the later time. Frank Sutherland, who conducted a Daily Inspection of Amy's Oxford, told her that the Duty Pilot had advised her not to take off and she replied that she would 'go over the top'. He was 'quite certain beyond any shadow of a doubt that Miss Johnson was the only person in the plane when it took off'. Her demeanour, he said, was 'perfectly normal'. This part of Amy's last journey is incontrovertible: she took off from Squire's Gate alone, just before noon and with full tanks. The weather was poor but she was determined to get through.

The end of her journey is open to greater interpretation. Not surprisingly, the crews of the convoy who raced to Amy's defence tell a much more confused and conflicting story. The weather was appalling – biting sleet, a freezing wind and a choppy sea; on top of this, immediately after the abortive rescue the men found themselves under attack from a stray Junkers. And most telling of all, they had to wait nearly three years to give their accounts. Six of the men questioned – five from the *Haslemere* – were adamant that they saw a second body in the water. However, it remains a far from clear picture: one of the sailors in the boat sent to rescue Fletcher said there was no body in the water, others were not aware of the parachutist, and there are discrepancies about how many times the Oxford circled and the manner in which it entered the sea.

Over the years 'Mr X' has taken several forms. Pauline believed that the door that Amy jettisoned when baling out, and which was hollow and would therefore have floated, may have seemed like a body as it bobbed up and down in the water.[22] Sir William Crocker was among those who believed – to me, most convincingly – that 'Mr X' was the zip-up pigskin case that Amy would probably have hurled out of the plane before she jumped.[23] The case, which has a rectangular base, a zip along its length and two large handles, measures eight inches by seventeen and is twelve inches deep. It floated for long enough to be picked up by a ship and in the poor visibility and heaving sea could easily have been mistaken for the top part of a man. There is also the possibility that the second corpse in the water belonged to the victim of one of the aerial battles that took place with such frequency over Kent and the Thames Estuary.

There is absolutely no evidence that 'Mr X' was a German friend whom Amy was delivering back to the Fatherland, although it is easy to see how a grain of truth may have helped spin this rumour into a full-blown theory. Amy's six-year relationship with Hans Arregger was well known in Hull; the ill-matched affair between a foreigner and the daughter of a highly respected businessman made tantalising gossip. Amy had even alluded to the friendship in her published writings. Hans may have been Swiss rather than German, but most people would have overlooked this nicety: Hans was a fairytale name that could hardly be more German.

Similarly, the extension of the Hans theory – that Amy was on an undercover mission – can be traced back to a few particles of truth. While she was stationed in Cardiff at the start of the war, she made occasional flights to France; on one particular visit to Rheims she was spotted by RAF pilots at the Hotel Lion d'Or and toasted with vintage champagne.[24] The story of the day Amy Johnson walked into a French bar made a titillating anecdote at a point in the Phoney War when there was little else to talk about. As the conflict continued few pilots would have remembered when exactly the event took place and it is probable that the Chinese whispers among the armed services transformed the episode into a much more thrilling encounter.

Amy did in fact contact Lord Vansittart, who helped set up the Special Operations Executive, before she joined the ATA in that frustrating period while she was casting around for interesting work.[25] He turned her down and it is easy to see why. Undercover agents needed to speak flawless French and to be able to blend seamlessly into ordinary life; Amy's experience of French society was limited to luxury hotels, *haute couturiers* and the beaches of the South of France. Even after her many visits to Paris, Amy still stood out as quintessentially English and it was not just her awkward phraseology. She was as much a hero in France as she was in Britain and it would have taken a very convincing disguise to hide her true identity.

The Airspeed Oxford was also exactly the wrong type of plane to take on a secret mission as its bright-yellow belly instantly identified it as a British aircraft. The Lysander was used for clandestine operations and was flown at night – rather than in the middle of a Sunday afternoon. If, as has been suggested, Amy stopped to pick up a passenger (which was strictly against ATA rules, although this regulation was occasionally broken), she would have struggled to find an airfield that was big enough for the Oxford to land on and then take off from. Any other large open space would have been blocked with something like a piece of agricultural machinery to keep out enemy planes.

Pauline was adamant that Amy had not picked up a passenger; she believed, instead, that Amy hit ice and tried to put down but could not find a break in the cloud.[26] Whenever I have asked former ATA pilots what they would have done in Amy's position, they have always responded with the same incredulity: they simply would not have ventured out in such appalling conditions.

But, even so, Amy was an experienced navigator and had taken courses in 'blind flying' to refresh her existing knowledge. It has been suggested that she took a risk that day because, as a famous pilot, she had felt she could not 'let the side down'. However, Amy's logbook shows that she was not afraid to abandon a trip in the face of bad weather – as she did on her flight north to Prestwick.

However, while her logbook for 1940 shows a strict adherence to the rules, the year finished with the tedium of being stranded in Prestwick for nearly a week over the Christmas period. By the time she left Squires Gate she may have run out of patience with the weather and the thought of getting back to Hatfield for some belated Christmas celebration may just have tipped the balance. Air Vice Marshal Sandy Johnstone remembers seeing her sitting alone at a table at the Orangefield Hotel in Prestwick.[27] She was depressed and frustrated at the weather that held her hostage in Scotland while she had so many social engagements in England.

On the face of it, Amy was an experienced navigator who had flown over large stretches of the world. But of her six major long-distance flights, three of them were made with a co-pilot (Jim) or a navigator-cum-mechanic (Jack). Significantly, for the three solo expeditions she flew light aircraft that were much easier to manoeuvre than the cumbersome Oxford. *Jason* bumped his way over to Australia; both pilot and plane were deft enough narrowly to avoid the sides of the Taurus Mountains as they loomed up out of the mist, and over the next three weeks their forced landings included touching down on a bamboo-pocked clearing, a parade ground and a football pitch. On her two trips to Cape Town Amy rarely lost sight of the ground. Her crashes or forced landings took place in bad weather, particularly fog, when visibility was poor. She broke her nose and dislocated a shoulder when she crashed her Beechcraft in fog at Chelsfield when she was returning from Paris. Her Polish accident happened in weather that was far worse than the sleet she experienced over the Thames Estuary, but Amy was still prepared to venture out in heavy snow that had grounded most of Russia's air fleet. Coincidentally, as she herself pointed out, most of her crashes took place on a Sunday.

In February 1999 Tom Mitchell, an eighty-three-year-old retired gardener living in East Sussex, finally unburdened himself of the sense of guilt that had been gnawing away at him for sixty years.[28] He told a local newspaper reporter that on the afternoon of Sunday, 5 January 1941 he had shot down what he had believed to be an enemy plane. He explained how an officer radioed the aircraft to request the 'colours of the day' – signal flares which the pilot was required to fire in the correct sequence (changed daily) from a Very pistol to identify an aircraft as friend, not foe. But, so Tom said, Amy gave the wrong colours and repeated her mistake when challenged a second time. The battery fired sixteen shells into the sky but were unable to see whether they had hit their target. When they read of Amy's death officers warned Tom never to tell anyone what had happened and his understanding of the scope of the Official Secrets Acts persuaded him to stay silent. When his sister died Tom re-read the wartime letters he had written to her in which he poured out his anguish about the incident and decided to speak out while he still had the chance.

There is no reason to doubt that Tom Mitchell truly believes that he shot down Amy Johnson's plane. However, the known facts show that he is mistaken. The most glaring hole in his version of events is that Amy's Oxford did not have a radio and she therefore could not have responded to the battery's request, let alone given the wrong colours of the day.

But, even if Tom Mitchell had simply misremembered this part of the story, practicalities still weigh against his account. He was stationed beyond the Isle of Sheppey, twenty miles away from the point at which Amy's plane went down – a distance well outside the guns' range. Even if the battery had fired when Amy's plane was nearer, they would have been highly lucky – or unlucky, as it happened – to hit the target in such dense cloud.[29] At least three witnesses, O'Dea and Dean on the HMS *Haslemere* and Lieutenant Ian McLaughlan on HMS *Berkeley*, remembered that the plane was under control when it struck the water; if it had been hit, the descent would have been more erratic. No one reported any sound of gunfire and official records show that the battery attacked much later that afternoon.

The nature of Amy's death – a celebrity who disappeared in wartime Britain – lends itself easily to conspiracy theories.[30] But the only possible suggestion of a 'cover-up' that I can detect is in the question of what exactly happened to Amy's body after it disappeared underneath HMS *Haslemere*. It seems probable that she died in the most horrific of circumstances, a victim of the ship's propeller, but that the crew, not surprisingly, saw no reason to make public the gruesome details of her final moments. Revealing the true nature of her death would only have added to the Johnson family's acute distress and would have transformed an heroic rescue attempt, which claimed their captain's life, into a humiliating blunder.

Seamen are notoriously superstitious and keeping a corpse on board is something they go to great lengths to avoid. The bodies of wartime casualties were traditionally disposed of at sea and this may have been what happened to Amy. In 1972 a former ATA pilot wrote to Amy's official biographer, Constance Babington Smith, to tell her that it had been on her conscience that Amy had been 'cut to pieces by the screw', but Constance decided to save Amy's parents the pain of this extra piece of information. This added detail has also started to emerge from wartime survivors although, unfortunately, their testimony is always second-hand.[31]

The other possibility is that the convoy itself was responsible for shooting the plane down. In February 1988 a sixty-six-year-old crew member of the *Berkeley* told the *Sunday Express*, 'I really believe, deep down in my heart, that we blew her out of the sky.' He went on to recount, in a bizarre and apparently superfluous detail, how the sailors had hung Amy's monogrammed underwear up to dry in the engine room; Molly's Christmas present to Amy was, of course, a set of satin underclothes. But, even if the sailors had turned laundrymen, it still seems unlikely that a whole convoy of ships, plus an American journalist, could have so successfully covered up a fatal attack.

Amy's death quickly became part of the war effort. A film, *They Flew Alone*, starring Anna Neagle and Robert Newton, told the story of Amy's life, while concentrating on her turbulent relationship with Jim, who was portrayed as a lovable, if drunken, rogue.[32] Anna Neagle had met Amy when they got drenched together at the start of the speedboat season at the Welsh Harp in North London, and as research for her film role she slept in the room at Molly's house where Amy had spent her last night – although it is difficult to believe that she managed a good night's sleep.[33]

Will and Ciss treated this latest, celluloid depiction of Amy as a celebration of her life, even though she had yet to be officially declared dead. It seemed appropriate that Amy, who herself had been so mesmerised by cinema, should have her life transplanted onto the screen. Just over a year after Amy's final flight they watched actors recreate the catastrophic phone call that had changed their lives. Their response was typically stoical: Will gave Ciss a biography of Marie Curie to mark the film's première.[34]

Amy dominated Will and Ciss's remaining years. They filled one room in their home in Beverley with mementoes of her and her flights, lining the walls with her image so that the corners of some photos became stained with rust from the drawing-pins that held them in place. When, in 1961, the bones of a woman were washed up on the beach at Herne Bay it seemed probable that they belonged to Amy Johnson, but it took five months to prove that the remains were those of a stranger.

Vera Brittain was keen to write an account of Amy's life but Will and Ciss decided to allow Betty to produce a biography.[35] Although Betty wrote several letters, trying to add to the information about her sister's death, her biography petered out shortly after Amy's marriage to Jim and was never completed. Betty, whose husband was killed in the war, took her own life in 1973, fortunately after her parents had died. Of the four sisters whose privileged background appeared to offer so many opportunities, only Molly survived to live into a comfortable old age.

Epilogue

In my search to revisit Amy's last hours I contacted Jennie Broad, the woman who narrowly missed accompanying Amy in her Airspeed Oxford. After leaving the ATA Jennie worked for BOAC in Egypt before becoming a sales pilot in South Africa and then flying an air ambulance in Australia. As she says, her 'last excitement' came at the age of seventy-five when she made a tandem parachute jump. Speaking to Jennie was like being instantly transported back to the 1940s. She dismissed the claim that Amy was on a secret mission, saying that she showed no signs of nerves when Jennie waved her off from Prestwick. Amy would not have offered Jennie a lift and the plane would have been camouflaged and fitted with long-range tanks if it had been destined for a clandestine errand. Jennie remembers the snow making it difficult to drive even a car that Sunday and believes that Amy got lost and ran out of fuel; like Pauline, she thinks the Oxford's door was 'Mr X'. Having dragged her back to the most exciting period of her life and abandoned her there, I put the phone down guiltily. Later she wrote to me, with the spirit of all former ATA pilots: 'Whoever said being old was the Golden Age should have his head put in a bucket of water.'

If Amy had given Jennie a lift she would probably not have risked taking off in such appalling weather conditions, but although Amy's death was undoubtedly tragic, it is difficult to imagine her living on into a twin-set-and-pearls old age. She came from a breed of pilots who tended to die young, even when their cause of death was nothing to do with flying. Tom Campbell Black suffered a dreadful accident while on the ground; Pauline died shortly after giving birth to twins; Dorothy Spicer was killed in a flying accident in South America and Winifred Spooner was struck down by flu. Amelia, Antoine de Saint-Exupéry and Smithy each flew into the wild blue yonder. Charles Scott, unable to adapt to life as a past celebrity, went through three divorces before shooting himself in 1946 while serving with a United Nations agency in Germany. Jim died in 1959 aged fifty-four, his last years tortured by ill health.

Amy always anticipated – even welcomed – a premature death. In an article written in 1937, and with Amelia's disappearance uppermost in her mind, she wrote: 'If I fail to find my Mid-Pacific island let no one grieve for me or wish me any other fate. We all must finish our lives some time, and I infinitely prefer this end to the flu or senile decay. Rather grieve if I never have the chance to try.'[1]

In the summer of 2002 the RAF Sub-Aqua Association, backed by Roy Nesbit's painstaking research of tides and naval records, began a search for the remains of Amy's Airspeed Oxford – principally, its two Armstrong-Siddeley Cheetah-X engines. Even if they manage to find their treasure, it is unlikely to prove more about Amy's death, although it may finally provide a full-stop to her life.[2]

The team of divers are as excited as the RAF pilots who used to crowd round Amy to ask for her autograph during the war. They are a jolly, purposeful group who, like their wartime predecessors, bear nick-names such as Gordon 'two sweets' Bucknall and whose metaphors are linked to food and drink. The weather is 'boil in the bag' hot and condi-tions on the seabed are 'like diving in tea'. It is a matter of pride to them that the RAF should find Amy's grave and the presence of the camera crews and newspaper journalists adds to their desire to reclaim one of their own – although, of course, Amy was never in the RAF. The search is run with military precision, but the busy shipping channels and the tides mean that each carefully planned foray leads to barely an hour on the seabed. When winter comes, the water returns to the treacherous conditions of 5 January 1941 and diving is abandoned until late spring. During the enforced break another theory emerges, based on the action of a Dutch galleon that sank in 1766 and which appears to have been dragged a mile along the seabed. It now seems likely that the Oxford's engines may have wandered away from their original resting place and that the divers may have been searching the wrong spot.

That same summer I persuaded a local sub-aqua club to take me out to the spot where Amy's plane went down as a sort of pilgrimage, or the nearest I would come to visiting her grave. It took almost a year before the weather and tides allowed us to venture out one Saturday afternoon. Herne Bay, now a fashionable retreat for retired East Enders and London's chattering classes searching for an alternative seaside, was full of shoppers and day-trippers; on board the speed-boat we were camouflaged with high-factor sun-cream lotion as we sped out to the spot where Amy's Airspeed Oxford went down. We sat quietly, gently bobbing up and down on a sea stirred by a passing container ship. Around us yachts and jet-skiers frantically squeezed every drop of enjoyment from their weekend. I felt nothing. This sun-dappled play-ground was not the grey, churning water where Amy Johnson died; it is difficult to imagine ghosts at the seaside in blazing sunshine: they belong to old buildings and stormy weather. Amy's grave lay beneath this world amid the hermit crabs and the underwater refuse site scattered with debris dating back to Roman times, a cemetery littered with wrecks and rubbish dumped from countless ships. The afternoon's biggest thrill was riding the waves back to Herne Bay, guided to safety by a GPS (Global Positioning System).

A small figure circles the playground, arms outstretched. While the boys kick a football about in a desultory fashion she gains speed, swooping over her friends playing marbles. 'I'm Amy Johnson, I'm Amy Johnson,' she chants. The other children barely glance up from their own games. For this inter-war generation of girls, wanting to be Amy Johnson was as natural as longing to be a princess or a Hollywood film star. Today their granddaughters dream of a fame found through music or movies, but their more attainable fantasy – and one that for most people is grasped at least every summer – is packaged in the form of a foreign holiday.

Amy Johnson's greatest legacy was that she made the world seem smaller and that, for the first time, women could play a part in the mechanical feat that brought about that reduction. Today's schoolchildren gazing up at *Jason* in the Science Museum are awed that anyone could fly to Australia in such a rickety piece of fabric and wood. But they are unfazed by the fact that the trip should have been made by a woman; it does not occur to them to see the accident of sex as a barrier to a long-distance flight. And that, too, is part of Amy's legacy – she was the first, 'ordinary' woman to perform extraordinary feats. She inspired W. E. Johns to create 'Worrals', a female Biggles who was capable of flying all kinds of aircraft, and to allow girls to dream of careers other than marriage.

Amy Johnson made it possible for women to be engineers and astronauts and to escape from whatever background they came from; she was the first woman to be seen as an international symbol of adventure and heroism. But her legacy is not confined to her sex; in daring to make the world smaller she changed our view of it from a patchwork, imperialist map to a globe criss-crossed with a cat's cradle of airline routes. Our perception of a country is measured first by how long it takes to fly there; an event is only real once a reporter has been dropped into a 'hotspot' to speak to us via a satellite link beamed into our sitting-room. Some of our best-loved entrepreneurs are those who make it easier and cheaper for us to fly wherever we want; a nation's 'air space' is as venerated as its soil.

When the wind from an open cockpit first 'messed up' Amy Johnson's hair, circling over Hull represented the very limits of her freedom; a lifetime later only a world war could keep her at home.

Notes

RAFM = Royal Air Force Museum
HCL = Hull Central Library
CBS = Constance Babington Smith

1. The Land of Green Ginger

1. *The British Colonist*, 10 December 1861, February 1862. RAFM.
2. AJK still exists as a business today.
3. See also: *Hull Daily News*, 22 September 1898; pocket account book, probably related to the Klondike Expedition; map of Atlin gold-fields and various other diaries and artefacts. RAFM.
4. 'The Diary of C. Olsen & Co., of their travels etc. after leaving Hull, England for the Klondyke Goldfields, January 26, 1897'. This is written in the third person, making it impossible to be sure which of the four men wrote it, although it seems most likely that Will Johnson was the author. RAFM.
5. 21 July 1898, RAFM.
6. According to *History of Seed Crushing in Great Britain*, by Harold W. Brace, p. 123, the brothers William and Henry Hodge ran a business between 1846 and 1851. William was previously an assistant to G. M. Bell. When the brothers went their separate ways in 1858, William ran Hodge Street Mill.
7. *Lost Houses of East Yorkshire*, by David Neave and Edward Waterson, p. 32, Georgian Society for East Yorkshire, 1988. Newington Hall was demolished in 1908.
8. Obituary, *The Hull Times*, Saturday, 16 November 1867.
9. Amy Johnson writing in *Myself When Young*, p. 131, edited by the Countess of Oxford and Asquith.
10. See *Superstitions: Folk Magic in Hull's Fishing Community* by Alec Gill. I am indebted to David Smith for drawing my attention to this explanation.
11. *Myself When Young*, p. 133.
12. Ibid., p. 134.
13. Ibid., p. 141.
14. Hull High School, where, four years earlier, a young Dorothy L. Sayers had taught French.
15. *Myself When Young*, p. 140.
16. *Dorothy L. Sayers, Her Life and Soul* by Barbara Reynolds, p. 91.
17. *The Letters of Dorothy L. Sayers (1899–1936)*, edited by Barbara Reynolds, p. 120.
18. CBS interview notes with Hans Arregger.
19. *Myself when Young*, p. 141.

2. Joy-riding (1919–25)

1. *Myself When Young*, p. 141. CBS believes that Amy did not take to the air until 1926 (see *Amy Johnson*, p. 68), when she and Molly went up with the Surrey Flying Services who were offering joy-rides at the Endike Lane flying ground near Beverley Road. Amy mentions going up in an aeroplane with Molly in a letter to Hans Arregger, dated Tuesday, 9 November 1926, in which she says they both enjoyed it but that Amy would have liked to have 'done some stunts' (HCL). Writing in 1938 (*Myself When Young*, p. 141), she gives the impression that the date of her first flight was shortly after the war and says that her fellow passenger was Irene, not Molly.
2. *Lindbergh* by A. Scott Berg, p. 82.
3. Alcock and Brown's feat, in June 1919, earned them a *Daily Mail* prize of £10,000. The prize had been unclaimed since it was first offered in 1913. The brothers Ross and Keith Smith received £10,000 from the Australian Government when they made the first flight from Britain to Australia; it took them nearly twenty-eight days.
4. Amy to Will, 25 June 1922, RAFM.
5. Amy to Hans, 3 October 1922, HCL.
6. Amy to Hans, 3 October 1922, HCL.
7. Amy to Hans, 9 October 1922, HCL.
8. Amy to Hans, 18 October 1922, HCL.
9. Amy to Hans, 9 October 1922, HCL.
10. Amy to Hans, 9 October 1922, HCL.
11. Amy to Hans, 9 October 1922, HCL.
12. Amy to Hans, 18 October 1922, HCL.
13. Amy to Hans, 17 January 1922, HCL.
14. Amy to Hans, early 1926, date uncertain,

HCL.

15. Quoted in *Marie Stopes and the Sexual Revolution* by June Rose, p. 117.
16. Amy to Ciss, summer 1923?, RAFM.
17. CBS interview notes, RAFM.
18. Amy to Hans, 8 February 1925, HCL.
19. Amy to Hans, 16 November 1922, HCL.
20. Amy to Hans, 16 November 1922, HCL.
21. Amy to Hans, 17 January 1923, HCL.
22. Amy to Hans, undated, HCL.
23. Amy to Hans, 5 March 1925, HCL.
24. Amy to Hans, 26 April 1925, HCL.
25. Amy to Hans, May 1925, HCL.
26. Amy to Hans, 10 May 1925, HCL.
27. Amy to Hans, 29 May 1925, HCL.
28. Amy to Hans, 13 May 1925, HCL.
29. Amy to Hans, 19 June 1925, HCL.

3. Sibling Rivalry (1925–6)

1. According to Government statistics the average age at which women got married for the first time was 25.59 in 1925 and 25.48 in 1932.
2. Amy to Hans, 10 November 1925, HCL.
3. Winifred had also decided against teaching; she wanted a job that offered more opportunities for promotion and travel. Amy applied for a position in Baden and considered working in America, giving her father a photo of her to take with him when he went there on business.
4. Letter to Will Johnson, 27 May 1924, RAFM.
5. Amy to Ciss, 8 October 1925, RAFM.
6. Amy to Hans, 18 October 1925, HCL.
7. Amy to Hans, 12 October 1925, HCL.
8. Amy to Hans, 10 November 1925, HCL.
9. Amy to Hans, 11 November 1925, HCL.
10. Amy to Hans, 25 October 1925, HCL.
11. Amy to Ciss, month uncertain, 1925, RAFM.
12. Amy to Hans, 10 November 1925, HCL.
13. Amy to Hans, 6 November 1925, HCL.
14. Amy to Hans, spring 1926, HCL.
15. Amy to Hans, November 1925, HCL.
16. Amy to Hans, 20 November 1926, HCL.
17. Irene to Will, 30 November 1926, RAFM.
18. Amy to Hans, 9 November 1926, HCL.

4. London (1927)

1. 'Thrilling incidents which shaped her destiny', a typescript for an article to appear in D. C. Thompson publications, December 1936 and April 1937, RAFM.
2. *A History of London* by Stephen Inwood, p. 724.

3. Quoted in *The Gazette*, 9 April 1977.
4. Amy to Hans, March 1927, HCL.
5. Amy to Hans, March 1927, HCL.
6. Amy to Hans, 23 March 1927, HCL.
7. Amy to Hans, 23 March 1927, HCL.
8. Amy to Hans, 30 March 1927, HCL.
9. *Britain in the 1920s* by Noreen Branson, p. 211.
10. Amy to Hans, 12 May 1927, HCL.
11. Will Johnson's diary and Amy's letters differ over her exact address: either 5e or 5c.
12. Amy to Hans, 25 April 1927, HCL.
13. Amy to Hans, 25 April 1927, HCL.
14. Amy to Hans, 29 April 1927, HCL.
15. Amy to Hans, 1 May 1927, HCL.
16. Amy to Hans, 17 April 1927, HCL.
17. Amy to Hans, 30 May 1927, HCL.
18. Amy to Hans, 10 June 1927, HCL.
19. Amy to Hans, 20 May 1927, HCL.
20. Amy to Hans, 20 May 1927, HCL.

5. A Room of One's Own (1927–8)

1. Amy to Hans, 13 August 1927, HCL.
2. 7 June 1927, HCL.
3. Amy to Hans, 3 November 1927, HCL.
4. Amy to Hans, 3 November 1927, HCL.
5. Amy to Hans, 3 January 1928, HCL.
6. Amy to Hans, 3 January 1928, HCL.
7. Amy to Hans, 16 January 1928, HCL.
8. A stone was laid on the site of the building works on 17 November 1928 by Lord Ampthill, Pro Grand Master of the United Grand Lodge of England. The building is now the School of Law at the University of Westminster.
9. *Myself When Young*, p. 153.
10. Amy to Hans, 9 January 1928, HCL.
11. Amy to Hans, 9 January 1928, HCL.
12. Amy to Hans, 23 January 1928, HCL.
13. Amy to Hans, date unclear, HCL and RAFM.
14. Amy to Hans, 22 April 1928, HCL.
15. Amy to Hans, 9 May 1928, HCL.
16. Amy to Hans, 9 May 1928, HCL.
17. Amy to Hans, 5 June 1928, HCL.
18. Amy to Ciss, 31 July 1928, RAFM.
19. Amy to Hans, undated, HCL.
20. *Myself When Young*, p. 154.

6. The Lipstick is Mightier than the Joystick (1928–9)

1. *Women with Wings* by Mary Cadogan, p. 95.
2. Quoted in *Amelia Earhart: A Biography*, by Doris L. Rich, p. 65.

3. Amy to Hans, 29 April 1928, HCL.
4. *The Tatler*, 31 October 1928.
5. Quoted in *Women with Wings* by Mary Cadogan, p. 168.
6. 13 March 1929.
7. *Myself When Young*, p. 150.
8. Amy to her father, 13 October 1928, RAFM.
9. *The Tatler*, no. 1399, 18 April 1928.
10. Lady Heath acquired her title when she married for the second time after the death of her first husband. She was a champion high-jumper and the founder of the Women's Amateur Athletic Association of Great Britain.
11. In 1927 Bailey set a women's altitude record for light aircraft when she took a Gipsy Moth up to 17,289 feet. Although she was of a class that did not have to worry about childcare, Bailey's flying exploits seemed all the more remarkable because she was the mother of five children.
12. Father's diary, Boxing Day 1928, RAFM.
13. Amy to Ciss, 11 March 1929, RAFM.
14. Part of a lecture given by Travers at the Royal Aeronautical Society on 3 November 1932, quoted in *Cross Country*, edited by E. Travers, p. 434.
15. *Cross Country*, p. 391.

7. Behind the Hangar Door (1929)
1. *Daily Express*, 20 May 1930.
2. He later built an observatory in his own garden from which, in 1933, he discovered a white spot on Saturn. He was made a Fellow of the Royal Astronomical Society for his timing of comets and, during the Second World War, he gave astronomy and navigation lessons to Royal Air Force cadets. See *Laughter in the Roar* by Brian O'Gorman, p. 6.
3. *Good Morning Boys: Will Hay, Master of Comedy* by Ray Seaton and Roy Martin, p. 70.
4. CBS interview with Will Hay, RAFM.
5. CBS interview notes with Winifred Irving, RAFM. It is not clear whether Jack was worried about Will Hay or someone else.
6. I am indebted to Martin Taylor, City Archivist at Hull City Archives, for details of Lake Drive.
7. Will to Irene, 5 May 1929, RAFM.
8. Irene to Will, 6 May 1929, RAFM.
9. On 19 June Irene wrote to her father – RAFM.

10. Will's diaries are held at RAFM.
11. Amy to her parents, 7 June 1929, RAFM.
12. Amy to her parents, 7 June 1929, RAFM.
13. *Going Solo* by Roald Dahl, pp. 83–4.
14. *DH: A History of De Havilland* by C. Martin Sharp, p. 112.
15. Will to Amy, 1 July 1929, RAFM.
16. Will to Amy, 11 July 1929, RAFM.
17. *Hull Times*, 3 August 1929, p. 5. Amy, Molly and their parents almost certainly knew what the letter said. Shortly after Irene's death Amy wrote to her father saying that she could not bring herself to wear colourful clothes 'despite what Irene said' (13 August 1929, RAFM).
18. Amy to Will, 13 August 1929, RAFM.

8. Where To? (1929–30)
1. Amy to Will, 6 September 1929, RAFM.
2. Will to Amy, 7 September 1929, RAFM.
3. On what the pilot thought was his final lap, the engine cut out, forcing him to glide slowly down to the water. It was only after he climbed out of the plane that he was told he had actually flown one more circuit than was necessary and that he had won the trophy for Britain.
4. Will to Amy, 7 September 1929, RAFM.
5. Amy to Ciss, 11 September 1929, RAFM.
6. Will to Amy, 12 September 1929, RAFM.
7. Amy to Will, undated, probably October 1929, RAFM.
8. Amy to Will, 3 October 1929, RAFM.
9. In Ireland Jimmy Martin had already designed a 'speed alarm' to warn a pilot that his airspeed was wrong, but he had no money to launch its production. When he moved to Acton he rented a barn in the grounds of a home for old horses, where he worked on ideas for planes and racing cars. He was mesmerised by the cars that roared round the track at Brooklands, and by 1928 he had become a regular at Stag Lane, where he took flying lessons with Baker.
10. Amy to her parents, 27 October 1929, RAFM.
11. Amy to Ciss, 19 November 1929, RAFM.
12. Amy to Ciss, 3 December 1929, RAFM.
13. Lady Heath trained as an 'air mechanic' in America and received a licence from the US Department of Commerce.
14. Amy to Will, 21 February 1930.
15. Light aircraft did not have VHF radio until 1945.
16. Amy to Ciss, 10 March 1930, RAFM.

17. Will to Amy, 13 January 1930, RAFM.
18. Will to Amy, 13 January 1930, RAFM.

9. *Jason* (1930)
1. Amy to Will, 5 February 1930, RAFM.
2. Quoted in *Solo, The Bert Hinkler Story* by R. D. Mackenzie, p. 100.
3. Amy to Will, 16 February 1930, RAFM.
4. Amy to Will, 5 March 1930, RAFM.
5. Will to Amy, 12 February 1930, RAFM.
6. Will to Amy, 25 February 1930, RAFM.
7. Will to Amy, 28 March 1930, RAFM.
8. 26 March 1930, RAFM.
9. 28 March 1930, RAFM.
10. Amy to Will, 4 April 1930, RAFM.
11. Amy to Will, 4 April 1930, RAFM.
12. *Cross Country*, edited by E. Travers, pp. 392–3.
13. Branks to Lord Wakefield, 4 April 1930, RAFM.
14. Amy to Ciss, 6 April 1930, RAFM.
15. Amy to Ciss, 6 April 1930, RAFM.
16. Amy to Ciss, 6 April 1930, RAFM.
17. 9 April 1930, RAFM.
18. Amy to Wakefield, 14 April 1930, RAFM.
19. Will to Lord Wakefield, 21 April 1930, RAFM.
20. Amy to Will, 27 April 1930, RAFM.
21. Amy went into great technical details about the flight during a lecture she gave to the Women's Engineering Society on 9 December 1930 and which was reprinted in *The Woman Engineer*.
22. *Sky Roads of the World* by Amy Johnson, p. 45.
23. Amy to Will, 23 April 1930, RAFM.
24. Amy to her mother, 1 May 1930, RAFM.

10. Journey's Start (5–7 May 1930)
1. Amy to Will, 24 April 1930, RAFM.
2. Lecture, 'How *Jason* and I Flew to the Land of the Golden Fleece' by Amy Johnson, RAFM.
3. This mistake was only revealed several years later.
4. Will to Jack, 6 May 1930, RAFM.
5. Jack to Will, 7 April 1930, RAFM.
6. 'How *Jason* and I . . .' by Amy Johnson, RAFM.

11. Basra to Baluchistan (7–10 May 1930)
1. 'How *Jason* and I . . .' by Amy Johnson, RAFM.
2. Amy actually recorded that the propeller stopped 'for a few agonising moments', but it is more likely that the blades slowed.

3. 'How *Jason* and I . . .' by Amy Johnson, RAFM.
4. Amy to Jack, 8 May 1930, RAFM.
5. Jack to Will, 8 May 1930, RAFM.
6. Will to Jack, 8 May 1930, RAFM.
7. RAFM.
8. *The Woman Engineer*, reprinted from a paper read to the Women's Engineering Society on 9 December 1930, RAFM.
9. Will to Jack, 9 May 1930, RAFM.
10. 'How *Jason* and I . . .' by Amy Johnson, RAFM.
11. *The Tatler*, 21 May 1930.

12. The British Girl Lindbergh (11–15 May 1930)
1. *Daily Mail*, 13 May 1930.
2. Ibid.
3. Ibid.
4. Ibid.
5. This was her explanation to an inquisitive young woman who asked the unaskable when she met Amy during the war. My thanks to Betsy Hughes for supplying this insight.
6. *Amy Johnson* by Constance Babington Smith, p. 204.
7. *The Times*, 28 May 1930.
8. *Amy Johnson* by CBS, p. 204.
9. Ibid., p. 205.
10. 11 May 1930, RAFM.
11. Lecture, 'How *Jason* and I Flew to the Land of the Golden Fleece' by Amy Johnson, RAFM.
12. *The Woman Engineer*, reprinted from a paper read to the Women's Engineering Society on 9 December 1930, RAFM.
13. 'How *Jason* and I . . .' by Amy Johnson, RAFM.
14. *The Times*, 14 May 1930.
15. *Daily Mail*, 14 May 1930.
16. 13 May 1930, RAFM.
17. 19 May 1930, RAFM.

13. Beastly Weather (16–24 May 1930)
1. 8 June 1930, RAFM.
2. *Daily Mail*, 19 May 1930.
3. Lecture, 'How *Jason* and I Flew to the Land of the Golden Fleece' by Amy Johnson, RAFM.
4. Photo caption, *New York Times*, 18 May 1930.
5. From a talk in the USA, 1934, RAFM.
6. 'How *Jason* and I . . .' by Amy Johnson, RAFM.
7. *Lindbergh* by A. Scott Berg, pp. 124–5.

8. *Shackleton* by Roland Huntford, pp. 695–7.
9. Lines from *The Waste Land* by kind permission of the estate of T. S. Eliot.
10. 19 May 1930, RAFM.
11. 19 May 1930, RAFM.
12. 21 May 1930, RAFM.
13. *Daily Mail*, 23 May 1930.
14. Ibid.
15. 'How *Jason* and I . . .' by Amy Johnson, RAFM.
16. *Daily Mail*, 24 May 1930.
17. *Daily Mail, Amy Johnson Souvenir Number*, 1930.
18. Ibid.
19. *Sunday Pictorial*, 25 May 1930.

14. The Gimme Gimme Girl (24 May – 7 July 1930)

1. Amy's stay in Australia lasted six weeks and by the time she was reunited with her family they had been apart for nearly two and a half months.
2. *Daily Mail*, 29 May 1930.
3. Unidentified cutting, RAFM.
4. *Sunday Pictorial*, 25 May 1930.
5. See *King Edward VIII* by Philip Ziegler, p. 128.
6. Francis Chichester admitted that he found it difficult to navigate his way around Australia. See *Solo to Sydney* by Sir Francis Chichester, p. 178.
7. *Daily Mail*, 28 May 1930.
8. *Scott's Book* by C. W. A. Scott, p. 88.
9. *Amy Johnson* by Constance Babington Smith, p. 243. Amy had always been troubled by the most extreme period pains and may well have been suffering from endometriosis, a condition in which parts of the lining of the womb become attached to other areas of the body, causing acute discomfort.
10. *Scott's Book* by C. W. A. Scott, p. 152.
11. *Daily Pictorial*, 29 May 1930. Sir Francis Chichester described suffering from a similar fear of crowds and strangers after completing his solo flight to Australia.
12. Readers of the *Daily Mail* suggested that a bronze statue of Amy should be erected in Hyde Park or Kensington Palace Gardens, claiming that she was as well loved as J. M. Barrie's Peter Pan. See *Daily Mail*, 27 May 1930.
13. *Newark Evening News*, 28 May 1930.
14. At least ten songs were written about Amy. For example: 'Amy, wonderful Amy', words by J. G. Gilbert, music by Horatio Nicholls; 'Johnnie, the Aeroplane Girl'; 'Queen of the Air' by W. T. Powell and P. Langley; 'Queen of the Air' by W. Alexander and L. Protheroe; 'Amy, Queen of the Air' by B. Norton and F. Hemingway; 'Heroine of the Air (Johnnie)' by H. W. Dury and H. Bull, which compares Amy to Grace Darling; 'When Johnnie goes Flying Home' by Patrius; 'Aeroplane Girl', a foxtrot by M. Vernon and M. Jones; 'The Lone Dove' by William Hodge (Amy's uncle); 'I heard a voice from heaven' by W. Roden.
15. Part of her speech can be heard on *The Century in Sound*, The British Library, Recordings from the National Sound Archive.
16. Joan of Arc was made a saint in 1920 and the decade that followed saw a growing interest in her, as all types of artists found a resonance in her life. Several silent films were made about her. Shaw's play was first performed in 1924 and Brecht invoked her name in *St Joan of the Stockyards*, a satirical attack on Germany.
17. *Daily Mirror*, 14 March 1932.
18. *Life in Britain Between the Wars* by L. C. B. Seaman, p. 61.
19. *Nhill Free Press*, 26 June 1930.
20. 7 June 1930, unidentified cutting, RAFM.
21. *The Times*, 30 May 1930.
22. *Graphic*, 7 June 1930.
23. *Daily Mail*, 4 June 1930.
24. *Daily Pictorial*, 5 June 1930.
25. Amy to Will, 3 June 1930, RAFM.
26. *Sun*, 5 June 1930.
27. *Daily Pictorial*, 5 June 1930.
28. *Newark Ledger*, 7 July 1930.
29. Many of the gifts fill a room at Sewerby Hall near Bridlington.
30. Unidentified cutting, RAFM.
31. *Truth*, front page, 22 June 1930.
32. *Truth*, 3 August 1930.
33. This is wildly inaccurate but Amy may not have realised the full extent of the gifts. The *Daily Mail* paid Amy £2000 for her exclusive story, plus a £10,000 fee that included a tour of Britain.
34. *Solo: The Bert Hinkler Story* by R. D. Mackenzie, pp. 91–3.
35. *The Times*, 20 June 1930.

15. Home Again (3 August – October 1930)

1. Betty Johnson and most newspapers estimated that 200,000 people turned up at Croydon Airport to greet Amy; other

papers put the total number who welcomed her home to London at a million.

2. *Airman Friday* by William Courtenay, p. 111.

3. Ibid., p. 123.

4. Ibid., p. 123.

5. Ibid., p. 114.

6. Will to Amy, 4 September 1930, RAFM.

7. Amy to Will, 19 August 1930, RAFM.

8. *Daily Mail*, 7 August 1930.

9. *New York Times*, 10 August 1930.

10. *Daily Mail*, 26 May 1930.

11. *Daily Mail*, 26 August 1930.

12. Amy to Will, 27 August 1930, RAFM.

13. Will to Amy, 26 July 1930, RAFM.

14. Amy to Will, 28 August 1930, RAFM.

15. Will to Amy, 26 August 1930, RAFM.

16. Will to Amy, 23 August 1930, RAFM.

17. Will to Amy, 23 August 1930, RAFM.

18. Amy to Will, 12 September 1930, RAFM.

19. Will to Amy, 15 September 1930, RAFM.

20. Vernon Wood to Will, 9 September 1930, RAFM.

21. Ciss to Mrs Glass, 7 October 1930, private collection.

22. Will to Amy, 3 October 1930, RAFM.

23. Wood to Amy, 31 October 1930, RAFM.

24. Will to Amy, 3 October 1930, RAFM. Will had received £264 from the *Daily Mail*, the *Daily Mirror*, the *Gaumont* and the *Pictorial* on Amy's behalf.

25. Amy to Ciss, 6/7 October 1930, RAFM.

26. Wood to Will, 10 October 1930, RAFM.

27. G. E. Moore to Wood, 22 October 1930, RAFM.

28. Will to Wood, 28 October 1930, RAFM.

29. Martin to Will, 23 October 1930, RAFM.

30. Amy to her parents, 23 October 1930, RAFM.

16. Tokyo (November 1930 – Autumn 1931)

1. See Amy's account in the *Sunday Dispatch*, 1932, RAFM.

2. *Hull Daily Mail*, 10 November 1930.

3. Amy to Ciss, 3 December 1930, RAFM.

4. Amy to Ciss, 4 December 1930, RAFM.

5. Amy to Ciss, 3 December 1930, RAFM.

6. RAFM.

7. Unidentified cutting, Smithsonian National Air and Space Museum.

8. *Daily Express*, date unclear, Smithsonian.

9. 25 January 1931, private collection.

10. Amy to Will, 24 October 1930, RAFM.

11. Jack to Ciss, undated, RAFM.

12. Will to Courtenay, 6 January 1931, RAFM.

13. Amy to Will, 31 January 1931, RAFM.

14. Leaving Belgrade, she was following a railway line when the track turned a sharp corner and disappeared into a tunnel; although she was doing 100 m.p.h. she managed to pull away at the last minute. When she could not find the aerodrome at Ankara she dropped smoke bombs over a sports stadium to clear the crowd and allow her to land there. Mrs Bruce's plane was exhibited outside Charing Cross tube station.

15. Amy to Ciss, 23 February 1931, RAFM.

16. *Round the World by Air and Steam.*

17. 26 February 1931.

18. Will to Amy, 26 February 1931, RAFM.

19. *Bernard Shaw, The Lure of Fantasy*, vol. 3: *1918–1950*, by Michael Holroyd, p. 30.

20. Ibid., p. 142.

21. Amy to Will, 9 March 1931, RAFM.

22. At the end of 1931 she had £3781 in the bank. By April 1932 this had dwindled to £106 before she went into the red. RAFM.

23. Will to Amy, 26 February 1931, RAFM.

24. Amy to Ciss, 14 July 1931, RAFM.

25. Amy to Will, 17 May 1931, RAFM.

26. From the manuscript of the autobiography of the architect Francis Johnson (no relation), whose uncle, Bernard Johnson, sold Brynmawr to Amy's parents. Francis Johnson's half-sister was a schoolfriend of Betty's and he remembered her as 'rather neurotic'. I am indebted to Doctor Neave for this information.

27. Throughout the journey the Russians supplied oil and petrol free of charge.

28. Jack's notes are held at RAFM.

29. The fly is curiously similar to the insect that the writer/director Billy Wilder introduced into his film of Lindbergh's crossing, *The Spirit of St Louis*. In the screen version the fly is a device to allow the actor James Stewart, who played the hero, to voice his feelings by talking to the stowaway. However, the actor found the concept so irritating that he threatened to quit. As it was too expensive to reshoot scenes, the co-star was allowed to stay as far as Newfoundland. See *Lindbergh* by A. Scott Berg, p. 502.

30. RAFM.

31. It was at Kazan, too, that the small Browning pistol that Amy had left there on the outward journey was returned to her.

32. As Dushka lived with Amy in Vernon Court, he was probably some sort of mixed breed, or even an Alsatian, rather

than a full-blooded wolf. He died a year
after arriving in Britain.
33. RAFM.

17. Jim Mollison (Winter 1931/2)
 1. *Death Cometh Soon or Late* by J. A. Mollison,
    p. 25.
 2. Ibid., p. 85.
 3. Ibid., p. 119.
 4. *Standard*, 29 March 1932.
 5. *Sketch*, 30 March 1932.
 6. Will Johnson's diary, Friday, 1 January 1931.
 7. *The Dark Valley* by Piers Brendon, p. 163.
 8. Amy to Will, 27 November 1931, RAFM.
 9. Amy to her parents, 3 December 1931,
    RAFM.
10. Amy to Egorov, chairman of the Osavi-
    akhim, January 1932, RAFM.
11. 21 January 1932, RAFM.
12. Amy referred to the operation in this way
    in an article she wrote for a series to
    appear in Thompson's *Weekly News*,
    December 1936 – April 1937. A wide range
    of papers, including foreign publications
    such as the *Washington Herald* (8 February
    1932), reported the operation. Jim's uncle,
    Dr Alexander Hislop, told CBS that Amy
    had had her uterus and ovaries removed;
    Molly confirmed that Amy had probably
    had a hysterectomy.
13. Official data for the average age at which
    women gave birth to their first child was
    first collected in 1938 when the figure was
    26.4 years; this included only legitimate
    births.
14. When CBS interviewed Amy's close
    friend Alice Hofer, she was emphatic that
    Amy was 'highly sexed'. Another friend,
    Peter Reiss, described her as 'very promis-
    cuous', although, of course, this is a
    highly subjective term. RAFM.
15. Will to Amy, 4 February 1932, RAFM.
16. Amy to Ciss, 1 March 1932, RAFM.
17. Amy to her parents, 27 March 1932, RAFM.
18. 27 March 1932, RAFM.
19. Amy to Jack, 17–27 March 1932, RAFM.
20. 'I was courted by cable', *Sunday Dispatch*,
    15 January 1933. In *Airman Friday* Courte-
    nay suggests that Amy wanted to cross the
    Atlantic alone but that her marriage pre-
    vented her from attempting this, p. 215.

18. Marriage (1932)
 1. Will's diary, Monday, 9 May 1932. RAFM.
 2. Amy to Will, 16 May 1932, RAFM.
 3. *Hull Times*, 14 May 1932.

 4. Amy to Hans, 9 May 1928, HCL.
 5. *Playboy of the Air* by Jim Mollison, p. 85.
 6. Jack to Ciss, 19 May 1932, RAFM.
 7. *The Times*, 19 and 26 February 1932. Jim
    claimed that he hit the porter after he had
    said, 'Take these two bitches out of here.'
    His companions were 'ladies of position'
    whose names were written on a piece of
    paper and passed to the Bench. The
    porter, who was wearing glasses, was
    badly injured and at one point it was
    feared he might lose the sight of one eye.
 8. Will to Amy, 14 June 1932, RAFM.
 9. 27 July 1932, RAFM.
10. Amy to Ciss, Moll and Bee, 25 July 1932,
    RAFM.
11. *The Tatler*, 6 July 1932.
12. Amy to Will, July? 1932, RAFM.
13. Will to Amy, 29 July 1932, RAFM.
14. Amy to her parents, 29 July 1932, RAFM.
15. Other famous names include the clown
    Joseph Grimaldi and Theodore 'Teddy'
    Roosevelt.
16. *Standard*, 29 July 1932.
17. 30 July 1932, RAFM.
18. 3 August 1932, RAFM.
19. Ciss to Amy, 5 August 1932, RAFM.
20. Amy to Ciss, 14 August 1932, RAFM.
21. 1 August 1932, private collection.
22. *Airman Friday* by Bill Courtenay, p. 220.
23. From *Aero-Digest*, quoted in *Death Cometh
    Soon or Late* by Jim Mollison, p. 256.
24. *Death Cometh Soon or Late* by Jim Mollison,
    p. 277.
25. Amy to Will, 5? September 1932, RAFM.
26. Will to Amy, 19 September 1932, RAFM.

**19. Solo to Cape Town (Winter 1932 –
Summer 1933)**
 1. *Sky Roads of the World* by Amy Johnson, p.
    83.
 2. Unidentified cutting.
 3. 7 November 1932, RAFM.
 4. *Sky Roads of the World* by Amy Johnson, p.
    88.
 5. Ibid., p. 91.
 6. RAFM.
 7. *Herald Tribune*, 19 December 1932.
 8. *New York Times*, 18 November 1932.
 9. *New York Times*, 19 November 1932.
10. *New York Times*, 19 November 1932.
11. Undated, RAFM.
12. *Washington Daily News*, 19 December 1932.
13. *Herald Tribune*, 19 December 1932.
14. *Herald Tribune*, 25 December 1932.
15. *Herald Tribune*, 19 December 1932.

16. *Washington Post*, 18 December 1932.
17. Capstack enjoyed photographing popular heroes such as the snooker player Joe Davis and film and theatre stars. See 'Blackpool Illuminations' by Lawrence Hole in *BJP*, 17 September 1997.
18. Amy to her family, 23 December 1932, RAFM.
19. 28 December 1932, RAFM.
20. 28 December 1932, RAFM.
21. *Playboy of the Air* by James Mollison, p. 219.
22. Mrs Bullmore to Amy, 5 March 1933, RAFM.
23. From correspondence from Crockers re Amy's and Jim's tax affairs, 23 January 1936, RAFM.
24. *Achievements* magazine, 1932.
25. A. E. Whitelaw, *New York Times*, 19 November 1932.
26. Amy to her mother, July? 1933, RAFM.
27. 1 May 1933. All letters concerning the Polish incident are held at RAFM.
28. H. G. Lane, editor of the *Sunday Dispatch*, to Perrin, 4 May 1933.
29. 21 April 1933, RAFM.
30. A news agency, Northern News Services, contemplated publishing a pamphlet that would tell the 'true' story of Amy's forced landing and hoped to sell it in Poland and all English-speaking countries. But the Royal Aero Club discouraged publication, saying 'no useful purpose would be served'. The affair resurfaced in November when a book about Amy edited by Hubert S. Banner retold the Polish incident as it appeared in the *Sunday Dispatch*. The Polish Aero Club and the mayor briefly considered suing.
31. 1 June 1933, RAFM.

20. The Water Jump (1933)
1. *Western Mail & South Wales News*, Tuesday, 4 July 1933.
2. *Western Mail & South Wales News*, Tuesday, 4 July 1933.
3. *Western Mail & South Wales News*, Tuesday, 4 July 1933.
4. *Airman Friday* by William Courtenay, p. 252.
5. *South Wales Evening Post*, Tuesday, 4 July 1933.
6. *Western Mail & South Wales News*, Friday, 7 July 1933.
7. *Daily Mail*, 5 July 1933.
8. *South Wales Evening Post*, 7 July 1933.
9. Quoted in *Airman Friday* by William Courtenay, p. 266.
10. *Playboy of the Air* by Jim Mollison, p. 102.
11. Quoted in *Playboy of the Air* by Jim Mollison, p. 101.
12. *South Wales Evening Post*, Saturday, 22 July 1933.
13. *South Wales Evening Post*, Saturday, 22 July 1933.
14. *Airman Friday* by William Courtenay, p. 212.
15. *South Wales Evening Post*, Saturday, 22 July 1933.
16. *Sky Roads of the World* by Amy Johnson, p. 107.
17. Ibid., p. 107.
18. Ibid., p. 108.
19. Ibid., p. 108.
20. Ibid., p. 108.
21. Ibid., p. 108.
22. Ibid., p. 108.
23. Eye-witness account.

For Amy and Jim's stay at Pendine, see the *South Wales Evening Post* and the *Western Mail & South Wales News*; the crash was covered in all national newspapers.

21. Looking for Work (1933–4)
1. *Amelia Earhart* by Doris L. Rich, p. 169.
2. *Evening News*, 24 July 1933.
3. *South Wales Evening Post*, 24 July 1933.
4. *Daily Mail*, 27 July 1933.
5. *Western Mail & South Wales News*, 25 July 1933.
6. *Airman Friday* by William Courtenay, p. 231.
7. *Playboy of the Air* by Jim Mollison, p. 109.
8. *Amelia Earhart* by Doris L. Rich, p. 116.
9. *Playboy of the Air* by Jim Mollison, p. 109.
10. *New York Times*, 31 July 1933.
11. *Playboy of the Air* by Jim Mollison, p. 109.
12. Ibid., p. 109.
13. *The Ninety-Niner* newsletter, No. 11, 15 August 1933.
14. She also visited MGM in Hollywood.
15. RAFM.
16. Amy to Will, 20 March 1934, RAFM.
17. Courtenay to Jim, 18 March 1934, RAFM.
18. Amy to Courtenay, 29 March 1934, RAFM.
19. Hillman's secretary to Amy, 5 March 1934, RAFM.
20. 8 December 1933, RAFM.
21. Amy to Will?, 18 May 1934, RAFM.
22. RAFM.

22. Mildenhall Madness (October 1934)

1. The brothers Ross and Keith Smith had won the first Great Air Race to Australia in December 1919 in a time of twenty-seven days and twenty-one hours.
2. It was claimed Germany had 24,000 skilled airmen. *Daily Mail*, 10 November 1934.
3. This Comet should not be confused with the De Havilland DH 106 Comet jet airliner that was first launched in 1949 and was grounded five years later after a series of fatal crashes.
4. Houses were built at Stag Lane.
5. Amy to Ciss, 11 October 1934, RAFM.
6. *Grosvenor House* can still be seen in its restored glory at the Shuttleworth Collection in Bedfordshire.
7. *Airman Friday* by William Courtenay, p. 309.
8. *Daily Mail*, 15 October 1934.
9. *Jackie Cochran: An Autobiography*, by Maryann Bucknam Brinley and Jackie Cochran, p. 100.
10. *Daily Mail*, 18 October 1934.
11. *Daily Mail*, 17 October 1934.
12. *Daily Mail*, 17 October 1934.
13. *The Great Air Race* by Arthur Swinson, p. 49.
14. *Florence Desmond by Herself*, p. 78. For Desmond's background see *The Call Boy* (British Music Hall Society), 'The Final Curtain', p. 14.
15. *Flying Matilda* by Norman Ellison, p. 143.
16. *Jackie Cochran: An Autobiography*, by Maryann Bucknam Brinley and Jackie Cochran, p. 144.
17. *Playboy of the Air* by James Mollison, p. 116.
18. *The Great Air Race* by Swinson, p. 101.
19. *The Times*, 20 October 1934.
20. *Daily Mail*, 19 October 1934.
21. *Millennium Child*, edited by Tinch Minter, p. 47.
22. *The Great Air Race* by Swinson, p. 114.
23. Ibid., p. 159.
24. Amy writing in the *Daily Mail*, 23 October 1934.
25. *Playboy of the Air* by James Mollison, p. 119.
26. Since the race rules stipulated that no one could take both prizes, the handicap went to Moll and Parmentier (see the official race programme). The plane carried three passengers and 25,000 letters.
27. Unidentified cutting.
28. *Daily Mail*, 8 November 1934.
29. *Daily Mail*, 9 November 1934.
30. *Daily Mail*, 10 November 1934.
31. *Daily Mail*, 23 October 1934.
32. In 1979 a few parts of *Black Magic* turned up in the outbuilding of a smallholding in Portugal. An engineer based on the Welsh border tried to rebuild the plane using a small piece of the fuselage, part of the tailplane, one seat, battered remnants of the wings and photocopies of the original drawings. The project was abandoned in 1982 after fire destroyed the tailplane. A new project to try to recreate *Black Magic* is currently underway.
33. *Daily Mail*, 14 November 1934.

23. In Search of an Image (1935–6)

1. Will to Amy, 16 November 1933, RAFM.
2. Will to Amy, 16 November 1933, RAFM.
3. Audrey Ronald, interviewed by CBS. Amy met her in Madeira and stayed at her home in St John's Wood for several months.
4. Petition by Amy alleging Jim's infidelity, RAFM.
5. Petition by Amy alleging Jim's infidelity, RAFM.
6. Amy to Will, 25 January 1935, RAFM.
7. Will to Amy, 5 February 1935, RAFM.
8. For local coverage of the accident and inquest see *The Hull Times*, 20 and 27 April 1935, and the *Hull Daily Mail*, 26 April 1935.
9. Amy to Wood, 20 April 1935, RAFM.
10. The charges were dismissed but she was fined forty shillings for failing to stop. *Daily Mail*, 1 September 1934.
11. Amy to Will, 1 May 1935, RAFM.
12. Spiro chartered the plane for a minimum charge of £25 a week plus £1 for every hour's flying. The cash was to be paid a month in advance and Spiro would pay for hangarage, oil and insurance.
13. See *Airman Friday* by William Courtenay, p. 222.
14. Courtenay to Amy, 16 January 1935, RAFM.
15. *The Dark Valley* by Piers Brendon, p. 271.
16. Amy had joined the Society before her Australia flight and was elected president in 1934; its members proved to be among her most loyal supporters.
17. Offers of work included a job at a precision engineering company, Screw Products, but this would remove her from London and aviation. She had also been asked to appear on the music-hall stage for £300 a week but still felt this was undignified. Phillips and Powis of Reading

wanted her to work for them. Amy discussed the idea of an 'aerial cruise' with Trevor. Although it would include such glamorous highlights as Copenhagen, Berlin, Budapest, Geneva, Paris and London, it would start and finish in Blackpool. Amy to Trevor, 19 March 1936, RAFM.

18. Several of Amy's business plans ran into legal problems. She instructed Crockers to recover £300 that she claimed a motor agent owed her as her share in the sale of a Delage car, and she had to call the firm in when Spiro's cheque for hiring the Beechcraft bounced. Eventually the solicitors extracted £60 from the businessman after deducting their fees of £15. Spiro also withdrew his tentative offer to buy a plane from Amy. On top of all this, De Havilland claimed that she and Jim owed them £436 for the *Seafarer* flight, but the couple argued that any goods and services supplied had been given in return for publicity.

19. Amy to her parents, 25 August 1935, RAFM.

20. Courtenay to Amy, 15 January 1935, RAFM.

21. Amy to Will, 10 February 1936, RAFM. Jacqueline Cochran also designed a make-up case that carried essential products for flying.

22. *My Reminiscences as a Cowboy* by F. Harris (published by Boni, 1930) is part of a collection of Amy's books that her parents donated to Kingston High School in Hull after her death. They were subsequently transferred to Hull Local Studies Library. Other books in the collection include *Sun up: Tales of the Cow Camps* (published by Scribner, 1932), *Cowboys North and South* (1931) and *Cow Country* (1934), all by W. James.

23. Amy to Will, 3 February 1936, RAFM.

24. Amy to Will, 4 February 1936, RAFM.

25. Will to Amy, 13 February 1936, RAFM.

26. Courtenay to Will, 24 March 1936, RAFM.

27. *Sunday Graphic*, 1 March 1936.

28. 13 March 1936, RAFM.

29. RAFM.

30. The manufacturers were lending Amy a Percival Gull which had been specially fitted with long-range tanks.

31. Amy to Kaplanski, 17 February 1936, RAFM.

32. Amy held shares in Phillips and Powis Aircraft and Boulton and Paul.

33. Draft press release, RAFM.

34. Percival agreed not to charge Amy for the repairs to the plane.

35. 9 May 1936, RAFM.

36. 9 September 1936, RAFM.

37. *Sky Roads of the World* by Amy Johnson, p. 60.

38. Ibid., p. 60. Jim and Teena met her at Croydon and Will recorded the whole event on his cine camera. It was the last family reunion.

24. France (1936–7)

1. Dupré's mother had divorced the Finance Minister, Joseph Caillaux, who was her second husband (the first was Dupré's father). Caillaux's wife was acquitted of murder in 1914.

2. Amy to Lord Swinton, 20 May, RAFM.

3. *In Vogue* by Georgina Howell (1978), p. 113.

4. Ibid., p. 113. The plane was a BA Eagle that she flew in the King's Cup.

5. *Calvacade*, 16 May 1937.

6. *Playboy of the Air* by James Mollison, p. 266.

7. *The Lives of Beryl Markham* by Errol Trzebinski, p. 153.

8. Wakefields' *Achievements* magazine, May 1936.

9. *West with the Night* by Beryl Markham, p. 281.

10. Amy to Will, 14 July 1936, RAFM.

11. Amy to Will, 10 October 1936. A fee of £30,000 had been talked about three years previously when a film of the assassination of King Alex was mooted. Fox dropped the idea of using a lone pilot but suggested that Amy might fly photographers to news 'hotspots', her fee depending on the risk involved.

12. Amy to Will, month uncertain, 1936, RAFM.

13. Amy to Will, month uncertain, 1936, RAFM.

14. In July Amy wrote to Colonel Jellicoe asking him to use his influence to try to persuade the Portuguese Government to sell *Black Magic* back to Amy so that she could use it in the Johannesburg Race. The event, which was due to start on 15 September, included 'control points' at Cairo and Vienna and would cover the East Africa route that Amy had recently flown.

15. *Daily Mirror*, 22 October 1936.

16. *Daily Herald*, 22 October 1936.

17. *Daily Mail*, 29 October 1936.

18. Unidentified cutting, RAFM.

19. *Daily Express*, 10 November 1936.

20. *France on Ten Words a Day* by H. McCarty Lee, published by Simon & Schuster, 1931.

21. The copy of *Courrier sud* may have lost its cover and become battered by schoolgirls who read it after Amy. However, it is the only book in the collection that is damaged in this way.

22. RAFM.

23. RAFM.

24. CBS interview notes, RAFM.

25. Unidentified cutting, RAFM.

26. *Daily Express*, 19 November 1936.

27. *The Bystander*, 16 December 1936.

28. Although he was born in Bradford, Cowan Dobson spent much of his adult life in Scotland. His paintings emphasised the ordinariness of his sitters. While at work he resembled what would now appear as a cliché of an artist, holding a huge palette and smoking a pipe. In his painting of Amy she wears a scarf and fur coat and looks more like a bored but wealthy housewife than a pilot.

29. RAFM.

30. Typescript, 'Part 4 – I become famous and desperately unhappy', early February 1937? RAFM.

31. *Daily Express*, 13 March 1937.

32. Until 1937 the only permissible ground upon which someone could petition for divorce was the other party's adultery (as per the 1923 Matrimonial Causes Act or 'Lord Buckmaster's Act'). The 1937 Matrimonial Causes Act liberalised divorce considerably so that other grounds could be pleaded: three years' desertion and cruelty were the main ones; others included incurable insanity and habitual drunkenness.

33. 15 March 1937, report from Jacks International Bureau, RAFM.

34. United Press, April 1937.

35. While she was in America Amy followed all leads that might produce work: she spoke to literary agents and considered a goodwill flight from England to Canada.

36. See 'That Man – Weems' in *Popular Aviation*, August 1938.

37. Although she would take a navigator with her, she wanted to master the sextant.

38. Amy to Will, 17 March 1937, RAFM.

39. *Daily Express*, 18 May 1937.

40. Eventually no name was cited in the divorce case (see High Court of Justice,

Folio 12 of 1938).

41. Florence to Amy, undated, RAFM.

42. Unidentified cutting, RAFM.

43. Amy to Will, 14 June 1937, RAFM. While she waited to move in, she stayed in a spacious suite on the third floor of the Trianon Palace Hotel overlooking the park in Versailles.

44. 30 June 1937, RAFM.

45. 1 July 1937, RAFM.

46. 16 July 1937, RAFM.

47. Amy to Will, 21 July 1937, RAFM.

48. Amy to Will, 30 July 1937, RAFM.

49. Amy to Will, 11 August 1937, RAFM.

50. Amy to Will, 11 August 1937, RAFM.

51. Amy to Will, 1 December 1937, RAFM.

52. Amy to Ciss, July 1937, RAFM.

53. Colonel Jellicoe to Amy, 25 June 1936, RAFM.

25. Speed (1938–9)

1. *The Cresta Run* by Michael Seth-Smith, p. 145.

2. *Sky Roads of the World* by Amy Johnson, p. 311.

3. *Wing-Tips*, 1938, RAFM.

4. She was fined £5 in August 1938 for driving at over fifty-five miles an hour at Worksop. She was towing a trailer at the time and was obviously in the middle of a gliding excursion. Her licence was endorsed; she already had two previous convictions for speeding. See *Sheffield Telegraph*, 5 August 1938. Amy also enjoyed watching speedway racing and tried dirt-track racing. *Northern Mail*, 15 May 1939 and *Sunday Chronicle*, 21 May 1939.

5. *Woman's Fair*.

6. *The Sketch*, 29 June 1938.

7. Amy also drove in the Empire Exhibition Scottish Rally in 1938, the Singer Motor Car Club Rally of June 1939 and was one of five women who entered a race held at Brooklands in September 1938 to mark the fiftieth anniversary of J. B. Dunlop's invention of the pneumatic tyre.

8. *Daily Mail*, 16 September 1938. The event, first organised by the Midland Automobile Club in 1903, continues today. A competitor recently clocked up the first climb in under twenty-five seconds.

9. The cottage was also known as the Old Vicarage and the Old Rectory.

10. Amy to Mrs Waller, 4 July 1938, RAFM.

11. *Playboy of the Air* by James Mollison, p. 172.

12. 24 September 1937, RAFM.

13. 17 November 1937, RAFM.
14. *Sky Roads of the World* by Amy Johnson, p. 260.
15. Quoted in *The Car in British Society* by Sean O'Connell, p. 2.
16. Quoted in *The Car in British Society* by Sean O'Connell, p. 46. The figure refers to Ministry of Transport figures for six areas.
17. Quoted in *The Car in British Society* by Sean O'Connell, p. 53.
18. Amy to Will, undated, 1938, RAFM.
19. Amy to Will, undated, probably January 1938, RAFM.
20. Amy to Will, undated, 1938, RAFM.
21. Amy to Will, undated, probably January 1938, RAFM.
22. On the day that Amy and Jim's decree absolute was finalised, at the end of August 1938, she was fined £50 and had her licence endorsed for driving a car and trailer at over thirty miles per hour on the road between London and Princes Risborough. For details of the Le Touquet incident see *The Times*, 6 June 1938 and 15 August 1938.
23. *Daily Sketch*, 25 August 1938.
24. An advertisement for the film.
25. *Modern Boy*, No. 12, 7 May 1938.
26. During her 1937 presidency of the WEA Amy praised Pauline Gower and Dorothy Spicer for gaining their mechanical qualifications without the aid of the RAF, and she admired Pauline's calm temperament and feet-on-the-ground approach.
27. *A Harvest of Memories* by Michael Fahie, p. 13.
28. She considered buying a Dragon Rapide from Mrs Victor Bruce but thought they were too expensive (Amy to Will, 11 May 1938). Amy crashed her plane at Hatton in October 1938 on the way home from a race meeting at Donnington. See *Warwick Advertiser*, 29 October 1938 and *Stratford-upon-Avon Herald*.
29. 10 September 1937, RAFM.
30. Amy to Will, 16 February 1939, RAFM.
31. 29 September 1939 and 23 June 1939, RAFM.
32. The speech was widely reported – see *Daily Sketch*, 8 September 1938, *Modern Woman* and *The Times*, 8 September 1938.
33. A speech at the Technical Institute in Lewisham reported in several newspapers on 16 September 1938. When she was elected president of the Women's Engineering Society for the third time in 1936 she made an astonishing speech which she intended as ironic: 'I am not a feminist, women have never been up to any good, and my candid opinion of the [female] species in general is that they have created little and destroyed much . . . I do not know of one who will put right the plumbing or the gramophone while her husband sits in his chair and smokes his pipe.' The speech was so badly received that Amy felt compelled to write to Lady Astor to explain herself. 'I was, as a matter of fact, quoting G. B. Shaw's technique – you remember when he came back from South Africa he said the solution of the problem of the "Blacks" was to intermarry with the "whites". I think such statements are colourful and enlivening. Where is some people's sense of humour?' The flippancy of her opening remarks meant that the rest of her speech – in which she suggested that, in the future, it would be possible to make a 'stratosphere flight' from London to New York in ten hours; that the world's population would soar out of control; and that 'synthetic birth' would lead to sextuplets born in a 'test tube' – went largely unreported.
34. 4 August 1938, RAFM.
35. See *Glasgow Weekly News*, 30 July 1938; *Sunday Graphic*, 11 September 1938; she spoke at a luncheon given in her honour at the Overseas Club in St James's (see *Daily Express*, 9 November 1938) and at the Women's Engineering Society on 8 November (see *The Aeroplane*, 16 November 1938).
36. *Picture Post*, 25 February 1939; *Daily Mirror*, 11 January 1939; *Flight*, 22 December 1939.
37. Quoted in *A Harvest of Memories* by Michael Fahie, p. 136.
38. *The Sunday Referee*, 18 September 1938.
39. Amy to Will, 14 February 1939, RAFM; see also *Daily Telegraph*, 10 February 1939.
40. Amy to Crockers, 23 February 1939. The bill covered advice on her income tax demand, Vernon Court and the Gate House, and her divorce.
41. Amy to Gloria, 16 May 1938, RAFM.
42. *Daily Herald*, 20 June 1939, 'Amy pilots 5/- ferry'; *Nottingham Journal*, 21 June 1939; *Liverpool Post*, 21 June 1939; *Sunday Graphic*, 18 June 1939; *Daily Mirror*, 20 June 1939.
43. Amy to Will, 15 August 1939, RAFM.
44. Amy to Will, 23 August 1939, RAFM.

45. Amy moved from Monks Staithe in August 1938 to Rossley Manor country club near Cheltenham, and then rented a cottage called Old Rowley at Stoke Orchard between Cheltenham and Tewkesbury. When she joined the IOW Ferry company she took lodgings in Portsmouth and then moved to a bungalow at Old Bosham.
46. Will to Amy, 24 August 1939, RAFM.
47. 24 August 1939, RAFM.
48. Will to Amy, 8 September 1939, RAFM.

26. War (1939–40)

1. Amy to her parents, undated, 1939, RAFM.
2. *Aeroplane* magazine, 19 October 1939.
3. Amy to Will, 28 November 1939, RAFM.
4. Amy to Will, 15 November 1939, RAFM.
5. Quoted in *The Forgotten Pilots* by Lettice Curtis, p. 12.
6. See 'The Very Few', an article about Russian women pilots in the *Guardian Weekend*, 15 December 2001.
7. *The Forgotten Pilots* by Lettice Curtis, p. 14.
8. The reasons why Batten was excluded from the ATA are discussed in *Jean Batten: The Garbo of the Skies* by Ian Mackersey, pp. 291, 293–6. While she claimed that her eyesight let her down, there were several ATA pilots who wore glasses, and one male pilot had a glass eye.
9. Amy to Will, December 1939, RAFM.
10. Reported in *The Woman Engineer*, March 1940.
11. Amy to Will, 6 March 1940, RAFM.
12. 29 February 1940, RAFM.
13. Cobham to Amy, 29 March 1940, RAFM.
14. Amy to Lady Astor, 21 March 1940, RAFM.
15. 27 March 1940, RAFM.
16. 3 May 1940, RAFM.
17. Amy to Will, 15 March 1940, RAFM.
18. *Evening Standard*, 10 April 1940.
19. *Sunday Express*, 21 April 1940; *Sunday Dispatch*, 21 April 1940; *Sunday Graphic*, 21 April 1940; *Star*, 20 April 1940.
20. Amy to Will, 9 May 1940, RAFM.
21. Lettice Curtis, interview with the author.
22. Amy to Will, 9 May 1940, RAFM.
23. Amy to Ciss, 11 May 1940, RAFM.
24. Amy to Will, 6 June 1940, RAFM.
25. Amy to Ciss, 25 May 1940, RAFM.
26. Reply from the factory, 22 May 1940, RAFM.
27. Amy to Moore-Brabazon, 1 May 1940, RAFM.
28. Amy to Ciss, 8 June 1940, RAFM.

29. Joy Muntz died during a conversion course before joining the ATA.
30. Amy to Ciss, 3 December 1940, RAFM.
31. In 2001 the jacket of an ATA uniform was given to the Wilberforce Museum in Hull.
32. Amy to Ciss, 25 September 1940, RAFM.
33. 18 October 1940, RAFM.
34. CBS interview with Alice Hofer and Lady du Cros.

27. The Final Weekend (4–5 January 1941)

The account of Amy's last flight is taken from sworn affidavits submitted for Grant of Probate, RAF Museum and interviews of witnesses by Messrs W. C. Crocker & Co., Solicitors, Public Record Office.

1. Amy to her mother, 26 December 1940, RAFM.
2. As testified by Pauline Gower in an affidavit submitted for Grant of Probate, RAFM; she described Amy's demeanour as 'perfectly normal'.
3. Correspondence between the author and Jennie Broad.
4. As testified by Molly in an affidavit submitted for Grant of Probate, RAF Hendon.
5. As testified by Molly in an affidavit submitted for Grant of Probate, RAF Hendon.
6. As testified by Molly in an affidavit submitted for Grant of Probate, RAF Hendon.
7. The Oxford's total fuel capacity was 156 gallons.
8. Philippa Bennett later testified in an affidavit submitted for Grant of Probate, RAFM.
9. *Bucks Free Press*, Friday, 10 January 1941. There have even been suggestions that Amy and Fletcher had met each other – *FlyPast*, November 2000, 'Amy Johnson and "Mr X"'.
10. See *Failed to Return*, p. 36 and *Missing Believed Killed*, by Roy Nesbit.
11. *Woman's Illustrated*, 13 August 1938.
12. Eyewitness account by American journalist Drew Middleton.
13. At Fletcher's inquest Dean reported the words as 'Hurry, please, please.'
14. As testified by Leading Seaman Nicholas Roberts in an affidavit submitted for Grant of Probate, RAFM.
15. Lieutenant Peter Loasby, commander of the ship that launched the lifeboat, put the

time at between five and ten minutes.

16. As testified by Vivian Gray, Seaman on the *Haslemere*, in an affidavit submitted for Grant of Probate, RAFM.

17. Walter Fletcher is buried in Woodlands Cemetery, Gillingham, Grave 1379.

18. In his biography, *Far from Humdrum*, Sir William Crocker confirmed that Williamson was an old friend of Will, p. 238.

19. Pauline to Will, 6 January 1941.

20. For contemporary coverage of Amy's death see: *Daily Express*, 7 January 1941, which quotes Drew Middleton; *Daily Express*, 8 January 1941, 'Mystery Man was with Amy'; *Daily Mail*, 8 January 1941, 'Unknown Man Died with Amy'; *Daily Express*, 9 January 1941, 'Where Did Amy pick up Mr X?'

21. Will to Vernon Wood, 16 May 1941, RAFM.

22. Reported in the *Daily Sketch*, 27 August 1941.

23. *Far from Humdrum*, p. 238. The pigskin bag can still be seen at Sewerby Hall, north of Bridlington, in the Amy Johnson Room that holds many of her treasures.

24. *Daily Mail*, 7 January 1941.

25. *The Mist Procession* by Lord Vansittart, quoted in *The Age of Illusion, Some Glimpses of Britain between the Wars* by Ronald Blyth, p. 84. See also *Amy Johnson* by Constance Babington Smith, p. 331.

26. As testified by Pauline Gower in an affidavit submitted for Grant of Probate, RAFM.

27. *Diary of an Aviator* by Air Vice-Marshal Sandy Johnstone, p. 35.

28. See *Guardian*, 6 February 1999; *Hull Daily Mail*, *Daily Mirror*, 10 February 1999; *Independent*, 15 February 1999; *Evening Standard*, 5 February 1999; *Press Association*, 5 February 1999; also correspondence with the author, 2 January 2001.

29. Peter Elliott, Senior Keeper, Department of Research and Information Services, RAF Museum, points out in a letter to *FlyPast*, January 2001, that at that stage in the war an average of 4000 rounds was fired for every unseen target brought down.

30. In the same month that Tom Mitchell made his confession, Graham Nicholson, a staff member who had worked at Squires Gate, came forward to recount how Amy had called him over to hand him her lunch in a brown paper bag, adding the ominous words, 'I won't be needing this where I'm going,' before winking at him. Nicholson believed that Amy intended to bail out of the plane to start a new life with another man after her unhappy marriage to Jim. However, all other evidence suggests that Amy had put her marriage behind her. Press Association, 10 February 1999.

31. In the BBC Leeds documentary, *Inside Out*, shown in November 2002, Derek Roberts, a former RAF Flight Clerk based at Sheerness, remembers the anguish of a sailor who told him how Amy had been inadvertently 'chopped to pieces' by the propeller. Tom O'Rourke, a retired boatman who was working near Southend when Amy died, says a sailor reported how a woman had been sucked under the boat. *Mail on Sunday*, 25 August 2002.

32. The film's première was held at the Dorchester Theatre, Hull, on 30 August 1942.

33. *Anna Neagle Says There's Always Tomorrow* by Anna Neagle, pp. 132–5.

34. *Madame Curie* by E. Curie, Heinemann, 1941, held in Hull Local Studies Library, Amy Johnson Collection. The inscription reads: 'To Ciss from Will after viewing the film, "They Flew Alone", 27.3.42.'

35. Quoted in *Vera Brittain: A Life* by Paul Berry and Mark Bostridge, p. 366.

Other articles on the death of Amy Johnson include: *FlyPast*, letters page, January 2001; 'The Last Flight of Amy Johnson, Blighty's Flying Sweetheart', by Midge Gillies, *Independent*, 6 January 2001; 'The Riddle of Amy Johnson's Last Day' by Diana Barnato Walker, Commodore, Air Transport Auxiliary Association, in *Army Quarterly & Defence Journal*, vol. 129, no. 3, July 1999; 'Amy's Last Flight' by Alison King, OBE, in *Aeroplane Monthly*, November and December 1980; 'What happened to Amy?' by Humphrey Wynn, *Aeroplane Monthly*, August 1973.

Epilogue

1. 'What Have I to Look forward to?' appeared in *Weekly News*, 20 March 1937.

2. For details of the dive see *Mail on Sunday*, 28 July 2002 and http://www.rafsaa.org

Sources

When the late Constance Babington Smith wrote her biography in 1967 she was fortunate enough to be able to interview many of the people who played a key part in Amy Johnson's life. Her notes from these interviews, together with thousands of other items relating to Amy and her family, including letters, diaries, newspaper cuttings and personal effects such as her wartime ration-book, have been carefully preserved at the RAF Museum in Hendon, north London. Her unpublished interview notes have added an important additional layer to my own research and have allowed me to piece together a picture of Amy as a passionate and complicated woman.

Such is the interest in Amy that items about her are held in collections around Britain and the world. The Central Library in Hull owns the letters she wrote to Hans Arregger, as well as many of her books. Sewerby Hall, set in a beautiful if desolate park which she opened in June 1936 and which overlooks the sea just outside Bridlington, houses a collection of trophies and mementoes as well as the infamous pigskin bag that she was carrying on her final flight.

In addition to the above, the following libraries, museums and other institutions have been extremely helpful and I am most grateful for their support: Bank of England; Local Studies Library, Brighton; British Film Institute; British Library; British Library Newspaper Collection; British Music Hall Society; Bromley Local History Library; Cambridge County Record Office, Cambridgeshire Collection; Castrol Archive; Sir Alan Cobham Archive; Croydon Airport Society; Ely Library; Herne Bay Library; Hull Coroner's Office; Hull City Archives; Hull Local History Unit; Hulton Archive; International Racing Bureau; Amy Johnson Appreciation Society; Musée de l'Air et de l'Espace, Le Bourget; Museum of Speed, Pendine; National Portrait Gallery; Law Society; John Lewis Partnership Archives; 99s Museum; Office for National Statistics; Princes Risborough Heritage Society; Public Record Office; Special Collections, The Libraries of Purdue University; Racing Collection, Newmarket Library; Roosevelt Museum; St Moritz Tobogganing Club; the Dorothy L. Sayers Society; Science Museum and Picture Library; Sheffield University; Shell Services International; Shuttleworth Collection; National Air and Space Museum, Smithsonian Institution; University Library, Cambridge; Women's Library; Wright State University; American Heritage Center, University of Wyoming.

Bibliography

Allen, Peter. *The 91 Before Lindbergh*, Airlife, Shrewsbury, 1984.

Allison, K. J. (editor). *A History of the County of York: East Riding*, volume II, Institute of Historical Research, Oxford University Press, 1974.

Atkins, Rev. William. *The Parish Church of Saint George, Hanover Square*, Richard Geiger, London, 1976.

Babington Smith, Constance, *Amy Johnson*, Collins, London, 1967.

Barrett, Norman (editor). *The Daily Telegraph Chronicle of Horse Racing*, Guinness Publishing, London, 1995.

Barty-King, Hugh. *Maples, Fine Furnishers: A Household Name for 150 Years*, Quiller Press, London, 1992.

Bedford, Duchess. *The Flying Duchess*, introduction by John, Duke of Bedford, Macdonald, London, 1968.

Berg, A. Scott. *Lindbergh*, G. P. Putnam's Sons, New York, 1998.

Bernier, Olivier. *Fireworks at Dusk: Paris in the Thirties*, Little Brown, London, 1993.

Berry, Paul and Mark Bostridge. *Vera Brittain: A Life*, Virago, London, 2001.

Binney, Marcus. *The Women Who Lived for Danger: The Women Agents of SOE in the Second World War*, Hodder & Stoughton, London, 2002.

Binion, Rudolf. *Defeated Leaders: The political fate of Caillaux, Jouvenel and Tardieu*, Columbia University Press, New York, 1960.

Birtles, J. Philip. *Hatfield Aerodrome, A History*, British Aerospace Regional Aircraft Ltd, Hatfield, 1993.

Blythe, Ronald. *The Age of Illusion: Some Glimpses of Britain between the Wars, 1919–1940*, Oxford University Press, Oxford, 1983.

Boase, Wendy. *The Sky's the Limit: Women Pioneers in Aviation*, Osprey, London, 1979.

Both, Rex. *Hull – The Fishing Years*, Breedon Books, Derbyshire, 1999.

Brace, Harold W. *History of Seed Crushing in Great Britain*, Land Books, London, 1960.

Branson, Noreen. *Britain in the Nineteen Twenties*, Weidenfeld & Nicolson, London, 1975.

Brendon, Piers. *The Dark Valley: A Panorama of the 1930s*, Pimlico, London, 2001.

Brinley, Maryann Bucknam and Jackie Cochran. *Jackie Cochran: An Autobiography*, Bantam Books, London, 1987.

Browne, Douglas G. and E. V. Tullett, *Bernard Spilsbury: His Life and Cases*, Companion Book Club, London, 1952.

Burnett, Tony. *Castrol Management in Australia*, Tony Burnett, 2000.

Cadogan, Mary. *Women with Wings: Female Flyers in Fact and Fiction*, Macmillan, London, 1992.

Colby, Reginald. *Mayfair: A Town Within London*, Country Life Limited, London, 1966.

Chance, Michael. *Whose Dog are You?* John Murray, London, 1938.

Chapman, Arthur. *The Story of a Modern University: A History of the University of Sheffield*, Oxford University Press, London, 1955.

Chichester, Francis. *Solo to Sydney*, Conway Maritime Press, Greenwich, 1982 (first published in 1930).

Clayton, Tim and Phil Craig. *Finest Hour*, Hodder & Stoughton, London, 1999.

Cluett, Douglas, Joanna Nash and Bob Learmonth. *Croydon Airport 1928–1939: The Great Days*, London Borough of Sutton Libraries and Arts Services, Sutton, 1980.

Collier, Basil. *Heavenly Adventurer*, Secker & Warburg, London, 1959.

Coster, Graham. *Corsairville: The Lost Domain of the Flying Boat*, Viking, London, 2000.

Coster, Graham (editor). *The Wild Blue Yonder: The Picador Book of Aviation*, Picador, London, 1997.

Cobham, Sir Alan. *A Time to Fly*, Shepheard-Walwyn, London, 1978.

Courcy, Anne de. *The Viceroy's Daughters: The Lives of the Curzon Sisters*, Phoenix, London, 2000.

Courtenay, William. *Airman Friday*, introduction by Amy Johnson and foreword by Marquess of Londonderry, Hutchinson, London, 1937.

Cowbourne, Donald. *British Rally Drivers: Their Cars and Awards, 1925–1939*, Smith Settle, Otley, 1996.

Crocker, William Charles. *Far from Humdrum: A Lawyer's Life*, Hutchinson, London, 1967.

Curtis, Lettice. *The Forgotten Pilots: A Story of the Air Transport Auxiliary 1939–1945*, G. T. Foulis, Oxfordshire, 1971.

Dahl, Roald. *Going Solo*, Penguin, London, 1986.

Dalrymple, William. *In Xanadu: A Quest*, Flamingo, London, 1990.

Denby, Elaine. *Grand Hotels: Reality and Illusion*, Reaktion Books, London, 1998.

De Havilland, Sir Geoffrey. *Sky Fever: The Autobiography of Sir Geoffrey de Havilland*, Airlife, Shrewsbury, 1979.

De Saint-Exupéry, Antoine. *Wind, Sand and Stars*, Penguin Modern Classics, London, 1969.

Desmond, Florence. *Florence Desmond by Herself*, George G. Harrap, London, 1953.

Dixon, Charles. *Amy Johnson – Lone Girl Flyer*, Sampson, Marston & Co., London, 1930.

Dring, Colin M. *A History of RAF Mildenhall*, Mildenhall Museum Publications, Mildenhall, 1980.

Drogheda, Lord. *Double Harness: Memoirs of Lord Drogheda*, Weidenfeld & Nicolson, London, 1978.

Dyhouse, Carol. *No Distinction of Sex? Women in British Universities 1870–1939*, University College, London, 1995.

Earhart, Amelia. *20 hrs. 40 min. Our Flight in the Friendship*, G. P. Putnam's, New York and London, 1928.

Edwards, Elizabeth. *A History of Bournemouth: The Growth of a Victorian Town*,

Phillimore, Chichester, 1981.

Ellis, Berresford Peter and Jennifer Schofield. *Biggles! The Life Story of Capt. W. E. Johns*, Veloce Publishing, Dorset, 1993.

Ellison, Norman. *Flying Matilda*, Angus & Robertson, Sydney, 1955.

Elton, Chris. *Hull City: A Complete Record 1904–1989*, Breedon, Derby, 1989.

Fahie, Michael. *A Harvest of Memories: The Life of Pauline Gower MBE*, GMS Enterprises, Peterborough, 1995.

Fairfax-Blakebrough, J. *Yorkshire East Riding*, Robert Hale, London, 1951.

Fitzgerald, Arthur. *Prix de l'Arc de Triomphe 1949–1964*, J. A. Allen, London, 1982.

Flanders, Allan, Ruth Pomeranz and Joan Woodward. *Experiment in Industrial Democracy: A Study of the John Lewis Partnership*, Faber & Faber, London, 1968.

Fox, James. *White Mischief*, Jonathan Cape, London, 1982.

Fox, James. *The Langhorne Sisters*, Granta Books, London, 1998.

Gibson-Smith, Charles H. *Aviation, An Historical Survey from its Origins to the End of World War II*, HMSO, UK, 1985.

Gill, Alec. *Good Old Hessle Road*, Hutton Press Ltd, Beverley, 1991.

Gill, Alec. *Superstitions: Folk Magic in Hull's Fishing Community*, Hutton Press Ltd, Beverley, 1993.

Gill, Alec and Gary Sargeant. *Village Within a City: The Hessle Road Fishing Community of Hull*, Hull University Press, 1986.

Gillett, Edward and Kenneth A. MacMahon. *A History of Hull*, published for the University of Hull by the Oxford University Press, 1980.

Graves, Richard. *Achievements: Land, Sea and Air: A Century of Conquest*, Bloomsbury, London, 1998.

Graves, Robert. *Goodbye To All That*, Jonathan Cape, London, 1929.

Graves, Robert and Alan Hodge, *The Long Week-end: A Social History of Great Britain, 1918–1939*, Hutchinson, London, 1940.

Gunston, Bill (editor-in-chief). *Chronicle of Aviation*, Chronicle Communications, London, 1992.

Hall, Carolyn. *The Thirties in Vogue*, Octopus Books, London, 1984.

Heath, Lady and Stella Wolfe Murray. *Women and Flying*, John Long, England, 1929.

Holroyd, Michael. *Bernard Shaw, vol. 2, 1898–1918: The Pursuit of Power*, Chatto & Windus, London, 1989.

Holroyd, Michael. *Bernard Shaw, vol. 3: 1918–1950, The Lure of Fantasy*, Penguin, London, 1993.

Honeycombe, Gordon. *Selfridges: Seventy-Five Years. The Story of the Store 1909–1984*, Park Lane Press, London, 1984.

Howarth, Stephen. *A Century in Oil: The 'Shell' Transport and Trading Company, 1897–1997*, Weidenfeld & Nicolson, London, 1997.

Howell, Georgina. *In Vogue*, Penguin Books, London, 1978.

Hughes, Lynn. *Pendine Races*, Gomer Press, Ceredigion, Wales, 2000.

Huntford, Roland. *Shackleton*, Abacus, London, 1996.

Inwood, Stephen. *A History of London*, Papermac, London, 1998.

Johnson, Amy. *Sky Roads of the World*, W. & R. Chambers, London, 1939.

Johnson, Brian. *Classic Aircraft*, Channel 4 Books, London, 2000.

Johnstone, Air Vice-Marshal Sandy. *Diary of an Aviator*, Airlife, Shrewsbury, 1993.

Kaplan, Fred. *Gore Vidal: A Biography*, Bloomsbury, London, 1999.

Kendall, Ronald. *Growing up on Spurn Head*, Elaine P. Walters, Corby, 1996.

Kersham, Ian. *Hitler: 1936–1945, Nemesis*, Penguin, London, 2000.

King, Alison. *Golden Wings*, White Lion Publishers, London, 1956.

Laurence, Dan H. and Danile H. Leary (editors). *Bernard Shaw, The Complete Prefaces, vol I: 1889–1913*, Allen Lane, London, 1993.

John Lewis Partnership, *John Spedan Lewis 1885–1963*, London, 1985.

Lomax, Judy. *Women of the Air*, John Murray, London, 1986.

Luff, David. *Mollison: The Flying Scotsman*, Lidun Publishing, Lytham St Annes, 1993.

Luff, David. *Amy Johnson: Enigma in the Sky*, Airlife, Shrewsbury, 2002.

Mackenzie, R. D. *Solo: The Bert Hinkler Story*, Angus & Robertson, London, 1963.

Mackersey, Ian. *Jean Batten: The Garbo of the Skies*, Macdonald, London, 1991.

Mackersey, Ian. *Smithy*, Little, Brown and Company, London, 1998.

Macmillan, Norman. *Sir Sefton Brancker*, William Heinemann, London, 1935.

Malkin, Larry, Ann Stothard and Dorothy Smith. *The School at Spurn Point (1893–1945)*, Countryside Publications, Chorley, Lancashire, 1984.

Mallowan, Agatha Christie. *Come, Tell Me How You Live*, Collins, London, 1975.

Markham, Beryl. *West with the Night*, Virago, London, 1984.

Markham, John and Martyn Kirby. *Hull – Impressions of a City*, Highgate Publications, Beverley, 1991.

Markham, John (editor). *Keep the Home Fires Burning*, Highgate Publications, Beverley, 1988.

Massingberd, Hugh (editor). *The Daily Telegraph Book of Obituaries*, Macmillan, London, 1995.

Mckee, Alexander. *Into the Blue*, Granada, London, 1981.

Meyrick, Mrs. *Secrets of the 43: Reminiscences by Mrs Meyrick*, John Long, London, 1933, and Parkgate Publications, 1994, with introduction.

Minter, Tinch (editor). *Millennium Child*, Cross Border Arts, Cambridge, 2000.

Mollison, James. *Death Comest Soon or Late*, Hutchinson, London, 1932.

Mollison, James. *Playboy of the Air*, Michael Joseph, London, 1937.

Mortimer, Roger. *The History of the Derby Stakes*, Michael Joseph, London, 1963.

Neagle, Anna. *Anna Neagle Says 'There's Always Tomorrow': An Autobiography*, W. H. Allen, London, 1974.

Neave, David. *Port, Resort and Market Town: A History of Bridlington*, Hull Academic Press, 2000.

Neave, David and Susan. *Bridlington: An Introduction to its History and Buildings*, Smith Settle, Otley, 2000.

Neave, David and Edward Waterson. *Lost Houses of East Yorkshire*, Georgian Society for East Yorkshire, 1988.

Nesbit, Roy. *Failed to Return*, Patrick Stephens, 1988.

Nesbit, Roy. *Missing, Believed Killed*, Sutton Publishing, 2002.

O'Connell, Sean. *The Car in British Society – Class, Gender and Motoring, 1896–1939*, Manchester University Press, 1998.
Ogilvy, David. *DH88 – De Havilland's Racing Comets*, Airlife, Shrewsbury, 1984.
O'Gorman, Brian. *Laughter in the Roar*, The Badger Press, Westbury, 1998.
Oxford and Asquith, Countess of (editor). *Myself When Young, by Famous Women of To-day*, Frederick Muller, London, 1938.
Overy, Richard. *The Battle*, Penguin, London, 2000.

Pearson, Gordon. *Hull and East Coast Fishing*, City of Kingston upon Hull Museums and Art Galleries, 1976.
Peacock, John. *Fashion Sourcebooks, The 1920s*, Thames & Hudson, London, 1997.
Popham, David and Rita Popham. *The Book of Bournemouth*, Barracuda Books, Buckinghamshire, 1985.
Porter, Lindsey. *The Peak District*, David and Charles, London, 1989.
Post, Wiley and Harold Gatty. *Around the World in Eight Days: The Flight of the Winnie Mae*, John Hamilton, London, 1931.
Pound, Reginald. *Selfridge: A Biography*, Heinemann, London, 1960.
Putnam, George Palmer. *Soaring Wings: A Biography of Amelia Earhart*, Harrap, London, 1940.

Reynolds, Barbara. *Dorothy L. Sayers: Her Life and Soul*, Sceptre, London, 1993.
Reynolds, Barbara (editor). *The Letters of Dorothy L. Sayers 1899–1936: The Making of a Detective Novelist*, Hodder & Stoughton, London, 1995.
Rich, Doris L. *Amelia Earhart: A Biography*, Airlife, Shrewsbury, 1989.
Robinson, John Martin and David Neave. *Francis Johnson, Architect: A Classical Statement*, Oblong, Otley, 2001.
Rose, June. *Marie Stopes and the Sexual Revolution*, Faber & Faber, London, 1992.
Rowbotham, Sheila. *A Century of Women*, Viking, London, 1997.
Ruthven, Malise. *Freya Stark in Iraq and Kuwait*, Garnet Publishing, Reading, 1994.

Saches, Albie and Joan Hoff Wilson. *Sexism and the Law*, Martin Robertson, Oxford, 1978.
Scott, C. W. A. *Scott's Book – The Life and Mildenhall–Melbourne Flight of C. W. A. Scott*, Hodder & Stoughton, London 1934.
Seaton, Ray and Roy Martin. *Good Morning Boys: Will Hay, Master of Comedy*, Barrie & Jenkins, London, 1978.
Seth-Smith, Michael. *The Cresta Run*, Foulsham, Slough, 1976.
Seymour-Ure, Kirsty. *Castrol – The First 100 Years*, Castrol Ltd in association with Bloomsbury, London, 1998.
Sharman, Sarah. *Sir James Martin*, Patrick Stephens, Somerset, 1996.
Sharp, Martin C. *DH: A History of De Havilland*, Airlife, Shrewsbury, 1983.
Schönburg, Janette. *She Who Dares Succeeds*, Saale Books, Exeter, 1993.
Shute, Nevil. *Slide Rule: The Autobiography of an Engineer*, William Heinemann, London, 1954.
Stark, Freya. *Beyond Euphrates: Autobiography 1928–1933*, The Century Travellers,

London, 1983.

Stevenson, John. *The Pelican Social History of Britain, British Society, 1914–1945*, Pelican, London, 1984.

Swinson, Arthur. *The Great Air Race*, Cassell, London, 1968.

Swoffer, Frank. *Learning to Fly*, Pitman, London, 1929.

Taylor, S. J. *The Great Outsiders: Northcliffe, Rothermere and the Daily Mail*, Weidenfeld & Nicolson, London, 1996.

Travers, E. (editor). *Cross Country*, Hothersall & Travers, Sittingbourne, Kent, 1990.

Trzebinski, Errol. *The Lives of Beryl Markham: Out of Africa's Hidden Seductress*, Mandarin Paperbacks, London, 1994.

Uglow, Jenny (editor). *The Macmillan Dictionary of Women's Biography*, Macmillan, London, 1991.

Walker, Diana Barnato. *Spreading My Wings*, Patrick Stephens, Somerset, 1994.

Warner, Marina. *Joan of Arc, The Image of Female Heroism*, Penguin, London, 1981.

Webster, Paul. *Antoine de Saint-Exupéry: The Life and Death of the Little Prince*, Macmillan, London, 1993.

Wertheimer, Alison. *A Special Scar: The Experiences of People Bereaved by Suicide*, Tavistock/Routledge, London and New York, 1991.

Wildridge, T. Tindall. *Old and New Hull*, M. C. Peck & Son, Hull, 1884.

Williams, A. Susan. *Ladies of Influence*, Penguin, London, 2000.

Williams, Betty. *Portrait of a Decade – The 1920s*, B. T. Batsford, London, 1989.

Wragg, David W. *A Dictionary of Aviation*, Osprey, Reading, 1973.

Yapp, Nick. *The Hulton Getty Picture Collection, 1920s*, Könemann, Cologne, 1998.

Yapp, Nick. *The Hulton Getty Picture Collection, 1930s*, Könemann, Cologne, 1998.

Young, Filson. *Growing Wings*, Michael Joseph, London, 1936.

Ziegler, Philip. *King Edward VIII*, Collins, London, 1990.

Miscellaneous items

Dictionnaire de Biographie Française, Librairie Letouzey, 1948, Paris, vol. 7.

Dictionnaire des Parlementaires Français, Presses Universitaires de France, Paris, 1963, vol. 3.

The Penguin Biographical Dictionary of Women, Penguin, London, 1998.

Encyclopaedia of Aviation, Reference International, London, 1977.

Amy's voice and an extract from 'Amy, Wonderful Amy' can be heard on the CD, *The Century in Sound, Recordings from the National Sound Archive/British Library*, NSA CD8, Track 13, '1930, The Story of My Flight'.

Unpublished manuscript, biography of Amy Johnson by Betty Falconar-Stewart (née Johnson), Wright State University Special Collections and Archives.

Castrol *Achievements* magazines (1930–37).

Stanford's London Atlas of Universal Geography, Whitehall Edition.

The British Racehorse, vol. XVIII, no. 3, September 1966.

The Bloodstock Breeders' Annual Review, vol. LV, 1966.

The official Amy Johnson website, produced by her descendants, can be found at:
www.amyjohnson.info

Television

Wonderful Amy (BBC North, 1974).

Inside Out (BBC, first shown 21 October 2002).

The Real Amy Johnson (produced by Lion TV for Channel 4, expected transmission 2003).

Films

The Spirit of St Louis (1957, Director, Billy Wilder).

They Flew Alone (1941, Director, Herbert Wilcox).

Index